PRAISE FOR *THE CREATION AND RE-CREATION OF CARDENIO: PERFORMING SHAKESPEARE, TRANSFORMING CERVANTES!*

"Gary Taylor and Terri Bourus make Shakespeare come alive with such enthusiasm, you'd swear the Bard himself was sitting in the room with them. Meticulous and passionate scholars, they don't shy away from questioning long-held theories and testing them—not only through extensive research—but also through the crucible of live performance. It does not surprise me that they would tackle the reconstruction of *Cardenio* or that Gary would take some twenty years to do it. When they're done, *Cardenio* will certainly stand as a testament to how painstaking line-by-line scholarship can combine with academic imagination to create pure joy."

—Jim Simmons, Producer/Writer of "Shakespeare
Lost/Shakespeare Found" TV documentary
about *The History of Cardenio*

"This persuasive book should put to rest nearly three hundred years of debate over the lost King's Men play of 1613. *Cardenio* was indeed a Fletcher/Shakespeare collaboration, based on episodes from Cervantes' bestseller *Don Quixote*. Lewis Theobald was not a forger: his 1727 adaptation *Double Falsehood* does derive from *Cardenio*. With meticulous scholarship and creative theatrical acumen the editors assemble a formidable case, and also triumphantly publish for the first time Taylor's 'unadaptation' of The History of *Cardenio*."

—David Carnegie, Emeritus Professor FRSNZ,
School of English, Film, Theatre, and
Media Studies, Victoria University of
Wellington, New Zealand; and co-editor of
The Quest for Cardenio: *Shakespeare, Fletcher,
Cervantes, and The Lost Play*

"Taylor and Bourus's team brings us closer to the lost *Cardenio* in four ways: they render the forgery hypothesis even less convincing, provide more evidence for Shakespeare's collaboration, enrich our understanding of Fletcher's dramatic art, and pay significant attention to the performative dimension."

—Brean Hammond, Professor of Modern English
Literature, University of Nottingham, UK; and
editor of the Arden edition of *Double Falsehood*

"The most up-to-date collection of essays about Shakespeare's lost play, with important new work on *Cardenio*'s composition, collaborators, reconstructions, and performances."

—Valerie Wayne, Professor Emerita, University of Hawaii, USA; and editor of the Arden edition of *Cymbeline*

"Taylor and Bourus's collaboration pairs textual studies and theatrical practice, literary analysis and performance studies, detective work and hypotheses scientifically tested with mathematical precision. Taylor's careful excavation of Fletcher and Shakespeare's language from Lewis Theobald's *Double Falsehood*, Bourus's thoughtful direction of the resulting script—two decades in the making—and the incisive analyses provided by all hands in these pages make of Fletcher and Shakespeare's labor of love lost a *Cardenio* found."

—Regina Buccola, Associate Professor, Roosevelt University, USA; and co-editor of *Chicago Shakespeare Theater: Suiting the Action to the Word*

THE CREATION AND RE-CREATION OF *CARDENIO*

PERFORMING SHAKESPEARE, TRANSFORMING CERVANTES

Edited by

Terri Bourus and Gary Taylor

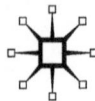

First published in 2013 by
PALGRAVE MACMILLAN®
in the United States—a division of St. Martin's Press LLC,
175 Fifth Avenue, New York, NY 10010.

Where this book is distributed in the UK, Europe and the rest of the world,
this is by Palgrave Macmillan, a division of Macmillan Publishers Limited,
registered in England, company number 785998, of Houndmills,
Basingstoke, Hampshire RG21 6XS.

Palgrave Macmillan is the global academic imprint of the above companies
and has companies and representatives throughout the world.

Palgrave® and Macmillan® are registered trademarks in the United States,
the United Kingdom, Europe and other countries.

ISBN: 978–1–137–34420–5 (pbk)—
ISBN: 978–1–137–34421–2 (hc)

Library of Congress Cataloging-in-Publication Data

The creation and re-creation of Cardenio : performing Shakespeare,
transforming Cervantes / edited by Terri Bourus and Gary Taylor.
pages cm
Includes bibliographical references and index.
ISBN 978–1–137–34421–2 (alk. paper)—
ISBN 978–1–137–34420–5 (alk. paper)
1. Second maiden's tragedy. 2. Shakespeare, William, 1564–1616—
Authorship. 3. Cervantes Saavedra, Miguel de, 1547–1616—Authorship.
4. Fletcher, John, 1579–1625—Authorship. I. Bourus, Terri, editor of
compilation. II. Taylor, Gary, 1953– editor of compilation.
PR2411.S3C74 2013
822'.3—dc23   2013013090

A catalogue record of the book is available from the British Library.

Design by Newgen Knowledge Works (P) Ltd., Chennai, India.

First edition: September 2013

Contents

Part I

Figures, Plates, and Tables

Figures

PLATES

between pp. 218 and 219

TABLES

ACKNOWLEDGMENTS

This book began with two events hosted, in April 2012, by the Indiana University School of Liberal Arts at IUPUI (Indiana University Purdue University Indianapolis). For both we are deeply grateful to Dean William Blomquist and his staff, particularly Genevieve Shaker and Julie Goldsmith. Both events were also supported by the research foundation at Florida State University. For bringing both together into this book and for compiling the index we are permanently indebted to Chad Andrews, an M.A. student in the IUPUI English Department and research assistant for the New Oxford Shakespeare in the 2012–2013 academic year, whose work above and beyond the call of duty has been indispensable.

The first event was a production of *The History of Cardenio,* performed in a new theater at the IUPUI Campus Center. Those six performances could not have happened without the dedication, creativity, and months of hard work by the talented actors, musicians, and crew of Hoosier Bard Productions; to each of them we extend our undying gratitude. Completion of the new theater was made possible by a large gift by an anonymous donor, who had a particular passion for live classical theater. Of the many people who helped to make this happen, we want especially to thank IU President Michael McRobbie, IUPUI Chancellor Charles Bantz, Tralicia Lewis (interim director of the Campus Center), Brian Fedder (light and sound technician), the IU Alumni Foundation, Women's Studies, and the departments of English, Communications, History, Philosophy, and World Languages.

The second event was an academic colloquium ("*The History of Cardenio*: Spain and England, Then and Now"). This colloquium tried to redress the balance of previous scholarship on *Cardenio* by soliciting work on Cervantes (as in chapters 1–4 of this book), Fletcher's relationship to Cervantes (as in chapters 5–8), and Fletcher's collaboration with Shakespeare (as in chapters 9, 10, and 13); because it coincided with the last weekend of performances, it also focused on issues of performance (as in chapters 12–16). Partial funding was provided by the office of the Vice-Chancellor of Research, Uday Sukatme. Much of the work of organizing the conference was done by our colleagues and staff in the New Oxford Shakespeare center at IUPUI: editors Francis X. Connor and Sarah Neville, research assistant Cassie Mills, and work-study student Tiffany Plourde. All the participants of the colloquium enriched our work on this volume, including Joe Cacaci, Suzanne Gossett, Christopher Marino, and Paul White.

Terri Bourus: In addition to our amazing cast, musicians, and crew, I wish especially to thank directors David Carnegie, Lori Leigh, Ralph Cohen, Joe Leonardo, and Wilson Milam. They all allowed me to watch them at work, and illuminated the challenges and joys of working with the evolving script of *The History of Cardenio*.

Gary Taylor: my work on *Cardenio* has been supported for seven years by research grants from Florida State University, and by the financial and human resources of the New York Public Theatre, the Williamstown Festival, the Blackfriars Theatre at the American Shakespeare Center, the Shakespeare Theatre in Washington, DC, the Chicago Shakespeare Theater, Victoria University of Wellington, and Shakespeare's Globe in London. Every member of every cast and crew has contributed to my understanding of the play. But I owe most to David Black and Joe Cacaci (who raised *Cardenio* from the dead and set it on its way), to David Carnegie (for the production and colloquium in New Zealand, and for shepherding *The Quest for Cardenio* to completion), and to Terri Bourus, who undertook the colossal task of opening a new theater with *Cardenio,* and who has taught me more about this play (and theater) than anyone else.

Some richer hand than ours requite you all.

TERRI BOURUS
GARY TAYLOR

Abbreviations

Ardila	Ardila, J. A. G., ed. *The Cervantean Heritage: Influence and Reception of Cervantes in Britain* (London: Legenda, 2009).
Bourus, "Stages"	Bourus, Terri. "'May I Be Metamorphosed': *Cardenio* by Stages." *Quest*, 387–403.
Chartier	Chartier, Roger. *Cardenio between Cervantes and Shakespeare: The Story of a Lost Play* (Cambridge: Polity Press, 2013).
CSI Shakespeare	*CSI Shakespeare*, WFYI Indianapolis, producer and writer Jim Simmons, original broadcast November 1, 2012, Comcast Xfinity and DVD and rebroadcast by American Public Television as "Shakespeare Lost/ Shakespeare Found."
DF	*Double Falsehood*, ed. Brean Hammond (London: Arden Shakespeare, 2010).
Doran and Álamo	Doran, Gregory, and Antonio Álamo. *Cardenio: Shakespeare's "Lost Play" Re-Imagined* (London: Nick Hern Books, 2011).
Doran, *Lost*	Doran, Gregory. *Shakespeare's Lost Play* (London: Nick Hern Books, 2012).
DQ	*The History of the Valorous and Wittie Knight-Errant, Don Quixote Of the Mancha*, trans. Thomas Shelton (London, 1612).
Fletcher	*The Dramatic Works in the Beaumont and Fletcher Canon,* gen. ed. Fredson Bowers, 10 vols. (Cambridge: Cambridge University Press, 1966–1996).
Fuchs	Fuchs, Barbara. "Beyond the Missing *Cardenio*: Anglo-Spanish Relations in Early Modern Drama," *Journal of Medieval and Early Modern Studies* 39 (2009): 143–59.
Hammond	Hammond, Brean. *DF* (introduction and commentary).
McMullan	McMullan, Gordon. *The Politics of Unease in the Plays of John Fletcher* (Amherst, MA: University of Massachussetts Press, 1994).

Middleton   Middleton, Thomas. *The Collected Works*, gen eds., Gary Taylor and John Lavagnino (Oxford: Clarendon Press, 2007).

Quest   *The Quest for Cardenio: Shakespeare, Fletcher, Cervantes and the Lost Play*, ed. David Carnegie and Gary Taylor (Oxford: Oxford University Press, 2012).

Shakespeare   Shakespeare, William. *The Complete Works*, gen. ed. Stanley Wells and Gary Taylor, rev. ed. (Oxford: Oxford University Press, 2005).

Stern 2011   Stern, Tiffany. "'The Forgery of Some Modern Author'? Theobald's Shakespeare and Cardenio's *Double Falsehood*," *Shakespeare Quarterly* 62 (2011): 555–93.

Taylor, "History"   Taylor, Gary. "A History of *The History of* Cardenio." *Quest*, 11–61.

THOC   Fletcher, John, William Shakespeare, and Gary Taylor, *The History of Cardenio* (1612–2012).

Foreword: Mr. Fletcher. & Shakespeare. [& Theobald]

Roger Chartier

The first contribution of this collection of essays—based upon a colloquium held in Indianapolis in April 2012—is to establish that Theobald was neither a liar nor a forger. He spoke the truth in his edition of *Double Falsehood*, published in December 1727, when he asserted on his title page that he possessed an old manuscript play "written originally by W. Shakespeare." His own intrigue deals with the drama of "love stories," in the plural, "built upon a novel in *Don Quixot.*" This "novel" tells of Cardenio, the young Andalusian lover of Luscinda, with whom he has exchanged a vow of marriage. Cardenio is betrayed by his friend, Fernando, a duke's son, who—although betrothed to Dorothea, the daughter of rich peasants—falls deeply in love with Luscinda and marries her. Nevertheless, all's well that ends well since, after many scrapes, regrets, and pardons, the couples first avowed to one another reunite.

As Theobald notes in the first edition of *Double Falsehood*, "unbelievers" have cast doubt on his assertions. Far from being "a dear relick" left by Shakespeare, "a Remnant of his pen," could this play, supposedly "revised and adapted" by Theobald, be nothing more than a forgery? Or rather, even if the manuscripts mentioned by Theobald were authentic, shouldn't the attribution really go to Fletcher, not Shakespeare, since even Theobald admits that Fletcher's "style and manner" are evident in the play? Or perhaps, in accord with Edmund Malone, we should attribute the work neither to Shakespeare nor to Fletcher but to Massinger?

For over fifteen years, textual critics have followed various clues to answer these questions. On the one hand, Jonathan Hope detects the presence of a seventeenth-century text within Theobald's piece. His contention rests on the frequent use of the "unregulated" auxiliary verb "do" in that text. On the other hand, Richard Proudfoot, Brean Hammond, and MacDonald P. Jackson discern the presence of Fletcher based on the presence in the play of contractions and "feminine endings" that characterizes his style. Their uneven distribution in the text would confirm Walter Graham's detection (in a foundational article published in 1916) of two distinct expressive styles in *Double Falsehood*.

Drawing on "the evidence of the [digital] machine," Gary Taylor and John V. Nance have established the presence of two layers of text in the play published in 1727. One is eighteenth-century, solely attributable to the pen of Theobald, and the second is seventeenth-century, attributable to Shakespeare and Fletcher. This finding results from the systematic computerized analysis of parallels between the verses, phrases, and word associations encountered in *Double Falsehood* and the same formulations in the works of Theobald, Fletcher, and Shakespeare. The search for parallels that occur among no other playwrights enables us to discern with certainty what belongs to each of them, not only in verse but also in prose. How pleasing to note that the comparison of parallel passages in different plays was one of the methods Theobald expressly demanded in his 1733 edition of the *Works of Shakespeare*: "I have constantly endeavored to support my Corrections and Conjectures by parallel Passages and Authorities from himself, the surest Means of expounding any Author whatsoever." Theobald would have undoubtedly profited immensely from the textual databases of our day— while regretting that their exploitation undermined his first attribution to Shakespeare alone.

The conclusions reached by Gary Taylor have multiple consequences. They should put an end to doubts arising from Moseley's "entry" in the Stationer's Register (September 9, 1653) establishing his "right in copy" for a play listed as "The History of Cardenio by Mr. Fletcher. & Shakespeare" *[sic]*. Of course, those prior suspicions were legitimate, given the uncertainties of the attributions in the entries in the Register at the time. Taylor's evidence authorizes the excision from the text of *Double Falsehood* of the fragments attributable to Theobald and without parallel to any other dramatist of the seventeenth century. It is thus possible to propose a plausible reconstruction of the play as performed at court in the winter of 1612–1613 (and possibly composed in the summer or autumn of 1612 according to bibliographical evidence established here by David L. Gants, which situates publication of Shelton's translation of *Don Quixote* in middle to late spring of 1612). Following Taylor's discoveries, the recovery of the lost play should respect the linguistic possibilities and the theatrical conventions of the era as well as the contemporary collaboration of the two playwrights who worked jointly on two other plays: *All Is True* and *The Two Noble Kinsmen*. More difficult is the "reconstruction" of the experiences of the first spectators of the play. As Elizabeth Spiller suggests, many of them—like Cardenio and Alonso Quijano in Cervantes' history—had read *Amadis de Gaula* and understood Fletcher and Shakespeare's *Cardenio* through remembering the pleasures and dangers of such reading.

The attention given to Fletcher is the second original contribution of this book. This was the right path to follow all along, as it should be remembered that Fletcher is named first in the "entry" for *The History of Cardenio* in the Register of the Stationers' Company. Moreover, Fletcher was far more familiar with Spanish texts than Shakespeare, commencing with Cervantes, and that influence turns up in one fashion or another among nine of Fletcher's own plays. Finally, from the very beginning of its performances, the play adapted by Theobald appeared to some viewers to be the work of Fletcher, in whole or part. However, during the last fifteen years *Cardenio*'s return to stage, to literary criticism, and to publication has largely effaced Fletcher's presence to the profit of Shakespeare, whose name alone suffices to justify any quest for the long-lost play. The contributions assembled here by Joyce Boro, Huw Griffiths, Christopher Hicklin, and Vimala Pasupathi happily correct that distorted perspective.

They do this by forcing us to reconsider what we thought we knew about Fletcher, especially his hispanophilia. Four of Fletcher's plays studied here were insired by Cervantes: *The Coxcomb*, based on *La novela del Curioso impertinente* (read aloud in *Don Quixote*); *The Chances* and *Love's Pilgrimage*, drawn respectively from *La novela de la Señora Cornelia* and *La novela de las dos doncellas* (both included in the *Novelas ejemplares*); and *The Custom of the Country* (where one encounters the characters of Ladislao and Transila from *Persiles y Sigismunda*). In each case, Fletcher apparently worked from a translation of Cervantes's work. Whence the two questions raised by Gary Taylor and Steven Wagschal: did Fletcher (and Shakespeare) read *Don Quixote* in its original language or (more likely) in Shelton's translation? And did Theobald instead use for his own contributions to *Double Falshood* the Spanish editions of *Don Quixote* (1611 and perhaps 1662), or the 1687 translation by John Phillips, all of which he owned?

In any case, as the textual analyses show, even if Fletcher was an attentive reader of Cervantes, he still appropriated with invention and originality the plot lines of the originals and subordinated them to his own dramatic preferences. Thus we see that the role of the protagonist is typically given to one or more male figures who become "author-characters" in the tale. A new accent falls on tensions linked to female sexuality contrasted with the stock figure of the "clever maiden in love." These essays stress also Fletcher's representation of different forms of masculinity, as manifest in martial values, libertine cynicism, or courtly love.

This last focal point permits further reevaluation of a prominent theme in plays written by Fletcher, either alone or in collaboration: the brutal destruction of a perfect friendship between two young men, often expressed in terms of erotic union, and ruined by the passion they share for the same woman. That is the story of Palamon and Arcyte in *The Two Noble Kinsmen*, of Memnon and Polidor in *The Mad Lover*, and of Fernando and Cardenio in *Don Quixote* (renamed Henriquez and Julio in *Double Falshood*). This theme is well known and, as Jeffrey Masten shows, interconnects the dramatic plots, the homo-social lifestyle of some playwrights, and collaborative writing especially when shared by two authors. But in this relation between lived experiences and staged works, one should not forget the parody Fletcher develops in some of his plays, *The Coxcombe* for example, where the ideal of a perfect amity between two men is rendered ridiculous, and discarded. The chivalric rhetoric of male friendship is merely dangerous, or laughable, since it is so opposed to contemporary social conventions demanding respect for rank and for the matrimonial links between families and clans.

The third original contribution of this book stems from its close connection to a new production of *The History of Cardenio* in Indianapolis in 2012. After professional readings or student performances of the play in various forms and venues, Terri Bourus' new staging made visible and audible Gary Taylor's most recent reconstruction of the once lost play. The playbill presented this as "The *History of Cardenio*, By William Shakespeare & John Fletcher, Inspired by Cervantes' *Don Quixote*, Recreated by Gary Taylor, Directed by Terri Bourus." As noted in the essays by Terri Bourus, Gerald Baker, and Ayanna Thompson, new connections developed here between theatrical practice and scholarly inquiry yield unprecedented intellectual opportunities for experiment and research. Brought to the stage with the constraints inevitably imposed by a particular theaterspace, a particular cast, and a finite university budget, this "recreation" by Gary Taylor reveals acutely the difficulties once encountered by Fletcher and Shakespeare and then later by Theobald when they sought to compose a play drawn from *Don Quixote*. The greatest challenge, then and now, is to link the "novel" of Cardenio with the "history" of Don Quixote. *Double Falsehood* avoided that difficulty by simply ignoring Don Quixote, Sancho, and their companions. But was that also happening in 1612–1613? Gary Taylor remains convinced that the comic exploits of Don Quixote constitute the "sub-plot" of a play that appears too short in its state as *Double Falsehood*. This is despite the arguments insisting on the troubles that would have been caused by a chivalric parody circulating contemporaneously with the death of Prince Henry, a figure deeply attached to the crusading ideals of knightly virtue. But Taylor may be right, especially given the choice made by other playwrights contemporaneous to Fletcher and Shakespeare who also staged versions of the novel of Cardenio. In Guillén de Castro's "comedia" *Don Quijote de la Mancha* and in the French plays by Pichou and by Guérin de Bouscal, Don Quixote is present, as a comic counterpoint to the sentimental novel. Gerald Baker's interpretation of Thomas Roe's allusion to "the various fortunes of Don Quixote" in a letter he sent to Elizabeth in 1630 reinforces the hypothesis that Don Quixote appeared in Fletcher and Shakespeare's play, if we accept that Roe referred to *The History of Cardenio*.

There remains the theatrical difficulty of integrating the two plots—much more challenging for an author and director today, who must confront the Quixote myth, the centuries-long accretion of a distinct and complex persona. The dramatists of the seventeenth century could more easily place in the margins of their plays an earlier version of that character, reduced to the role of a "*gracioso de comedia*" or extravagant jester. Just as in the music that might accompany the unfolding of the plot, the risk here becomes a Spanish exoticism, certainly seductive but far too easily stereotyped (as in the flamenco music utilized by Greg Doran in his version of *Cardenio* for the Royal Shakespeare Company, here analyzed by Carla Della Gatta). As Borges would have said, one doesn't need "professional Spaniards" to make or to get the Hispanic references.

Theater experience—or, as Terri Bourus puts it here, live theater as itself a "research discipline"—clarifies with greater acuity than mere reading the tensions, historic and dramatic, of a play. This is certainly the case with the marriage scene between Fernando and Luscinda. *Double Falsehood* gets round the difficulty it poses by interrupting the nuptials before the sacramental vow is pronounced. The priest has not done his work, and Don Bernard declares: "Let the Priest wait." In 1612–1613, did Fletcher and Shakespeare do the same? Or were they more loyal to *Don Quixote*, where the two young people are actually twice married: once by the priest in Luscinda's house, but also before (to another spouse) through the binding promises of marriage exchanged between Luscinda and Cardenio and between Fernando and Dorotea. In Cervantes, this double marriage forms the main spring of the plot, because Dorotea and then Cardenio can hope for an annulment of the never-consummated union between Fernando and Luscinda. But this double marriage created a real inconvenience for seventeenth-century playwrights, especially if they were Catholics. They sought to avoid the theological problem either by weakening the sacramental force of a marriage promise (held to be a solemn, irrevocable engagement in traditional definitions of marriage prior to the Council of Trent), or by interrupting the ceremony uniting Luscinda and Fernando before the exchange of vows before a priest. Gary Taylor has had to confront the same problem faced by Guillén de Castro, Pichou, and Theobald.

There is another serious challenge: Fernando's sexual liaison with Dorotea. In *Don Quixote*, this is treated as an exchange of vows made before sacred images of the saints and the Virgin, as well as in the presence of a human witness, the "*doncella*" of Dorotea. After carnal consummation of the verbal union, Fernando confirms the matrimony with a ring that he places on the young woman's finger. This scene is not shown in *Double Falsehood*, merely evoked in passing by a Henriquez already in love with Leonora. He himself introduces the supposition of a sexual violation ("Was it a rape then?"). But he immediately challenges that definition: "True, she did not consent; as true, she did resist; but still in silence all. 'Twas but the coyness of a modest bride/ Not the resentment of a ravish'd maid." Any staging of this encounter has to navigate in one way or another between two extremes. Moreover, as stressed by Lori Leigh, even a decision to leave this (or any other) action unstaged produces an "unscene," a narrative that itself creates a particular perception of the story. Once again, the exigencies of staging oblige reconsideration of multiple texts, all sedimentary and contradictory, that have communicated to us the history of Cardenio. As Ayanna Thompson demonstrates, this necessity acquires an even greater edge for modern audiences when a "reconstruction" like Taylor's introduces an element not present in either *Double Falsehood* or *Don Quixote*: an identification of Violanta/Dorotea as "a mixed-race country girl," designated in the play as a "gypsy," "Egyptian," or "half-black" woman.

The Indianapolis experiment, in its modernity, sends us back to the conditions that regulated the representation of theatrical works in England over the period 1576–1642. Rewriting *Double Falsehood* to recover the text as written by Fletcher and Shakespeare, cleansed of Theobald's anachronistic varnish, means that Gary Taylor is, in effect, rewriting himself. His *History of Cardenio* printed here differs from the text performed in 2012, which itself varied from eight other versions read or staged between 1992 and 2011. Collaborations across time and space, constant revisions, the sheer malleability of the text shaped his writing habits just as they governed those of Fletcher, Shakespeare, and Theobald.

As the work of Terri Bourus demonstrates, material constraints in the theater and in representation itself reproduce today the same challenges confronted by seventeenth-century troupes of actors. Thespians must make the best use possible of all simple stage devices in public amphitheaters, like the Globe, with their projecting platforms and their galleries, and in the private halls, like the Blackfriars, with their indoor, rectangular, artificially lighted spaces. They must excite the imagination of audiences without recourse to imposing sets or heavy stage machinery. Representation onstage, yesterday and today, is the fundamental test through which the text must pass, constantly reworked as the rehearsals and performances unfold just as in Gary Taylor's *History of Cardenio*. It is the staging that manifests the real force of the play (as in the potent scene of Luscinda's and Fernando's marriage), as well as its inherent difficulties (as in the dense and complex denouement, demanding great visual and dramatic invention).

Plays are made to be performed. That's what Renaissance dramatists reiterated in their admonitions that served, paradoxically, also to justify editions solely destined for reading. Their conventional rhetoric, however, was doubly correct. First, it made stage production the essential measure by which to judge any play's effectiveness. But it also permitted spectators who became readers—and readers who were never spectators—to encounter in their reading a trace, partial but real, of the acting and the emotions such vivid performances inspired. The same may be said for this book, which displays all the traces of a vibrant colloquium and a fine production.

Trans. by
KEVIN C. ROBBINS

Part I

Cervantes, Fletcher, Shakespeare, and Performance

The Passion of Readers, the Imitation of Texts: The History of Reading in the Quest for *Cardenio*

Elizabeth Spiller

The quest for Cardenio has been the story of a lost text. This text itself has a kind of instability—perhaps "Cardenno," maybe "Cardenna," or simply *The History of Cardenio*—that seems particularly appropriate as a textual afterlife to the fictional hero whose own name was not Quixote, but rather Quesada, or perhaps Quixada, Quijana, or Quixano.[1] Much of the excitement of this quest has involved reading backward from Lewis Theobald's *Double Falsehood* (1728) and forward from Thomas Shelton's translation *The History of the Valorous and Wittie Knight-Errant Don-Quixote of the Mancha* (1612), to the text that may have stood between them. Yet, these recent critical acts of readers—and the remarkable and evolving readings of the play text that have emerged from them—remain modern ones. But Cervantes' *Don Quixote* articulates and practices its own, decidedly early modern, theory of reading. This theory of reading emerges out of an engagement with the one text that is very much not missing from this story, at least as Cervantes imagined it and as early modern audiences to *The History of Cardenio* would have experienced it: the romance of *Amadis of Gaul*.

Threatened by the inquisitorial fire of the barber and the priest in Cervantes' version and torn apart onstage to make an improved "second" edition in the Taylor rendition (*THOC* 1.6), *Amadis of Gaul* was the most widely read of the Renaissance romances. For early modern readers *Amadis* also became the central text in contemporary debates about the nature and consequences of reading. Quixote, Quesada, Cardenio: they are each overcome by the passion of reading this book, a passion that is tied to acts of *imitatio*. They were not alone. In Spain, *Amadis* went through about 100 bibliographically distinct editions and was arguably the first modern best seller; in France, there were as many as half a million readers of the Herberay translations; in England, copies of the romance were collected by readers from Philip Sidney and Robert Burton to Robert Boyle. The story of *Amadis*—whether told within and across the pages of the story of Cardenio or in the experiences of historical readers—connects acts of *imitatio* to humoral imbalance in ways that are at the heart of early modern understandings of reading. This essay will outline key developments in contemporary attitudes toward reading and the consequences that reading theory and practice might have had on this story about reading.

What does it mean for later scholars, writers, or editors to recreate an early modern text? Jorge Luis Borges asks us to consider this question when he imagines the "interminably heroic" quest by which "Pierre Menard, Author of the *Quixote*" sets out to write chapters 9, 38, and parts of 22 of the first part of the *Quixote*, "word for word and line for line."[2] In this meditation on the nature of mimesis and fiction, Borges begins by suggesting that there are two forms of imitation that Menard might pursue: copying the text or copying the author. The first Menard rejects out of hand: "he never contemplated a mechanical transcription of the original; he did not propose to copy it" (91). The second—in which one would need to "Know Spanish well, recover the Catholic faith, fight against the Moors or the Turk, forget the history of Europe between the years 1602 and 1918"—involves copying not the text but Cervantes himself. This, too, Menard rejects as "too easy" (91).

Both of these forms of imitation resonate across various attempts to create, recreate, or edit an original literary text, whether the *Quixote* or *The History of Cardenio*. Menard's initial choices suggest that the frame for thinking about such possibilities depends on one's assumptions about the nature of authorship. Menard, however, decides to at once remain himself and yet also "reach the *Quixote*" through his own experiences. What starts as a comic meditation on the nature of authorship thus becomes a reflection on reading. In concluding that "every man should be capable of all ideas," Menard echoes Quixote's own convictions about the truth of the imagination. Menard also follows Quixote's method of imitating his heroes primarily through his acts as a reader. Borges gives us a story that seems to be about authorship but turns out to be about reading because, for him, acts of authorship are always forms of reading. With this comes the related lesson that, far from being "a contingent work" and "not necessary" in the way that the decidedly French Menard imagines (91), the *Quixote* is in some sense the only story: all stories begin with the reading of *Quixote*, and the most powerful forms of imitation come from and through its reading.

Shakespearian editor John Kerrigan has suggested that any such lessons about reading have not been well learned by textual scholars. Taking W. W. Greg's "The Rationale of the Copy-Text" (1950) as his point of departure, Kerrigan notes that an editorial practice that charges the editor with the goal of identifying and eliminating textual corruption tends to assume a highly idealized notion of the text as intended by the author, one "free from historical contingency and the accidents of material circumstance." While this critique of traditional bibliographic methods is a familiar one, Kerrigan also argues that this approach necessarily "pays little or no attention to the role of the reader," if only because the reader becomes largely irrelevant when the goal of the editor is to arrive at the text that most closely approximates the intentions of the author.[3] It is perhaps not a coincidence that *both* of Menard's initial approaches to creating the *Quixote*, the first with its commitment to the achievement of a perfect text and the second with its intentionalist suppositions, have affinities with the editorial assumptions of Fredson Bowers, G. Thomas Tanselle, and other editors working in the tradition of Greg.

Yet, for Kerrigan, the same charge can also be made against Jerome McGann. Kerrigan identifies McGann's inclination to overlook both the act and history of reading as a "grave deficiency" in his work (104). His assessment of McGann's attitude toward reading is worth detailing because it provides a framework for thinking about why having a history and theory of reading might be important, especially in the case of texts such as *Quixote* and *Cardenio*. McGann's *The Textual Condition* (1991) was primarily interested in offering a model of reading to align with the editorial practice that he developed in such works as *A Critique of Modern Textual Criticism* (1983). In keeping with his corrective to traditional editorial theory, McGann was committed to articulating a material, rather than transcendent, model of reading. Addressing those who would suggest that reading, as he depicted it, is "an affair of the mind alone, of the individual standing silent before the mute text, building invisible cities of meaning to unheard melodies of truth," McGann insisted that the act of reading is not separable from the physical: "Reading appears always and only as text, in one or another *physically determinate* and socially determined form...Textuality cannot be understood except as a phenomenal event, and reading itself can only be understood when it has assumed *specific material constitutions*" (my emphasis).[4]

In tethering reading to the physical reality of the text itself in this way, though, McGann constructs a model of reading in which readers tacitly disappear into the text: "Various readers and audiences are hidden in our texts, and the traces of their multiple presence are scripted at the most material levels" (10). In assuming that the physical reality of reading is nothing other than the material fact of the text, McGann unintentionally assumes a surprisingly ahistorical model of reading. As Kerrigan notes, McGann is "damagingly indifferent to the synchronic variety and historical complexity of reading practices" (104). Another Pierre Menard.

Equally important, McGann's interest in correcting for transcendence and textual idealism leads him to an arguably narrow and rigid view of the physical: despite his references to the phenomenal, he tends to assume that the text alone comprises the physical. Even as he derides those who would ignore the physicality of text to comprehend reading as "an affair of the mind alone," his reader remains strangely disembodied. In the early modern period, though, any such account of reading would have been largely incomprehensible. Quixote's windmills of the imagination seem like the perfect image for reading as "an affair of the mind alone," but within early modern faculty psychology, the act of reading happened not just in the mind but in and to the body, and Cervantes makes clear that reading changes Quixote's blood and complexion at least as much as it transforms his mind.

Both traditional and recent editorial theory too often overlooks the role and importance of readers. In a scholarly field that has largely continued to focus on the production and transmission of texts in ways that have sometimes seemed to suggest that actually reading what is *in* a book may be entirely beside the point, readers are relegated to the third and last place in the cycle of the "sociology of texts." Yet, authors often, and editors must, begin *as readers*. As Alberto Manguel makes clear, reading always comes before writing.[5] This lesson is particularly acute in this case, which is a labyrinthine *mise en abyme* of readers reading readers. The Taylor *History of Cardenio* is compelling as an experiment in editorial and performance practice, but it is also a kind of reading laboratory, an achievement of an act of reading that emerges out of and through a whole archaeology of earlier readers and other reading practices.

Working through this history of readers, to get back, as it were, to Shakespeare and Fletcher, let alone Cervantes and Quixote, one must go through Lewis Theobald. It is worth pausing over Theobald here because his activities as a reader fundamentally determined the shape and texture of *Double Falsehood* and may give us some sense of why and how the play he staged differed from the play that Shakespeare and Fletcher might have written after reading Shelton and Cervantes. Theobald certainly wrote differently than Shakespeare or Fletcher or Cervantes. Less obviously, though, he also read differently. Indeed, much of what Theobald misses in his adaptation arises out of the disparity between his model of reading and those of Cervantes, Shelton, Shakespeare, Fletcher, and, indeed, Quixote himself. About a month after Theobald's death in 1744, Charles Corbett published a detailed bookseller's catalogue of his library as it was being put up for auction.[6] This catalogue can give us some answers to what texts Theobald may have had access to. Thus, it does seem worth calling attention to the fact that Theobald owned three editions of *Don Quixote*, two of those Spanish versions and the third a previously overlooked English copy in John Phillips' (admittedly somewhat odd) 1687 translation.[7] Such information can be invaluable in tracing sources and influences that are central to a nuanced understanding of the writing practices of authors, editors, and translators. Yet, Theobald's library does not just offer us evidence of what he read (or could have read), but of *how* he read. As historians of reading have made clear, libraries are collections of books, both read and unread, that stand as a material archive of how we approach and understand the act of reading—of what we think reading is, why it matters, and how it works.

In this context, Theobald's library is revealing because it suggests how differently he read than did the original audiences of either Cervantes' novel or Shakespeare and Fletcher's likely play. In some ways Theobald's collection is entirely expected. He owned the works of almost all the major playwrights, both classical and modern—Seneca, Sophocles, Aeschylus, Plautus, Euripides, Aristophanes, Shakespeare, Jonson, Moliere, Racine, Fernando de Rojas, Heywood, Samuel Daniel, Tasso, among others—and usually in multiple editions and languages. He also owned a number of works in literary criticism, including Jonathan Richardson's *Explanatory Notes and Remarks on Milton's Paradise Lost* (1734), Pierre Brumey's *Le Theatre des Grecs* (1730), and Thomas Blackwell's *An Enquiry into the Life and Writings of Homer* (1735).[8] His library is rich in dictionaries, variorums, and "delphins"— useful in translations and editions.[9] This emphasis on original plays, literary criticism, and translation in Theobald's library is understandable—between his copy of *Mechanici de Machinis Bellicis* (1572) and the volume of "one hundred ninety-five old English Plays in Quarto...all done up neatly in Boards," his collection contains what would have amounted to a remarkable play-making toolkit.[10] Yet, whatever else it is, this library is fundamentally an eighteenth century one, rather than a Renaissance one. Despite key works by Livy, Tacitus, and Plutarch, Theobald's collection is much lighter on moral philosophy than were the great humanist libraries of the Renaissance. History, cosmography, geography, and theology—also at the core of such libraries—are likewise underrepresented. Perhaps most startling, though, in the context of a discussion of how Theobald might have read a work such as *Cardenio* is the almost complete absence of examples of the genre at the heart of *Don Quixote*: the romance.[11] Theobald's library does not include a copy of *Amadis de Gaul*, or, indeed, copies of *any* of the romances that the barber and the priest threw into the fire. Regardless of whether Theobald read the Spanish Quixote, used the Shelton translation, or worked from a "manuscript copy of an original Play by William Shakespeare," what he wrote emerged out of a very different set of experiences and assumptions than those shared by the thousands of readers of *Amadis* that Cervantes invoked, mocked, and imitated in his novel.[12] For those, like Theobald, who were not romance readers, key features of this story about reading remain unintelligible.

For this reason it makes sense to turn to some of the other readers standing between the perhaps originary 1604 reader of *Quijote*, the publisher and bookseller Francisco de Robles, and Theobald. These readers certainly include Edmund Gayton and John Locke. In *Pleasant Notes upon Don Quixot* (1654), Gayton was quick to warn would-be readers that romances are "noxious to the brain," but Locke counted works of "diversion, and delight" as the last "use of reading" and recommended *Quixote* as exemplary in "usefulness, pleasantry, and a constant *decorum*."[13] They also include readers such as Lady Mary Wroth, whose 1621 *Urania* drew from the Shelton translation and created a court scandal about whether and how romances should be read, and Lady Anne Clifford, who included a clearly labeled copy of Shelton's translation in the 1646 Appleby triptych, a portrait that used Clifford's reading of romances to document her intellectual and material lineage with the Herbert family.[14] It seems possible, if unlikely given the construction of his library, that Theobald might have encountered Locke's "Thoughts Concerning Reading and Study." He is certainly less likely to have known of Wroth, Clifford, or Gayton. Yet, they are there, just as much as Shelton and Shakespeare and Fletcher. What is important about these examples is not that they give us insight into what some seventeenth-century

English readers thought about *Quixote*, insight that might seem to hold hints that might allow one to extrapolate something about how Shakespeare and Fletcher might have read and experienced Cervantes. What is important here—whether in Wroth's engagement with an allegorical mode of romance reading or in Gayton's insinuations about connections between wandering Jews and "errant" knights and the need for the "vigorous" reading he associates with English romances (*Pleasant Notes*, 20–1)—is that these examples tell us as much about what these authors thought about reading as they do what they thought about *Quixote*.

These early responses to *Quixote* make sense, since whatever else it is, *Quixote* is a book about reading, a laboratory both for creating readers and for readers to discover and study themselves as readers. A novel in which arguably the only thing that happens in Part II is that the characters have now read Part I, *Quixote* repeatedly asks us to think about what reading is and does. Reading is at the heart of both the practice and subject of Cervantes' novel. Reading is at the heart of most seventeenth-century English responses to *Quixote*. It does not, however, have a role in *Double Falsehood*. This omission is perhaps reason enough to indict Theobald as a reader and would-be re-writer of either Cervantes or Shakespeare. Other of the inset tales within the *Quixote* ask the reader to engage a range of other genres (the picaresque in the case of Ginés de Pasamonte, or the pastoral in that of Gristóstomo and Marcela, for instance), but the encounter with Cardenio is the one episode in Part 1 in which Quixote encounters someone who is in a way reading from the same text that he is: Cardenio and Quixote are readers of *Amadis* and it is this book that creates both the text and genre of their adventures. It is perhaps out of this affinity that, as I have argued elsewhere, Quixote and Sancho become not just an audience to Cardenio's story, but characters within it.[15]

Cervantes' own sly overturning of diegetic levels within the narrative, across the pages as it were of *Amadis*, may thus help explain how a novel about Quixote and Sancho might have become a play about Cardenio and Lucinda. In this context, it is worth noting that the most substantial change the Taylor version of *The History of Cardenio* makes to *Double Falsehood* is to add "Don Quixot" and "his boy" Sancho back into the narrative.[16] The second most significant change involves recognizing that reading is a part, rather than a consequence, of the story. In the play's second scene, we are introduced to Cardenio when he enters, "reading a book." Later, Quesada, soon to become Don Quixot, enters the play carrying another copy of the same book (1.6). Between those two scenes, Cardenio, overcome with love and "unlanguaged" by despair, parts from Lucinda (1.4), leaving her with only his book:

> Read this and you read me: *The History*
> *Of Amadis of Gaul*, mirror of heroes
> And passion's pattern unsurpassable.
> Let Amadis remember you my promise.

Quesada, later, transforms himself into "Don Quixot" and sets out to fight dragons and rescue maidens after Lucinda's father, Don Bernard, rips apart his copy of *Amadis* (1.6). Introducing reading—by way of this paired set of *Amadis* book props—functions dramatically to integrate plot and sub-plot. Thematically, the introduction of *Amadis* into the play also provides a reminder that, in the early modern period, reading was understood to arise out of various forms of passionate imitation. As Quixot insists,

> Does not a painter, when he learns his art,
> Follow and imitate the most famed masters?
> So every knight-apprentice-errant copies
> Th'original of manhood, Amadis of Gaul. (*THOC* 4.1)

Reading creates passion, and that passion is not original but mimetic. In Cervantes, Quixote most closely achieves the passion of his heroes when he reads, rather than when he loves and fights. Reading here is, as it was for early modern readers such as Wroth, Gayton, Clifford, and Locke, a fundamentally aesthetic practice, both an act and an art.

Like other early modern theater companies, the King's Men often used books as props. It is impossible to know whether on June 8, 1613, one of those props was used in the production of "Cardenna" before the ambassador(s) of Savoy. We cannot know whether Shakespeare and Fletcher's characters were depicted as readers of *Amadis*. What we do know, though, is that *Amadis* was in some way part of that production. In Cervantes' novel, *Amadís de Gaula* is the joint text of Cardenio's and Quixote's passions. Early modern audiences shared this passion. *Amadis* was the mostly widely read secular book in Europe, so regardless of whether the actors brought books onto the stage in 1613, members of the audience would themselves in some way have brought *Amadis* to the playhouse through their own experiences as readers. This reading context, not obviously shared by Theobald, was necessarily a part of whatever play was written and, equally important, part of whatever play was performed and watched in 1613.

To understand what readers and audiences may have brought to the play, it is helpful to understand who read *Amadis* and how it became part of a larger argument about the nature and consequences of reading. *Amadís de Gaula* was a long romance cycle, centered on the adventures of Amadis and his beloved Oriana. Originally written by multiple authors, sometime before 1379, this cycle was rewritten and extended by Garci Rodríguez de Montalvo and published starting in the 1490s.[17] The first extant edition, containing the first four books, was published in Saragossa in 1508. Between 1508 and 1586, nineteen editions were published, mostly in Seville and Saragossa. After 1503, Seville held important overseas trade monopolies, and some of these editions (1511, 1526, 1531, 1535, 1539, 1547, and 1551) were almost certainly printed for shipment to the New World. *Amadis* also spread quickly across Europe, particularly in France in Nicolas de Herberay's influential translations. English readers and writers knew *Amadis* through the Herberay

translations, but Anthony Munday also published English-language translations of the first and second books in 1590 and 1595, with the third book
to come in 1619. Italian, German, and Dutch translations likewise appear
through the close of the sixteenth century.

The impact of the Amadis cycle was unprecedented. Thousands of readers, and listeners, read and heard *Amadis*. In Spain, *Amadis* was "the most
popular work of fiction in the Golden Age." Outside Spain, there may well
have been as many as 500,000 readers for the French editions alone.[18] Who
were those readers? The question of whether Shakespeare or Fletcher, or any
other author, may had access to and been shaped by a text like *Amadis* is of
course always at at the heart of traditional source study.[19] Yet, once one starts
thinking about texts from the perspective of the reader, it may be equally
relevant to think more widely, focusing not just on those who came to texts
as writers but on those who may, Quixote-like, have brought their reading
experiences with them from romance to romance, from novel to play, or simply from printed word to lived experience.

For this kind of question it is thus worth thinking about the evidence
about readers and their practices that may appear in library collections and
bookseller's catalogues, and marginalia, *adversaria*, and commonplace books.
Isabella d'Este, the Marchionesse of Mantua, had copies in her famed *stu-
diolo*, as did the English mathematician John Dee, in his extensive library at
Mortlake. It is perhaps unsurprising that Mary, Queen of Scotts, owned "the
first buik of Amadis de gaule" and "the levint buik of Amadis de gaule," but
it is more unexpected to discover that William Cecil, Lord Burghley, pur-
chased a copy of the Herberay translation in 1554.[20] In 1599 Robert Sidney
was "very earnestly" writing to acquire a "Spannish Amadis de Gaule," and
in 1617 Fynes Moryson describes buying "the fourteenth Booke of *Amadis
de Gaule* in the Dutch tongue, to practise the same."[21] The reach of *Amadis*
extended beyond courtly readers and aristocratic libraries. In interviews with
the Inquisition, farmers, itinerant glass blowers, wool dyers—about 80 percent of those questioned—admitted to reading or owning *Amadis* and other
romances of chivalry. Among those who could not read, these romances
were one of the few categories of books that people acknowledged having
heard read aloud.[22]

Amadis probably changed early modern reading practices. *Amadis* certainly became a metaphor for those changes. The numbers and availability of printed books increased exponentially during the sixteenth century,
and reading became a newly important and often highly contested activity.
Among a range of competing and coexisting models of reading—important
in creating faith, acquiring knowledge, or achieving economic success—the
two most important here are humanism and Galenism. These two commitments intersect in *Quixote*, and they do so around the text of *Amadis*.

For humanists, reading was at the heart of the imitation and creation
of virtue. Humanistic pedagogy primarily focused on the creation of civic
virtues—scholars have thus rightly focused attention on how Renaissance
humanists read authors such as Cicero, Plutarch, Tacitus, and Livy.[23] Yet

humanistic *imitatio* also carried over to other kinds of literature. Machiavelli, as John Locke will do later, speaks of reading for pleasure as well as for virtue. With Dante and Petrarch and Ovid, Machiavelli reads avidly: "I read about their amorous passions and about their loves. I remember my own, and I revel for a moment in this thought." Identifying this 1513 letter as a "document in the history of reading," Anthony Grafton stresses that this second form of reading was as essential to Renaissance humanism as was its commitment to more familiar philological and philosophical scholarly forms of reading.[24]

I would emphasize, though, that while such modes of reading differ in purpose and content, they each depend primarily on acts of imitation. Whether in emulating Ciceronian virtue or in re-experiencing Ovidian passion, Machiavelli reads himself in and through these texts. Authors, translators, and publishers of the *Amadis* cycle consistently encouraged their readers to follow this form of humanistic *imitation*. The Parisian publisher and bookseller Denis Janot thus aligned his editions with humanistic reading practices by replacing the black letter fonts and double-column pages with an elegant Garamond and a single-column format, while plates that depicted particularly intense emotional moments were re-used and transferred from one character to another in ways that encouraged readers to model the characters and script themselves into a narrative of imitative passion.

While humanism spoke to the Renaissance commitment to this idea of the creation of the individual as what Ernest Burckhardt classically described as a "work of art," Galenic medicine translated the virtues and qualities that readers might create in themselves into a physiological framework.[25] In the sixteenth century, reading came to be accepted as one of the "non naturals," implicitly classified alongside the six external factors that Galenic medicine had always identified as components of humoral balance.[26] Because humoralism was a materialist psychology that understood the body as a site for the concocting and digestion of the four elements, reading could alter readers physically, changing the quality of spirits in the blood and the temperature and complexion of the body as a whole. What and how one read was as important as what one ate or where one lived in altering one's humoral balance. While humanism emphasized the moral qualities that reading might create, humoralism stressed the physical character it produced.

Amadis became a text that intensified the overlay of imitation onto passion that was implied by these two models of reading. Juan Luis Vives complained that romances like *Amadis* "kyndle and styr up covetousness, inflame angre, & all beastly and filthy desyre."[27] He was not alone: Juan de la Cerda, Luisa María de Padilla Manrique, Benito Remigio Noydens, Antonio de Guevara, Francisco Cervantes Salazar, Montaigne, Ambroise Paré, Jacques Amyot, Thomas Blount, Thomas Hobbes, and Robert Boyle all warned would-be readers against such dangers. The complaints of such critics stress that romance encouraged intense imitative responses and did so in ways that were humorally dangerous. These complaints focus not just on the moral consequences of romance but also on its physiological ones. In tempering the reader's body, romances were understood initially to produce heat ("kyndle," "inflame," "fevered"), but that heat ultimately burned away, leaving a dry and now cold body (described in one account as the "furious ardour" that "dries up and desiccates the greenest and most flourishing part"). For these writers, reading romances produced love-sickness. A form of melancholy, love-sickness was a malign humoral imbalance that arose when an image (presumably that of the beloved) led to a malfunctioning of the brain. Ordinarily, visual images came into the *sensus communis*, the moist first ventricle of the brain. These images would normally then be transferred first to the central ventricle, the site of reason and imagination and the hottest part of the brain, and then later moved to the cool, dry third ventricle, to be stored for later use. In those who suffered from love-melancholy, though, these transfers do not happen: instead, the "estimative faculty" of the second ventricle seemed to focus intensively and persistently on the image of the beloved, drawing heat and moisture from the other parts of the brain and body, causing the body to overheat and dry out.[28]

While romances like *Amadis* encouraged imitation by readers, Cervantes' *Quixote* asks us to imagine the "furious ardour" that might come with such acts of reading. Early modern warnings about what might happen to those who *read* romances sound suspiciously like a version of the passion that often afflicts the characters *within* the romances themselves. This is not a coincidence, but rather suggests how strongly *Amadis* became a text through which Renaissance readers explored the intersection of a model of reading that demanded imitation with one that produced passion. Cervantes draws on this model of passionate imitation when he describes how, for Quixote, "through his little sleepe and much reading, he dryed up his braines in such sort as he lost wholly his judgement" (1.1.4). As Cervantes construes it, it is *in the act of reading itself* that Quixote most closely emulates his fictional heroes. Love dries out Orlando's brain when he become enamored by the image of Angelica, but it is reading that dries out Quixote's when he becomes enthralled by the words on the page.

Yet, what the critics of *Amadis* saw as the danger produced by reading, Cervantes offers us as what I would suggest are its possibilities. Passion and imitation: it is out of this intersection of passion and imitation that *Quixote* was constructed. It is almost certain that it is out of this intersection that Renaissance audiences, with their experiences as readers of *Amadis* and their understanding of the similar theories of humoral affect that shaped theatrical production, would have experienced whatever version of *Cardenio* may have been staged in 1613.[29] As historical models of reading that we may find in the Renaissance, what are the lessons for us, as editors or as teachers? It seems clear that Borges, and Taylor, are right that we can only "reach the *Quixote*" as readers, by starting with reading rather than by ending with it.

It is consistently worth remembering what the Renaissance knew so well. Reading happens not just in our minds, but in our bodies, and it is precisely for this reason that it produces the passions that connect us to lived experience.

NOTES

1. See *DQ*, 1.1.2; 1.1.6; 1.4.32 and *The Second Part of the History of the Valorous and Witty Knight-Errant, Don Quixote* (London, 1620), 74.497, for multiple and conflicting accounts of Don Quixote's original name; for a history of the different titles that may have been used to refer to the English play, see Taylor, "History," 4, 12–14, 22–4.

2. Jorge Luis Borges, "Pierre Menard, Author of the *Quixote*," in *Labyrinths: Selected Stories Collected Fictions*, ed. Donald A. Yates and James E. Irby (New York: New Directions, 1964), 91.

3. John Kerrigan, "The Editor as Reader: Constructing Renaissance Texts," in *The Practice and Representation of Reading in England*, ed. James Raven, Helen Small, and Naomi Tadmor (Cambridge: Cambridge University Press, 1996), 102.

4. Jerome McGann, *The Textual Condition* (Chicago: University of Chicago Press, 1991), 4–5.

5. Alberto Manguel, *A History of Reading* (New York: Viking Penguin, 1996), 7–8.

6. Charles Corbett, *A Catalogue of the Library of Lewis Theobald, Deceas'd* (London, 1744).

7. Corbett, *Catalogue*, nos. 28, 193, and 472. In his discussion of Theobald's library, Roger Chartier comments on Theobald's likely reliance upon one of his Spanish-language editions of *Quixote* but does not note that he also owned at least one English edition: *Cardenio between Cervantes and Shakespeare: The Story of a Lost Play* (Cambridge: Polity Press, 2013), 118. For a further discussion of what edition(s) Theobald may have been using, see also chapter 2 in this volume by Gary Taylor and Steven Wagschal.

8. Corbett, *Catalogue*, nos. 32, 281, and 35.

9. Corbett, *Catalogue*, tp.

10. Corbett, *Catalogue*, nos. 126 and 460.

11. In ways that differ from our expectations, Renaissance readers were much more likely to own copies of romances like *Amadis* than they were plays. See, for examples, the inventories in Robert J. Fehrenbach, E. S. Leedham-Green, and Joseph Laurence Black, *Private Libraries in Renaissance England: A Collection and Catalogue of Tudor and Early Stuart Book-Lists* (Binghamton, NY: Medieval & Renaissance Texts & Studies, 1992), vols. 1–7.

12. "Royal License," *DF*, 162; *DQ*, ¶2r; J. A. G. Argile, "The Influence and Reception of Cervantes in Britain, 1607–2005," in *The Cervantean Heritage: Reception and Influence of Cervantes in Britain* (London: Legenda, 2009), 4–5. See also chapters 2, 3, and 10 in this volume by Gants, Taylor and Wagschal.

13. Edmund Gayton, *Pleasant Notes upon Don Quixot* (London, 1654), 19–21; John Locke, "Some Thoughts Concerning Reading and Study for a Gentleman," in *A Collection of Several Pieces of Mr. John Locke* (London: 1720), 244.

14. Elizabeth Spiller, *Reading the History of Race in the Renaissance* (Cambridge: Cambridge University Press, 2011), 154–5.

15. Elizabeth Spiller, "Cervantes *avant la Lettre*: The Material Transformation of Romance Reading Culture in *Don Quijote*," *MLQ* 60.3 (1999): 317.

16. For arguments that the Jacobean play contained Quixote and Sancho, see Taylor and Nance, "Four Characters in Search of a Subplot," *Quest*, 192–213; for "Quixot" as the preferred English rendition of the name in the seventeenth century, see Taylor, "History," 17.

17. Edwin Place, "Preface," in Edwin Place and Herbert Behm, trans., *Amadis of Gaul: Books I and II* (1974: Lexington: University Press of Kentucky, 2003), 9.

18. Sara Nalle, "Literacy and Culture in Early Modern Castile," *Past and Present* 125 (1989): 80; Marian Rothstein, *Reading in the Renaissance: Amdis de Gaule and the Lessons of Memory* (Newark: University of Delaware Press, 1999), preface, n.p.

19. For a classic account of the literary influence of *Amadis of Gaul* in England that largely pursues this kind of source study, see John J. O'Connor, *Amadis de Gaul and Its Influence on Elizabethan Literature* (Camden: Rutgers University Press, 1970); for a more recent focus on Shakespeare's reading practices generally, see Robert S. Miola, *Shakespeare's Reading* (Oxford: Oxford University Press, 2000). The speculation that Shakespeare drew from the ninth volume of the French *Amadis* cycle in the *Tempest* was first advanced by the nineteenth-century translator of *Amadis*, Robert Southey; Henry Thomas, *Shakespeare and Spain* (Oxford: Clarendon, 1922), 22. Fletcher certainly knew *Amadis*, referring to it in *The Elder Brother*, 5.2.64 ("is growne an *Amadis*"); in *The Wild-Goose Chase*, 1.1.110–1 ("Beleeve them? Beleeve *Amadis de Gaule/* The *Knight* o'th'*Sun*"); and 4.3.55–6 ("Who am I?—You are Amadis de Gaule, sir"). My thanks to Gary Taylor for calling my attention to these references.

20. Cited in Alex Davis, *Chivalry and Romance in the English Renaissance* (London: D.S. Brewer, 2003), 28–9.

21. Michael G. Brennan and Noel J. Kinnamon, *A Sidney Chronology, 1554–1654* (Basingstoke: Palgrave Macmillan, 2003), 163; Fynes Moryson, *An Itinerary* (London, 1617), 56–7.

22. Nalle, "Literacy and Culture," 89.

23. See, for example, Anthony Grafton and Lisa Jardine, "'Studied for Action': How Gabriel Harvey Read His Livy," *Past and Present* 129 (1990): 30–78.

24. Anthony Grafton, "The Humanist as Reader," in Guglielo Cavallo and Roger Chartier, eds., *A History of Reading in the West*, trans. Lydia G. Cochrane (Amherst: University of Massachusetts Press, 1999), 180.

25. Jacob Burckhardt, *The Civilization of the Renaissance in Italy*, trans. Samuel George Chetwynd Middlemore (1860; Swan Sonnenschein: London, 1904), 4, 354.

26. The six non-naturals established by Galenic medicine were diet, air and climate, sleep and wakefulness, retention and evacuation, and "perturbations" of the mind and passions.

27. Juan Luis Vives, *Office and dutie of an husband*, trans. Richard Hyrde (London, 1585), O7v.

28. Spiller, *Reading and the History of Race*, 23–45. See also Barry Ife's classic *Reading and Fiction in Golden-Age Spain* (Cambridge: Cambridge University Press, 1985), 1–38.

29. The role that humoral physiology played in both the construction of character and in creating a humoral ecology among actors and audiences has been the focus of much recent attention: see, among others, Gail Kern Paster, *Humoring the Body: Emotions and the Shakesperean Stage* (Chicago: University of Chicago Press, 2004). One might also consult Stephen Gosson's *Plays Confuted* (London, 1582), D5v, for an example of contemporary concern about how staging the dangerous "humors" of printed romance brought their distempers and poisons to theater audiences.

2

READING CERVANTES, OR SHELTON, OR PHILLIPS? THE SOURCE(S) OF *CARDENIO* AND *DOUBLE FALSEHOOD*

Gary Taylor and Steven Wagschal

Strangely and sadly, Cervantes is almost entirely ignored by modern scholarship on the seventeenth-century play *Cardenio* and the eighteenth-century play *Double Falsehood*.[1] His name and his novel are often invoked. But the words critics quote and analyze are those of Thomas Shelton, the first translator of the Spanish *Don Quijote*. Scholars compound this confusion (of the Spanish text with the English translation) by assuming that the eighteenth-century *Double Falsehood* and the seventeenth-century *Cardenio* had the same source. But why must we, or should we, make that assumption? The Spanish text was available in England, and being read by Englishmen, in 1612, 1727, and every year between. If we remove these self-imposed blinders, we can learn a lot about *Double Falsehood* and its relationship to Cervantes.

Richard Farmer in 1727 first noted that *Double Falsehood* could be based either on Cervantes or Shelton's 1612 translation. But in 1911 Rudolph Schevill challenged that orthodoxy.[2] He argued that the play published by Theobald late in 1727 was based on *The Adventures on the Black Mountains*, an adaptation of the Cardenio narrative published in London in 1729 in a large collection of abridged novels and histories edited by Samuel Croxall.[3] Although Schevill was a professional Hispanist, his inquiry was "based entirely on an examination of Shelton's *Don Quixote*, Croxall's *The Adventures*, etc., and *Double Falsehood*" (270). He demonstrated that the anonymous *Black Mountains* indisputably plagiarizes the Shelton translation. Schevill found "no evidence whatsoever" that would connect it to "the Spanish original" (277). *Black Mountains* for the most part reproduced Shelton word for word, sentence for sentence, and paragraph by paragraph, but it "tried to bring the Elizabethan English of Shelton somewhat up to date by changing the forms which at the time of the 'translation' were most apparently obsolete" (275). More significantly, *Black Mountains* omits Don Quixote, Sancho, the barber and the curate, as does *Double Falsehood*. Schevill conjectured that Theobald had pre-publication access to the manuscript of *Black Mountains*, and to nothing else. If this hypothesis is true, then the eighteenth-century play had an eighteenth-century source, and can tell us nothing about the seventeenth-century play.

But Schevill's claim was soon discredited. In 1916, Walter Graham demonstrated that at least seven passages of *Double Falsehood* depend on parts of the Shelton translation that were *not* included in *Black Mountains*.[4] Graham's proof demolishes the argument that Theobald's 1727 text derives from the 1729 novella. Instead, the novella appears to have used the printed text of *Double Falsehood* (which it specifically acknowledges) as a framework for reorganizing the multiple, intertwining, reported accounts that Cervantes/Shelton used to tell the Cardenio story. Nevertheless, Graham's evidence does not, in itself, prove Theobald's claim that *Double Falsehood* was based on an unpublished seventeenth-century play. After all, since the unknown translator/adapter who produced *Black Mountains* made use of Shelton's translation, Theobald too might theoretically have used the 1725 reprint of Shelton in order to create a new play that he then falsely attributed to Shakespeare. Moreover, Graham inherited from Schevill a focus exclusively on Shelton, and exclusively on the Cardenio story. He did not look for sources of *Double Falsehood* elsewhere in the novel. He never considered the obvious fact that the key passages, absent from *Black Mountains* but present in Shelton and *Double Falsehood*, are also present in *Don Quijote* itself.

Subsequent scholarship has inherited that Anglophone assumption. John Freehafer's influential 1969 essay on *Cardenio* demonstrated that no other English translation, except Shelton, can account for certain parallels between *Don Quixote* and *Double Falsehood*.[5] But Freehafer never compared Shelton to the Cervantine original. Indeed, the first explicit comparison between Shelton and Cervantes, in relation to this play or plays, was not published until 2012. Freehafer had shown that the full title of the play attributed in 1653 to Fletcher and Shakespeare, "The History of Cardenio", reproduces verbatim a phrase from Shelton's translation, which does not occur in any other seventeenth- or eighteenth-century translation. In *The Quest for Cardenio*, Gary Taylor demonstrated that the title phrase must come from Shelton, because Cervantes has, at that point in the text, *cuento* (account, tale), not *historia* (history).[6] Taylor limited his examination of the Spanish text to the paragraph cited by Freehafer from Shelton. Steven Wagschal has now searched, digitally, the entire Spanish text of the 1605 *Don Quijote*, confirming that the phrase "historia de Cardenio" appears nowhere in Cervantes. Thus, the only four words of the early-seventeenth-century English play for which we have indisputable documentary evidence come from Shelton, not Cervantes.

However, this evidence tells us nothing about *Double Falsehood*. Theobald's text never uses the phrase "the history of Cardenio." Nevertheless, Theobald did know that story. Using "novel" in the early sense of "novella" or "in-set story," Theobald's preface acknowledged that "the tale of this play" was "built upon a novel in *Don Quixot*" (*DF* Pre.28–9). Theobald then proceeded to note that "*Don Quixot* was published in the year 1611"

(Pre.31). In the second issue of his Preface, he corrected this initial statement, observing that "the *First* Part of *Don Quixot*, which contains the Novel upon which the Tale of this Play seems to be built, was published in the year 1605" ("Eleven Years" before Shakespeare's death in 1616).[7] This self-correction establishes that, when the play was first performed and published, Theobald did not know the date of the original publication of Cervantes' novel. Moreover, the revision "1605" refers to the Spanish text, rather than the English translation of 1612. So, apparently, does Theobald's original "1611". A Spanish-language edition of the novel was published in 1611 in Brussels, and at the time of his death in 1744 Theobald owned a copy of that 1611 Spanish octavo. His library, at the time of his death, also included another, undated, two-volume, illustrated octavo edition of the Spanish novel, and the 1687 folio translation by John Phillips. But it did not contain a copy of Shelton.[8]

Theobald refers to one sentence in the novel twice in his 1733 edition of Shakespeare. On both occasions he quotes the Spanish text, and then supplies his own translation, which differs substantially from Shelton's (and Phillips's).[9] It is always difficult to prove a negative proposition, and we cannot prove that Theobald *never* possessed a copy of Shelton. But there is no evidence that he ever did. Tiffany Stern claims that "Theobald was a Cervantes fanatic" (592), a characterization most Hispanists would find exaggerated. What is the evidence of this alleged fanaticism? John Fletcher demonstrably read and used Cervantes far more than Theobald did. *The Happy Captive* (1741) is very loosely based on the captive's tale in *Don Quijote*, but most of Theobald's play bears no relationship to the novel: it preserves only the basic scenario of a young woman in Algiers who falls in love with a Spanish captive there, and runs away with him against her father's wishes. We have not found a single verbal parallel linking Theobald's play to either the Shelton or the Phillips translation. The only detail that varies significantly is the name of the heroine: "Zorayda" in Theobald and Cervantes, "Zoraida" in Shelton and Phillips. We possess abundant documentary proof for Theobald's knowledge of Spanish, and his possession of Spanish texts of Cervantes. By contrast, the claim that he ever read Shelton is purely speculative.

Critics like Stern, who assume or insist that Theobald possessed a copy of Shelton, have a transparent agenda: they want to prove that he could have forged *Double Falsehood*. But it seems improbable that anyone would have forged a play based on Shelton. The 1725 reprint claims, on the title page of each of its four volumes, to have been "Translated into *English* By *THOMAS SHELTON*, and now printed *verbatim* from the 4*to* Edition of 1620." Every reader of Rowe's edition, or Pope's, knew that Shakespeare died in 1616, and Theobald's Preface to *Double Falsehood* reminded them of that date. Why would Theobald forge a play using a source that, so far as he or the general public knew, had not been published until four years after Shakespeare's death? If he were using Shelton, why not correct the 1725 reprint, by telling his readers that *Don Quixote* had been translated in 1612, instead of referring to a Spanish edition of 1611? Why base a forgery on a work that Shakespeare is not known to have used elsewhere? Why not forge a play based on North's translation of Plutarch's *Lives,* or Holinshed's *Chronicle?*

But instead of rhetorical questions, let's consider one that can be tested: Does the alleged evidence of *Double Falsehood*'s dependence on Shelton survive a comparison with the Spanish text, or with Phillips's translation? To answer this question, we have re-examined all parallels between the play and Shelton cited by other scholars, and in each case we have compared the play to the original Spanish and to Phillips. In order to avoid bias, the Spanish text has been checked by Wagschal, who has no investment in the disputed relationship between *Double Falsehood* and the seventeenth-century play, and for whom *Double Falsehood* belongs to the long history of appropriations and adaptations of Cervantes.

Fourteen of the twenty-four verbal parallels between *Double Falsehood* and Shelton, collected by previous scholars, could in fact come from either the Spanish or the English text, because Shelton and Phillips are both close to Cervantes, or because the parallel is situational rather than verbal.[10] But there remain at least nine verbal details of *Double Falsehood* that point clearly to Shelton rather than Cervantes or Phillips. In the following list, we ignore elements of the parallel that could have come from any of the three texts, focusing instead on pertinent differences between them.

1. *DF* 3.1.6–13: She bids me fill my memory with her danger.

   SHELTON 3.13.271 (Lucinda's letter to Cardenio): I beseech Almighty God that this may arrive unto your hands before mine shall be in danger to join itself with his.

Shelton's "in danger" is much closer to *Double Falsehood*'s "danger" than to the Spanish *condición* (1.27.336). Phillips (3.13.129) has no equivalent for this sentence, and differs from Shelton, Cervantes, and the play in the rest of this passage.

2. *DF* 3.2.164: Don Bernard, this wild Tumult soon will cease.

   SHELTON 3.13.275: All the house were in a tumult for this sudden amazement.

The word "tumult" does not appear in Phillips (3.13.131) or in the Spanish (*"Alborotáronse todos con el desmayo de Luscinda"*).[11]

3. *DF* 4.1.181: So sad a story

   SHELTON 4.2.300: her sad story
   PHILLIPS 4.2.144: her doleful story

In Shelton the story is Dorotea's; in the play, it belongs to her equivalent, Violante. The Spanish contains no equivalent of "sad story" in either context.

4. *DF* 4.2.5: solitary places

CERVANTES 1.23.287: lo más cerrado desta sierra
SHELTON 3.9.214: solitary places
PHILLIPS 3.9.106: remote and private Retirements

The Spanish here is singular rather than plural, and not synonymous with the English.

5. *DF* 4.2.38: How much more grateful are these craggy mountains

SHELTON 4.1.282: How much more gratefull companions will these crag-ges and thickets prove

Shelton's "grateful" differs significantly from the Spanish *agradable* ("agree-able, pleasant") in *Quijote* (1.28.344). Nothing in Phillips (4.1.135) cor-responds to this sentence, and his translation differs from Cervantes and Shelton in the rest of the speech.

6. *DF* 4.2.86–7: Can it be possible / That you are Violante?

SHELTON 4.1.291: is it possible that you are named *Dorotea*.

Cervantes (1.28.352) contains nothing comparable to "can it be possible" or "is it possible." Neither does Phillips (4.1.140).

7. *DF* 5.2.172–4: Here is a letter, Brother…The Writing, yours.

CERVANTES 1.36.451: *la firma que hiciste.*
SHELTON 4.9.404–5: Witness shall also be thine own hand writing.

The Spanish does not refer to the handwriting of the letter, but instead specifies, literally, "the signature that you made."[12] Phillips omits all refer-ence to the letter (4.9.200). Shelton and the play assume that the entire letter was written by Fernando personally; Cervantes, perhaps more credibly for someone of Fernando's rank, presupposes that only the signature is his.

8. The Duke's elder son, not named in *Don Quixote*, is called "Roderick" in the Dramatis Personae list and in *DF* 1.1, 3.3, 4.1, 5.1, and 5.2.

Freehafer noted that this name occurs in Shelton's marginal note at 3.13.267, which explains that "Julian" (in Cardenio's list of traitors, to whom Fernando might be compared) was "One who for the rape of his daughter, committed by Rodericke King of Spaine, brought in the Moores and destroyed all the Countrey." On this same page, Cardenio explains that Fernando sent him to "his eldest brother" (allegedly "to get some money of him, for to buy six great horses"). So the unnamed elder brother, and his crucial role in the betrayal plot, are mentioned on the same page as this villainous "Rodericke" in the marginal note.

This parallel is more persuasive and important than Freehafer realized. Phillips omits the note, and the whole passage that prompted it. Neither Shakespeare nor Fletcher uses the name elsewhere, so it cannot have been interpolated or forged by Theobald in order to make his attribution to Shakespeare more plausible. If plugging in a suitably Shakespearian name were a forger's intention, "Roderigo" would have been readily available to anyone familiar with *Othello*. The name does not appear in D'Urfey's *Don Quixote* either, so Theobald would not have needed to change it to avoid associations with that popular farce.[13] Since there is no discernible reason for Theobald or anyone else to have forged or substituted the name, it presumably belonged to the seventeenth-century play.[14] "Roderick" had not been used for a character in any extant English play before 1613, so it's not simply a conventional Spanish name that the author(s) of *Cardenio* could have picked up anywhere. It seems most likely to have come from Shelton.

But Shelton also uses "Rodericke" elsewhere (*DQ* 1.5.33), where it appears three times in one paragraph. There, it refers to "the Moor, Abindaraez, when the constable of Antequera, Roderick Narvaez, had taken him and carried him prisoner to his castle." This chapter of the novel has nothing to do with Cardenio, which perhaps explains why Freehafer and other English scholars overlooked the parallel. The passage refers to a Moorish tale in the pastoral romance *"Diana of Montemayor"* (as Cervantes and his translators explain). The Moor fights with Don Roderick, and Roderick wins and captures him. But the Moor was on his way to get married to a Moorish woman, and Rodrigo as a demonstration of his chivalry makes arrangements for the wedding to take place. Hence, in the tale to which *Don Quixote* alludes, "Roderick" is responsible for a marital happy ending – just like "Roderick" in *Double Falsehood,* but unlike the elder brother in the Cardenio episodes of *Don Quixote*. The name thus helps to explain the play's expansion of the elder brother role, and it provides a chivalric role model for that character (allowing spectators to make comparisons with the chivalric Prince Henry). The name cannot come from the Spanish text or Phillips; neither contains Shelton's marginal note, and both name the constable "Rodrigo" instead of Shelton's "Roderick" (Phillips 1.5.20). So does Montemayor, in the Spanish and in the English translation of *Diana,* which most scholars believe was the source of Shakespeare's *Two Gentlemen of Verona*.[15] Since Cervantes and his translators both name the source of the story, this detail might well have stood out for Shakespeare.

9. *DF* 4.1.125–6: He pull'd at it as he would have dragg'd a bullock backward by the tail

   SHELTON 1.6.40: A thiefe that used to steale cattell and pull them backeward by the tayles

Shelton's marginal note, explaining the text's reference to "Cacus", has not been noticed by previous scholars. The note does not appear in Cervantes or Phillips, and the phrase is extremely rare: there are no parallels for the verb "pull" near "backward by the tail(s)", referring to cattle, in any period or genre of Literature Online, or Early English Books Online, or Theobald.

These nine elements of *Double Falsehood* all derive from the same source as the title of the seventeenth-century play: Shelton. By contrast, among the parallels noted by other scholars we have found only two that are closer to Cervantes than to Shelton. We have also noticed two additional features of the play that link it to the books Theobald owned, rather than to Shelton.

> A. DF 3.2.73, 159, 160: Shews a dagger…What dagger means she?…Here is the dagger.
>
> SHELTON 3.13.272: I carry hidden about me a ponyard…thou carriest a poniard
>
> SHELTON 3.13.274: I hoped that she would take out the Poynard to stab her selfe
>
> SHELTON 4.1.296: a ponyard that was found hidden about her in her apparrell…Don Fernando…attempted to kill her with the very same ponyard

Shelton uses "poniard" five times, describing one object associated with one person. But although Cervantes used both words elsewhere, the Spanish in all these passages uses *daga* (dagger) instead of *puñal* (poniard). All three English playwrights (Fletcher, Shakespeare, and Theobald) use both English words elsewhere; both occur in stage directions throughout the period. The repeated word here in *Double Falsehood* cannot come from Shelton. But it could come from Cervantes ("una daga" 1.27.337, "la daga" 1.27.339, "una daga" 1.28.356) or Phillips ("this dagger" 3.13.130, "her dagger" 3.13.131, "a Dagger" 4.1.142).

> B. *DF Dramatis Personae*: Master of the Flocks.
>
> *DF 4.1.0.1: Enter Master of the Flocks, three or four Shepherds.*
>
> SHELTON 4.1.299: my Master came at last to the notice that I was no man but a woman, which was an occasion that the like evill thought sprung in him, as before in my servant. And as fortune gives not always remedie for the difficulties which occurre, I found neyther rocke nor downefall to coole and cure my Masters infirmitie, as I had done for my man

As Freehafer noted (502), Shelton calls this character "Master" twice, whereas other translators call him a "Countryman" (Phillips 4.1.144) or "Rustick." In the passage quoted above, "Master" correctly translates the Spanish *amo*, twice used in verbal contrast to the *criado* ("Servant") who had previously tried to rape her. No such contrast occurs in the play, which does not dramatize the attempted rape by the servant. Thus the word "Master" here differentiates Shelton from the other English translators, but not from Cervantes. However, the play does make use of a passage, a few sentences earlier (Shelton 4.1.298), which introduces and identifies this character.

> I found a Heardman, who carried me to a village seated in the midst of these rockes, wherein he dwelled and intertained me, whom I have served as a Sheepheard ever since, procuring as much as lay in me to abide still in the fielde…

This differs significantly from the Spanish (1.28.358):

> ha no sé cuántos meses, que entré en ellas, donde hallé un ganadero que me llevó por su criado a un lugar que está en las entrañas desta sierra, al cual he servido de zagal todo este tiempo, procurando estar siempre en el campo...

Here Dorotea is the servant (*criado*), but the man is not called master; he is instead "a Heardman." One word refers to his specific relationship to her; the other to his occupation, his economic and social identity. "Heardman" (or herdsman) in English does not necessarily imply owner. The first example in the *Oxford English Dictionary* comes from *The General History of the Turkes* (1603): "Who yet with their wives and children, as heardsmen, wander up and downe the countrey" (133). "Herdman" fits the representation of the character in the play's dialogue: he is present in the mountains with the other shepherds, who seem to include him among the generic collective vocatives "neighbors" (4.1.108, 123, 127) or "sirs" (24). Although one of them calls him "sir" (7), he in turn calls all of them "sirs" (137), so the scene does not establish a hierarchical difference between him and the other shepherds. The dialogue makes it clear that Violante is "[his] boy" (4.1.21, 156), and that he is her "master" (4.1.158, 4.2.50), but it does not make him anyone else's boss. Roderick addresses him simply as "Shepherd" (4.1.186), and later calls him "the surly Shepherd" (5.1.58), not differentiating him from the others. The dialogue of *Double Falsehood* is thus perfectly compatible with Shelton's translation "Heardman."

By contrast, *un ganadero* is a livestock owner or rearer, usually of more than one herd, which could be of sheep, goats or cattle. Cervantes distinguishes *ganadero* from *pastor* (used for literary shepherds like Crysostom and his friends) or *cabrero* (a more vulgar word, used for the actual goatherds encountered by Cardenio and Quixote). Since he owns more than one herd, *un ganadero* cannot be out in the fields or mountains, herding them all. Indeed Cervantes and Shelton both locate him in a "village" (*lugar*), in contrast to Dorotea, who stays as much as possible "in the field" (*en el campo*), the better to hide from him her true sexual identity. "Master of the Flocks" is actually a better translation of *ganadero* than "herdman" (or "Countryman").

C. In three chapters of the novel (*DQ* 3.10, 3.13, 4.1), Shelton consistently uses the word "city" to describe the place where Cardenio and Luscinda live, where Fernando tries to wed her, and where Dorothea goes to seek him.

Shelton accurately translates the repeated *ciudad* of Cervantes (*DQ* 1.24, 1.27, 1.28). Phillips instead consistently calls it a "village" (Spanish *lugar*). Among many other places, *lugar* appears in the first sentence of the first chapter of *Don Quijote*, but is never used in reference to Luscinda's or Cardenio's home. The contrast between Cervantes/Shelton ("city") and Phillips ("village") corresponds with a contradiction in *Double Falsehood*. As

David Carnegie has pointed out, the dialogue uses the word "City" (3.3.66), and stage directions and speech prefixes designate a character who dwells in that place as "Citizen" (2.4, 3.1, 3.3). *Citizen* here means "inhabitant of a city (or town), esp. one possessing civic rights and privileges" (*OED* 1), and it contrasts with the word "villager" (1.3.24), associated with the farmer's daughter Violante. But the scene locations in *Double Falsehood* repeatedly refer to the "Prospect of a Village" (1.2, 2.1, 2.3, 3.1, 3.3).[16] These scene directions represent anachronistic theatrical conventions, which would not have been present in a play manuscript of 1613 or 1653; they must have been added to the text at some time after 1660. Stage directions for a "prospect of" occur thirteen times in six other plays by Theobald. But that theatrical convention would have been satisfied by a "Prospect of the City," as in Theobald's *Persian Princess* (1715), or by the very common scene location "A Street," as in Theobald's *Merlin*. By contrast, "prospect of a village" first appears here in *Double Falsehood*.[17] The choice of "Village," as the locale for those scenes, cannot derive from theatrical convention, or from Cervantes, or Shelton, or a pre-1642 play manuscript. But it could derive from Phillips.

> D. In Shelton, Cardenio addresses the Barber and Curate as "Good sirs" (3.13.264) and "Sirs" (265), and at the end of the chapter addresses one as "Sir."

This translates accurately the "*señores*" of Cervantes (1.27.331, 1.27.332). But in the same sentences, Phillips has "Gentlemen...Gentlemen" (3.13.128) and "Gentlemen" (3.13.132), which more closely corresponds to Spanish *señores hidalgos* or *señores caballeros*. In the corresponding scene (4.2.1–7), *Double Falsehood* does not have these vocatives, but it replaces the Curate and Barber with "*two Gentlemen*" in the opening stage direction, and with subsequent speech prefixes for "*Gent.*"

Taylor and Nance have argued that Theobald invented these "Gentlemen," as a consequence of his deletion of the original subplot containing Quixote, Sancho, the Curate, and Barber.[18] Two phrases in the opening lines, "compose yourself" (4.2.1) and "this interval" (4.4.4), occur elsewhere in Theobald but not in Shakespeare or Fletcher.[19] However, like other scholars, Taylor and Nance simply assumed that both *Cardenio* and *Double Falsehood* were based on Shelton's translation. The original play cannot have drawn upon the Phillips translation, but *Double Falsehood* could. Needing to remove the Barber and Curate, but also requiring some companions for Cardenio in this scene, Theobald might have turned to Phillips for inspiration, and there discovered an alternative generic identity for the two characters.

What are we to make of this contrasting evidence? *Double Falsehood* seems to owe nine features to Shelton, and four to some other source: Phillips (two), Cervantes (one), Phillips or Cervantes (one). But these different sources are distributed in an interesting pattern. All nine Shelton parallels affect the play's dialogue, and in particular affect dialogue that shows no sign of eighteenth-century interference.[20] The first two come from scenes usually attributed to Shakespeare; the next five, from scenes usually attributed to Fletcher; the last two link Shakespeare scenes to Fletcher scenes, and presumably reflect decisions made in the initial scenario, before writing began. One of them links *Double Falsehood* to another text Shakespeare read. By contrast, the four elements that point away from Shelton are all connected to the play's unspoken paratext, an element of the play strongly associated with Theobald and the process of theatrical adaptation.

The "two Gentlemen," the "Prospect of a Village," and the "Master of the Flocks" occur only in the paratext of *Double Falsehood*. Neither Shakespeare nor Fletcher used scene locations, and neither used the phrase "of the flocks," and neither ever produced a *dramatis personae* list like the one in *Double Falsehood*. The speech prefixes in 4.1 identify Violante's employer only as "Master," and that same label might have been used in the original stage direction for his entrance. Indeed, if that original stage direction read "Shepherds Master and Violante," without punctuation, Theobald might have consulted his 1611 edition of *Don Quijote* to clarify the sense.

"*Shows a dagger*" also occurs first in a stage direction, apparently designed to clarify an ambiguity in the dialogue ("see—I'm armed"). Like his editorial predecessors Rowe and Pope, Theobald routinely added such directions, to make explicit stage action merely implied by Shakespeare's dialogue. Again, Theobald might have turned to his Spanish text, or Phillips, to clarify the ambiguity. The subsequent appearances of "dagger" in the dialogue (3.2 159–60) could also be the result of Theobald's adapting hand.

> What dagger means she? Search her well, I pray you.
> *Don Bernard.* Here is the dagger. O the stubborn sex!

The phrase "stubborn sex" occurs in Theobald's *Perfidious Brother* (1715), but nowhere in Shakespeare, Fletcher, or any other English playwright.[21] One of the two lines that contains "dagger" thus has certainly been adapted or interpolated. "What dagger means she?" followed by "Here is the dagger," at a climactic dramatic moment, is too commonplace to attribute to anyone in particular, but whoever wrote it was not inspired. The one element of the two lines that might most plausibly be attributed to the original play is the five-word-string "her well, I pray you," which occurs in *Othello* 5.1 but nowhere else in English drama before 1750. Of the four short sentences here, only one seems likely to be Shakespeare's, and it does not mention the weapon.

What might have caused Theobald to intervene at this point in the wedding scene? Perhaps simply a desire to clarify the action. But in Cervantes and his translators at this point, Don Fernando takes Luscinda's weapon and attempts to kill her with it. That certainly would have provided the scene with a more dramatic ending, and provided the tragicomedy with a more powerful mid-play lurch toward tragedy. However, Theobald, or his leading actor, may well have baulked at the idea of a "distrest lover" acting so despicably. Robert Wilks, who played the role, was also one of the tri-umvirate of managers that ran Drury Lane. For the "twenty years" of his tenure there, Wilks would not support production of any play "wherein it was not his Fortune to be chosen for the best Character," and "any Author who brings a Play to *Drury-Lane*, must...flatter Mr. *Robert Wilks*."[22] All the Shakespearian parallels for "Rash e'vn to madness" (3.2.161) refer to the madness of men, not women.[23] Moreover, Leonora/Luscinda has not acted rashly, on the spur of the moment; her suicide was carefully premeditated. In the novel, it is Fernando who acts rashly here, violently reacting to the discovery that she would rather die than sleep with him. The clunky "What dagger means she?...Here is the dagger" might have replaced something much more dramatic, and "Rash e'vn to madness" might originally have been a comment on male rage, not female resistance.

These conjectures about the motive for Theobald's intervention in the text are, necessarily, speculative. But the overall pattern of indebtedness here is not at all speculative. The original play's title links it to Shelton. Shelton's influence is also demonstrable in the dialogue of *Double Falsehood*, in scenes which on other grounds have been attributed to both Shakespeare and Fletcher. But *Double Falsehood*'s links to the novel are not confined to Shelton. Four features of the play link it to Cervantes or Phillips; three of those are confined to stage directions and speech prefixes, and the fourth originates with a stage direction. One of those features (the scene direc-tions for a village) cannot have originated with Shakespeare or Fletcher, and all four could easily be the responsibility of a post-Restoration theatrical adapter. The most economical explanation is to assume that those four fea-tures all originated with Theobald, who referred in 1727 to two Spanish edi-tions of *Don Quijote*, who quoted the original Spanish of *Don Quijote* twice in 1733, who followed the Spanish spelling of the name *Zorayda* in 1741, and who at the time of his death in 1744 owned editions of the Spanish text and of the Phillips translation.

This evidence does not in itself prove that different authors used differ-ent sources, more than a century apart. The original Jacobean playwright(s) might theoretically have consulted both the Shelton translation *and* the Spanish original. Alternatively, Theobald might have used Cervantes, Phillips, *and* Shelton to forge a play that he then attributed to Shakespeare. But why would Shakespeare and Fletcher consult the Spanish text, if a fresh new translation was available? A forger might write dialogue based on a Jacobean translation (if he knew it predated Shakespeare's death), but why in the world would a forger consult the Spanish original and a Restoration translation for stage directions?

The Anglophone assumption that the original play was based on the Shelton translation does, after all, make sense. Even Ben Jonson acknowledged that Shakespeare had "small Latin, and less Greek," and modern scholars also generally agree that some of his plays are based on a reading knowledge of French and Italian texts, too. But there is no generally accepted evidence that Shakespeare read Spanish.[24] Edward M. Wilson and others have argued that

Fletcher did.[25] However, the best evidence for Fletcher's use of an untranslated Spanish source comes from *Rule a Wife and Have a Wife*, licensed on October 19, 1624, and presumably written shortly before that date, making it "one of the last plays that Fletcher wrote."[26] That Fletcher probably read Spanish in 1624 does not prove that he could read it before 1613, when the King's Men were performing *Cardenio*. Although some Englishmen certainly encountered the Spanish text of *Don Quijote* within months of its publication, no early English playwright seems to have read the novel in Spanish. No Jacobean English play shows any close indebtedness to the language of the Spanish original. Most early dramatic references to the novel could be based on secondhand conversation about its most famous elements, or upon the 1608 French translation of the inset "Tale of the Curious Impertinent," which has always enjoyed a life independent of the rest of *Don Quijote*.[27]

Finally, an intriguing detail of *All Is True; or, Henry VIII* suggests that at least one of its authors had recently been reading *Don Quixote*. *All Is True* was a "new" play, which had been performed only "two or three" times, when the Globe Theatre burned down on June 29, 1613. That was only three weeks after *Cardenio* was performed by the King's Men for the ambassadors from Savoy. In the court of Henry VIII, a Chamberlain enters "reading this letter," which begins "My lord, the horses your lordship sent for, with all the care I had I saw well chosen, ridden and furnished. They were young and handsome and of the best breed in the north" (2.2.1–4). As editors of the play have noted, "There is no source for this letter in Holinshed"; a proposed source in Samuel Rowley's *When You See Me, You Know Me* complains about the Cardinal's confiscation of "commodities," but has no "horses" being "sent for" by a "lordship."[28] But anyone familiar with the story of Cardenio, in any language, will recognize an uncanny echo of its dramatic moment of betrayal, which depends on a collocation of horses, a letter, and a lord sending a faithful subordinate on a mission doomed to be frustrated by a higher power at court (Shelton 3.13.268–9).

Just a coincidence? Who can be sure?

NOTES

1. For the more general problem of critics of English Renaissance literature ignoring its relationship to Spanish literature, see Fuchs.
2. Farmer, *An Essay on the Learning of Shakespeare*, 2nd ed. (Cambridge, 1767), 29; Schevill, "Theobald's *Double Falsehood*?" *Modern Philology* 9 (1911): 269–85. The first edition of *Double Falsehood* is dated on the title-page as "1728", but it was printed by December 24, 1727: see Brean Hammond, "After Arden," in *Quest*, 69–71.
3. *A Select Collection of Novels and Histories*, ed. Samuel Croxall, 6 vols. (London, 1729), 1: 313–44.
4. Graham, "The *Cardenio-Double Falsehood* Problem," *Modern Philology* 14 (1916): 260–80, esp. 271–3.
5. Freehafer, "*Cardenio*, by Shakespeare and Fletcher," *PMLA* 84 (1969): 501–13. Because he did not know of the 1611 Spanish edition, Freehafer constructed

an elaborate conjecture about Theobald consulting and misunderstanding the Stationers' Register; this misled scholars for four decades.

6. Taylor, "History," 13–14.

7. We cite the line-numbering from Hammond's Arden edition, but quote the original spelling and punctuation. Hammond's collations do not record the change from "1611" to "1605," and he silently modernizes "Quixot" to "Quixote."

8. Charles Corbett, *A Catalogue of the Library of Lewis Theobald, Esq. Deceased* (London, 1744), items 28 ("Don Quixot in Spanish, with cuts, 2 vols. a neat letter," undated, octavo), 193 ("Don Quixot in Spanish—1611," octavo), and 472 ("Phillips' History of Don Quixot—1687," folio). Hammond identifies the catalogue's undated copy as "the first 1605 edition" (81), but that edition did not contain "cuts" (engraved illustrations) and was not in two volumes. On the basis of the quality of Theobald's collection, Chartier believes "we may assume" that it was the first Spanish illustrated edition (2 vols., Brussels, 1662). "Less probably," because of the "more mediocre quality," it might have been the illustrated Madrid edition of 1674, or one of its descendants (117).

9. Volume 3, *Winter's Tale* 3.3, note 18 ("*Entre el si y el no de la Muger no me atreveria yo à poner una punta d'alfiler.* Between a Woman's *ay* and *no* I would not undertake to *thrust a pin's point*"); Volume 5, *King Lear* 4.6, note 52 ("*Entre el* Si *y el* No *de la muger, no me atreveria yo à poner una punta d'Alfiler.* Betwixt a Woman's *Yea,* and *No,* I would not undertake to thrust a Pin's Point"). On both occasions, Theobald's translation of *Part Two,* chapter xix, differs substantially from the translations by Shelton ("betweene a womans I, and no, I would be loth to put a pins point") and Phillips ("as for a woman's *I* and *No,* I would not undertake to put the point of a Needle between 'em," 381). In both notes, Theobald is cautious about whether "our Author had *Don Quixote* in his mind here," and Stern takes this caution as evidence that "Theobald seems to hope (rather than know) that Shakespeare shared his fascination with *Don Quixote*" (580). But the Second Part of *Don Quixote* was not published until 1615, and not translated into English until 1620, so Theobald was right to be cautious about whether it could have influenced *King Lear* or *Winter's Tale.* His caution about Shakespeare's knowledge of *Part Two* does not constitute evidence that Theobald was retracting his claim that Shakespeare based a play on *Part One.* It is Stern who is confused here, not Theobald.

10. See A. Luis Pujante, "*Double Falsehood* and the Verbal Parallels with Shelton's *Don Quixote,*" *Shakespeare Survey* 51 (1998): 95–105. Pujante provides a numbered list of twenty parallels, collected by previous scholars or noted by him for the first time. Of these twenty, twelve (2, 4, 6, 7, 9, 11, 12, 13, 15, 16, 18, and 19) do not discriminate between Shelton, Phillips, and Cervantes. Pujante discusses (but does not separately enumerate) two further parallels, cited by Freehafer: "Rodericke" (our Shelton parallel number 8) and "Andalusia" (which appears in both the Spanish and English texts). Another parallel noted by Taylor ("History," 57) is also indifferent.

11. Miguel de Cervantes, *El ingenioso hidalgo don Quijote de la Mancha,* ed. Luis Murillo, fifth edition, 2 vols. (Madrid: Castalia, 1978), 1.27.340. Subsequent references to the Spanish text cite this edition. There are no substantive variants in seventeenth-century Spanish editions of the parallels we have examined here.

12. Pujante notes that the whole business with the letter in *Double Falsehood* "is not based on a letter, note or document mentioned by Dorothea in *Don Quixote,* but

only on this brief reference at the end of the Cardenio episode which involves a contradiction in Cervantes" (104). The play therefore solves an apparent problem Cervantes had created. The final scene is clearly written by Fletcher, but the earlier scene with the letter (*DF* 2.2) seems to have been written by Shakespeare; if so, they collaborated on this narrative improvement.

13. For Theobald's need to change some Cervantine names (strongly associated with D'Urfey's popular play), see Taylor, "The Embassy, The City, The Court, the Text: *Cardenio* Performed in 1613," in *Quest*, 305–8.

14. From his earliest work on *The History of Cardenio* through the 2012 Indianapolis production, Taylor changed "Roderick" (the name of the elder brother in *Double Falsehood*) to "Ricardo" (the name of the Duke in *Don Quixote*) throughout the play. When he began work on the reconstruction, he did not see the relevance of the Roderick marginal note, and he was trying wherever possible to restore Spanish names. But the character is responsible for re-uniting Fernando to Violante, and thus (since 2010, when Taylor decided that Violante should be a mixed-race character) the play's Roderick is responsible for racial mixing in the Spanish ruling class. The play's elder brother thus echoes the historical "Roderick," whose actions led to centuries of Spanish-Moorish mixing. As a result of our study of the sources, the text of *The History of Cardenio* included in this volume reverts to "Roderick." This also makes it possible to restore the Cervantine "Ricardo" as the name of the Duke: Theobald might have changed the name because a Duke Ricardo appears in Durfey's *Second Part of Don Quixote*.

15. For the pastoral romance, see Jorge de Montemayor, *Los siete libros de la Diana*, ed. Asunción Rallo (Madrid: Cátedra, 1991); for the four extant versions of the anonymous interpolated tale, see Francisco López Estrada, "*El Abencerraje y la hermosa Jarifa*": *cuatro textos y su estudio* (Madrid: Publicaciones de la Revista de Archivos, Bibliotecas y Museos, 1957). For Montemayor and *Two Gentlemen*, see among many others Geoffrey Bullough, *Narrative and Dramatic Sources of Shakespeare*, 8 vols. (London: Routledge & Kegan Paul, 1957–75), 1: 206. Shakespeare could have read Montemayor in French translation, or in English in manuscript. The earliest surviving edition of Bartholomew Yong's translation of *Diana of George of Montemayor* was printed in 1598. Curiously, the character is introduced in a sentence that Shakespeare might have remembered, and that links Rodrigo/Roderick to Fernando, as Cervantes never does: "In the time of the Valiant Prince *Don Fernando*, who was afterward King of Aragon, lived a knight in Spaine called *Rodrigo* of *Narvaez* (Yong, 107).

16. Carnegie, "Locale in *Cardenio, Double Falsehood, Don Quixote,* and Wellington," *Shakespeare* 7.3 (2011): 344–51.

17. The stage direction "a prospect of" first occurs in Aurelian Townshend's masque *Albion's Triumph* (1632); it first appears in play-texts by Davenant. "Prospect of a Village" first appears in *Double Falsehood*; but "a street" shows up as early as Dryden's *Rival Ladies* (1664), and another thirty-four times by 1727.

18. Gary Taylor and John V. Nance, "Four Characters in Search of a Subplot: Quixote, Sancho, and *Cardenio*," *Quest*, 297–8.

19. See "compose your self" (*Clouds* 2.1, twice), "this interval" (*Orestes* 5.1, *Fatal Secret* 3.1). This second phrase may also reflect Theobald's source. Where Shelton has "when they meet me in my wits" (3.13.278), Phillips has "in my lucid Intervals" (3.13.132); *Double Falsehood*'s "He's calm again. I'll take this interval" effectively means "this calm interval," which is certainly closer to Phillips than to Shelton. Shelton is much closer to Cervantes' "cuando me encuentran

con juicio" (1.27.342). The phrase in Phillips translates *lúcidos intervalos*, which occurs twice in *Part Two* (2.1, 2.18), but never in the 1605 *Quijote*.

20. Stern claims that "passages generally agreed to be purely by Theobald still contain fragments of Shelton's work" (592). But we have found no evidence of Shelton in parts of the text attributed to Theobald by the consensus of attribution scholars.

21. The only other example in Literature Online comes from the anonymous "The Tunbridge Prodigy" in *Poems on Affairs of State* (1697–1716)—which was certainly written in Theobald's lifetime, and conceivably even by Theobald himself.

22. *An Apology for the Life of Mr. Colley Cibber, Written by Himself,* ed. Robert W. Lowe, 2 vols. (London: Nimmo, 1889), 2: 227–8; Lowe cites in a footnote the corroborating comment, by John Dennis, about flattering Wilks (2:226).

23. Compare "ev'n to madness" (*Othello* 2.1.310), and the collocation of "heady-rash" and "mad" (*Errors* 5.1.217–18) and "rash choler" and "madman" (*Caesar* 4.3.93–4).

24. Robert S. Miola, in *Shakespeare's Reading* (Oxford: Oxford University Press, 2000), endorses the consensus view that Shakespeare read Latin, French, and Italian (165–8), but never mentions Spanish.

25. Wilson, "*Rule a Wife and Have a Wife* and *El Sagaz Estacio*," *Review of English Studies*, 24 (1948): 189–94, and "Did John Fletcher Read Spanish?" *Philological Quarterly* 27 (1948): 187–90. See also Lee Bliss, "*Don Quixote* in English: The Case for *The Knight of the Burning Pestle*," *Viator* 18 (1987): 377, and Trudi L. Darby and Alexander Samson, "Cervantes on the Jacobean Stage," in Ardila, 209–10.

26. George Walton Williams, ed., *Rule a Wife and Have a Wife*, in *Fletcher*, 6:485–6.

27. For the first decade of the novel's reception in English, see Valerie Wayne, "*Don Quixote* and Shakespeare's Collaborative Turn to Romance," in *Quest*, 217–38. As Wayne notes, Shelton's translation was written in Brussels, probably for an English exile there, so its circulation in England before 1612 is uncertain; Wayne calls the novel a "catalyst," rather than a "source," between 1607 and 1612. For the 1608 French translation of the "Curious Impertinent," see *The Second Maiden's Tragedy*, ed. Anne Lancashire, Revels Plays (Manchester: Manchester University Press, 1978), 30, 77–8.

28. See *King Henry VIII*, ed. Gordon McMullan (London: Arden Shakespeare, 2000), 279.

3

THE 1612 *DON QUIXOTE* AND THE WINDET-STANSBY PRINTING HOUSE

David L. Gants

Some time in late 1612 or early 1613 a play titled *Cardenio* was performed by the King's Men at the court of James I.[1] It might well have been performed in the commercial London theater before its court performance. Because this lost play was likely based on episodes from Thomas Shelton's translation of *Don Quixote* (STC 4915),[2] establishing a publication date for the romance would aid scholars in attempting to pinpoint more closely when the play was first written and staged.

Accurately dating early modern printed books poses a number of problems to students of the period, beginning with conflicting calendar schemes. Depending on the venue, a title-page, colophon, or dedicatory epistle might bear a date according to the regnal (beginning with the coronation anniversary of the current monarch), legal (beginning on Lady Day, March 25), or calendar (beginning January 1) year. Adding to the confusion was the older Julian calendar still used in England, which in the seventeenth century ran ten days ahead of the Gregorian calendar employed on the continent, a reckoning dissonance that could produce apparent contradictions arising from current events or dates found within a book's text (for an example, see note 14 in this chapter). Entries in the Register of the Company of Stationers, the de facto copyright system observed by booksellers at the time, could signal any number of events besides a title's imminent publication (see below).[3] As well, not all titles were registered, in particular later editions of works already entered. Beyond title-pages, dedications, colophons, and Stationers' Register entries, evidence to help establish publication dates is sporadic at best and found mainly in presentation inscriptions or external documentary references.

W. W. Greg has noted two habits practiced by early modern printers that both help and hinder in dating a book. With the exception of law books and official publications, he observed, "most printers, and in particular printers of popular literature, adopted the new year-number on New Year's Day" when setting a title-page imprint. At the same time, they often postdated works, "anticipating the date of the new year on books printed and actually issued near the end of the old,"[4] perhaps as early as November. Thus each piece of information, each title-page date or entry in the Stationers' Register, is not a point but rather a circle of possibilities within a larger Venn diagram that is a book's publication history. This essay locates its discussion of *DQ*'s publication within the variabilities and ambiguities of London's early-seventeenth-century book trade, suggesting as far as the evidence permits, the most likely period during which Shelton's translation was at press.

When the bookseller Edward Blount and his partner William Barrett[5] contracted with the establishment at the sign of the Cross Keys operated by John Windet and William Stansby to produce *DQ*, they did so at a time of transition and expansion for the printing house. Windet, freed by John Allde on April 13, 1579,[6] was nearing the end of his career, having printed books under his name for twenty-five years. He had begun in 1584 as a master printer in partnership with John Judson,[7] first using equipment acquired from the estates of Henry Bynneman and John Day, and subsequently in the early 1590s adding to his stock with material from John Wolfe's house, either by buying it outright or merging with Wolfe's business.[8] Upon Wolfe's death in 1601, Windet succeeded him as Printer to the City of London, and for the rest of the decade ran a successful if modest operation printing a wide variety of religious works as well as official publications, travel narratives, popular science and husbandry, history, and a smattering of popular literature.

Stansby had been bound to Windet as an apprentice during Christmas 1589 and made free of the company on January 7, 1597.[9] While other of Windet's apprentices left to work as journeymen or occasionally became master printers in their own right when they gained their freedom, Stansby remained at the house at Cross Keys, apparently becoming a partner in 1609 through the purchase of a large quantity of english-body type.[10] This expansion of typographic resources allowed the new partners to broaden the scope of their enterprise, with "an increased emphasis on composition over press-work" that enabled them to contract for larger projects and adjust their production schedule to accommodate more concurrent printing.[11] Mark Bland estimates the average annual output between the years 1603 and 1608 at 280 edition sheets,[12] while average output for the years 1610–1612 jumped to over 700 (based on my calculations).

Windet died late November or early December of 1610, and the terms of his will confirm that the 1609 partnership agreement gave Stansby one-half ownership in the business as well as the right to purchase the other half upon Windet's death from his heirs.[13] Although Windet likely had been involved in the negotiations over *DQ* with Blount and Barrett—the title was registered with the Stationers on January 19, 1611, barely a month after Windet's passing,[14] and books identifying Windet as printer appeared as late as October 1610—responsibility for the production of the volume fell to the new master of Cross Keys. Stansby had worked with Windet for over twenty years, as an apprentice, journeyman, and finally partner, and was thus familiar with the publishers[15] who provided the bulk of the capital necessary to undertake a printing job. Of the various elements that went into book production in early modern London, none required as much long-term investment as paper, which by various estimations accounted for 40–50 percent of a volume's total direct costs.[16] A publisher had to purchase all the necessary paper, financed either through personal funds or a loan, and he did not begin to see a return until the completed volumes were out of the printing house and into the wholesaler's warehouse for distribution to retailers. A profit, if any, could take years to appear. Thus a printer such as Stansby, most of whose business depended on contracting to work on projects initiated by booksellers, needed to maintain good relations with his network of publishers in order to survive.

During the three-year period when the publication of *DQ* was being planned, its printing carried out, and the finished volumes distributed to the booksellers, 113 distinct editions identified as coming from the Windet-Stansby house survive, a total of over 2,100 edition sheets.[17] Based on evidence derived from title-pages and entries in the Stationers' Register, 38 stationers at one or more times acted as publishers for those editions,[18] but of that group, 8 individuals or partnerships financed over half the total output:

> Eleazar Edgar, Ambrose Garbrand, and John Browne, 14 titles, 251 edition
>   sheets;
> Edward Blount and William Barrett, 4 titles, 179 edition sheets;
> John Smethwicke, 8 titles, 140 edition sheets;
> Matthew Lownes, 1 title, 127 edition sheets;
> Walter Burre and Thomas Thorpe, 6 titles, 114 edition sheets;
> John Budge and Richard Bonian, 15 titles, 114 edition sheets;
> Nathaniel Butter and Martin Clerke, 4 titles, 95 edition sheets;
> Nathaniel Fosbrooke, 2 titles, 94.5 edition sheets.

Burre's importance increases dramatically when his financing of Walter Ralegh's massive *History of the World* (STC 20637) is taken into account. He entered the 394-edition-sheet folio on April 15, 1611, and it was not published until nearly three years later, March 29, 1614.[19] It is likely that a significant portion of the *History* was at press during *DQ*'s printing, perhaps 125 edition sheets or more.

Overall, then, a small group of important publishers commissioned the bulk of the work Windet and Stansby undertook from 1610 through 1612, men in whose good graces Stansby needed to remain as he took over mastership of the printing house. Inevitably when dealing with multiple investors whose interests do not always coincide, conflicts over priorities will develop, especially as Stansby tried to establish himself and his business after the death of his partner. One reason for the changes in *DQ*'s printing arrangements (discussed later) may have been just such a conflict. As one might expect, this cohort of financiers also brought most of the large projects to Cross Keys: Blount and Barrett contracted for an expanded reprint of John Florio's dictionary *Queen Anna's New World of Words* (STC 11099, 179 sheets, roughly split between Stansby and Melchisidec Bradwood) and *DQ* (78 sheets); Fosbrooke commissioned *Saint Peter's Prophesy of These Last Days*, by John Hull (STC 13933, 78.5 sheets); and Matthew Lownes another edition of Richard Hooker's *Of the Laws of Ecclesiastical Polity* (STC 13714, 127 sheets). When attempting a reconstruction of the Windet-Stansby workflow, these and other lengthy volumes can provide a framework (especially those with dates) into which other more elusive pieces of the puzzle might be placed.

Table 3.1 presents a list of the books known to have been in the Windet-Stansby house during the years 1610–1612, ordered chronologically based on estimates derived from documentary evidence. Providing a picture of the Windet-Stansby printing office both before and after *DQ* was at press provides context, helps identify production patterns, and allows for a better understanding of how projects that span calendar years fit into the overall schedule.

Table 3.1 Dating evidence of production in the Windet-Stansby printing house 1610–1612

STC	Size	Dating Evidence
18640	34.5	SR entry June 16, 1609; dedication dated March 27, 1610
17942	10.0	SR entry October 26, 1609; title-page dated 1610
7048	54.0	SR entry December 2, 1609; title-page dated 1610
13564	8.0	[a]Sermon preached December 3, 1609; title-page dated 1610
12649	20.0	SR entry January 16, 1610
4637	40.0	SR entry January 24, 1610
5112	3.0	[a]SR entry February 21, 1610
5777	32.0	[a]Assigned to Browne March 1, 1610
5917	16.5	[a]SR entry March 31, 1610
21028.5	8.0	[a]SR entry March 31, 1610
18183	22.0	SR entry April 27, 1610
7333	3.0	SR entry May 8, 1610
11123	12.0	SR entry May 8, 1610; dedication dated June 6, 1610
19565	2.0	[a]SR entry May 14, 1610[b]
6965	9.0	SR entry June 1, 1610
13161	6.0	Describes masque performed June 5, 1610
7322	63.0	SR entry June 7, 1610; author's (not translator's) preface dated January 20, 1610
5118	3.5	Pageant performed April 23, 1610; SR entry June 12, 1610
13005a.5	44.0	Assigned to Garbrand June 15, 1610
11795	2.0	SR entry June 25, 1610
24950	4.0	SR entry July 4, 1610
8449	0.5	[a]Proclamation dated July 30, 1610
5862	3.0	[a]SR entry August 13, 1610
53	9.0	Sermon preached July 8, 1610; SR entry October 11, 1610
12663.4	10.0	SR entry October 4, 1610; title-page dated 1611
14816	3.5	[a]Dedication dated October 13, 1610
13140	2.0	[a]Refers to coronation of Louis XIII on October 17, 1610
24833	9.0	SR entry November 8, 1610
5808	118.0	SR entry November 26, 1610; title-page dated 1611
13933	78.5	Two variant title-pages dated 1610 and 1611, but SR entry January 21, 1613[c]
877	7.0	Title-page dated 1610; assigned to Stansby September 11, 1611
2533.5	14.0	[a]Title-page dated 1610

Table 3.1 Continued

STC	Size	Dating Evidence
5768	6.5	Title-page dated 1610
6945.2	24.0	Title-page dated 1610
7220	31.5	Title-page dated 1610
12274	11.0	Title-page dated 1610
12567	16.0	Title-page dated 1610
12582.24	17.0	[a]Title-page dated 1610
13018	6.0	[a]Title-page dated 1610
14736	8.0	Title-page dated 1610
15687	32.5	Title-page dated 1610, date uncertain
19436.3	6.0	[a]Title-page dated 1610
21073	14.0	[a]Title-page dated 1610
22385	4.0	Title-page dated 1610
12996	20.0	[a]Title-page dated 1599, STC speculates ca. 1610
4915	**78.0**	***Don Quixote*: SR entry January 19, 1611; title-page dated 1612**
9226	5.5	Patent dated March 5, 1611; SR entry April 16, 1611
20758	6.0	SR entry March 19, 1611; dedication dated April 16, 1611
6591	9.0	Sermon preached April 14, 1611; SR entry September 20, 1611
20637	393.0	SR entry April 15, 1611; title-page dated 1614
15514.5	22.0	Dedication dated May 14, 1611
24622	39.0	SR entry May 17, 1611
23200.5	6.0	SR entry May 17, 1611
23201	5.5	Title page dated 1611
23201.5	7.5	Title page dated 1611; patent for book dated August 1, 1611[d]
17840	5.0	SR entry June 6, 1611; sermon preached June 10, 1610
5807	11.0	SR entry June 7, 1611[e]
6906	6.5	SR entry June 7, 1611
18019	3.0	SR entry July 2, 1611; title-page dated 1612
6585	7.0	Sermon preached July 7, 1611; SR entry September 3, 1611
8470.5	0.5	Proclamation dated July 22, 1611
8470.7	0.5	Proclamation dated August 1, 1611
3568	7.0	SR entry August 9, 1611
17924	7.0	Sermon preached August 25, 1611; title-page dated 1612
932.5	13.0	Assigned to Stansby September 11, 1611; title-page dated 1612
13714	127.0	Assigned to Stansby September 11, 1611[f]
3149	102.0	SR entry September 11, 1611; title-page dated 1613
12618	14.0	SR entry September 19, 1611; title-page dated 1612
4705	14.5	SR entry August 26, 1611; dedication dated October 18, 1611
24027	12.0	Dedication dated November 5, 1611; SR entry December 9, 1611; title-page dated 1612
21016	36.5	SR entry December 6, 1611; title-page dated 1612
23350	13.0	SR entry December 13, 1611; title-page dated 1612
19507	23.0	SR entry December 16, 1611; title-page dated 1612
54	53.0	Title-page dated 1611
745	16.0	Title-page dated 1611
3777	24.5	Title-page dated 1611
4980	10.0	Title-page dated 1611
6375	9.0	Title-page dated 1611
7022	2.0	Title-page dated 1611
10221	1.5	Title-page dated 1611
11099	90.0	Title-page dated 1611

continued

Table 3.1 Continued

STC	Size	Dating Evidence
12229	10.0	Title-page dated 1611
12255.5	16.0	Title-page dated 1611
13142	4.0	Title-page dated 1611
14759	14.0	Title-page dated 1611
16650.5	3.0	Title-page dated 1611
22740	7.0	Title-page dated 1611
23548	56.0	Title-page dated 1611[g]
22397	20.0	SR entry January 7, 1612; dedication dated January 26, 1612
24852	26.5	SR entry February 10, 1612
21024	8.0	SR entry March 23, 1612
4994	10.0	SR entry April 17, 1612
4923	15.0	SR entry May 19, 1612
5742	32.0	SR entry May 19, 1612; dedication dated June 13, 1612
25163	8.0	Sermon preached June 21, 1612; SR entry June 23, 1612
19458.5	9.0	Dedication dated June 27, 1612; SR entry July 6, 1612
15324	12.0	SR entry July 6, 1612
14308	65.5	SR entry July 23, 1612, title-page dated 1613
20505	201.0	SR entry August 7, 1612, title-page dated 1613
11207	149.0	SR conditional entry May 4, 1611; SR entry August 12, 1611; title-page 1612
18014	13.0	SR entry August 14, 1612
20138	23.5	SR entry November 7, 1612; dedication dated November 16, 1612
9227	5.0	Title-page dated 1612
10207.3	1.5	Title-page dated 1612
10258	2.0	Title-page dated 1612
11856	20.0	Title-page dated 1612
16670	14.0	Title-page dated 1612
19083a	3.0	Title-page dated 1612
22863	18.0	Title-page dated 1612
23203	8.0	Title-page dated 1612
23545	11.0	Title-page dated 1612
25084	52.0	Title-page dated 1612

[a]The title-pages of these books identify Windet as the printer; the remainder were the responsibility of Stansby or the both of them jointly.

[b]Sharp-eyed readers may have noticed that the title, which concerns the assassination of Henry IV of France, was entered on the same day the event occurred, May 14, 1610. However, France had switched to the Gregorian calendar in 1582, while England still employed the older Julian one. Thus the assassination took place on May 4, 1610, according to English reckoning, although the text retained the French Gregorian date.

[c]The 1613 SR entry for Fosbrooke describes this as "A booke formerly prynted by him": Edward Arber, *A Transcription of the Registers of the Stationers' Company of London 1554–1640*, 5 vols. (London: Privately Printed, 1874–94), 3.512.

[d]Stansby entered STC 23200.5 with the Stationers, often an indication that he also bore the costs. However this later edition from the same year includes a copy of the royal patent that begins "Wheras *Arthur Standish* Gentleman, hath taken much paines and beene at great charges in composing and publishing [this book]," it appears likely Standish provided financing (A2ʳ). Furthermore, the patent seems to have been awarded after the publication of the first and probably the second, editions which provides further evidence for dating all three.

[e]The title-page identifies this as "the second course to his Crudities" (A1ʳ), indicating it was published after STC 5808.

[f]The assignment likely marks the completion of Hooker's book and was part of a mass assignment to Stansby of the late Windet's titles.

[g]The Stationers' Company bought the rights for this title from Edward Weaver on July 23, 1610 (*Records of the Court of the Stationers' Company 1602 to 1640*, ed. William A. Jackson (London: The Bibliographical Society, 1957), 43.

The dating information for each of these titles provides at best a calendar range, an approximate span of time during which production occurred. Entry in the Stationers' Register usually corresponded with the beginning of a project (as seems to be the case with *DQ*), although it could also be done when a volume was completed, or as in the case of the massed September 11, 1611, entries of Hooker's *Laws* and others,[20] an administrative action noting the transfer of rights from one stationer to another. The same holds true for dated dedicatory epistles, which were often the last text supplied by the author and, as part of the prefatory material, usually printed last. References to external events such as the date a masque was performed or sermon preached also contribute to our picture of the printing house workflow. By placing each approximate range derived from this information onto a timeline it becomes possible to detect patterns and likelihoods.

Figures 3.1–3.3 represent an attempt to create a timeline covering the years 1610–1612, displaying each title as a horizontal line whose position along the chronological continuum derives from its accompanying dating information and whose length corresponds to its size in edition sheets. During the three-year period under examination, Windet and Stansby machined an average of fourteen edition sheets per week or a little less than sixty per month. Estimates of the number of works concurrently printed at any one time ranged in the area of four to six, which when combined with the production average indicate that the printing house typically machined around 10–12 edition sheets per month of any one title. These estimations are the basis for determining the magnitude of each line representing a book project. However, one large unknown looms over the timeline, the matter of the editions for which we only have a title-page date. Specific placement on the annual work schedules would only obscure the larger picture, so they have been placed below the timeline as lines indicating their approximate size.

Figures 3.1 (1610) and 3.3 (1612) show distinctive types of clustering that may help place *DQ* more accurately on the timeline. During the late winter and early spring of 1610, and again during the summer and fall of 1612, the printing house seems to be sequencing its jobs in an overlapping fashion. At other times it commences multiple large projects (July 1610) or a group of smaller projects (December 1611–January 1612) simultaneously. This is an indication of the production ebb and flow typical of an essentially craft business, one where factors such as weather, labor difficulties, frequent holidays, availability of capital and raw materials, and market fluctuations all had a greater and immediate impact on the trade than today. At times, projects smoothly dovetail together, while at other times events conspire to create potential logjams. The latter seems to be the case in Figure 3.2 (1611), where a mixture of large and small projects in the summer and fall likely made for a difficult work schedule.

An analysis of skeleton forme re-use patterns in *DQ* indicates sequences of regularity as well as possible disruptions and frequent changes that map roughly onto the reconstruction of the printing house schedule in 1611 and

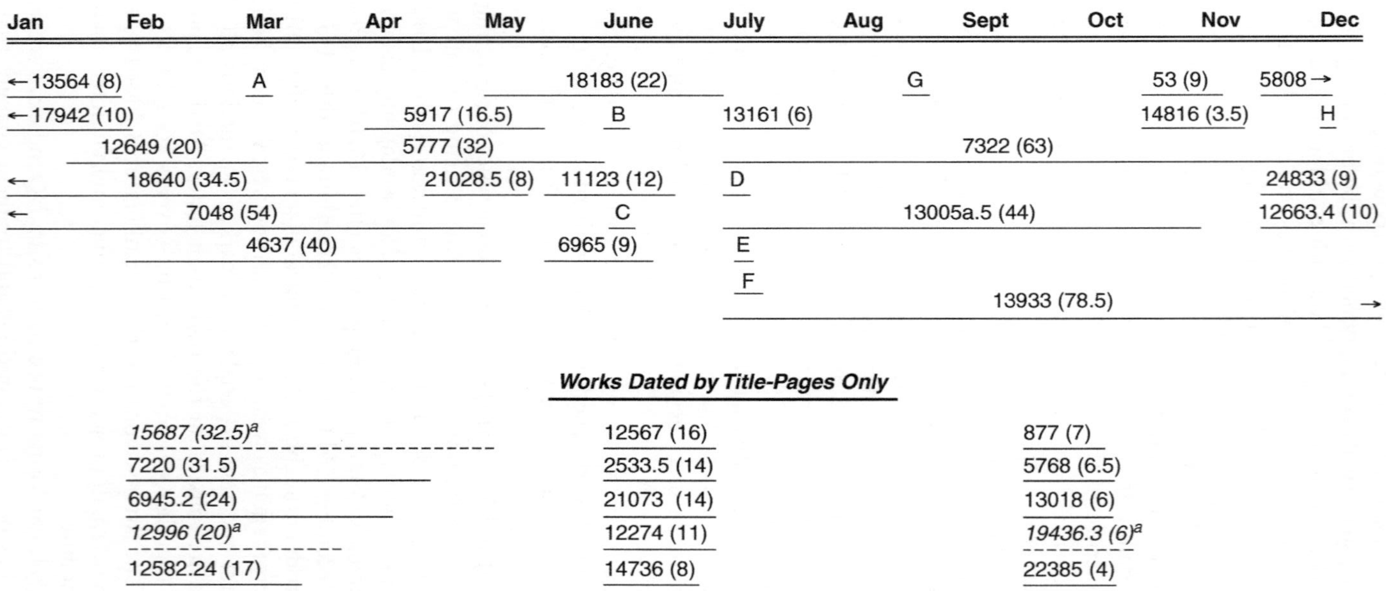

Jan	Feb	Mar	Apr	May	June	July	Aug	Sept	Oct	Nov	Dec
←13564 (8)					18183 (22)			G		53 (9)	5808→
←17942 (10)		A	5917 (16.5)		B	13161 (6)				14816 (3.5)	H
12649 (20)			5777 (32)					7322 (63)			
18640 (34.5)			21028.5 (8)		11123 (12)	D					24833 (9)
7048 (54)					C	13005a.5 (44)					12663.4 (10)
4637 (40)					6965 (9)	E					
						F		13933 (78.5)			

Works Dated by Title-Pages Only

12567 (16)	877 (7)
2533.5 (14)	5768 (6.5)
21073 (14)	13018 (6)
12274 (11)	19436.3 (6)[a]
14736 (8)	22385 (4)
15687 (32.5)[a]	
7220 (31.5)	
6945.2 (24)	
12996 (20)[a]	
12582.24 (17)	

Key to shorter items: A = 5112 (3), B = 7333 (3), C = 19565 (2), D = 5118 (3.5), E = 11795 (2), F = 24950 (4), G = 5862 (3), H = 13140 (2).

Figure 3.1 Reconstruction of Windet-Stansby House workflow, 1610.

[a]Uncertainly dated 1610 by STC.

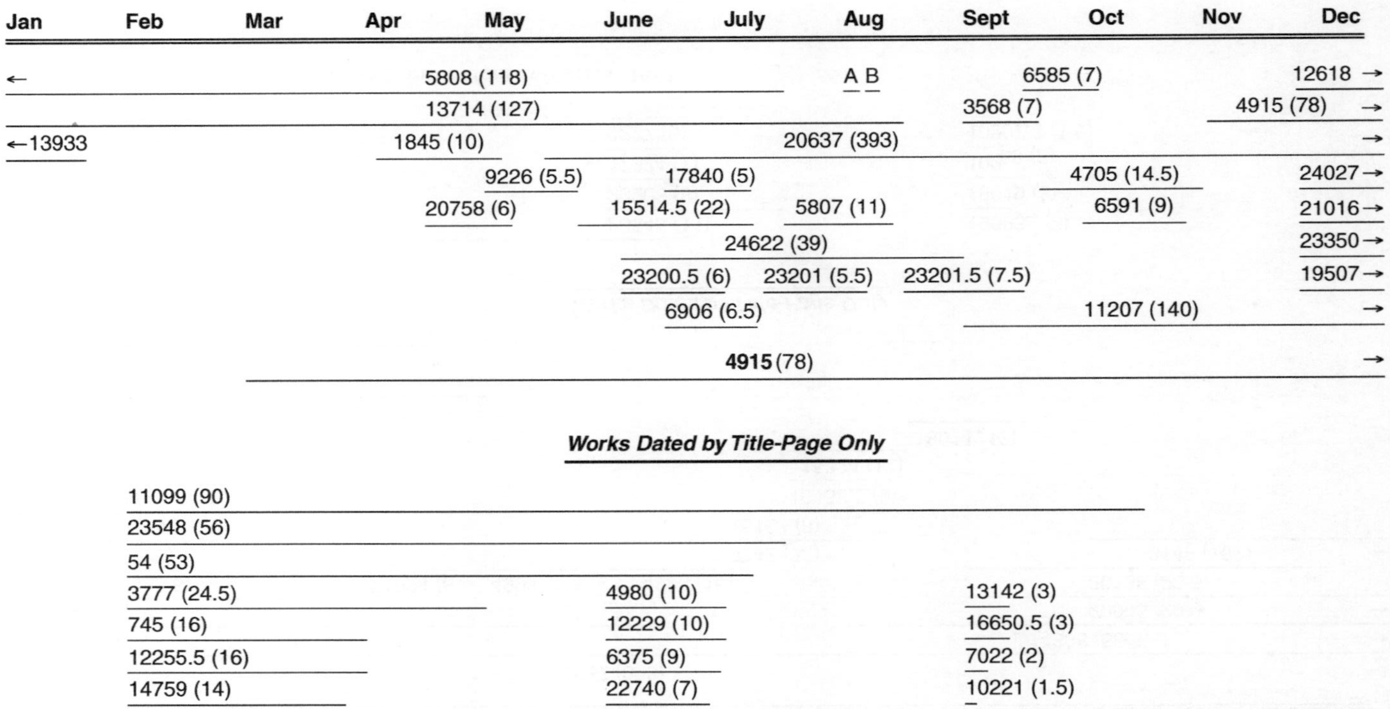

Jan	Feb	Mar	Apr	May	June	July	Aug	Sept	Oct	Nov	Dec
			5808 (118)				A B	6585 (7)			12618 →
			13714 (127)					3568 (7)		4915 (78)	→
←13933			1845 (10)			20637 (393)					
				9226 (5.5)	17840 (5)				4705 (14.5)		24027 →
				20758 (6)	15514.5 (22)	5807 (11)			6591 (9)		21016 →
					24622 (39)						23350 →
					23200.5 (6)	23201 (5.5)	23201.5 (7.5)				19507 →
					6906 (6.5)				11207 (140)		→
						4915 (78)					→

Works Dated by Title-Page Only

June	Sept
4980 (10)	13142 (3)
12229 (10)	16650.5 (3)
6375 (9)	7022 (2)
22740 (7)	10221 (1.5)

11099 (90)
23548 (56)
54 (53)
3777 (24.5)
745 (16)
12255.5 (16)
14759 (14)

Key to shorter items: A = 8470.5 (0.5), B = 8570.7 (0.5).

Figure 3.2 Reconstruction of Windet-Stansby House workflow, 1611.

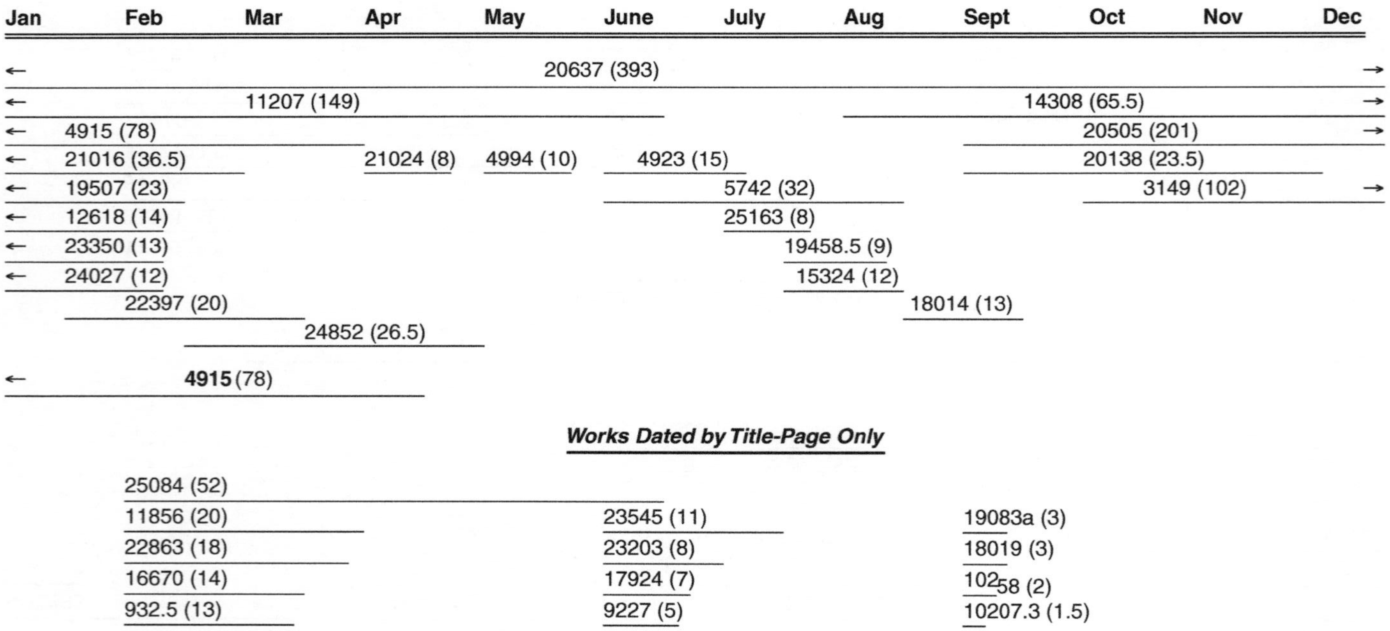

Jan	Feb	Mar	Apr	May	June	July	Aug	Sept	Oct	Nov	Dec

20637 (393)

11207 (149) 14308 (65.5) →

4915 (78) →

21016 (36.5) 21024 (8) 20505 (201) →

19507 (23) 20138 (23.5) →

12618 (14) 4994 (10) 4923 (15) 3149 (102) →

23350 (13) 5742 (32)

24027 (12) 25163 (8)

22397 (20) 19458.5 (9)

24852 (26.5) 15324 (12)

18014 (13)

4915 (78) →

Works Dated by Title-Page Only

25084 (52)

11856 (20) 23545 (11) 19083a (3)

22863 (18) 23203 (8) 18019 (3)

16670 (14) 17924 (7) 102_58 (2)

932.5 (13) 9227 (5) 10207.3 (1.5)

Figure 3.3 Reconstruction of Windet-Stansby House workflow, 1612.

early 1612. The structure of the volume itself is described bibliographically as follows:

4°: ¶⁴ A-2O⁸ 2P² [$4 (+¶3,4) signed]; 302 ll., pp. [24] 1–61 [62] 63–279 [280] 281–336, 335–423 [424] 425–431, 468–469, 454–594 [595–598] [=580], misnumbering 46 as 64, 47 as 65, 78 as 77, 79 as 78, 254 as 244, 255 as 245, 269 as 273, 337 as 335, 338 as 336, 339 as 337, 347 as 348, 412 as 413, 413, as 412, 426 as 446, 431 as 451, 562 as 522, 579 as 597.

DQ was printed as a quarto-in-eights, which means each gathering consisted of four separate formes of type (a total of sixteen pages) machined onto two sheets of paper, with both sheets folded twice and one nested within the other. Each page of the edition is separated into four ruled compartments: the main text on the "inner" edge of the page (i.e. closest to the gutter); the headline directly above the main text; the pagination on the upper-outer corner; and a tall, vertical area below the pagination for explanatory glosses. Because little of this format required adjustment during printing (only the pagination and the section numbers needed changing), compositors saved time and labor by reusing the shell of compartments and headlines, called skeletons. Over time, types and brass rules become damaged through repeated use in ways that can render them distinctive, allowing bibliographers to track them as they appear over and over in a book. The skeleton forme distribution in *DQ* falls into five stages:

B–D: Stansby's compositors used at least two different skeletons as they began work on the quarto, with the first gathering somewhat jumbled and the second and third settling into a semblance of a pattern.

E–R: These thirteen gatherings show Stansby's house setting and printing by formes, that is, the compositor setting one side of a sheet and sending it to the press before beginning work on the other side. This requires setting the pages out of order, not a difficult task in an establishment able to cast-off text[21] accurately, and only employs a single skeleton forme.

S–Y: The forme arrangements abruptly become more complicated at this point. A number of new page skeletons appear, and their placement on the forme is no longer consistent, indicating the house was no longer setting strictly by formes.

Z: One gathering with a single forme showing the same regularity as gatherings E–R.

2A–end: The jumbled forme arrangement of gatherings S–Y resumes, with new page skeletons appearing, moving around on forme, and periodic exchange of typographic materials from one skeleton to another.

The sudden change in skeleton forme usage between gatherings R and S seems to signal a shift in *DQ*'s place on the work schedule. Evidently when the project began, the compositors and pressmen laboring on the book had established a rough equilibrium between the two tasks of typesetting and machining that setting by formes supports. Such a balance might occur when compositors had sufficient time to set and proof all four pages while the pressman dealt with the prior forme, and vice versa. As they reached gathering S, however, that equilibrium was upset, possibly by the arrival of new printing jobs and a reshuffle of the work schedule. Figure 3.2 indicates that around June 1611, a cluster of new titles appear on the docket, including Ralegh's substantial (and politically important[22]) *History of the World*, financed by one of Stansby's significant publishers Walter Burre. Utilizing the ten-sheet-per-month production rate estimate for an edition at press, approximately 30–35 edition sheets of *DQ* would have been printed between the time work commenced around February and when the *History* arrived; in fact, the sixteen gatherings in B-R total thirty-two edition sheets. Commencing with gathering S, the four skeleton pages on a forme no longer remained as an intact unit but instead were treated as individual parts of a growing collection of skeletons, used in a seemingly random manner by the compositors. The most likely explanation for this shift is that the addition of a large number of new printing jobs (many commissioned by booksellers with whom Stansby did a large amount of business) slowed progress on *DQ* and disrupted the regularity of production, with compositors dividing their time among different projects, leaving multiple pages set aside until they could be imposed and printed.

Evidence from another book in the printing house supports this scenario. One of the rules used in *DQ*'s textual frame bore damage that makes it distinctive, and its last appearance on its original skeleton page occurs in gathering Y. The next gathering (Z) suddenly reverts to the earlier pattern of an intact single skeleton forme on both sheets, as had taken place in E–R. This regularity only occurred for one gathering, and from 2A to the end of the project, the previous random use of page skeletons resumes. One possible explanation for this aberration is that another project of similar format demanded the press's time and typographic resources. Sometime in late September or early October, work began on John Denison's sermon *The Sin against the Holy Ghost* (STC 6591), financed by John Budge, another of Stansby's frequent publishers).[23] The same damaged rule found in the framing compartments of *DQ* prior to Z also appears in five of the first seven gatherings of Denison's book. When the rule again shows up in *DQ*, it is in a different skeleton page. It seems that Denison's book, also a quarto with a four-compartment frame, superseded *DQ*'s place on the production schedule, borrowing many of its rules or complete page skeletons along the way, leaving only a single skeleton with which to print gathering Z as time allowed. Once work on the sermon came to an end, the borrowed skeleton materials returned to *DQ*, jumbled and reworked into new skeleton pages.

If, as it appears, Denison's *Sin* was the cause of the disruption in *DQ*'s production, it means that by October 1611, only forty-four editions sheets of the book had been completed, leaving another thirty-four to be composed, imposed, and printed. The skeleton forme evidence from gatherings 2A–end show no indication of a change in the overall slowdown in production that

began with gathering S. Calculating forward using the production rate estimates derived from gatherings S–Y, it appears likely that *DQ* was completed
some time in middle to late spring of 1612, perhaps about the time production of the dovetailed sequence of jobs around May or June commenced.

The history of *DQ*'s printing and publishing, then, is not unusual for a
book produced by a printing house managed by a new and ambitious master printer trying to expand a business recently taken over from a deceased
partner. Stansby solicited new projects, stumbled at times when conflicts
over production priorities emerged, but proved flexible enough to accommodate publisher demands.[24] In late 1610 he (and most likely Windet to some
degree) reached an agreement with Blount and Barrett to print Shelton's
translation. Production commenced in late winter of 1611 and proceeded
smoothly until new work arrived in the summer that took greater precedence
on the schedule. Printing was interrupted in the early fall to accommodate a
sermon by Denison, then resumed at the former, slower pace until *DQ* was
finally published some time in the spring of 1612.

For historians of early modern theatre, this reconstruction establishes that
the lost *Cardenio* could have been completed weeks or months before the
death of Prince Henry on November 6.[25] It also helps place *Cardenio* in
the larger narrative of Shakespeare's late career.[26] The chronology of the
Shakespeare canon has been the subject of scholarly labor and controversy
for more than two centuries. Nevertheless, a few things are clear.[27] First,
because so many scholars have worked on the problem, we have better evidence for the chronology of the Shakespeare canon than the Fletcher canon.
Second, we know that *All Is True* (also known as *Henry VIII*) was a "new"
play, which had been performed only a few times, in late June 1613, when
the Globe theater burned down; it was not performed during the fully documented court season from November 1, 1612, to April, 1613. Third, we
know that *The Tempest* was performed at court on November 1, 1611. Fourth,
there is widespread consensus that three or four others belong to the period
1608–1611. Simon Forman saw *Cymbeline* in April 1611 and *The Winter's
Tale* in May 1611; a variety of circumstantial evidence puts *Coriolanus* in
1608–1609, and *Pericles* in early 1608.[28] The most recent Arden edition also
puts *Timon of Athens* in 1607 or early 1608.[29]

We can therefore be reasonably confident that Shakespeare worked on at
least one play a year in the five years from 1607 to 1611 (*Pericles, Coriolanus,
Winter's Tale, Cymbeline, Tempest*), even if we do not include *Timon*. This
makes financial sense: the King's Men would want at least one new play a year
from their leading dramatist. But, unless scholars have completely misjudged
the evidence, no canonical Shakespeare play seems to have been premiered
in the nineteen months between November 1, 1611, and June 1, 1613. The
gap may be even longer than this, because *The Tempest* could have been completed a year or more before its first recorded court performance: most scholars agree that it draws upon William Strachey's *A True Reportory of the Wracke
and Redemption of Sir Thomas Gates, Knight*, dated July 15, 1610. But even
if we assume that *The Tempest* was brand-new when it launched the court's

winter season of 1611–1612, we have a nineteen-month gap between plays, an empty interim longer than any other in the Shakespeare canon. The foregoing investigation strongly suggests that Stansby's edition of *Don Quixote* was published during that gap. Shakespeare could easily have written part of a play based on that novel in the summer or autumn of 1612, in anticipation of the need for a new play for the winter court season of 1612–1613.

Even if all these chronological conclusions are correct, they would not prove that Shakespeare collaborated with Fletcher on the lost *Cardenio*. But the bibliographical evidence I have surveyed here does make that scenario *possible*. In doing so, it would also fill a hitherto-unexplained, uniquely long gap in the chronology of Shakespeare's career.

NOTES

1. For the date of the court performance, see Gary Taylor, "The Embassy, The City, The Court, The Text: *Cardenio* Performed in 1613," *Quest*, 286–308. For the relationship between Shelton's translation and the lost play, see the essay by Taylor and Wagschal, chapter 2, in this volume.
2. Alfred W. Pollard, Gilbert R. Redgrave, and Katherine R. Pantzer. *A Short-Title Catalogue of Books Printed in England, Scotland and Ireland and of English Books Printed Abroad 1475–1640*, 3 vols. (London: The Bibliographical Society, 1976–1991).
3. The Stationers' Register follows the legal calendar, but for the purposes of this essay, all entry dates have been modernized.
4. W. W. Greg, *A Bibliography of the English Printed Drama to the Restoration*, 4 vols. (London: For the Bibliographical Society, 1939–59), 4.xciv. Philip Gaskell also cites the printer and author John Nichols who, in his early-nineteenth-century collection *Literary Anecdotes*, observed as common practice among stationers in the eighteenth century, "that when a Book happens not to be ready for Publication before November, the date of the ensuing year is used"; *A New Introduction to Bibliography* (Oxford: Oxford University Press, 1972), 317–18.
5. Blount was the older of the two, having commissioned his first publication in 1594, while Barrett entered the trade in 1608. The two were partners from 1608 to 1613.
6. Edward Arber, *A Transcription of the Registers of the Stationers' Company of London 1554–1640*, 5 vols. (London: Privately Printed, 1874–94), 2.680.
7. *Records of the Court of the Stationers' Company 1576 to 1602*, ed. W. W. Greg and E. Boswell (London: The Bibliographical Society, 1930), 14.
8. See Mark Bland, "Johnson, Stansby and English Typography" (DPhil thesis, Oxford University, 1995), especially 121, 135–7.
9. Arber, *Transcription of the Registers*, 2.173, 2.717.
10. See Mark Bland, "William Stansby and the Production of *The Workes of Beniamin Jonson, 1615–16*," *Library*, 6th ser., 20 (1998): 4–5. The amount of english-body type Stansby brought to the house was quite large, enough to allow Stansby on one occasion to set aside at least thirty-seven folio pages in late 1616 while he worked on a different project; Johann Gerritsen, "Stansby and Jonson Produce a Folio: A Preliminary Account," *Essays and Studies* 40 (1959): 52–5. Thirty-seven pages totals over 400 lbs. of type; compare this with

William Jaggard, who printed the entire Shakespeare Folio "with a worn fount of type which can have weighed no more than about 90 kg. (200 lb.)"; Gaskell, *A New Introduction*, 38.

11. Bland, "William Stansby," 5.
12. Bland, "Johnson, Stansby and English Typography," 1.165.
13. Kevin Bracken, "William Stansby's Early Career," *Studies in Bibliography* 38 (1985): 214–16.; Bland, "Johnson, Stansby and English Typography," 2.302.
14. Arber, *Transcription of the Registers*, 3.451.
15. The term "publisher" is anachronistic when discussing the early modern book trade as it had not yet developed as a distinct professional activity. In this essay I use publisher to identify the person or persons who initiated the project, arranged its financing, and wholesaled the completed volumes to the trade. Most publishers were stationers or holders of patents, but a non-stationer could act as a silent partner to a stationer.
16. For a detailed breakdown of costs, see Peter Blayney's thought experiment in "The Publication of Playbooks," in *A New History of Early English Drama*, ed. John D. Cox and David Scott Kastan (New York: Columbia University Press, 1997), 394–413.
17. Assessing a printing house's productive capacity presents a number of challenges, not the least of which concerns the unit of measurement. Counting titles tells you nothing about the relative size of the volumes in question, and pagination merely enumerates a structure whose size varies with format—it takes much more work to produce a twelve-page folio than a twelve-page duodecimo. In order to estimate the Windet/Stansby establishment's printing resources, this study employs "edition sheets," that is, the number of sheets of paper used in an exemplar volume as an indication of the total press resources required to machine the entire print run. Thus a 16-page folio, a 32-page quarto, and a 64-page octavo all contain four sheets per volume and likely took approximately the same amount of time to print. While not perfect, edition sheets do provide valuable insight into how efficiently a house managed its limited number of printing presses. Given the establishment's more than ample typographic resources, the primary limitation facing Windet and Stansby was the number of presses they owned. A two-man press crew could only machine a set number of sheets per day, no matter how many formes of type were composed. A Stationers' Company inventory in 1586 showed that Windet owned three presses (Arber, 5.lii), while after a series of complaints, a 1615 decree limited most printers (including Stansby) to two working presses (Arber, 3.699).
18. This includes Thomas Coryate, who while not himself a stationer, paid the publication costs for his *Coryates Crudities* (STC 5808). Blount and Barrett entered the work with the company on November 26, 1610 (Arber, 3.449).
19. Arber 3.457; Dana F. Sutton's hypertext edition of William Camden's *Diary*, www.philological.bham.ac.uk/diary.
20. Over three dozen titles were transferred to Stansby, likely as part of a settlement with Windet's heirs.
21. Casting-off involves setting a sample page of text, counting the number of words on that page, and using the estimate to predict where the breaks occur in the manuscript, thereby enabling them to set the text out of order.
22. *The History of the World* did prove politically important, although not in the way Ralegh and Burre anticipated. The Archbishop of Canterbury sent a letter

to the Master and Wardens of the Stationers' Company dated December 22, 1614, ordering the suppression of the book and all copies delivered to him or the Bishop of London (*Records*, Jackson, 355). John Racin, Jr. notes the reason for the suppression in a letter dated January 5, 1615, where John Chamberlain writes the book "is called in by the Kinges commaundment, for divers exceptions, but specially for beeing too sawcie in censuring princes"; "The Early Editions of Sir Walter Ralegh's *The History of the World*," *Studies in Bibliography* 17 (1964): 200. This was followed up in September of 1616 by a letter to the Stationers from James I ordering them to deliver all copies in their possession to John Ramsay, one of the king's favorites (357).

23. Sermons commanded a large market, comprising 7 percent of the total London printing output in Jacobean London (calculated in edition sheets), the same as books of history or complete Bibles, one-and-one-half times that of popular prose literature, and over four times the amount of dramatic publishing.

24. Stansby continued to run this productive house for another quarter century, only retiring in 1636 when he sold the establishment to Richard Bishop for £700.

25. On the relationship of *Cardenio* to Henry's death, see Taylor, "Embassy," *Quest*, and Richard Wilson, "Unseasonable Laughter: The Context of *Cardenio*," in *Secret Shakespeare: Studies in Theatre, Religion and Resistance* (Manchester: Manchester University Press, 2004), 230–45. By contrast, both *Henry VIII* and *Two Noble Kinsmen* undoubtedly postdate Henry's death and his sister Elizabeth's wedding: among the many discussions of that context in relation to the post-*Tempest* plays, see Julia Briggs, "Tears at the Wedding: Shakespeare's Last Phase," in *Shakespeare's Late Plays: New Readings,* ed. Jennifer Richards and James Knowles (Edinburgh: Edinburgh University Press, 1999), 210–27.

26. *Cardenio* was first linked with Shakespeare in a Stationers' Register entry of September 9, 1653, when Humphrey Moseley registered a large number of plays, including "The History of *Cardenio*, by Mr Fletcher & Shakespeare"; G. E. B. Eyre and G. R. Rivington, *A Transcript of the Registers of the Worshipful Company of Stationers; From 1640–1708 A.D.*, 3 vols. (London: Privately Printed, 1913–1914), I.428.

27. The most recent systematic survey of the documents relevant to the entire chronology remains Gary Taylor, "The Canon and Chronology of Shakespeare's Plays," in Stanley Wells, Gary Taylor, et al., *William Shakespeare: A Textual Companion* (Oxford: Clarendon Press, 1987), 69–144, esp. 130–4 (1608–1613). Although scholars continue to debate whether *Cymbeline* preceded or followed *Winter's Tale*, there is a strong consensus about the plays Taylor identifies as Shakespeare's last: see for instance *Late Shakespeare, 1608–1613*, ed. Andrew J. Power and Rory Loughnane (Cambridge: Cambridge University Press, 2012).

28. Taylor dates *Pericles* in the "five first months of 1608" (130); in her edition of the play (London: Arden Shakespeare, 2004), Suzanne Gossett specifies "between April and June 1608" (12–18).

29. Anthony B. Dawson and Gretchen E. Minton, eds., *Timon of Athens* (London: Arden Shakespeare, 2008), 54–70.

4

QUIXOTE ON THE ENGLISH STAGE: A NEW GLIMPSE OF *THE HISTORY OF CARDENIO*?

Gerald Baker

On October 29, 1630, the diplomat and parliamentarian Sir Thomas Roe wrote to Elizabeth Stuart, the Winter Queen. He had been a member of Elizabeth's household probably since her coming into England after her father's accession, and had continued to be a correspondent and ally after her marriage and departure from England in 1613. On this occasion he wrote concerning the recent plague season:

> [A]nother general calamitye, we have had no playes this six moneths, & that makes our grate men see the goodness of them ... : for if our heads had beene filled with the loves of Piramies & Thisbe, *or the various fortunes of Don Quixotte,* we should never have cared, who had made peace or war but on the stage. But now every foole is enquiring what the French doe in Italy, & what they breake in Germany.[1]

This piece of correspondence has been available in easily accessible sources, but has not been previously noted in relation to the nexus of evidence that begins to define the shape of the lost King's Men play, *The History of Cardenio.* In talking about the absence of plays (the theaters were prohibited from opening because of plague) and giving examples of staged narratives that would fill up the mental space "every foole" now devotes to political speculation, Roe refers here quite clearly to a *play* that includes Don Quixote, not to the novel, and he refers to the *character* and his "fortunes," rather than to the title of the play, for a title cannot have "fortunes."[2] I suggest that there are grounds for taking this otherwise unknown play to be that *History of Cardenio.*

First consider the allusion he couples to the "Quixotte" reference. It is entirely reasonable to take his other reference to "Piramies and Thisbe" as an allusion to the King's Men play *A Midsummer Night's Dream.* We know that the profile of the play was high and that the material concerning the mechanicals and their interlude were popular. A variety of allusions attest to that material's continuing visibility in the Stuart theater. Sharpham's *The Fleer* (1606) contains a reference that likely puts us in touch with a piece of original stage business, "[L]ike *Thisbe* in the play, a has almost kil'd himselfe with the scabberd." John Gee in 1624, *New Shreds of the Old Snare,* has clearly *seen*, not merely read, the play: "As for flashes of light, we might see very cheape in the Comedie of *Piramus* and *Thisbe*, where one comes in with a Lanthorne and Acts *Mooneshine*." In 1646 James Shirley uses the *Dream* mechanicals preparing an entertainment as the blueprint of the antimasque in his *Triumph of Beauty*. And in 1661 the title page of the (separately published) derived droll *Bottom the Weaver* witnesses to amateur performance as well as its presence in the prewar King's repertory. Bentley, in *Shakespeare & Jonson: Their Reputations in the Seventeenth Century Compared*,[3] numbers eighteen allusions to the play, comparable to *Merry Wives* (22) and *Romeo and Juliet* (15), though because of his presentation it is not possible to allocate these accurately to pre-1642 and post-Restoration periods, nor to particular threads or sections of the play.

We can be openminded about what triggered Roe's mentioning it at this particular time: it might be the company's presentation of it at court less than a fortnight before, on October 17[4] (whether he'd seen it or merely heard about it): it might be having seen it elsewhere in the not-too-distant past (I consider below the opportunities Roe would have had for seeing plays in London). But it is clear that he could expect his correspondent to recognize what he was talking about.

The play featuring Don Quixote, mentioned in the very same context and indeed sentence must then have either (a) had a similar familiarity or recognition factor to *Dream*, or (b) been recently in its company's active repertory, or perhaps both. His reference in the case of the Quixote play, however, is not triggered by a performance in the current court season (we know and have extant all of the other plays performed before the date of his letter). That does not preclude some other performance, or memory of performance, recent or older, acting as trigger. And it is possible that an aspect of *Dream* called to mind a Cervantine play. Roe is, interestingly, not the only person to link Pyramus and Thisbe to Don Quixote. Roger Chartier, in considering the way in which Edmund Gayton handles the Cardenio story in his *Pleasant Notes upon Don Quixote* (1654), tells how Gayton adds "new themes" to his verse paraphrase of Cardenio's narration.[5] At the point where Luscinda's father is denying Cardenio access to his daughter, Shelton's translation describes the parental action as "imitating in a manner therein *Tisbi*, so much solemnized by the Poets, her parents" (*DQ* 3.10.221). But Gayton amplifies this with: "Like *Pyramus* and *Thisbe* then,/ Through crannies we did Court,/ And chinks and holes, conveigh'd our Sport,/ (Made stronger by her Fathers pen)" (130). As well as adding Pyramus to the reference, he goes on in subsequent stanzas to add a whole stage to the narrative. Where Cervantes' lovers, confronted by the entirely precautionary confinement, move straight to conversing in letters, Gayton envisages a sequence where they first have clandestine face-to-wall-to-face conversations before moving to correspondence. We know from numerous references that Gayton's mind-scape includes numerous plays; there are examples in this very chapter on page129, referring to *Epicoene*, *The Knave in Grain* and (perhaps) *George a Greene*.[6] So it may be that the additional conversations derive from memories of watching or reading *Dream*—his vocabulary of "crannies," "chinks," and "holes" repeats the vocabulary of the mechanicals' interlude. But whatever the source of Gayton's addition to the narrative sequence, the thing we should note is that two writers, nearly a quarter of a century apart, link together aspects of *Dream* and aspects of *Quixote*. And this is remarkable because we know that in the collaborative closing phase of his writing, *A Midsummer Night's Dream* for whatever reason loomed large for Shakespeare: not very many months after this first collaboration with Fletcher, he would revisit characters, locations, and situations from *Dream* in *The Two Noble Kinsmen*. In Gayton's quatrain 8 we might be looking at a relic of an earlier stage of that process. And Roe then opens the window on that mindscape a little further: his words associate Pyramus and Thisbe with not just the book but the *person* of Don Quixote.[7]

It is reasonable to suppose that Roe's play was a King's Men play, both for its juxtaposition in his letter to *Dream* and because of the company's dominance of court schedules by 1630. It includes Quixote as a character, but it need not be named for him and he may not be its main concern, any more than Pyramus and Thisbe are the main concern of *Dream*, or for that matter Hotspur the ostensible main concern of *1 Henry IV*, or Benedick and Beatrice of *Much Ado About Nothing* (and there are references to both these other plays by these characters' names).[8] And in his copy of the 1632 Folio Charles I himself marked several titles on the catalogue page with characters' name as alternate identifiers: for example, "Malvolio" against *Twelfth Night*, and "Pirimus & Thisby" against *Dream*.[9] Quixote's appearance then does not preclude the play containing other narrative material that does not directly involve him: Chartier has pointed out that the first two known plays to contain the character of Don Quixote (one Spanish, one French) also dramatized the Cardenio narrative from the novel.[10] Moreover, Gary Taylor and John Nance have argued independently of Chartier that *Double Falsehood*, Theobald's eighteenth-century adaptation of a claimed early modern original, contains remnants of a Jacobean Quixot/Sancho subplot.[11]

There might be two objections to the idea that in an English play featuring Quixote additional narrative material might also derive from Cervantes's novel. The first is that collaborators could not work from the same book at the same time.[12] It seems naïve to suppose that professionals might not *each* supply themselves with a personal copy, and the more so when one considers that this particular book was widely known and alluded to, from very soon after its publication. And we can certainly see cases where collaborators are using the same source book in their respective shares.[13] The second objection could be that other adaptations of material from the novel (Field's *Amends for Ladies*, Beaumont and Fletcher's *The Coxcomb*, Middleton's *The Lady's Tragedy*) do not include Quixote as a character. But these all derive directly or indirectly from the same 'History of the Curious-Impertinent' that appears as a narrative *read out* to the characters (and moreover read out while Quixote is asleep), an entirely separate narrative unit. But in almost any other extractible section of the book, Quixote interacts with the characters to a greater or smaller extent and his presence would enhance a dramatization of any narrative segment, whether or not he was the protagonist of that segment.

That character and novel were quickly and widely recognized in England is clear from the variety of allusions gathered by Randall and Boswell, and that playwrights were amongst the first to be aware is obvious not only from the general similarity to Cervantes of the basic concept of Beaumont's *The Knight of the Burning Pestle*, but from the windmill allusions in Middleton's *Your Five Gallants* and Wilkins's *The Miseries of Enforced Marriage*, all to be dated around 1606/1607, a year or two after the book's first publication. Jonson and Webster provide further indications in the years 1610/1615 that dramatists especially were picking up and remarking on features of the book.[14] Taken together with the three adaptations of the Curious-Impertinent, which fall within the same date range, it is clear that Cervantes' book was very much part of playwrights' mental landscape within a decade of the book's appearance. But when one considers which elements in the book were being mentioned specifically, it is less easy to see *what* might form the basis of a play if a playmaker was moved actually to dramatize the title-character himself. Those early allusions to the windmills incident in chapter eight of Part One point us to what was, for the seventeenth century and possibly for every generation since, the most frequently mentioned incident in the book. However, we do find as well visual reference to Mambrino's helmet (in the frontispiece to Blount's second edition of Shelton's translation), and verbal references to "water milles" like "Scotch bagpipes" (Webster 1615)—these may be the water mills of Part Two's chapter twenty-nine, but at that date refer more probably to the fulling mills Quixote and Sancho encounter in chapter twenty of Part One. There is also reference to Quixote's penance in the Sierra Morena (in May's *The Heir* of 1620). All of these are single incidents, however, almost single images described at length. There is not matter to furnish a play-length story in any of them and very little narrative thread beyond the presence and interaction of Quixote and Sancho. For a modern reader, those interactions and their discourses may often be the meat of the book, but this seems not to be the case for first-generation readers. We find references that can be read as being quite dismissive or can seem to be taking the story as if it was quite as serious as *Amadis of Gaul* itself, missing the humour and parody entirely.[15] It seems that what would be of most interest, in the first quarter century of the novel's existence, for a dramatizing of Quixote himself would be the physical comedy and incidents. And this would actually make the material analogous to that other play Roe cites, where he highlights the physical and burlesque elements of *A Midsummer Night's Dream* in the mechanicals' "Pyramus and Thisbe" interlude. So it is possible in the light of contemporary readers' responses to envisage somewhere in the first decade or so of *Don Quijote*'s existence (where playwrights' responses gather chronologically) a play that includes Quixote, probably presented in comedic mode, but which includes other narrative material. Of all the various other narrative elements in Part One—Marcela and Chrysostom, the Curious-Impertinent, the Captive, and more—the one which most directly impacts on Quixote and in which he has a significant role himself is the thread that tells of Cardenio and Dorotea and their loves and betrayals: not because of the Don's presence when the story comes to resolution in the inn with the arrival of Fernando and Luscinda, but because of the knight's meeting with Cardenio and of Dorotea's involvement in the scheme to de-humor Quixote. A play with Quixote that contained other narrative material would most conveniently draw that material from the Cardenio plot in the same book, as Guillén de Castro did by 1610 and Pichou did in 1628.[16] The King's Men play *Cardenno* or *Cardenna* appears in the King's Chamber accounts exactly where frequency and kind of allusion by playmakers invite us to expect a Quixote play.

Even accepting the likelihood that the King's Men's play contains both Cardenio and Quixote material does not prove that this is the play which Roe is thinking of in his letter to Elizabeth. There is after all a quarter of a century between the publication of Cervantes' book and the writing of Roe's letter. Within those years, from 1605 to 1630 inclusive, *Annals of English Drama 975–1700* lists over 125 lost plays, in most cases known to us only by title (and these of course are only a fraction of the output, most of which has left no trace).[17] I am referring to playhouse output here, not to academic or closet plays and not to masques or civic entertainments. In a very few cases, we do know enough about the content of the play to be able to say confidently that it is not *Quijote*-related—1624's *The Late Murder in Whitechapel* by Dekker, Ford, Webster, and Rowley being the most obvious, where we have papers in the law suit that followed outlining the script's narrative line; or the alleged Shakespearian *Iphis and Iantha*, placed by *Annals* in 1613, with its clear reference to the story in Ovid. A good number of others exclude themselves by defining their historical period or geographical location in their title—for example: Beaumont's *Madon King of Britain* placed in 1606, the anonymous *Richard Whittington* of 1605, the Fletcher/Field/Massinger collaboration of 1617, *The Jeweller of Amsterdam*, the anonymous *The Dumb Bawd of Venice* in 1628. Altogether, thirty-four titles exclude themselves by virtue of known content, indicated historical period, or suggested location.[18] The titles of many others contain no element that suggests any relation to Quixote material or indeed run counter to that suggestion. Examples include 1608's *The Silver Mine*, *The Proud Maid's Tragedy* in 1612, *The Owl* and *The Noble Grandchild* both in 1614, *The Man in the Moon Drinks Claret* of 1621, *Two Kings in a Cottage* from 1623, and two titles placed in 1624, *The Parricide* and *The Angel King*. Given the allegiances (or perhaps one should more accurately say "most usual employers") of the writers who evince an interest in *Quijote* by alluding to it, we might also exclude titles definitely associated with amphitheater houses other than the Globe.[19] Titles associated with the King's Men and therefore that house in the period are *The Spanish Maze* 1605*,[20] *The Twins' Tragedy**, *The Nobleman** and *A Bad Beginning Makes A Good Ending** and *The Knot of Fools** 1612, *The Woman's Plot** and *The Woman Is Too Hard for Him* 1621*, *The Dumb Bawd, The Spanish Duke of Lerma*, and *The Buck Is a Thief* 1623, *Shank's Ordinary* and *The Spanish Viceroy* 1624, *The Judge* 1627, *The Lovesick Maid** and *Minerva's Sacrifice* 1629*, *Beauty in a Trance** and *An Induction for the House* 1630*. At the indoor Cockpit, converted to playhouse usage in 1616–1617, and not excluded by content or setting or period is *The Man in the Moon Drinks Claret* Prince's 1621*, *The Black Lady* and *The Valiant Scholar* Lady Elizabeth's 1622, and perhaps *The Dutch Painter and the French Branke* Prince's 1622, *The Cra[fty?] Merchant* Lady Elizabeth's 1623, *The Spanish Contract* 1624, and perhaps for Queen Henrietta's in 1625 and 1626 respectively *A Fool and Her Maidenhead Soon Parted* and the first of the two plays Shirley titled at different times *The Brothers*. There is nothing in these lists that seems an obvious derivative from *Quijote* material and not many titles that indicate *any* elements of Cervantine material. The case remains the same if we extend inspection to houses not within the usual fashionable beat and to titles whose company or venue are not known. *The Younger Brother* was possibly a Prince's Men play in 1617, an unknown company had *The False Friend* in 1619 and the Palsgrave's *Honour in the End* in 1624. These might relate to elements we find in *Quijote* narrative, but imply situations or characters that appear in many narratives not written by Cervantes. Beyond these the pirates, painters, Welsh travellers and angel kings who populate the lost play titles take us nowhere near a deluded knight and his narrative *compadres*.

While one recognizes the absence of any information at all about much of the repertory, it does seem unlikely that a play as recognizable as Roe expects his to be and on such a widely familiar subject would have left no trace at all of itself in the record, and *The History of Cardenio* performed in 1613 by the King's Men seems to match the indicators reviewed so far. Its title links it to *Don Quijote* material, it comes from the span of years when playwrights in England were especially conscious of the book's contents, the title signifies the narrative complexity that a play would need and that the knight's adventures alone do not provide. But one can nevertheless question whether a play from 1613 would still be current in 1630. We have of course scarcely any detailed information about the King's or any other company's repertory in the period that would enable us to say whether any given play was being performed in any given year, and particularly whether an *older* play would be. There are two indicators for the King's, however, and they certainly do not exclude the possibility. The first is the bill for court performances in the fall of 1630,[21] which lists twenty plays: only three of these are less than five years old, and four of them (20 percent) are within the sixteen-to-twenty-year-old range that would include *The History of Cardenio*. It is reasonable, though not provable, to think that the plays presented at court were from the current repertoire—"current" in this case being what had been performed publicly before the plague closure in April, or was being prepared for performance when playing was resumed. The other indicator is the list of plays sent by Essex as Lord Chamberlain in August 1641 to the Stationers' Company forbidding their printing without the King's Men's consent.[22] These were presumably those scripts that the company wanted to remain inaccessible because they were proven, reliable pleasers in their recent repertory. Of these sixty-one titles, almost half are indeed Caroline scripts but only thirteen of them five years old or less. The sort of range in which *Cardenio* would fall (twenty-six to thirty years) contributes as many as seven titles. Although there is nothing on the list that can certainly or even plausibly be related to *Cardenio*, the 1641 list does confirm that in the Caroline period it was by no means only novelty that was in request.

It is unlikely in any case that what Roe was referring to was a novelty. His opportunities for London playgoing were limited (but not nonexistent) throughout the quarter century in question. It will be helpful at this point to outline his general whereabouts, for there were major and lengthy diplomatic missions that took him abroad for years at a time. In 1605 itself he was one in the several hundred strong retinue that accompanied Nottingham to Spain to ratify the recent peace treaty and may thus have been exposed to *Quijote* fever very early on. There is a short spell in the Netherlands later that year, and then he was in England until his voyage to Guiana between February 1610 and July 1611. After that he was in England again through to April of 1613, when he accompanied Elizabeth and her husband to Heidelberg, the Palatinate's capital. Various errands kept him on the Continent till January 1614, when he returned home and stayed (save for a short spell soldiering in the Netherlands in the summer of 1614) until February 1615. At that point he set sail to India as ambassador to the Mughal court, returning in September 1619. In July 1621 he was appointed ambassador to the Sultan in Constantinople, leaving in October. Although he began his return journey in June 1628, that journey was largely overland from Italy onward and he was not in London again until January 1629. In June of the same year he went on another mission to Northern and Central Europe that lasted until June 1630. When the theatres were closed for the plague in mid-April of that year, Roe was still in Danzig[23] and could thus have seen no *public* playing in the months between his return in June and his writing to Elizabeth at the end of October. A Quixote play, if it was new and not *Cardenio*, must fall within the periods of his stays in England, or if an older play must have sustained itself in the repertory so as to be performed during one or more of those stays. These chronological constraints, combined with the titles already excluded by subject matter, locale or period, at once reduce the list of possible alternatives to *Cardenio* from the list of 125 lost plays to about three dozen: and if the list is restricted to King's and Cockpit plays, as suggested earlier, to no more than a dozen (the asterisked items in the list above). The chronological and geographical constraints make the period between publication of Cervantes' book and April 1613 the most likely time when Roe could have seen a Quixote play, but fall 1619 to fall 1621 and the first half of 1629 are also possibilities. Before April 1613 knowledge of the play would be available to Elizabeth too (and indeed the possibility of actually seeing it), and revival in the first half of 1629 would make it a recent reference point for Roe.

There is one other reason why Roe might especially recognize or remember this particular play. Although there is no direct connection documented between Roe and Fletcher, they had people in common: Ben Jonson, for one. Jonson contributed a poem to the paratext of Fletcher's *Faithful Shepherdess*, as Fletcher did to Jonson's *Volpone* and *Catiline*. And Jonson addressed two of his *Epigrams* (xcviii and xcix) to Roe, who may have contributed complimentary verses to *Sejanus* (as "Th. R") and *Volpone* (as "T. R."). More importantly, Roe and Fletcher shared the acquaintance—and patronage—of the Earl and Countess of Huntingdon. Not manifest from the large body of Fletcher's dramatic texts and their preliminaries, he nevertheless had patronage relations with the Huntingdons. Dating from perhaps 1620 and published in 1930, a verse letter from Fletcher to the Countess displays both familiarity with the household at Ashby and sympathy with the non-court politics of the Earl.[24] Strachan reports that by 1620 Roe was "now clearly identified as a member of the court party" (124), at least in relation to the business of the Virginia Company with which the Earl was by then involved. But earlier connections existed and were apparently cordial. One of the first letters to survive from a British subject in India is from Roe to the Countess in October 1616, which alludes to previously received patronage and to political opinions quite in line with the Protestant and country party views of the Huntingdon circle centered at Ashby, as well as indicating a social familiarity with the household at least comparable to Fletcher's.[25] Even without postulating Roe having direct personal contact with Fletcher, it is easy to see that he would have cause enough to take an interest in his work that went beyond the interest one would take in the dominant playwright of the decade. McMullan describes the "symmetries…apparent between the country-based, feminocentric, uncourtly environment cultivated by the Huntingdons at Ashby and the politics of [Fletcher's] plays, which are cynical of court and assertions of absolutism, and are fascinated both with negotiations of city and country and with issues of gender, in particular with female dominance and agency" (35). Even in the attenuated, adapted half-life *Cardenio* suffers as *Double Falsehood*, there is partial congruence between the situations of the play and the ethos of the Huntingdon-Fletcher circle as McMullan describes it: a skepticism of the court not only in Fernando/Henriquez's exploitation of his princely glamor among rural folk but also in the questionable stratagem of his older brother abducting a novice from a nunnery; negotiations of city and country in the interactions of the two sets of characters; and an environment, not feminocentric to be sure, but that has bred women who at least demonstrate independent spirits and a will to resist. There is reason for a person—especially one like Roe with at least one other attested theatrical connection—in the Huntingdon milieu to remember the play and to recognize it in any future incarnations it chanced to have.

That recognition factor may of course have been a factor between Roe and Elizabeth themselves, rather than a public recognition (or as well as a public recognition). Roe had been a member of Elizabeth's household before she came to reside at Court at the end of 1608,[26] and despite his overseas missions he had been in England from July 1611 through to April of 1613, when he had joined her and the Elector Frederick on their post-wedding journey back to Heidelberg. So knowledge of what the playing companies were performing during that period would have been available to both of them. In addition, James I had made Roe a Gentleman of the Privy Chamber by 1614 (the exact date is unknown). His closeness, or perhaps simply usefulness as evidenced by his company on the Heidelberg journey, combined with his nearness to the Court as evidenced by his Privy Chamber role makes it likely he would have been in attendance during the betrothal and wedding celebrations that included the first recorded performance of *Cardenio*.[27]

There are two other occasions before the date of the letter when they were in the same place at the same time. In December 1628 Roe "no doubt" visited the couple in their exile in the Netherlands, on the overland leg of his return trip from years as ambassador to the Sultan, and in the latter part of 1629 he saw them again at their estate in Gelderland, at Rhenen, though on this occasion the stay was limited to two nights.[28] We are told that "occasionally her children and visitors even performed a play or masque at her residence" (*Oxford Dictionary of National Biography*) so there is a possibility of theatrical activity or shared theatrical memories forming a part of their interactions on these visits. This is not to suggest that *Cardenio* itself would have been part of such activity, but simply to indicate the likelihood that a shared interest might trigger continuing references to shared or common experiences during Roe's visits and in later correspondence.

Whether or not Roe refers to something high in the public consciousness or merely to an experience he shared with Elizabeth, he attests to the existence of a play, written between 1605 and 1630, with Quixote as a character. Given their respective whereabouts between 1605 when *Don Quijote* was first published and the date of Roe's letter,[29] it is unlikely that either of them would have seen or have prominent in their minds the French or Spanish plays on the subject. An English play, then, which Roe could assume would distract the English public from international news: and in the standard scholarly listing of lost plays in the range 1605–1630 there is very little that might be a Quixote play and nothing that definitely is. The most direct link of any play title to Quixote is *The History of Cardenio*.

We cannot exclude the possibility that whatever Roe was referring to has left no trace of its existence, but with the likelihood that by the Caroline period fewer new plays were required to fill the repertory because of the accumulated back list this is less probable than in the earlier part of the Stuart period.[30] Roe's remark does seem to point to the King's Men having a play with a similar visibility to the comic and burlesque *Dream* that was not only drawn from *Don Quixote,* but which also brought the character himself onstage. We know separately that they had a play whose title linked to *Quixote*, and that the names of their two most prominent writers were attached to it—and they would be the playwrights most likely to produce something with that high a recognition factor. Fletcher and Shakespeare's *History of Cardenio* seems to match the specification Roe's reference implies without any need to suppose a second play to explain his remark. We might therefore surmise, however tentatively and provisionally, that it was still live in the King's Men repertory close to or in 1629/1630 (thus causing Roe to make it an example in writing to Elizabeth), and that the play did include some actual embodiment of Don Quixote himself. The Roe allusion is also consistent with Gary Taylor's suggestion that Edmund Gayton had seen a performance of the lost *Cardenio,* most probably during the reign of Charles I.[31]

It is possible to weave these various suppositions into the web of what we already know about *Cardenio* and its metamorphosis into *Double Falsehood*. *The History of Cardenio* dramatizes the Cardenio-Fernando material from *Don Quijote* and also presents the knight himself as a character. It is as recognizable (at least to an informed playgoer) as the mechanicals' play in *A Midsummer Night's Dream*. Even if not still performed by 1629/1630, an allusion to it can be made with the expectation it can be recognized. And it may still be in the repertory then. This new strand then takes *Cardenio* sixteen or seventeen years nearer to Moseley's entry, and of course closer to the point where John Downes or Betterton would be working on it,[32] and the popularity its continuing presence in the repertory implies gives them a *reason* to be working on it. And that same popularity, causing a demand (in the absence of a printed edition) for manuscripts as happened with *A Game at Chess* or *The Wild Goose Chase*,[33] also makes a degree more feasible the existence of the *multiple* manuscripts that Theobald claimed to have in his possession.[34] *The History's* history may be a bit more coherent and a bit more plausible.

NOTES

1. National Archive, State Papers 16/174/102, cited here from Dale B. J. Randall and Jackson C. Boswell, *Cervantes in Seventeenth-Century England* (Oxford: Oxford University Press, 2009), 69: my emphasis.
2. And therefore he cannot be referring to the "Cartel pour les courreurs du Cuveau" of D. Jocquet in 1613 (noted in Randall and Boswell, *Cervantes*, 20), which is an address-in-character and not a play, and which does not represent Quixote's adventures or "fortunes." Randall and Boswell give other extracts from the Roe/Elizabeth correspondence in 1636 (84), 1637 (85), and 1639 (92), which are not indicated as play references and seem to be triggered by the novel: but these do not cast doubt on *Roe's* application here since they all come from *Elizabeth's* side of the correspondence.
3. Chicago: University of Chicago Press, 1945, I 109.
4. Bentley, *The Jacobean and Caroline Stage*, 7 vols. (Oxford: Clarendon Press, 1941–1968), I, 27.

5. *Cardenio between Cervantes and Shakespeare: The Story of a Lost Play* (Cambridge: Polity Press, 2013), 98.

6. Gary Taylor provides listings of Gayton's references in Taylor, "History," 34.

7. Taylor's and Chartier's work, carried out independently of one another, as well as the occasional use of Gayton by other scholars indicate how useful and desirable an authoritative and scholarly edition of *Pleasant Notes* would be.

8. Both of these usages are found in the same Chamber Account Warrant of May 20, 1613, which is the first documentary record of *Cardenio*. Note also the records from Herbert's Office Book for a performance of "Malvolio" on February 2, 1623, and of "The First Part of Sir John Falstaff" on January 1, 1625: N. W. Bawcutt, ed., *The Control and Censorship of Caroline Drama: The Records of Sir Henry Herbert, Master of the Revels 1623–73* (Oxford: Clarendon Press, 1996), 140, 159.

9. T. A. Birrell, *English Monarchs and Their Books: From Henry VII to Charles II: The Panizzi Lectures* (London: The British Library, 1986), 44–45.

10. Chartier, "*Cardenio* without Shakespeare," in *Quest*, 312–13 and 315.

11. Taylor and Nance, "Four Characters in Search of a Subplot: *Cardenio,* Quixote, and Sancho," in *Quest*, 192–213. The essay draws together various kinds of evidence, especially structural and linguistic, which converge to make a strong demonstration of the case, and therefore no single citation does justice to it.

12. Hammond, *DF*, 43, suggests that "purely on the pragmatic level" this would entail "an awkward arrangement."

13. Taylor and Nance give examples from Shakespeare's and Fletcher's canons in the essay in *Quest* cited in note 11, 194–5.

14. All of these references, previously needing to be hunted down across editions of the dramatists involved, are conveniently gathered together in Randall and Boswell's collection *Cervantes*. For Beaumont, Middleton, and Wilkins, see 6–7: for Jonson, 8–9: for Webster, 25–6 (a nondramatic allusion) and 52–4. Later allusions are given from Massinger and Dekker on 48–9 and from May on 49. Valerie Wayne has a larger discussion of the pre-1613 allusions in her *Quest* essay, "*Don Quixote* and Shakespeare's Collaborative Turn to Romance," 217–38, but does not include Webster.

15. For example, "I:Cocke" in 1615, "…whose witts best treasury/ Lyes in *Don Quixot, Amadis de Gaule,/ Huon* of *Burdeaux,* and those other small/ Slight Pamphleters" (Randall and Boswell, *Cervantes,* 24–5), or William Crosse, in 1625 apposing "meere *Quixotes*" to "*Rodomantading* braves" (57).

16. Chartier, "*Cardenio* without Shakespeare," loc. cit.

17. Alfred Harbage, rev. S. Schoenbaum, third edition rev. Sylvia Stoler Wagonheim, *Annals of English Drama 975–1700* (London: Routledge, 1989), 92–129 (for all lost plays considered in this paragraph). On pp. xvii–xviii of this edition, Wagonheim states: "Sometimes the year in which a play has been placed is merely a median point between a forward and a backward limit, but usually there are better reasons for its chronological position than this." I have not attempted for my purpose here to distinguish between more accurately positioned titles and those whose median placing is merely indicative.

18. In addition to those listed above, *The Bold Beauchamps* 1606, *The Battle of Hexham* 1607, *Torrismount* 1608, *St. Christopher* 1609, *Belinus, Brennus* 1610, *Richard II* 1611, *A Yorkshire Gentlewoman and Her Son, Machiavel and the Devil, The Arraignment of London, Duke Humphrey, King Stephen, Raymond Duke of Lyons* all 1613, *Perkin Warbeck* (not the Ford play), *Titus and Vespasian*

1619, *Guy of Warwick* (assuming this Day and Dekker collaboration is not the same as the script published in 1661) 1620, *Osmund the Great Turk* (if this is not Carlell's play) 1622, *The Bellman of Paris, The Devil of Dowgate, Richard III, The Duke of Guise, St George for England, The Plantation of Virginia* all 1623, *Henry I, Henry II, The Bristow Merchant, The London Merchant, The Fair Star of Antwerp* all 1624, *St. Alban's* 1625. In many cases, *Annals* has further information on writer and/or company. I exclude from this count Webster's *Guise*. If this was a tragedy based on recent French history, as it has frequently been surmised to be, it could be added to the total: but Archer in his play-list of 1656 listed it as a comedy (as in [dis]guise?). This is entirely possible, since Webster's output contains more plays that are comedies or tragicomedies than the outright tragedies with which we most frequently associate him.

19. Beginning in 1632 (admittedly after the date of Roe's letter) Sir Humphrey Mildmay reports no visits to any amphitheater but the Globe in his record of fifty-seven visits to playhouses. That, coupled with Gurr's assertion—in *Playgoing in Shakespeare's London,* third edition (Cambridge: Cambridge University Press, 2004), 90—that the "evidence consistently says that by 1630, though not much before, the amphitheaters in the northern suburbs...served a distinctly less gentlemanly clientele than the hall playhouses in the city...and in summer the Globe on the Bankside," justifies one in concentrating the search for candidates for a Quixote play on venues or companies likely to have been at the forefront of the attention of someone of Roe's class.

20. The significance of asterisked items in this paragraph is explained later in the text.

21. Bentley, *The Jacobean and Caroline Stage., loc. cit.*

22. Ibid., I 65–6.

23. Strachen, *Sir Thomas Roe 1581–1644* (Wilton: Michael Russell, 1989), 208.

24. The full text is included in McMullan, 17–18. I am obliged to Gary Taylor for pointing out to me the Huntingdon connection of both men.

25. McMullan, 25–6, describes and quotes from the letter, which is described in Strachan, *Sir Thomas Roe,* 313.

26. Details of Roe's and Elizabeth's whereabouts and movements are taken from the respective *ODNB* entries, by Michael Strachan (Roe) and Ronald G. Asch (Elizabeth), with additional information from Strachan, *Sir Thomas Roe.*

27. His presence on the trip precludes him from having been at the performance before the Savoy ambassadors on June 8, as the party did not reach Heidelberg until June 7.

28. Strachan, *Sir Thomas Roe,* 187, 197.

29. Elizabeth in England till her marriage, then the Palatinate, Bohemia, and Netherlands exile: Roe on a voyage to Guiana (in the planning of which Prince Henry was closely involved), and extended diplomatic missions in India and Constantinople, followed by treaty negotiations in Northern Europe.

30. Andrew Gurr suggests in *The Shakespearian Playing Companies* (Oxford: Clarendon Press 1996) that "[i]n 1632 Herbert licensed only two new plays for them [the King's Men]. Throughout the 1630s that number rarely rose to more than four" (378).

31. Taylor, "History," 34–5.

32. As Theobald indicates in his "Preface of the Editor" they were: see *DF* 167–8, ll. 10–16.

33. Harold Love considers the practice of scribal publication generally in "Thomas Middleton: Oral Culture and the Manuscript Economy" in Gary Taylor and John Lavagnino (eds.), *Thomas Middleton and Early Modern Textual Culture: A Companion to the Collected Works* (Oxford University Press, 2007), 98–109, and records the production of six manuscripts of *A Game at Chess* between the play's suppression and its first print publication. *The Wild Goose Chase* was not published in this way, but its twenty-year persistence in the repertory combined with Moseley's story of a "Person of Quality" borrowing it from the actors and not returning it indicates an active demand for manuscripts of unprinted popular plays. *Fletcher*, VI. 227, conveniently gathers together the details of its pre-publication history.

34. For Theobald's account of the manuscripts he possessed, see *DF* 167–9, ll. 8–26. For those still sceptical that it is likely he might possess multiple copies, it may be salutary to mention an item in the Abraham Hill list of manuscript plays (B.M. Add. MS. 2893), discussed by Bentley, *The Jacobean and Caroline* Stage, IV. 864–6. At some point between 1677 and 1703, Hill possessed *two* copies of *The Cloudy Queen and Singing Moor,* a script of which no other record survives. In the light of this, it is entirely reasonable to suppose Theobald could have had several copies of a manuscript of a play with the comparatively high profile a *Quijote* adaptation would have.

5

Blessed with a Baby or "Bum-Fidled with a Bastard"? Maternity in Fletcher's The Chances and Cervantes' Novela de la señora Cornelia

Joyce Boro

Fletcher's sustained attraction to Spanish literature is incontestable. Seventeen of his approximately fifty-four plays derive from Spanish sources, thirteen of those from Cervantes' oeuvre, making Fletcher the most prolific English ambassador for Iberian literature.[1] While Fletcher's Hispanophilia is readily apparent, his Hispanophobia is less visible. Indeed, despite Fletcher's "twenty-year obsession with Cervantes' writings," he "was also determinedly Protestant and anti-Spanish."[2] This duality of fascination and aversion is typical of the early modern English response to Spanish literature. "English interest in Spain," Alexander Samson concludes, "was not mutually incompatible with political prejudice."[3] As a Catholic superpower, Spain was viewed with great suspicion in post-Reformation England. However, notwithstanding heightened Anglo-Spanish tension and the abundance of documented hostility toward Spain, translators, adapters, and readers continued to enjoy Spanish literature and steadily increasing numbers sought to learn the language.[4] Often, as in Fletcher's *The Chances*, Spanish characters are subjected to English nationalistic bigotry: they are ridiculed, morally debased, or depicted as Catholic or Moorish Others. For instance, in her analysis of *Rule a Wife and Have a Wife*, Barbara Fuchs reveals Fletcher's "strident nationalism" and discusses "how the playwright weaves a jingoistic thread into his *translatio*" (152, 155). Similarly, Trudi L. Darby and Samson uncover traces of "Fletcher's political hostility to Spain" throughout his works.[5]

It should not, therefore, come as a surprise to discover that while *The Chances* closely adheres to the plot of *La señora Cornelia*, the play also reflects

Fletcher's religious and nationalist biases. Fletcher's adaptation reflects contemporaneous anxieties regarding the fraught category of motherhood from
a uniquely English, Protestant perspective. Recalling the Violenta/Fernando
storyline from *The History of Cardenio*, both *The Chances* and *La señora
Cornelia* center on a woman secretly engaged to a man whose child she
has borne out of wedlock, yet the mothers are treated dichotomously.[6] The
novela invokes the traditions of idealized maternity and the nursing Virgin
Mary to underscore Cornelia's and her baby's virtues and innocence. In contrast, Fletcher's Constantia is distanced from the Catholic icon and linked
to more animalistic conceptions of motherhood and her infant is presented
as an unwanted burden. In both texts, the reception of Cornelia/Constantia
and her baby is mediated through Cervantes's Juan and Antonio (Fletcher's
"John" and "Fredrick"), who occupy author-character functions.[7] Because
these pairs of characters inhabit opposing positions on the moral spectrum,
they hold divergent views of women and maternity, which are reflected in
their respective texts. Whereas Cervantes' pair are ideal Spanish gentlemen scholars with a healthy respect for women, their English counterparts
reflect Hispanophobic bigotry as they are transformed into lascivious, greedy
students, more interested in drinking and whoring than in their books.[8]
According to the landlady, their nationality explains their behavior: "They
are Spaniards, Lady, Gennets of high mettle,/ Things that will thrash the
devill, or his dam,/ Let 'em appear but cloven."[9] As the only Spaniards
in either text—both play and *novela* are set in Bologna—Juan and Antonio
(Fletcher's John and Fredrick) are represented as emblematic of their country. In order to explore how Fletcher transforms and Anglicizes maternity,
I will investigate early modern conceptions of the peripartum, which includes
pregnancy, childbirth, and lactation. This historical contextualization will
illuminate what is at stake in the alternative presentations of the mothers and
babies, and it will equally shed light on Fletcher's working methodology.
A clearer grasp of how Fletcher adapts his sources will lead to a fuller appreciation of his dramaturgy and to a more nuanced assessment of the reception
of Spanish literature in early modern England, which, ultimately, will help
to unravel the *Cardenio* problem. Of particular relevance to an understanding (and reconstruction) of *Cardenio* is Fletcher's attitude toward Spain, his
treatment of sexuality, his use of obscene language, and, more generally,
his tendency toward cultural Anglicization and the foregrounding of female
characters and concerns, all of which are elucidated through this analysis of
The Chances.

The Chances's lively, incredible plot is drawn from *La señora Cornelia*, one
of twelve *Novelas Ejemplares* written by Cervantes between 1590 and 1612
and published in 1613. *The Chances* was based on either the Spanish original or its French translation (1614–1615).[10] Indeed, there are so few verbal
parallels between *The Chances* and the *novela*, and the French and Spanish
editions are so close, that it is impossible to determine which Fletcher used.
Originally printed in the 1647 Beaumont and Fletcher folio, *The Chances*
was first staged in 1625 (and again in 1630 and 1635).[11] It continued to be

popular through the interregnum and into the Restoration. It inspired the mid-century droll entitled *The Landlady*, collected by Francis Kirkman in *The Wits* (1672). With the reopening of the theaters Fletcher's play returned to the stage; Samuel Pepys attended three performances of *The Chances* (in 1660, 1661, and 1667). The play was also adapted thrice: George Villiers, second Duke of Buckingham's version was staged in 1682; the second adaptation was presented by David Garrick in 1773; and *Don Juan, or The Two Violettas*, a musical by Frederic Reynolds, was performed in 1821.

An investigation of the later adaptations of *The Chances* renders Fletcher's anti-Spanish bigotry more conspicuous, and it simultaneously evokes questions regarding the presentation of Hispanism in *Double Falsehood and Cardenio*. Hispanophobia is absent from Villiers', Garrick's and Reynolds' texts, just as it is missing from Theobald's. While John and Fredrick are still the only Spaniards in the post-Restoration versions of *The Chances*, their Spanishness is presented as neither a character flaw nor as a redeeming attribute. The plot requires that John and Fredrick be foreign so that they are unknown to the other protagonists and uninvolved in the play's backstory: their precise nationality is irrelevant. Fletcher's negative association of the Spaniards with lechery, as evinced in the landlady's comment quoted above, is omitted from the adaptations. Indeed, John and Fredrick are no longer depicted as lewd Spaniards, but they are invested with respectability. Fredrick becomes "Mr. Modesty," and John's reformation is dramatized over the course of the play, as he refutes his "former vanities" and resolves to "Change the wild wanton, for the sober plan,/ And like my friend— become a *Modest* man."[12] In Fletcher's drama, John relinquishes his illicit desire for Constantia only to replace it with lust for a prostitute (the second Constantia); in the adaptations, however, he progresses from carnal longing for Constantia to sincere love for the second Constantia, who is refashioned as a thoroughly respectable woman. With his penchant for whoring and his attempt to use his financial and social status to coerce the second Constantia, Antonio (a member of Constantia's brother's entourage) replaces John and Fredrick as the plays' debauched lech. Since Antonio's role and agency are limited, his immorality does not infiltrate the fabric of the play in the manner of John and Frederick's licentiousness in *The Chances*. Thus, in the adaptations, the Spaniards' rehabilitation concomitantly ameliorates the presentation of Spain itself, and it also adjusts the moral tone of the play. As a result of John and Fredrick's transformation, the adaptations are sanitized; many instances of lewdness, obscene puns and jokes, and frank discussions of sex are eliminated from their source. This is typical of eighteenth-century revisions of early modern plays, and accordingly, Taylor's *The History of Cardenio* is teeming with sexual jokes and innuendo that are absent from *Double Falsehood*, and which are very reminiscent of Fletcher. Likewise, the revised depiction of Hispanism in the adaptations of *The Chances* is suggestive in the context of *Cardenio* and *Double Falsehood*. Set in Spain and peopled exclusively by Spanish characters, Theobald's *Double Falsehood*, like the adaptations of *The Chances,* is void of anti-Spanish prejudice. It is impossible to draw any conclusions regarding *Cardenio*'s vision of Spain from this analogy, but the adaptations of *The Chances* indicate that although Hispanophobia is absent from *Double Falsehood,* it may have played a role in *Cardenio.* A thorough exploration of how Fletcher's Hispanophobia fares in the other eighteenth-century adaptations of his plays would certainly help to resolve this question.

*   *   *

The maternal body simultaneously encodes selfless nurturing and the more instinctual side of corporeal existence. Paradoxically, motherhood is a blessed state epitomized by the Virgin Mary, but the animalistic act of birth itself enacts Eve's punishment.[13] Although married mothers were obviously not virgins, received Biblical wisdom stressed their chastity.[14] The fertility of wives, the fulfillment of their conjugal duty, and their ability to create and nurture families were emphasized by early modern writers.[15] In contrast, the sinfulness of sex was at the vanguard of discussions of unwed mothers, who were labeled whores and "bastard bearers," and were subject to harsh penalties.[16] But for all mothers, the sinful, animalistic facet of birth lingered. "The language of childbirth was peppered with the imagery of the stalls; pregnant women were often likened to farrowing sows" and said to be "got upon the nest" or "breeding"; "the period of lying in after childbirth was referred to as being 'in the straw.'"[17] Lactation similarly associated mothers with animals. "Like the mess and pain of birth itself, the involuntary nature of lactation affirmed woman's ambiguous affinity with the natural world."[18] Moreover, lactation was generally perceived as an activity performed by animals; suckling a puppy was a treatment for engorgement; human and goat milk were used for medicinal purposes; and stories of witches nursing familiars abounded.[19] "[N]ursing could either be constructed as occupying a dangerous and uncivilised place where maternity was threatening and monstrous, or understood as evidence of God's benevolence through the operation of natural instinct."[20]

The sexuality and bestiality of motherhood coupled with female authority over the peripartum instilled anxiety at the heart of maternity.[21] From the later seventeenth century onward, the licensing of midwifes fell within the jurisdiction of male ecclesiastics and there was an increase in the availability and popularity of male practitioners, but in Cervantes' and Fletcher's societies, women still dominated the perinatal.[22] Male practitioners (i.e. surgeons) would only be summoned to a birth in the eventually of a serious, usually mortal, complication. Typically, women attended the mother during labor, delivery, and most of the lying-in interval.[23] This extensive female role often resulted in a tense power dynamic between the sexes. The mother's involvement in childrearing imbued her with authority over her offspring, which began during pregnancy[24]: "the pregnant mother, then the nursing mother, rose above the passive role imposed on her at the time of conception: she nourished the child she carried with her blood and, after his birth, with her milk, which was presented as directly derived from menstrual blood [...] The nursing mother thus continued to shape the child in her own image."[25] Lactation was a conduit of physical and spiritual nourishment. Therefore, by breastfeeding, women performed the religious education of their children, transmitting piety to them through their milk. Texts by Elizabeth Hoby, Dorothy Leigh, and Elizabeth Clinton, for example, show how maternity can inspire women to subvert gender stereotypes in ways such as writing, asserting control over their children, and breastfeeding despite their husbands' prohibitions.[26] Countering female authority, husbands took charge of infant nutrition, determining feeding schedules, and hiring and supervising wet nurses.[27] Despite the known medical and spiritual benefits of mother's milk, husbands often prevented their wives from breastfeeding for economic, social, and genealogical reasons.[28] Since most husbands desired their wives to return to their pre-partum state quickly, a yearning to breastfeed may put mother and baby in conflict with the "greater" needs of the family, thereby highlighting the incompatibility of the roles of good mother and wife.

Lactation also represents a site of spiritual tension. Breastfeeding evokes Eve's original sin since, like childbirth, it recalls the bestial aspects of the female body.[29] Nevertheless, veneration for the Virgin Mary rehabilitated breastfeeding among Catholics.[30] The *madonna lactans* is "*nutricula nostra*, nurse of the faithful" and a powerful symbol of humility.[31] Furthermore, the nursing relationship of Mary and baby Jesus is an allegory of communion. As Jesus suckles his mother's whitened blood, the Eucharist is recalled, emphasizing the Catholic obligation to be nurtured by Christ's body and blood.[32] However, Protestants, who denied Mary's sanctity and rejected the doctrine of transubstantiation, highlighted the nutritional and spiritual benefits of breastfeeding, underscoring the transmission of moral qualities through mother's milk. But while Catholics retained a more positive perception of breastfeeding and viewed it as a spiritually valuable activity, the rates of maternal breastfeeding were higher amongst reformed populations, largely because of the greater imperative amongst Catholics to resume sexual activity for the means of procreation. As such, Catholics were more likely to employ wet nurses.[33]

* * *

In both *La señora Cornelia* and *The Chances*, the Spaniards (Cervantes' Juan and Antonio and Fletcher's John and Fredrick) perform the role of midwife, caring for the postpartum mother and child, but they do so very differently. Discussing the *novela*, Thomas Pabón writes: "Receiving Cornelia's child, Don Juan is symbolically cast as midwife standing beside her door to receive the new child."[34] His role extends to verbal midwifery, as he narrates the newborn into existence by telling his landlady and Antonio about his neonatal discovery. Behaving like a traditional midwife, Juan carries the baby to safety. He marvels at the baby's beauty prior to ensuring that the infant has a proper midwife, wet nurse, and adoptive parents. In middle- or upper-class families, authority over the newborn was transferred from midwife to wet nurse and back to the parents, under the supervision of the father who had ultimate control over the infant. Recognizing that he has interfered with natural postpartum progression, Juan excises himself from the birth story. He provides his landlady with ample funds before ordering her to conceal his actions and to deliver the baby to a midwife, who, he affirms, will know how to find a wet nurse and new parents. Juan's concern with secrecy suggests feelings of shame regarding his involvement. Not only does he realize that he has erred, but there may also be a deeper recognition of transgression into the largely female sphere of childbirth.

Cervantes' Antonio fulfils a similar role as he discovers Cornelia wandering the streets in search of her fiancé. He acts as midwife by safely enclosing the new mother in his chambers and caring for her during her lying-in. Paralleling Juan's relationship to the baby, by recounting his meeting with Cornelia, Antonio is implicated in her metaphorical birth. In an influential essay, Peter Dunn reveals how the *novela* is structured according to dichotomies such as darkness and light, separation and union, interior and exterior.[35] These polarities recall the language of childbirth, which is figured as a movement from the dark, interior, hidden isolation of the womb to the presence of light and familial and social interaction. Understood in these terms, Antonio becomes Cornelia's symbolic midwife, delivering her from one metaphorical extremity to the other. He transforms Cornelia from dark unknown to bright known: from "a black outline of a person" to a "woman in a long habit" to "the greatest beauty that human eyes had ever seen" to a face as bright as the moon or sun.[36]

Shortly after Cornelia and her baby are safely ensconced in the Spaniards' rooms, mother and child are unwittingly reunited in an emotional, pivotal scene, which Fletcher significantly omits. Moved to tears at the sight of the seemingly unknown infant, Cornelia is overcome by a natural inclination to breastfeed the baby. The men watch in silence, and a poignant tableau, reminiscent of the *madonna lactans*, is created.

> She took him in her arms and looked at him attentively, his face as well as the poor but clean cloths in which he was swaddled. And then, unable to restrain her tears, she placed the veil from her head over her breasts to nurse the baby modestly. And bringing him to her breasts, she placed her face next to the child's. And with the milk she sustained him, and with the tears she bathed his face. And in this way she remained, without raising her face for the time that the baby did not want to leave the breast. During this time all four remained in silence. The baby nursed. But it was not thus, because new mothers cannot breastfeed, and so realizing this she returned the baby to Don Juan.[37]

As in paintings of the nursing virgin, the mother's downward gaze reinforces the intimate connection of mother and child. The assembled watch in silence, affirming the pictorial qualities of the scene. Sexual voyeurism is absent, as Cornelia's *"honestidad"* is stressed.

After performing this semblance of feeding the baby, Cornelia's ethereal qualities continue to be accentuated, further linking her to the Virgin Mary:

> She lowered to her shoulders a veil that she wore on her head, leaving her face free and uncovered, showing it to be like the moon, or to be more accurate, the very sun when it shows itself as the most beautiful and bright. She cried liquid pearls from her eyes, and she wiped them with the whitest linen and with hands such that between them and the linen one must have been of great discernment to differentiate between the whiteness.[38]

The white luminance of her skin recalls paintings of the Virgin and saints and symbolizes moral cleanliness. Her tears further link her to Mary since pearls are a Christian symbol of purity and the Incarnation. In this state of glowing, white, pearly purity, Cornelia recounts her story of premarital sex and the birth of her illegitimate son. Despite her sexual narrative, the Spaniards' reception of her story is discussed in terms of service, compassion, pity, and obligation, reminiscent of the adoration of the Virgin. The religiosity is reinforced by Cornelia's nun-like costume: she wears an "*hábito*," a nun's habit, and a "*toca*," a veil or a wimple.

Yet the more sinful aspects of motherhood are also included in Cornelia's portrayal. At the conclusion of the "breastfeeding" scene, quoted above, after what appears to be a description of Cornelia nursing the baby, we discover that she did not actually feed him. The narrator explains: "But it was not thus, because new mothers cannot breastfeed, and so realizing this she returned the baby to Don Juan." With this problematic sentence, our expectations are undercut through one of many "tantalizing false lead[s]" that structure the *novela*.[39] By stating that new mothers cannot breastfeed, the *novela* reminds us that Cornelia is producing colostrum because her milk has not yet come in. Colostrum *is* the ideal sustenance for a newborn, but in the period it was deemed harmful to babies. It was thought to block the intestines, and new mothers were believed to be dirty while they were still experiencing postpartum bleeding (lochia), which could occur for several weeks after delivery: to breastfeed while sullied by impure blood would morally damage the infant. Cornelia may resemble the Virgin, but she is, after all, a postlapsarian woman tainted with Eve's sin. Additionally, by claiming that Cornelia is unable or unfit to feed the baby, her maternal authority is undermined and she is prevented from inhabiting the important role of physical and spiritual attendant to her baby.

The scene in which Cornelia appears to breastfeed her infant is of crucial importance because it epitomizes Cornelia's characterization in the *novela* and it foregrounds her motherhood. According to the typology of the Virgin Mary, Cornelia's maternal role signifies her moral purity even though memories of Eve's transgression linger. Cornelia openly discloses her motherhood and her relationship with the duke; she is reunited with her son before he is delivered to a wet nurse; and, at the story's conclusion, we learn that she later has two daughters. In *The Chances*, however, Constantia never discusses her birth story and only briefly interacts with her son in the final scene as she delivers the boy to his father. Constantia's maternal role is downplayed in favor of her sexualized presentation. Seen through the Spaniards' eyes, her motherhood contaminates her moral character, marking her as unchaste and unredeemed. Ultimately, Constantia's transformation stems from Fletcher's governing cultural imperatives: his Hispanophobia compels him to debase the Spanish and to efface Catholic ideology from his text, which profoundly affects Constantia's characterization.

In *The Chances,* the Spaniards' corruption is intrinsically linked to the representation of Constantia and her baby. When John is handed Constantia's swaddled baby, he initially thinks he has acquired a fortune. Discovering an infant in the bundle, he is horrified, but he rejoices over the wealth represented by the child's rich clothing and jewels, believing them to be the harbingers of additional financial gain. Rather than compliment the infant's beauty, John stresses the newborn's illegitimacy and the burden that the baby represents. John declares himself to have been "bum-fidled with a Bastard" (1.5.16) and tricked into accepting this "lumpe of lewdnesse" (2.1.69). He laments having "to raise a dayrie/ For other mens adulteries" (1.6.28–9). He associates breastfeeding with animals, discussing the nurturing of the baby according to the agricultural terminology of raising milk cows. Like Juan, John performs the role of midwife, conveying the baby from birth-chamber to wet nurse, but his corrupt, uncaring attitude obscures his nurturing role. Throughout the scene he flaunts his copious sexual experience, boasting of "the dire massacre of a million/ Of Maiden-heads" (1.5.18–19). His monologue (1.5.1–48) highlights his lasciviousness as well as his sexualized masculinity, thereby distancing him from the female sphere of childbirth.

Fredrick and Constantia's encounter retains none of the imagery of light and dark, enclosure and revelation from *La señora Cornelia*, yet Fredrick still acts the midwife, delivering Constantia to safety and presiding over her lying-in, albeit with a threatening, Hispanophobic undertone. The emphasis throughout is on the dangers plaguing Constantia, who thinks the disrespectable Spaniards are honest. When Constantia reveals her face, Frederick "grow[s] wilde" and must force himself to "be temperate" and "look off" (1.10.28, 30, 31). Constantia's sexual vulnerability is compounded when John also begins to lust after her. Constantia's naïveté is stressed as their dishonesty is made increasingly apparent: John blatantly declares: "I am not honest, nor desire to be [...] 'tis impossible I should be honest" (2.3.51, 58).

Once Fredrick and John discover that Constantia is a mother, "that there has been stirring/ Fumbling with Linnen," their perception of her shifts (2.4.68–9). "[H]er fame [as] pure as fire" dissipates (2.4.70). They declare: "That pure fire/ has melted out her maiden-head: she is crackt" and "whord" (2.4.70–1, 3.4.41), and "loose ith'hilts" (2.3.75). She is a "Hens *[sic]*," a "Pullet," (2.4.65), a "mare" (3.4.71), "a fowle at souse" (4.1.14). And her child is nothing to them but a "Bastard" (1.5.16). Even though the Spaniards know that Constantia had sex "upon vow of marriage," the activity trans-forms the mother into an impure, animalistic bastard-bearer (2.4.76). She is not redeemed until the play's conclusion, when she is reunited briefly with her fiancé and baby. Throughout *The Chances*, Constantia's motherhood remains in the background.

This duality of purity and corruption visible in the representations of both Fletcher's Constantia and Cervantes' Cornelia lies at the disjunction of different understandings of motherhood. In *The Chances*, separation of mother and baby is prolonged, which facilitates Constantia's disempowerment and her sexual objectification by the Spaniards. The nurturing, chaste aspects of the maternal role are deemphasized in order to highlight Constantia's sexuality. Her characterization bears witness to the anxiety associated with motherhood, which stems from two main sources: first, the paradoxical understandings of childbirth and lactation as simultaneously chaste and redemptive, bestial and sinful; and second, the fraught relationship between the sexes due to female authority over the peripartum. These same anxieties emerge in the *novela*, specifically in the retraction at the conclusion of the "breastfeeding" scene. The abnegation recalls the impurities of maternity and prevents Cornelia from inhabiting an authoritative nurturing role. Even though Cornelia is modeled on the Virgin Mary, she is not exempt from the taint of corrupted maternity.

In reworking his source, Fletcher amplifies the tensions inherent in maternity, thereby increasing his engagement with the troubling category of motherhood. This magnification of gender issues is typical of Fletcher's "feminocentric approach."[40] Equally representative of Fletcher's methodology is the cultural Anglicization of his Spanish source, which, in this play, is intrinsically related to his religious and nationalistic prejudice. Indeed, Fletcher's interest in women and his Hispanophobia dovetail in the character of Constantia. She permits him to investigate maternity while expounding a Protestant, Anglo-centric worldview. Fletcher's depictions of maternity and of the Spaniards are consonant with post-Reformation, anti-Catholic English discourse. Cervantes' exemplary characters, Juan and Antonio, are unrecognizable because they are morally corrupted through the lens of anti-Spanish sentiment. With the transformation of their ethical core, their attitude toward Constantia shifts and the audience's perception of Cornelia/Constantia is likewise altered since her character is mediated through the Spaniards' perspective. Constantia behaves morally throughout the play and her name is a potent reminder of her constancy, but the Spaniards' language and attitude obscures her virtue and reconfigures her as a morally corrupt example of motherhood, and of female sexuality more generally. By debasing the Spaniards, Fletcher not only ridicules their nation by associating Spanishness with libertine behavior, but their altered characterization enables him to meditate upon the more animalistic, troubling aspects of motherhood, and permits him to convert his heroine, distancing her from the problematic (from his Anglo-Protestant viewpoint) Marian adoration inherent in Cervantes' Catholic vision of motherhood. Fletcher's Hispanophobia lurks

behind his transformation of Cervantes' text. It is unfortunate that his prejudices lead him to negate Cervantes' reverential vision of maternity in favor
of a bawdy, highly sexualized depiction of motherhood, and it is both tragic
and ironic that the Spanish are held accountable for this shift, when it is their
culture and religion that enable a celebration of maternity.[41]

NOTES

1. For a list of these plays and statistics see McMullan, 259; Trudi L. Darby
   and Alexander Samson, "Cervantes on the Jacobean Stage," in Ardila, 211.
   Important studies of the relationship between Fletcher and Cervantes include:
   Taylor, "History" and Valerie Wayne, "Don Quixote and Shakespeare's
   Collaborative Turn to Romance," in *Quest,* 217–38; Trudi Darby, "Cervantes
   in England: The Influence of Golden-Age Prose Fiction on Jacobean Drama,
   c. 1615–1625," *Bulletin of Hispanic Studies* 74 (1997): 425–41; Diana de Armas
   Wilson, "Of Piracy and Plackets: Cervantes' *La señora Cornelia* and Fletcher's
   The Chances," in *Cervantes for the 21st Century,* ed. Francisco La Rubia Prado
   (Newark: Juan de la Cuesta, 2000), 49–60; Alexander Samson, "Last Thought
   upon a windmill"?: Cervantes and Fletcher', in Ardila, 223–33; Darby and
   Samson, "Cervantes"; Edward M. Wilson, "*Rule a Wife and Have a Wife* and
   El sagaz Estacio," *Review of English Studies* 24 (1948): 189–94.
2. Wilson, "Of Piracy," 51–3; Taylor, "History," 18.
3. Samson, "A Fine Romance: Anglo-Spanish Relations in the Sixteenth Century,"
   Journal of Medieval and Early Modern Studies 39 (2009): 66.
4. On the fraught Anglo-Spanish relationship see, for example, Sampson, "Fine";
   Barbara Fuchs, *Exotic Nation: Maurophilia and the Construction of Early
   Modern Spain* (Philadelphia: University of Pennsylvania Press, 2009). On
   learning Spanish see, Joyce Boro, "Multilingualism, Romance, and Language
   Pedagogy: Or, Why Were So Many Sentimental Romances Printed as Polyglot
   Texts?" in *Tudor Translation,* ed. Fred Schurink (Palgrave Macmillan, 2012),
   18–38.
5. Darby and Samson, "Cervantes," 211 ff.
6. Feliciana de la Voz in *Persiles y Sigismunda*, Dorotea in *Don Quijote*, and
   Teodosia in *La dos doncellas* suffer similar plights.
7. On their role as author-characters see Ruth El Saffar, *Novel to Romance: A Study
   of Cervantes's "Novelas ejemplares"* (Baltimore: The Johns Hopkins University
   Press, 1974), 121–2. Cyrus Hoy discusses this character type in "Fletcherian
   Romantic Comedy," *Research Opportunities in Renaissance Drama* 27 (1984):
   3. Roderick in *The History of Cardenio* and DF are typical Fletcherean male
   characters, who manage the play's action and for whom there is no parallel
   in *Don Quijote*. Unsurprisingly, Fletcher apparently wrote all but the first of
   Roderick's scenes.
8. On their differences, see Wilson "Of Piracy," 54–5. She offers an interesting
   reading of the *novela*, but unfortunately her essay devotes little space to *The
   Chances*, which she dismisses as "a 'hasty pudding' of a play . . . with little chance
   of being read save as a pirated version of *La señora Cornelia*" (58).
9. John Fletcher, *The Chances,* ed. George Walton Williams, in *Fletcher,*
   3.3.24–6.
10. On Fletcher's knowledge of Spanish see Wilson, "*Rule,*" 189–94.

11. Hoy believes it to be Fletcher's final play: see "Fletcherean," 11; *Fletcher* IV: 544.
12. David Garrick, *The Chances. A Comedy. With Alterations* (London: Printed for the Proprietors, 1773; Cambridge, Chadwyck-Healey, 1994), 3.4.74 and 5.3.263, 265–6, accessed June 13, 2012, Literature online, http://gateway .proquest.com.
13. Felicity Dunworth, *Mothers and Meaning on the Early Modern English Stage* (Manchester: Manchester University Press, 2010), 10; Margaret L. King, *Women of the Renaissance* (Chicago: University of Chicago Press, 1991), 1–2.
14. On the redemptive power of motherhood and a wife's obligation to bear children, see: 1 Timothy 2:14–15; Psalms 127:3; Proverbs 31:28; Exodus 20:12; Leviticus 19:3; Deuteronomy 5:16.
15. Sara Mendelson and Patricia Crawford, *Women in Early Modern England, 1550–1720* (Oxford: Oxford University Press, 1998), 148–9.
16. Mendelson and Crawford, *Women*, 150; Dunworth, *Mothers*, 202; David Cressy, "Purification, Thanksgiving and the Churching of Women in Post-Reformation England," *Past and Present* 141 (1993): 131; Merry E. Wiesner-Hanks, *Women and Gender in Early Modern Europe*, third edition (Cambridge: Cambridge University Press, 2008), 64–70.
17. Keith Thomas, *Man and the Natural World: A History of the Modern Sensibility* (New York: Pantheon Books, 1983), 43, 99; Dunworth, *Mothers*, 116.
18. Dunworth, *Mothers*, 115.
19. Chris Laoutaris, *Shakespearean Maternities: Crises of Conception in Early Modern England* (Edinburgh: Edinburgh University Press, 2008), 166–7.
20. Dunworth, *Mothers*, 86.
21. Naomi J. Miller, "Mothering Others: Caregiving as Spectrum and Spectacle in the Early Modern Period," in *Maternal Measures: Figuring Caregiving in the Early Modern Period*, ed. Miller and Naomi Yavneh (Aldershot: Ashgate, 2000), 5.
22. Mendelson and Crawford, *Women*, 153, 315–18.
23. Adrian Wilson, "Participant or Patient? Seventeenth-Century Childbirth from the Mother's Point of View," in *Patients and Practitioners: Lay Perceptions of Medicine in Pre-Industrial Society*, ed. Roy Porter (Cambridge: Cambridge University Press, 1985), 138; Teresa Ortiz "From Hegemony to Subordination: Midwives in Early Modern Spain," in *Art of Midwifery, The: Early Modern Midwives in Europe*, ed. Hilary Marland (London: Taylor and Francis, 1994), 95–114; Perry, *Gender*, 64–5.
24. Mendelson and Crawford, *Women*, 162; Dunworth, *Mothers*, 112; King, *Women*, 19–22.
25. Christiane Klapisch-Zuber, "Blood Parents and Milk Parents: Wet Nursing in Florence, 1300–1530," in *Women, Family, and Ritual in Renaissance Italy*, trans. Lydia G. Cochrane (Chicago: University of Chicago Press, 1985), 161. On the use of menstrual blood to nourish the fetus and its transformation into milk postpartum, see James Hart, *Klinike* (London: 1633), 330; Jacob Rueff, *The Expert Midwife* (London, 1637), 53.
26. Laoutaris, *Shakespearean*, 227–35. For comparable Spanish examples see Lisa Vollendorf, *The Lives of Women: A New History of Inquisitional Spain* (Nashville: Vanderbilt University Press, 2005), 41–3, 132–4. On the link of maternity and authorship see King, *Women*, 22–3.
27. Klapisch-Zuber, "Blood," 155–9.

28. See Dunworth, *Mothers,* 116; Klapisch-Zuber, "Blood," 160; Ambroise Paré, *The Workes of that Famous Chirurgion Ambrose Parey* (London: Cotes and Young, 1634), 909; cf. Walter Harris, *An Exact Enquiry into, and Cure of the Acute Diseases of Infants* (London: Clement, 1693), 17. Cf. Wiesner-Hanks, *Women,* 91–2. On aversions to breastfeeding across Europe see King, *Women,* 12–15.

29. Dunworth, *Mothers,* 28ff. On the Virgin and maternity in Spain see Mary Elizabeth Perry, *Gender and Disorder in Early Modern Seville* (Princeton: Princeton University Press, 1990), 37–43.

30. Valerie Fildes, *Breasts, Bottles and Babies: The History of Infant Feeding* (Edinburgh: Edinburgh University Press, 1986), 105.

31. Naomi Yavneh, "To Bare or Not too Bare: Sofonisba Anguissola's Nursing Madonna and the Womanly Art of Breastfeeding," in Miller and Yavneh, *Maternal Measures,* 70, 69.

32. Yavneh, "To Bare," 70.

33. Fildes, *Breasts,* 105; Robert Cleaver and John Dod, *A Godly Form of Householde Government* (London, 1598); William Gouge, *Of Domesticall Duties* (London, 1622). Cf. Rachel Trubowitz, "'But Blood Whitened': Nursing Mothers and Others in Early Modern Britain" and Emilie L. Bergmann, "Nurture and Instruction: Language and 'Mother's Milk': Maternal Roles and the Nurturing Body in Early Modern Spanish Texts," in Miller and Yavneh, *Maternal Measures,* 107.

34. Thomas Pabón, "Secular Resurrection through Marriage in Cervantes 'La Señora Cornelia,' 'Las dos doncellas,' and 'La fuerza de la sangre,'" *Anales cervantinos* 16 (1977): 111.

35. Peter N. Dunn, "Las Novelas ejemplares," in *Suma cervantina,* ed. J. B. Avalle-Arce and E. C. Riley (London: Tamesis, 1973), 81–118.

36. Miguel de Cervantes, "La Novela de la señora Cornelia," in *Novelas ejemplares,* ed. Harry Sieber, vol. 2 (Madrid: Cátedra, 1994), 247, 251. All translations are mine.

37. Cervantes, "Novela," 251.

38. Cervantes, "Novela," 251.

39. Melveena McKendrick, "The Curious and Neglected Tale of *La señora Cornelia,*" *Bulletin of Hispanic Studies* 82 (2005): 707.

40. McMullan, 35.

41. I am very grateful to Valerie Wayne, Alexander Samson, Gary Taylor, and Terri Bourus for their insightful comments on this essay.

6

GIRLS ON THE RUN: *LOVE'S PILGRIMAGE,* *THE COXCOMB,* AND *DOUBLE FALSEHOOD*

Christopher Hicklin

This essay examines two overlooked Fletcherian plays that have many elements in common with *Double Falsehood*, but lack the Shakespearian connection that has brought it so much attention. *Love's Pilgrimage* and *The Coxcomb* share a similar textual history with *Double Falsehood*. All three plays were based on stories by Cervantes, cowritten by John Fletcher between 1609 and 1616, not published during the lifetimes of the playwrights, and printed only in a revised state.[1] However, the ur-text behind *Double Falsehood* is widely supposed to have been a collaboration with William Shakespeare, while *The Coxcomb* and *Love's Pilgrimage* are attributed to Fletcher's partnership with Francis Beaumont.[2] As a result there is a mass-market edition of *Double Falsehood*, along with a number of adaptations and productions, but even Beaumont and Fletcher specialists say little about *The Coxcomb* and less about *Love's Pilgrimage*.

A theme shared by these three plays is the repercussions of broken marriage promises, which degrade not only the lovers involved but also the binding social conventions of friendship and hospitality. In each play one or two women are deceived by a prospective husband, pursued by an unwanted suitor, and at some point run away (often disguised as a boy). In *Double Falsehood*, Henriquez promises to marry Violante, but rapes her when she refuses to have premarital sex.[3] He then leaves her to pursue a marriage with Leonora, who then runs away to avoid him. Violante runs away disguised to work as a shepherd, and is nearly raped again. In *The Coxcomb,* Viola is almost gang-raped by her drunk fiancé Richardo and his friends, and runs away, though not disguised as a boy. She is robbed and bound before she is rescued by Valerio, but he only wants to help her if she agrees to be his concubine. Valerio, in a reversal of expectations, respects Viola's consent and accepts her refusal, though this leaves her once again abandoned and alone. In *The Coxcomb*'s other plot, Antonio's wife Maria goes to the country as part of her complex power struggle with her husband, and, in a twist on usual gender roles, she lies to her husband's friend Mercury (pretending to be a widow, promising to marry him) so that he will sleep with her. *Love's Pilgrimage* features two women, Theodosia and Leocadia, who independently disguise themselves as boys to pursue the same runaway husband, Marc Antonio. These girls on the run engage in the pastoral pattern of movement from the town or home to the country, and are examples of Fletcher's fascination with the manipulations of pastoral and romantic conventions, as seen in plays such as *The Faithful Shepherdess*.[4]

When comparing *Double Falsehood* and *Love's Pilgrimage* to the Cervantes stories on which they are based, one notices that the elements of all four plots are very similar. There is no simple answer to the question this raises: what would motivate Fletcher to not only repeat himself, but also to adapt similar stories from the same author? A brief and obvious answer would be that this kind of material was successful in the theater and worth repeating. A full answer would involve a closer examination of the sources and plays than is within the scope of this esssay, but the situation does mirror Fletcher writing *The Woman's Prize*, a sequel to *The Taming of the Shrew*, and then, years later, combining the basic patterns of *Shrew* and *Woman's Prize* into (the also partly Cervantes-based) *Rule a Wife and Have a Wife*. Additionally, the similarities between the plots of *Double Falsehood* and *Love's Pilgrimage* cannot be used to argue that Fletcher had no hand in the source-text of *Double Falsehood*; rather, we should expect such repetitions and variations on a theme.[5]

Love's Pilgrimage was probably written between 1614 and 1616 and revised in 1635.[6] It is based on "Las dos doncellas" from Cervantes's *Novelas Exemplares*, which was allowed for publication in Spain in August 1613. It was first printed in the Beaumont and Fletcher folio of 1647, probably from the revised version of 1635 since stage directions contain the names of minor actors associated with the King's Men in the 1630s, and two passages are appropriated from Ben Jonson's *The New Inn*, performed by the King's Men in 1629 and printed in 1631. It is not known for which company the play was originally written. As editor L. A. Beaurline writes: "That we are dealing with the revised form of *Love's Pilgrimage* complicates any interpretation of authorship."[7] The same problem is magnified with *Double Falsehood*. A tendency in the criticism of the Beaumont and Fletcher canon is that the more complex or uncertain the authorship of the play, the less attention it receives outside of attribution studies (unless Shakespeare is involved). *The Coxcomb*, which was probably inspired by the tale of the curious impertinent in *Don Quixote*, was performed by the Children of the Queen's Revels in November 1612. It may have been written a few years earlier. It was certainly acquired later by the King's Men, who performed it at court in 1622 and 1636.[8] Like *Love's Pilgrimage*, it was not printed until the 1647 folio, and the text printed is somewhat abridged. The prologue calls it a "Comedy long forgot" which the "ignorant multitude...condemn'd for the length./ That fault's reform'd" (Prologue 1, 12, 16–17).[9] Again all that survives is a collaborative Fletcher play in a text filtered through a later reviser, like *Love's Pilgrimage* and *Double Falsehood*.[10]

These three texts, altered at different times, allow us to compare changes made for audiences of the 1620s and 1630s with changes made for audiences of the 1720s. For example, the revised *Love's Pilgrimage*, unlike *Double Falsehood*, does not cut out material extraneous to the main action, but adds incidental comic dialogue. In the first scene material from Ben Jonson's *The New Inn* is interpolated.[11] These segments are inserted into a scene that develops the setting of a desolate one-room inn on a little-traveled road with dialogue between a down-at-heels innkeeper, his hardworking cunning wife, and a hungry and intermittently officious bailiff. The only action relevant to the plot is the appearance of the two weary travelers who appear separately and rent the only available room, and yet this scene occupies the first four of the play's twenty-six pages in the Beaumont and Fletcher folio of 1647.[12] Another folio page is given to 2.4, which may be another interpolation.[13] It features more food and inn-based dialogue by the bailiff, innkeeper, yet another innkeeper, and a second hostess at a new inn. Humorous minor characters and their byplay were not excised by the reviser(s) of the 1630s. Scene-setting accomplished through the dialogue of minor characters is mostly absent in *Double Falsehood*, which is able to substitute the physical scenery and machinery of the eighteenth-century stage.

Also absent for the most part from *Double Falsehood* are the extended bouts of sexual imagery and bawdy wordplay that are hallmarks of Beaumont and Fletcher plays. For those familiar with Fletcher, the experience of reading *Double Falsehood* is similar to that of watching censored broadcast versions of shows like *The Sopranos* or *Sex and the City*. The editing of the episode results in jarring dubbed audio and noticeably awkward scene and shot transitions. The brevity of *Double Falsehood* contributes to this sense of incompleteness, along with the absence of more explicit humor. Some relatively tame bawdy does remain in *Double Falsehood*, such as the reference to syphilitic noses falling off (4.1.126–7), the fathers arguing about their daughters' possible pregnancies (5.2.20–6), or Camillo's response to Violante while she is still disguised as a boy: "Nature, sure, meant thou shouldst have been a wench—/ And then't had been no marvel he had bobb'd thee" (5.2.149–50).[14] The bawdy in these examples, however, is confined to minor comic characters and is either obscure or restrained to the point that the Arden editor only allows that the last example "may have carried a sexual innuendo" (5.2.150n). Then there are lines such as the beginning of Julio's mad-scene, "Horsemanship! Hell—riding shall be abolish'd" (4.1.27), where one expects a development of "riding" as a sexual metaphor or something more like Gary Taylor's version of this line, "Horsemanship? Whore! Riding shall be abolished."[15] Compare the rhetorical question in *Love's Cure*: "doe [court ladies] love to ride great horses, as you doe? No, they love to ride great asses sooner" (2.2.93–5).[16] Julio's boast in *Double Falsehood*, "Wear I not a sword?/ Ne'er on man's thigh rode better" (3.2.56–7), could be bawdy, but as a martial double entendre it pales in comparison to *Love's Pilgrimage*: "There be Trenches/ Fitter, and warmer for your years, and safer/ Then where the bullet plays" (2.3.39–41).[17] *Double Falsehood* contains nothing like the extended bawdy of *Love's Pilgrimage*, where female thieves seduce men in the forest with "the sport of all sports...turning up of taffetaes" so that men are "stript and bound,/ Like so many Adams, with fig leafs afore 'em" (2.2.16–37), and a young man is advised, "he that ventures/ Whilst they are fit to put him on, has found out/ The everlasting motion in his scabbard" (2.1.148–50).[18] In *Double Falsehood* the Master does vaguely eroticize Violante's hand once he suspects her true gender, "This is a fine hand,/ A delicate fine hand...and a woman's hand" (4.1.169–71), but this does not compare to the more obvious manual innuendos found in both *Love's Pilgrimage* and *The Coxcomb*: "Hostess,/ I kiss thy hands through which many a round reckoning/ And things of moment have had motion" (*Love's Pilgrimage* 2.4.64–6) and "by this light, for one use that shall be nameless, tis the best wanton hand that ere I lookt on" (*Coxcomb* 2.2.156–7). Henriquez's apostrophe when Violante appears at the window verges on erotic imagery, "O taper, graced by that midnight hand" (1.3.27), where the phallic shape of the taper contributes to the metaphor, but the missed opportunity suggests excised material.

In the preceding examples, one assumes that a later reader (Theobald) understood the bawdy of the original text all too well, and censored it out, whereas the earlier revisers of the other plays were content to let much of it stand. I will now examine a few readings of *Love's Pilgrimage* and *The Coxcomb* that show later critics misunderstanding characterization and the dramatic strategies of Fletcherian theatre. By improving some readings of known Beaumont and Fletcher plays, we can avoid similar mistakes when searching for Fletcherian elements in *Double Falsehood*. The following examples appear in useful studies of the plays of Beaumont and Fletcher, but the few discussions of *The Coxcomb* and *Love's Pilgrimage* have left some misconceptions unanswered. While analysis of the sexuality and politics in Beaumont and Fletcher has advanced considerably, there is still short shrift given to plot and characterization, which appealed to Beaumont and Fletcher's audience as much as their witty bawdy, emotional patterning, coded political commentary, and manipulation of theatrical convention.

In the title plot of *The Coxcomb*, Antonio is so comically committed to renaissance ideals of friendship that he insists his newfound friend Mercury should have sex with his wife Maria, so that the two men can have shared everything. Mercury, however, is bound by the ideals of hospitality, so that he is reluctant to cuckold a man who has invited him into his home. Engineering a conflict between incompatible ideals, especially when the character's allegiance to the ideal is comically exaggerated, is a typical strategy in the Beaumont and Fletcher collaborations. Mercury attempts to remain loyal to his ideal: he does not sleep with Maria until he believes Antonio is dead, and Mercury repents only when he discovers that Antonio is alive. William Appleton's description of the conclusion of the play is slightly misleading on this point, "The story ends on a curious note. Maria's simulated lust finally cures Mercury's passion for her, but Antonio, consistent to the last, apologizes for his wife's obstinate virtue."[19] In this interpretation Maria only "simulated lust" in order to cure Mercury (with the implication that they did not sleep together), and Antonio apologizes to him that she has not (because of her "obstinate virtue"). This is not what happens. Mercury agrees in principle to sleep with Maria only after he believes her husband is dead (3.1.71, 84–5, 95–8). Antonio confirms his own death via a letter in 4.6, and Maria, goaded by her husband's antics, *does* have sex with Mercury between 4.6 and 4.8. Mercury then delivers a soliloquy that is a pitch-perfect mix of postcoital regret ("Now what am I the better for enjoying/ This woman that I lov'd so?" [4.8.1–2]) and cocky self-congratulation ("this it is/ To thresh well" [4.8.28–9]), including the mock complaint as Maria calls him back to bed, "The Devill cannot keep these women off,/ When they are fletched once" (4.8.21–2).[20] Mercury even scolds her lightly for delaying their marriage until after they have sex: "it was your fault, that it came/ To this pinch now...I offer'd you/ To marry you first, why did you slacke that offer?" (4.8.32–5). Maria, like Henriquez and Marc Antonio, uses an insincere promise of marriage to maneuver someone into bed. Antonio's apology, referred to by Appleton, "I am sorry my wife is so obstinate" (5.3.226) is *not* for his wife's obstinate virtue in refusing to sleep with Mercury, but because she makes no sign of agreement or conciliation to Antonio's request, "ah, good wife, love my friend, friend, love my wife, harke friend" (5.3.221–2). Antonio is resolutely unembarrassed that his wife has cuckolded him and he is, as Appleton notes, consistent to the end, boasting, "such a wife as thou, had never a man, and such a friend as he, beleeve me wife, shall never be" (5.3.220–1). Mercury has "lost that passion" (5.3.228) not because he is cured by aversion to Maria's feigned lust, but because he no longer wishes to accept favors of any kind from Antonio (5.3.226–7). He believed that Antonio was dead and that Maria would marry him. He even worries that she killed her husband for his sake (5.3.147–9) and remains speechless for fifty lines after Maria tells him "my husband lives, I know it, and I see him" (5.3.150–1). Mercury realizes he has inadvertently cuckolded a man he was indebted to for generous, if oppressive, hospitality (cf. 1.1.35–43, 1.2.57–73).

The mechanics of the plot involve Antonio pretending to be dead, and his wife pretending that she does not know that he is pretending to be dead. The final scene of *The Coxcomb* is a contest between Maria and Antonio to see who will give up this game first. He finally gives up his disguise as an Irish footman when Maria attempts to have him whipped (5.3.200–9). (He is a cuckold fantasist, not a sadomasochist.) However, Antonio gets everything he wants and is not punished. He has co-opted everyone into his sexual role-playing game. Maria, I argue, is silent in the end because she is angry that her husband is not humiliated or shamed, and so she has not won the struggle.[21] Antonio cannot feel humiliation for what Maria and Mercury have done: a cuckolding (or rather, the sharing of his most precious possession with his best friend) is exactly what he wanted.[22] As Eugene Waith notes, "unlike the fools of Jonsonian comedy, [Antonio] is never put out of his humor."[23] There is even a sense of "here we go again" when he then turns to his cousin Curio: "you and I must be better acquainted" (5.3.229).

But Waith adds that at the end of the play Antonio "is unaware that he is a cuckold"—however, Antonio never indicates that he believes he is not a cuckold. Rather, Waith does not credit Antonio's pride in his cuckoldom and underestimates the perversity of Antonio the same way he discounts Maria's agency in seducing Mercury: "[Maria] gives in to [Mercury] in order to make him see what a beast he is."[24] It is Mercury who gives in to Maria (she manipulates him, as discussed above), and she does not much care what Mercury feels; she wants her husband to feel like a fool and give up his desire to be a wittol.[25] Appleton and Waith understate the level of perversity in the play because they also underestimate the consistency, or even existence, of characterization in the play.

Another example of such underestimation is found in a very brief comment by Kathleen McLuskie, describing the end of *Love's Pilgrimage*: "as the plot hurries to its conclusion, a character [Theodosia] who has deceived her own brother [Philippo] with her disguise for four acts is instantly recognized by her father [Alphonso], who has pursued her through the play and must be reconciled to her before a satisfactory conclusion can ensue."[26] However, the second scene in *Love's Pilgrimage* is a long dialogue between Theodosia and her brother Philippo in which they both reveal their identities to each other, and they spend the play working together to find her runaway fiancé, Marc Antonio. In fact, it is *Leocadia*'s father who sees through *her* disguise (5.4.142), shortly after Theodosia's father Alphonso recognizes his son Philippo, Leocadia's companion (5.4.138). When Alphonso recognizes Theodosia in the final scene (5.6.110), she does not seem to be disguised.[27] McLuskie's reading makes the end of the play appear ridiculous in a clumsy and uninteresting way; in fact, the ending is ridiculous in an absolutely fascinating way. Two old men, fathers to the two girls who have been engaged to Marc Antonio, decide to duel with pistols and poniards, but since one is chair-bound (and choleric—he often commands his servants to carry him toward other characters so he can beat them), the other is also tied to a chair to make a fair fight (5.6.17–89). The duel is interrupted when, under the direction of Eugenia, the governor's wife, the two daughters enter and (the dialogue implies) place themselves between their two fathers in a silent Solomonic tableau (5.6.102–11). The burlesque violence of two cranky old men dueling while tied to chairs shudders to a halt as the fathers must either give up their feud or murder their daughters. This conclusion is a striking change from "Las dos doncellas" where the four newlyweds, returning from a pilgrimage, find the fathers of Leocadia and Theodosia jousting in turn with the father of Marc Antonio, and the conflict is broken up by the two young men, not the young women, "putting themselves in the midst betweene those that fought."[28] Beaumont and Fletcher change the story to underline the affection between the fathers and daughters, rather than the young mens' new relationships to their fathers-in-law. In addition, this final sequence in *Love's Pilgrimage* is preceded by a powerful exchange in which Philippo tests the sense of honor of his sometime rival and future brother-in-law, Marc Antonio:

Philippo. Brother let's speak with you; you were false unto her [Leocadia].
Mark-antonio. I was, but have ask'd pardon: why do you urge it?
Philippo. You were not worthy of her.
Mark-antonio.   May be I was not;
    But tis not well, you tell me so.
Philippo.   My sister
    Is not so faire.
Mark-antonio.   It skills not.
Philippo.   Nor so vertuous.
Mark-antonio. Yes, she must be as vertuous.
Philippo.   I would faine—
Mark-antonio. What brother?
Philippo.   Strike you.
Mark-antonio.   I shall not beare strokes,
    Though I do these strange words.
Philippo.   Will you not kill me?
Mark-antonio. For what good brother?
Philippo.   Why, for speaking well
    Of Leocadia.
Mark-antonio.   No indeed.
Philippo.   Nor ill
    Of Theodosia?
Mark-antonio.   Neither.
Philippo.   Fare you well then. (5.6.92–102)

This is the closest thing to Harold Pinter I have read in early modern drama (just mentally add a "*Pause*" stage direction every few lines). Upset that his fiancé Leocadia continually runs away from him, and unimpressed by the quick moral conversion of his new brother-in-law, Philippo quietly attempts to humiliate Marc Antonio by exposing his cowardice. This is unlike Cervantes' story, where the analogous friendship resumes with no problems. On the other hand, the exchange also exposes Philippo's immaturity and conventional sense of honor (both regular targets of criticism in Beaumont and Fletcher plays). This subtle power struggle is an astonishing prelude to the fathers' duel. *The Coxcomb* too ends with an exceptionally chilly exchange between Richardo and his father-in-law Andrugio, who greets him with only, "Say nothing to me, for thy peace is made" (5.3.236). It is the vacillation between the ridiculous, menacing, and sublime that makes the conclusion of *Love's Pilgrimage* and *The Coxcomb* so interesting; it is meant to exhilarate the audience with vertiginous fluctuations of tone while simultaneously flattering an informed reflexive knowingness on the part of avid theatergoers. But the dramatic power of these odd, ambivalent conclusions can only be understood if readers and audiences are willing to take seriously the consistent yet baroque characterization that does exist in the Beaumont and Fletcher plays.

Unfortunately, it is difficult to apply this insight to *Double Falsehood*, since any jarring tonal juxtapositions may be either the residue of *Cardenio* or the product of the severe abridgment and revision applied by Theobald. Still, strong indications remain, such as in 4.1 where, as Brean Hammond notes, "there is precisely the dramatization of surprising incident and shifting emotion that one associates with Fletcher" (49). Many of today's readers and audience members may miss the Fletcherian moments in *Double Falsehood* because they do not know to look for them, or for what to look. The ever more fine-grained attribution of authorship for *Double Falsehood* helps us to recognize Fletcher's hand in the play, but I have tried here to contribute to a necessary and complimentary task, to pay more attention to the Fletcher plays themselves.

NOTES

1. There is space in this essay to discuss only briefly the specifically Cervantine aspects of these plays; I use their origin as a selection principle. The most detailed examination of Fletcher's use of Cervantes is Joan F. McMurray, "John Fletcher and His Sources in Cervantes" (PhD diss., University of Rochester, 1987), though it does not examine *Double Falsehood*. See also T. L. Darby, "Cervantes in England: The Influence of Golden-Age Prose Fiction on Jacobean Drama, c. 1615–1625," *Bulletin of Hispanic Studies* 74 (1997): 425–41, available online at *Early Modern Spain*, www.ems.kcl.ac.uk. Darby briefly discusses the staging of the first scene of *Love's Pilgrimage*.

2. Cyrus Hoy, "The Shares of Fletcher and His Collaborators in the Beaumont and Fletcher Canon (VII)," *Studies in Bibliography* 15 (1962): 86. Though Hoy's methodology has been criticized, this series of articles in *SiB* 8–9, 11–15, available online at http://etext.virginia.edu/bsuva/sb/, remains a useful starting point for attributions.

3. She is not raped in the corresponding scene of *Don Quixote*, and whether she was raped in the Jacobean play has been disputed: see Taylor, "History", 40–4. In *DF* Henriquez describes his treatment of Violante: "By force alone I snatch'd th'imperfect joy,/ Which now torments my memory. Not love,/ But brutal violence prevail'd…Shame, shame upon it!" (2.1.26–31). He then rationalizes his act: "Was it rape then? No. Her shrieks, her exclamations then had drove me from her. True, she did not consent: as true, she did resist; but still in silence all" (2.1.36–9). Though he decides that her behavior was "but the coyness of a modest bride,/ Not the resentment of a ravish'd maid" (2.1.40–1), he still acknowledges a trespass, even if only by dismissing it: "The loose escapes of youthful nature known,/ Must wink at mine, indulgent to their own" (2.1.60–1). Violante feels the shame and the double bind produced by this displaced guilt: "There's not a maid whose eye with virgin gaze/ Pierces not to my guilt. What will't avail me/ To say I was not willing?/ Nothing, but that I publish my dishonour,/ And wound my fame anew" (2.2.2–4).

4. The pastoral scenes in *Double Falsehood* are those most commonly attributed to Fletcher. On Fletcher's reworking of pastoral and romantic conventions in *The Faithful Shepherdess*, see Lee Bliss, "Defending Fletcher's Shepherds," *Studies in English Literature, 1500–1900* 23 (1983): 295–310, and on the manipulation of genre and convention in the Beaumont and Fletcher canon, see Eugene Waith, *The Pattern of Tragicomedy in Beaumont and Fletcher* (1952; reprint, New York: Archon Books, 1969).

5. One other connection between *Cardenio* and *Love's Pilgrimage* is F. G. Fleay's discredited claim that *Love's Pilgrimage* was the "Cardenna/o" of the 1613 performance records, because (in both the play and Cervantes) Leocadia claims she is "Francisco, son to Don-Henriques/ De Cardinas" [2.2.163–4]): see Fleay's *Biographical Chronicle of the English Drama 1559–1642* (London, 1891), 1:194. G. E. Bentley countered this claim, arguing that Humphrey Moseley would not have registered *Love's Pilgrimage* in 1646 and re-registered the same play as *Cardenio* in 1653 (*Jacobean and Caroline Stage* 3:370). Conclusive evidence that *Love's Pilgrimage* was not originally *Cardenio* is that Cervantes's "Las dos doncellas" was not licensed for print in Spain until August 1613, so the documents of May and June 1613 cannot refer to a play based on it.

6. G. E. Bentley, *The Jacobean and Caroline Stage* (Oxford: Oxford University Press, 1956–1968), 3:367.

7. Beaurline, ed. *Love's Pilgrimage,* in *Fletcher,* 2:571.

8. E. K. Chambers, *The Elizabethan Stage* (Oxford: Clarendon Press, 1923), 3:223—24. A. S. W. Rosenbach is skeptical that Cervantes is a source, "The Curious-Impertinent in English Dramatic Literature before Shelton's Translation of Don Quixote," *Modern Language Notes* 17 (1902): 181–2. Joan F. McMurray argues that "the general parallels between the characters and the plot [are] strong enough to demonstrate that Fletcher used in a highly inventive way the serious Spanish story as the model for the coxcomb story in the play," in "John Fletcher and His Sources in Cervantes," 217. Rosenbach's skepticism is evidence of the extent to which Fletcher (at least when collaborating with Beaumont) was willing to depart from a Cervantine source.

9. *The Coxcomb,* ed. Irby B. Cauthen, Jr. in *Fletcher,* 1:269. It is difficult to infer from the text what exactly has been cut, but it was not a masque. See Suzanne Gossett, "The Term 'Masque' in Shakespeare and Fletcher, and *The Coxcomb,*" *Studies in English Literature, 1500–1900* 14 (1974): 285–95.

10. On evidence for abridgment, see John Frehafer, "*Cardenio,* by Shakespeare and Fletcher," *PMLA,* 84, 501–13, and Taylor and Nance's "Four Characters in Search of a Subplot" in *Quest,* 192–214.

11. See *Fletcher,* 3:572 and Michael Hattaway, ed., *The New Inn,* The Revels Plays (Manchester: Manchester University Press, 1984), 229–30.

12. *Comedies and Tragedies written by Francis Beaumont and John Fletcher, Gentlemen* (London, 1647), sigs. 8Ar–*8D1v.

13. The scene begins with an erroneous stage direction that belongs to the next scene, 3.1. Beaurline discusses the possible interpolation in *Fletcher,* 3:674–75.

14. Gordon Williams provides both transitive and intransitive examples of the verb "to bob" (a "sexual encounter") in Fletcher's plays, *A Dictionary of Sexual Language and Imagery in Shakespearean and Stuart Literature,* 3 vols. (London: Athlone, 1994), 1:123–4.

15. For many examples of the sexual pun on "riding," see Williams, *Dictionary of Sexual Language,* 3:1154–5.

16. The joke refers to the proverbially well-endowed animals. See, for example, the Geneva Bible translation of Ezekiel 23:20: "For she doted vpõ their seruants whose members are *as* the members of asses, and whose yssue is *like* the yssue of horses."

17. For the phrase in *DF,* compare "Behold, I have a weapon—/ A better never did itself sustain/ Upon a soldier's thigh." *Othello* 5.2.258–60.

18. *Love's Cure* contains a similar image: "remember Mistresse: nature hath given you a sheath onely, to signifie women are to put up mens weapons, not to draw them" (2.2.89–90). The action of *Love's Cure* undercuts this sort of gender essentialism.

19. Appleton, *Beaumont and Fletcher, A Critical Study* (London: George Allen & Unwin, 1956), 45–6.

20. "To fletch" is "to fit (an arrow) with a feather" (*OED v.*), playing on the common image of the penis as an arrow (Williams, *Dictionary of Sexual Language*, 1:41). The passive construction of this phrase, however, seems to reverse the image, so that the woman is the arrow, the penis the feather. The unusual image is more than made up for because "fletched" in this context has the advantage of sounding similar to "fucked" while also playing on Fletcher's name. (Those who fletch are fletchers.) Fletcher's name is the aural link between "fletched" and "lecher" and brings to mind the satirical lines about Fletcher's father's second marriage, attributed to Sir John Davies: "devide the name of Fletcher:/ He my Llord F, and she my Lady Letcher" (qtd. in McMullan, 9).

21. Her last line, "O my lov'd husband" (5.3.210), follows Antonio's revelation of his identity (though she was aware of it well earlier). It is a line ripe for comic understatement in performance.

22. When Mercury tells Antonio that he is in love with his wife, Antonio responds, "I am resolv'd, go thy wayes, a wife shall never part us, I have consider'd and I finde her nothing to such a friend as thou art...Sir, you are not every man, now to your taske, I give you free leave, and the sinne is mine if there be any in it" (2.1.129–36).

23. Waith, *The Pattern of Tragicomedy in Beaumont and Fletcher* (1952; reprint, New York: Archon Books, 1969), 19.

24. Ibid.

25. Not that she does not give her husband many opportunities to correct his behavior. The terms of the contest are set in 2.3 when he approaches her disguised as an Irish footman with a letter supposedly from Mercury. She sees through his disguise, and has him imprisoned. After she confirms that Mercury is not involved in the deception (and he reveals his desire for her) in 3.1, she agrees to go to the country with him, hoping this will cure Antonio (3.1.93–4). Antonio again approaches her as the footman in 4.6, and she hopes the game is over and "my husband hath reveal'd himselfe, and in this hast sent after me" (4.6.2–3). But only after he instead delivers news of his death and urges her to let Mercury "bee your right hand in all things" (4.6.22) does she resolve to have sex with him: "I am provided for you my fine youth" (4.6.43). Mercury's feelings are secondary to her desire to dishumor Antonio.

26. McLuskie, "The Plays and the Playwrights: 1613–42," in *The Revels History of Drama in English*, gen. eds. Clifford Leech and T. W. Craik (London and New York: Methuen, 1975–1983), 4:182.

27. Deciphering the action of the final scene relies on embedded rather than explicit stage directions, which do not specify that Leocadia and Theodosia enter undisguised and dressed as women (5.6.103sd). However, the final scene makes better sense if this is the case.

28. [James Mabbe, trans.] *Exemplarie Novels...by Migvel De Cervantes Saavedra* (London, 1640), 51–2.

7

FURIOUS SOLDIERS AND MAD LOVERS: PLOTTING FLETCHER AND THE HISTORY OF CARDENIO

Vimala C. Pasupathi

Notions of John Fletcher's "essential" dramatic style have circulated since the seventeenth century; in the 1647 Folio, Fletcher's friends and near-contemporaries spoke of his distinct "sound," deeming it "So his owne,/ That twas his marke," and claiming that "he was by it known."[1] Sir Aston Cokaine invoked Fletcher's "own unequal[e]d Language" (a3r), a form so exemplary that Robery Staplyton claimed: "The Native may learne English from his lines" (a4r). Even before the publication of the Folio, John Ford had claimed that any poet seeking "Fame by desert.../ Must write like Fletcher"—that is to say, with the imitable style and authentic voice invoked in the 1637 quarto of *The Elder Brother*, whose Prologue assured readers that they would be able to "heare *Fletcher* in it."[2]

More recently, electronic databases have allowed us to qualify and quantify what that Prologue described as "his true straine,/ And neate expressions." Such databases have also significantly enhanced the kinds of assessments we can make about Fletcher's role in Theobald's *Double Falsehood*.[3] Whereas readers were once simply expected to "heare" Fletcher's authorship in a play printed more than a decade after his death, we have the tools now to *see* rather convincing evidence of his style in Theobald's dramatic interpretation of the Cardenio story—despite the fact that Theobald himself was loathe to admit the younger playwright's role (*DF* Pref.34–42).

But the fact that *Double Falsehood* contains stylistic matches with (and verbal echoes from) several of Fletcher's other works invites us to look more closely at Fletcher as a potential author, and raises questions about the extent to which Theobald's 1727 text bears any resemblance to what audiences would have recognized as characteristically Fletcherian plots. Indeed, the verses commending Fletcher in the 1647 volume more frequently invoke his plots than his language, describing the characters and storylines from dramatic works—often identified explicitly by name and title—as well as offering up shorthand versions of a particular character's fate. For instance, H. Howard's verse describes the plots of *A King and no King*, *The Maids Tragedy* and *The Faithful Shepherdess*; Richard Lovelace references the plots of nearly ten plays, whose titles the typesetter reproduces in the margins alongside their description. Robert Herrick also describes *The Mad Lover*, *Philaster*, and *A King and no King*, ascribing the last play's storyline to Fletcher in his parenthetical comment, "and the rare plot thine."[4] The fact that not one of the "thirty foure witnesses" assembled by Moseley in the Beaumont and Fletcher Folio of 1647 makes reference to the plot or titular character from the apparently missing collaboration by Fletcher and Shakespeare should not surprise us—after all, none of these verse contributors makes any reference to *The Two Noble Kinsmen*, a known and extant collaboration by the two playwrights, or to *All Is True (Henry VII)*, which is now widely accepted as a Shakespeare–Fletcher collaboration.[5] Nor should this fact deter us from considering how the particular aspects of Cardenio's story—in both *Double Falsehood* and the source for the seventeenth-century play about him, Thomas Shelton's translation of *The History of The Valorous and Wittie Knight-Errant, Don Quixote of the Mancha* (1612)—might have resonated with Fletcher's interests as they manifest in his many solo-authored plays.

In her essay on the subject of written scenarios ("plots") and *Double Falsehood*, Tiffany Stern casts doubt on many aspects of Theobald's claims about his possession of a manuscript by Shakespeare as well as his own writing process. Yet even she concedes at several points in her discussion that elements in *Double Falsehood* may indeed be attributed to Fletcher. Although she is careful to remind us that "*Cardenio* itself may not have contained any Shakespeare—and perhaps no Fletcher either," she allows for the possibility that the plot "may well have been Fletcherian" and makes the same claim of the play's "structure."[6] *Cardenio*, she admits, "mimics the particular plotting habits he displays elsewhere," since "at least ten of his other plays contain stories taken from Spanish sources," including "at least three from sources by Cervantes."[7]

Documentary evidence leads Stern to an intriguing set of conjectures: that Fletcher was "more plot-reliant" than Shakespeare, and, additionally, that we may even assume that he "*liked* to compose" the scenarios of plays (121, emphasis mine). But because her essay is focused solely on what material evidence can teach us about the enterprise of scenario-writing, Stern ultimately has little interest in examining the Cardenio plot *as* a plot. And so, aside from briefly referencing Fletcher's "plotting habits" and his reliance on Spanish sources, her essay makes no attempt to identify particular elements in the Cardenio story or in *Double Falsehood*'s plot that would have resonated with Fletcher in 1612 or 1613. My own essay attempts to do some of that work, albeit with the acknowledgment that such an endeavor may ultimately invite challenges to claims for distinctly Fletcherian plots as much as it can support them. Very broad comparisons, at least, would no doubt raise the objection that the same might be found in numerous other works from the same period.

In his excellent edition of *Double Falsehood*, Brean Hammond makes note of numerous instances in Theobald's text that resonate with Shakespeare's works; in addition to the passages from Shakespeaean drama Hammond provides in annotations on the playtext itself, the edition's introduction attends to motifs and plot devices that resemble those in Shakespeare. He links, for instance, Violante's disguise to the male garb donned by Viola, Portia, and Imogen, and points out verbal and tonal elements in the play's songs that share resonance and purpose with those in *The Tempest* and *The Winter's Tale* (Hammond 28–9). Additionally, Hammond compares the omission of the figures of Don Quixote and Sancho in *Double Falsehood* to the absence of Pyrocles and Musidorus in Shakespeare's adaption of Sidney's *Arcadia* for the Gloucester plot of *King Lear*; he also suggests that the eighteenth-century play's additions to Cervantes's plot are in keeping with Shakespeare's dramatic interests, if not easily ascribed to his hand. For example, the "increased participation of the fathers," which enables the play's emphatic "reunion of fathers with daughters," is one instance in which the play develops "a motif much more prevalent in other Shakespeare plays of this period than in *Don Quixote*" (45). Certainly, Hammond is to be commended for the sensitivity and the caution with which he approaches the parts of *Double Falsehood* that could speak to Shakespeare's role in the play; yet it is also worth noting that he has far less to say about Fletcher's possible contributions other than to note that "the somewhat trite in Providential interference" was "more commonly discovered" in his works, and that a favored conceit, in which "powerful, independent protagonists will have their loyalty to a corrupt leader tested to the full, sometimes by that leader's attempt to seduce the protagonist's loved one," is "presented only in domestic terms" in *Double Falsehood* (48). In fact, one of the plot conceits Hammond describes as a "particularly Shakespearean resonance," the instance in which Leonora urges Julio behind an arras, is one that appears in multiple plays by Fletcher in addition to Shakespeare's *Hamlet*.[8]

Of course, outside of the context of *Cardenio*, Fletcher's plots and plot-devices have already received a significant amount of attention from scholars of early modern drama. Indeed, critics have done well to note, as Robert Herrick did in his verse in the Folio, Fletcher's penchant for plots with long journeys and surprising twists. They have also pointed to the witty and resourceful female characters that populate his works, as well as his propensity to dramatize plots that involve alternately competing and doting pairs of male friends. All these Fletcherian elements, and others, can be found in *Double Falsehood*; they also feature in Shelton's 1612 translation of *Don Quixote*.[9]

To the rather long list of Fletcherian preoccupations that scholars have already noted, I will add in this essay two aspects of his plots that I think are particularly relevant for the study of *Double Falsehood* and *The History of Cardenio*. First, Fletcher's plots often demonstrate his investment in staging the positive psychological impact of having friends—a facet of his drama that stands in stark contrast to Shakespeare's plots and to the Cervantine plot of the Cardenio story. Second, Fletcher's plots also tend to demonstrate the cultural importance of occupationally affiliated social networks, groups and professional communities whose members work collaboratively to sustain and care for individuals who are mad, depressed, or otherwise in need.

With respect to the second feature, readers might well object that Thomas Dekker was in fact just as attuned to the restorative function of such networks, and indeed, to a large extent, his *Shoemakers Holiday* (1599) offers us an ur-plot of sorts (about shoemakers) for the kinds of dramatic plots that Fletcher would ultimately go on to write and re-write himself (about soldiers). More specifically, Fletcher went on to write plays over the course of a decade that reflect a keen interest in the social dynamics of demobilized martial collectives. As I will suggest in this essay, placing what we know of the enigmatic *Cardenio* in conversation with these plays—produced on his own in the years preceding and shortly following his collaborative work with Shakespeare—can open up new ways of thinking about Fletcher as a dramatist and allow us to see the utility and appeal of Cervantes's story for a playwright who liked to devise and re-imagine a plot.

FLETCHER'S PLOTS VERSUS SPANISH CAMPAIGNS

Fletcher's interest in martial collectives is perhaps unsurprising given the fact that he was writing, for much of his career, during a protracted (and for some subjects, frustrating) period of generally peaceful relations with Spain and other Catholic powers. But even as expressions of concern for the plights of cashiered soldiers were typical in works by sixteenth- and seventeenth-century playwrights and poets, his approach to staging their problems was not. Whereas other playwrights typically addressed these problems by dramatizing the experiences and often-tragic downfall of exceptional soldiers (exemplified by Shakespeare's *Coriolanus*, George Chapman's *Bussy D'Ambois*, and, less tragically, Heywood's *The Royal King and the Loyal Subject*), Fletcher instead wrote primarily tragicomic works in which groups of soldiers help redeem the most vulnerable of their number by offering encouraging solidarity and sustaining mirth. In plays such as *The Captain*, *The Mad Lover*, and *The Loyal Subject*, all written between 1609 and 1618, troubled individuals escape the errors and ill-fates that might befall them in isolation in large part owing to productive—and in some cases explicitly performative—collaboration. In short, they work together to protect one another from depression and violence that, in other playwrights' works, accompanies soldiers as they suffer on their own.[10]

As I've articulated it here thus far, this distinctly Fletcherian interest in supportive martial collectives may seem to have little to no bearing on how we imagine the missing *Cardenio*. Unlike the extant *Two Noble Kinsmen*, which contains a Shakespearian nod to his younger colleague's interests in a lengthy lament on "th'unconsider'd solder" (1.2.31), *Double Falsehood* does not feature a single soldier, let alone whole armies; and though its source material was rife with elements that would allow for chivalric burlesque, the

Cardenio story in Cervantes's novel and *Double Falsehood* seems to afford little opportunity to celebrate the camaraderie and pleasure afforded by the presence of others connected by shared labor, if not other forms of social equality. In fact, as I have already noted, the sense of friendship offered by *Double Falsehood* and the Cardenio story—that it must inevitably be tested or ruined by acts of betrayal—is a pattern more readily discernable in plays by Shakespeare.[11]

Moreover, by most standards of comparison, the plays that are exemplary of Fletcher's plots about friendships among demobilized soldiers have little in common with those he wrote based on works by Cervantes; indeed, we would be hard pressed to link his interest in soldiers in peacetime with his appreciation for *Don Quixote*, the *Novelas Ejemplares*, or even Anglo-Spanish relations, except very loosely. The 1679 Folio identifies the setting in *The Captain* rather confusingly as Venice, Spain, but aside from Spanish names for characters and the brief indicator of the location for the action, there is nothing in the play itself that demands a Spanish setting or presents a scenario that applies to Spain exclusively.

As members of the largest standing army in Europe, Spain's soldiers were both a source of envy and a cautionary tale for English subjects during Fletcher's lifetime. While they were renowned for their martial prowess and discipline, contemporary accounts of their violent response to missing wages in Antwerp also emphatically warned of their destructive, rebellious, and murderous side.[12] But even if Fletcher was willing to articulate an "overt wish for war" with Spain in private correspondence, he was also capable of "detach[ing] enjoyment of Spanish literature from Spanish politics," and was apparently able to imagine the plight of demobilized armies without necessarily thinking simultaneously of the famous tercios or of war with Spain.[13] In fact, the problems experienced by Fletcher's martial collectives in each play—their lack of employment and appropriate forms of compensation, their need for validation from the state in times of peace, as well as their vulnerability to abuse by those in power—are problems that were equally, if not more so, endemic to soldiers in England.

Significantly, Fletcher avoids leaving audiences with the impression that armed collectives, Spanish or otherwise, will inevitably engage in murderous riot and pillage. In *The Loyal Subject* especially, he raises the possibility that they can live as contentedly at home as in the camp—not in spite of their status within a martial community, but rather, because of the care and support that this community of military professionals affords them. This premise informs both *The Captain* and *The Mad Lover*, plays whose respective titular anti-heroes descend into depression and madness shortly after they return from war. As in *The Loyal Subject*, the men in these earlier plays rally around their distracted officers, not only offering encouraging words to facilitate their mental recovery but also taking active steps to help set that recovery in motion. *The Mad Lover* is especially remarkable along these lines, for multiple soldiers find new employment putting on masques and other performances designed to bring their love-sick general, Memnon, back to his wits. As he does in *The Captain* and *The Loyal Subject*, Fletcher suggests that members of a newly extraneous labor force can perform significant cultural work off the field as much as they were able to do when the state called them to it. *The Mad Lover*, especially, emphasizes these soldiers' collaborative efforts to prevent a comrade from courting the disasters that can come from their seclusion in social isolation. More so than other plays, I will suggest, *The Mad Lover's* plot and subplots can be read as martially themed re-visions of the pastoral portions of the Cardenio story—including the very scenes of *Double Falsehood* that attribution scholarship has assigned to Fletcher.

SHEPHERDING MAD LOVERS

Cardenio is not explicitly identified as a soldier in Shelton's translation of *Don Quixote*, but in *Double Falsehood*, his counterpart Julio vows to be one if he is called upon as he leaves for Duke Angelo's court: "If war, I come thy soldier" (1.2.119). Regardless of whether Julio's father is justified in questioning the quality of his horsemanship, his distracted behavior (like that of Cardenio in the Shelton translation) contains a number of as-yet unidentified parallels with the titular mad officer of Fletcher's play. Like Shelton's Cardenio, Fletcher's Memnon writes anguished love poetry, and increasingly shows signs of madness thereafter. Both characters share features with *Double Falsehood's* Julio as they are each led to suspect the motives of the men who have claimed to woo on their behalves. Additionally, the plots of all three texts resolve the conflict between the mad protagonist and his rival (who selfishly pursues his friend's beloved for himself) by staging the surprise return of the rival's former love, a woman in each text who affirms her own undoing by the rival's hand. And, most significantly, all three characters are prevented from harming themselves through the intervention of collectives explicitly described as "friends" and identified as affiliated with a particular vocation or labor.

Whereas in Fletcher's play those friends are identified as the protagonist's fellow soldiers, the characters that offer the mad protagonist relief in *Double Falsehood* and Shelton's *Don Quixote* are shepherds and goatherds. Similar to *The Mad Lover's* Chilax, a rank-and-file soldier who initially is inclined to make jokes at his superior officer's love-sick antics, these Cervantine helpmates are quickly drawn into sympathizing with a man who appears both to be their social better and a person in distress. In Shelton's version, the goatherd mentions that after hearing Cardenio's "so feeling laments," they "kept him company" (3.9.215) and continue to care for him and provide him with meat (if sometimes from a distance). Indeed, they do so despite the fact that he has caused some of their number physical harm after acting violently from the "madness [that] comes to him at times" (216)—that is, in sudden, unpredictable bouts. In one instance, the Goatherd claims, Cardenio "stopt and grew silent," while "staring and beholding the earth...fixedly" (215); yet shortly thereafter he "[rose] from the ground," seemingly unprovoked, and "with great furie[,]...set vpon him that sat next vnto him, with such courage and rage, that if wee had not taken him away, he would have slaine him with blows and bites" (215). These men might understandably avoid any contact with him, and yet, as the Goatherd informs Quixote, "I and foure others, whereof two are my men, other two my friends, resolued Yesterday to search vntill we found him; and being found...we will haue him cured, if his disease may be holpen." (216).

Double Falsehood loses the sentimentality that Shelton's translation roots in the Goatherd's invocation of friendship and occupational obligation. One shepherd refers to his fellow shepherds as "neighbours" rather than friends (4.1.108, 121) and though these neighboring herders all "desire [Julio] to eat" (4.1.112), they undertake no effort (beyond allowing him to take their meat) to cure him. Still, the play maintains the novel's sense that the shepherds sympathize with Julio as a victim of love and "too much foul play" (4.1.21), in spite of the fact that he "takes [their] victuals" and then "beats [them] well and soundly" (4.1.11–13). Here, *Double Falsehood* renders the Goatherd's earnest account in *Don Quixote* to great comic effect, providing stage directions indicating that Cardenio "seizes on the [second] Shepherd" and pulls on his nose, occasioning the victim's complaint that he has been given "such a devilish dash o'er the mouth" that he will be unable to "whistle to [his] sheep again" (128–30).

In *The Mad Lover*, Memnon's mental agitation manifests in some of the same behaviors that we see in the two accounts of the Cardenio story, though we do not see neat or direct verbal parallels in the way such behaviors are described. Whereas Julio "wonders strangely" (4.1.23) at the shepherds in *Double Falsehood*, Fletcher's soldiers note that Memnon "starts strangely" (5.2.3), though they also describe him in the preceding line as "wondrous sad." They also note that he "weeps often too" (5.2.2), but here their use of the adverb means that he does so in addition to other actions, and so their account is not exactly comparable to Julio's admission to the disguised Violante in *Double Falsehood* that he "weeps sometimes too" (4.2.81).

Still, Fletcher's representation of a disturbed mind ultimately works to the same effects that we see in the other two works' mad lover plots. Like the Cardenio in Shelton's translation, in one moment still and silent and at another full of "courage and rage," the general's behavior is unpredictable and marked by sudden fits; according to Chilax, "sometimes he rages,/ And sometimes sits and muses" (4.5.6–7). Additionally, much like Cardenio's fits, which consist of "words...addrest to the dispraise of that Fernando" that not only "attach him of treason and untruth" (216) but also reveal him as the cause of the madman's strife, Memnon's outbursts reveal his anger and pain at being betrayed by Polidor, the brother he accuses of wooing the Princess Calis for himself. As he rages, we are told, he "calls on *Polidor*," and "Swears a will not be fool'd" (4.5.6–7).

As a result of the madness that comes with his thwarted love, Memnon also threatens the lives of the men who have committed to helping him regain his sanity; and yet, even when he expresses his intent to kill his entire company in a disturbing vision of murder-suicide, these men continue to attempt to help him and refuse to allow him to isolate himself or carry out his terrible plan. To be sure, *The Mad Lover*'s depiction of Memnon's madness is considerably darker than what we see in either of the Cardenio stories.[14] His threats of violence go beyond the comical blows that pervade *Double Falsehood* and its Cervantine origins, and so in this respect, Fletcher's plot bears greater resemblance to the soldiers' tragedies depicted by Shakespeare.[15] Yet Fletcher also stages a lighter version of Memnon's violence by way of a theatrical avatar, effectively displacing the Quixotic beatings, or rather re-integrating them, presenting them in another dramatic register: at one point, the soldier named Chilax entertains the members of his cashiered company by acting the part of the "The strangest Generall that ere thou heardst of" (2.2.49–50). "I'll play Memnon" (2.2.49), he says, and then takes a comical-violent course on the Foole who stands by. He explains, "'tis the nature/ Of this strange passion when't hits to hale people/ Along by th'haire, to kick'em, breake their heads" (2.2.72–4). When the Foole protests, "Do ye call this Acting, was your part to beat me" (75), Chilax persists, claiming, "Yes, I must act all that he does" (76).

This brief meta-theatrical fiction in Fletcher's play does little to help the titular Mad Lover, but it sets in motion a series of additional command performances that work to produce positive outcomes for nearly every character involved. As the soldier Stremon claims later of their plays and masques, the activities "get [the soldiers] all employment" (4.1.110) and therefore ensure they are occupied and ultimately peaceful civilians while they are between campaigns. More significantly, their second and third performances in the play help turn Memnon's rage and despair into laughter, while a fourth theatrical ruse provides the means for resolving conflicts with the friends who have fallen for his beloved and have consequently turned to rivals. The Foole describes their collaborative endeavors as "do[ing] something,/ To satisfie the Gentleman," and suggests that they do so because "hee's mad . . . /. . . And must have men as mad about him" (4.1.104–7). But what they actually do is not just fooling around; like the efforts to protect the lonely Cardenio that Shelton's Goatherd ascribes to his friends and his men, the soldiers' shared sense of sympathy and obligation to a pathetic (if also potentially dangerous) melancholy lover solidifies their resolve to help.

It is perhaps worth noting as well that such help in both dramatic works involves the use of music. The soldiers believe that Memnon "shall not this day perish, if his passions/ May bee fed with Music" 4.1.2–3), giving Chilax the opportunity to describe the "silver sound" for which Taylor notes analogues in other Fletcher-authored songs as well as Shelton's translation, and, more significantly, in the Robert Johnson song that may have originally appeared in the lost *Cardenio*.[16] This sound makes Memnon's "spirit . . . a little quieter" (4.1.8).[17] Similarly, in *Double Falsehood* (but not *Don Quixote*) a Shepherd claims of Julio [Cardenio] that he "knew our music would allure him" (4.1.20), and in the next scene the singing of Violante [Dorothea] does indeed initiate his return to sanity.

In addition to the texts' use of song to abate the symptoms of madness, we also find a compelling plot convergence in the plays' deployment of a theatrical ruse in which the villain is made to atone for all his sins by marrying the woman he first deflowers and then abandons. Unlike Fernando or Henriquez, Polidor steadfastly refuses to act upon his desire for Memnon's beloved Calis, even as she reciprocates his feelings. But in constructing a virtuous sibling in this way, Fletcher rewrites the ending that took the lives of one of his and Shakespeare's *Two Noble Kinsmen*, while again displacing elements of the Cardenio story onto another character. In this case, Fletcher gives us a soldier named Siphax, who, like Polidor, promises to act as a go-between to Calis for Memnon. Much like the figures of Don Fernando and Henriquez, Siphax's lust and ambition get the better of him when he sees her and so he begins to plot to gain the princess' hand by devious means. As with Memnon's more murderous plan, Siphax's scheme is prevented by Chilax, who ingeniously seizes (for the second time) upon the opportunity presented to him in the arrival of Cloe, a camp whore.

Just as Dorothea's fluency in the tropes of chivalric romance makes her the perfect actress to star in the fiction intended to cure the madness of Don Quixote in Cervantes' tale, Chloe's familiarity with the camp makes her an excellent collaborator with the soldiers in Fletcher's play. But more importantly, she resembles Dorothea in the fact that her first sexual encounter was with Siphyx, a figure who (like Fernando in Cervantes and Henriquez in *Double Falsehood*) cavalierly uses and abandons her, thereby initiating a virgin's undoing. Just as Theobald's Roderick easily enlists Violante to help expose his younger brother's sins, Cloe is quickly convinced to take part in a ruse that will secure her own marriage with Syphax: "Why should I not?" she asks rhetorically, adding, "he had my Maiden head/ And all my youth" (4.2.9–10). Later, Cloe describes their staged coup against Siphax as the perfect form of justice, praising "the law of Armes, that ever/ Rewards the Souldier with his own sins" (5.4.194–5); if this law does not easily apply to Don Fernando and Henriquez, we may nonetheless recognize that they are subject to a similar law governing the laws of friends.

CONCLUSION

Many of the elements of the three plots I have described here might also be manifest in other plays written during Shakespeare and Fletcher's lifetimes. As I noted at the outset of this essay, neither plot tropes nor narrative situations can, in and of themselves, be taken to indicate the presence or contribution of any given writer. But Moseley did name Fletcher as primary author of *The History of Cardenio*. Based on Fletcher's other works, we can see how the playwright might have liked a number of elements in the Cervantine plot, and imagine that he would return to reconfigure them as he explored his other interests. *The Mad Lover* and other plays whose plots revolve around soldiers suggest that Fletcher would have been drawn to the Cardenio story in *Quixote* for reasons that were distinct from those which would have interested Theobald or Shakespeare. Whereas Shakespeare might have found occasion therein to exploit favored tropes of false friends and the woman-as-lad in disguise—a trope that Fletcher was clearly less enamored with—Fletcher may have instead recognized the opportunity to stage and revisit the tragicomic situation of a furious lover whose friends take steps to see to his cure.[18]

It is also worth noting that no scholar has satisfactorily identified a source for Fletcher's *The Mad Lover*. While the similarities with *Double Falsehood* and Shelton's translation that I have presented here do not prove that the play's basic conflicts derived from *Don Quixote*, they nonetheless allow us to contemplate a version of the playwright's methods and encourage us to see plots as richly adaptable and in constant evolution. Claims such as these can never be more than conjectural, of course, but they can open up new lines of inquiry about the missing seventeenth-century play as well as possibilities for staging (or adapting) *Double Falsehood*. The Indianapolis production of *The History of Cardenio* made Cardenio's madness darker throughout, and increased the use of music to cure him (*THOC* 4.1, 4.3, 5.2); in both respects, Taylor's adaptation brought the play closer to *The Mad Lover*. The adaptation's subplot, incorporating the novel's story of Quixote's madness, also included the meta-theatrical efforts of his friends to cure him, and all those scenes of positive friendship occurred in the second half of the play, usually attributed to Fletcher. Since performances in Indianapolis, Taylor has further revised the script, making Roderick a general, Gerald a corporal, and Roderick's "train" soldiers.[19] Again, all this material comes in the Fletcherian half, and these changes bring into the play the kind of benevolent martial community that Fletcher elsewhere dramatizes. They also contrast Quixote's romantic ideal of chivalric singularity with Roderick's modern military collective.

Taylor's changes to *Double Falsehood* are necessarily speculative and, unless someone discovers more documentary evidence about the seventeenth-century play, we will never know whether they resemble in any way what was performed at court in 1613. But we can say that Taylor has made the second half of the play's *plot* even more Fletcherian than *Double Falsehood*. Until we have learned all that can be learned from the plots we have, no play is ever truly lost.

NOTES

1. *Comedies and Tragedies Written by Francis Beaumont and Iohn Fletcher* (1647), d2.
2. "Elegy on John Fletcher" (1625?) in *English Literary Criticism*, ed. Brian Vickers (Oxford: Oxford University Press), 545; *The Elder Brother* (London, 1637), Av.
3. See essays by Nance and by Taylor, chapters 9 and 10 in this volume, and essays by Jackson, Proudfoot, and Taylor in *Quest*.
4. *Comedies and Tragedies*, sig. E1r. Robert Gardner's verse (*Comedies and Tragedies*, sig. c2r.) also describes the plots of multiple plays. It might be worth

noting here that this facet of the folio's front matter stands in marked contrast to the verses preceding the works of Shakespeare in both the First and Second Folios, which extoll the playwright's virtues but offer only a single reference to specific characters from a specific play, *Romeo and Juliet*.

5. The description of the writers of the commendatory verses as witnesses is Moseley's, in his verse "The Stationer" (*Comedies and Tragedies*, sig. g2r).

6. Stern, "'Whether one did Contrive, the Other Write,/ Or one Fram'd the Plot, the Other did Indite': Fletcher and Theobald as Collaborative Writers," in *Quest*, 115–30 (quoting 121, 129, 124).

7. Stern (121) names only *Love's Pilgrimage*, *The Chances*, and *The Coxcomb*. Most scholars identify seventeen Fletcher plays based on Spanish sources, of which thirteen come from Cervantes: see Boro's essay, chapter 5 in this volume.

8. Characters eavesdrop or conceal themselves behind an arras in *The Noble Gentleman*, *Woman Pleased*, and *The Mad Lover*; in the last of these, the title character also sees through the disguise of another and, in exposing her, declares that she "Stinkes like a poyson'd Ratt behind a hanging" (4.5.44).

9. Citing multiple critics, Gary Taylor argues that "The adventures of Cardenio and his fellow characters, set in Andalusia and the Sierra Morena, would also fit Fletcher's aesthetic and political commitment to a 'country-based, feminocentric, uncourtly environment'...and his 'traveling instinct,' his fondness for plots of 'perpetual motion,' of 'constantly coming and going.' The intense and complicated relationship between Cardenio and Fernando would attract a playwright who liked stories about 'pairs of friends'; both Cardenio and Sancho would have appealed to his interest in characters dominated by hunger; both Dorothea and Luscinda epitomize his 'favorite character type,' the 'clever maiden in love,' possessed with a 'more generous...intellectual endowment' than the female characters of Shakespeare or Beaumont. Fernando, on the other hand, abundantly possesses the 'romantic charisma' and 'breezy moral complacency' of the 'uninhibited and highly resolute young male' at the center of so many Fletcherian comedies" ("History," 18).

10. See Vimala Pasupathi, "Shakespeare, Fletcher, and the Gain O'The Martialist," *Shakespeare* 7 (2011): 297–309.

11. Tom McFaul discusses Shakespeare's characteristically skeptical view in *Male Friendship in Shakespeare and His Contemporaries* (Cambridge: Cambridge University Press, 2007). Of course, it is worth noting here that *Double Falsedhood*'s treatment of friendship along these lines is primarily advanced over the course of the play's first half—that is, the parts typically ascribed to Shakespeare.

12. Prominent examples of accounts depicting the so-called Spanish fury include Gascoigne's *The Spoyle of Antwerpe* (London, 1576) and the anonymous play *A larum for London* (London, 1602).

13. McMullan, 257. His case for Fletcher's bellicosity may be somewhat overstated. The lines from the letter that occasion McMullan's assertions about Fletcher's "overt wish" are part of a list of subjects Fletcher "overpasse[s]" in order to emphasize a more important subject, his desire to be amongst the Countess and her attendants at Ashby. It is this peaceful desire that causes him to pass over all other desires, including the urge to discuss "whether ytt be true/ wee shall have wars wth Spain," a phrase he follows with the parenthetical comment, "(I wolde we might)." In my reading, the phrase's "might" renders the comment less forceful or fervent than McMullan suggests. More objectively, however, I would

note that the statement should be read in the context of the verse itself. The parenthetical statement functions, amongst other instances, as playful rhetorical posturing, and exists at least in part to provide additional syllables to preserve the rhyme scheme and enable a rhyme with the next line's "write." Whether the verse can be said to reflect Fletcher's actual opinions on war, it's worth nothing that at least one play that may date from around the same time as the letter, *The Humorous Lieutenant* (ca. 1618), offers a much more ambivalent sense of what might be gained from England's intervention in Protestant campaigns on the continent. See Vimala Pasupathi, "The King's Privates: Sex and the Soldier's Place in John Fletcher's *The Humorous Lieutenant,*" in *Research Opportunities in Medieval and Renaissance Drama* 47 (2008): 25–50.

14. Such elements might have been particularly vulnerable to alteration by Theobald to suit eighteenth-century audiences; in conversations about this essay, Terri Bourus has suggested to me the prospect that Theobald would have needed to cut them in order to make the part amenable to the famously dignified acting style of Barton Booth.

15. On Shakespeare's tragic Jacobean soldiers, see Paul Jorgensen, *Shakespeare's Military World* (Berkley: University of California Press, 1956) and Richard Ide, *Possessed with Greatness: The Heroic Tragedies of Chapman and Shakespeare* (Chapel Hill: University of North Carolina Press, 1980).

16. Taylor, "History," 28–33.

17. According to John P. Cutts, *The Mad Lover* features "the most extensive example within a single play of the use of musical sound and imagery in the depiction and cure of madness": "Music in *The Mad Lover,*" *Studies in the Renaissance* 8 (1961): 237.

18. Although the woman-as-lad figures in several plays with Fletcher's name attached, they date before 1612/1613, and all of them are thought to be collaborative. In *Double Falsehood*, both Cardenio and the Master of the Flocks see through the disguises adopted by female protagonists in a scene (4.1) attributed to Fletcher; in *The Mad Lover*, Memnon also sees through the ruse designed to get him to accept a whore disguised to look like his beloved princess. Both may be instances of Fletcher's meta-theatrical comment on the convention, related to his refusal to use it after 1612–1613. I am indebted to Gary Taylor, Terri Bourus, and Gerald Baker for these observations.

19. For Shelton's translation and the change in Roderick's identity, see Taylor and Wagschal's essay in this volume. Taylor also informs me (privately) that my work on Fletcher's martial characters influenced his post-Indianapolis revision.

8

"Shall I Never See a Lusty Man Again?": John Fletcher's Men, 1608–1715

Huw Griffiths

In 2009 I wrote an essay on *Cardenio*.[1] I argued that in considering the nature of any play called *Cardenio*, written by Shakespeare and Fletcher, then one important area of investigation might be the modifications made to the narrative of interrupted male friendship between its apparent source in Cervantes and its eighteenth-century adaptation in *Double Falsehood*. Where the former celebrates an idealized male friendship, at times through the kinds of homoerotic representations of male beauty common to the classical and Renaissance traditions, the latter eschews this in favor of a celebration of a more domesticated and bourgeois heterosexuality. Theobald's adaptation sidelines the homoerotic potential of early modern male *philia*, associating it with the rapacious aristocratic sexual appetites of the villainous Henriquez, whose characterization might readily be identified with what Thomas King terms "residual pederasty." In the later period status-driven homoeroticism comes to be understood as tyrannical and corrupting and, crucially, as outmoded.[2] In arguing that an original Shakespeare and Fletcher play could not have worked in quite this way but, as in the Cervantes original, would have afforded much greater affective power to the friendship between Cardenio and Don Fernando, my main touchstones were the powerful portraits of male friendship available in the Shakespearian canon, from *The Two Gentlemen of Verona* and *The Merchant of Venice*, to the more generically comparable *The Winter's Tale* and *The Two Noble Kinsmen* (the latter, of course cowritten by Fletcher).

I now want to revise and complicate this argument by looking at what happens to certain aspects of Cervantean romance in two plays from the Fletcher canon: *The Coxcomb* and *The Custom of the Country*. In my earlier essay, I had already indicated that in Fletcher's *Monsieur Thomas* (where, as in *Don Quixote*, *Two Gentlemen*, and *Two Noble Kinsmen*, two male friends are rivals for the love of one woman) something slightly different happens.

Instead of the reconciliations of the comic narrative being achieved through recognition (belated or otherwise) of the men's love for each other, in *Monsieur Thomas* the comic ending is achieved though the recognition that the two rivals are, in fact, father and son. The father gives up the contested bride in favor of his son and reconciliation is achieved in the bourgeois haven of a paternally sanctioned marriage, rather than through the idealized textual space of male *philia*. In the chapter on *Cardenio*, I argued that the greater presence of the fathers in *Double Falsehood* than in the original Cervantes story was an important aspect of the way in which the eighteenth-century adaptation might have revised any earlier version of the play, as was the greater emphasis placed on the class distinctions between all the male protagonists, with the bourgeois values of Julio and his father, Camillo, triumphing over the aristocratic imperiousness of Henriquez and his father, Duke Angelo. However, when analogous texts from the Fletcher canon are looked at, a picture emerges that is more complex than a simple dichotomy between a late-sixteenth and early-seventeenth-century idealization of male friendship and a later seventeenth- and eighteenth-century rejection of those values and relationships.

In a seminal book on the connections between homoeroticism, homosociability, and collaborative authorship for the early modern stage, Jeffrey Masten demonstrated that social, cultural, political, and sexual relationships between men in the late sixteenth and early seventeenth centuries structured the dramatic narratives onstage and modes of collaboration offstage. In particular, the aspiration to gentlemanly status on the part of playwrights saw them adapt the concept of *philia*, usually associated with the aristocracy, as an aspirational model both for their own professional and personal relations, and as a structuring dynamic in the plays themselves. My turn, here, to consider Fletcher alongside or even in front of Shakespeare does not refute Masten's important argument but it does begin to turn it in a slightly different direction. Masten himself admits that, for him, "Shakespeare...is a prime location for a reconsideration of collaboration and the emergence of authorship" and that it is with Shakespeare "that there is the most to be realized through revisions of textuality and sexuality in the study of early modern drama."[3] And of course he is right; Shakespeare has long been a focus for vexed questions around sexual identity in the period. However, it is also the case that Fletcher, as much as Shakespeare, often turned his attention to the possibilities and problematics of male friendship in his plays, whether he was writing collaboratively or not. My argument will be that even as Fletcher necessarily operated within the same paradigms as his collaborators, some of his work suggests a class-based resistance to the valorization of male *philia* that is in evidence elsewhere in early modern drama. However, what I attempt to do, rather than focus on one author as a site for imagining collaborative relationships and homosocial identifications, is to trace identifications and rejections of love and friendship across and between collaborators contemporary with each other (Fletcher and Shakespeare; Fletcher and Beaumont; Fletcher and Massinger) as well as, somewhat more briefly, cross-temporal identifications and rejections between men, as post-Restoration dramatists adapt these earlier plays, within new contexts. There are broad implications for this way of working in terms of how we conceive of the relationship between a longer history of the early modern stage, its texts, their afterlives and a history of early modern sexuality. I try to suggest some of those implications at the close of the chapter but, for the most part, the work lies in attempting to trace exactly what work is done when stories of male–male relationships are adapted first into drama from romance origins, and then from Elizabethan and Jacobean drama into Restoration and eighteenth-century drama.

In *The Coxcomb* and *The Custom of the Country*, as Cervantean romance narratives are adapted for the Jacobean stage, concepts of sexual morality and of ideal masculine identity are transformed. Looking at Fletcherean, rather than Shakespearian, parallels might allow us to see that the side-lining of some forms of masculinity, a process that could more clearly be associated with the later seventeenth and early eighteenth century, is already there in some aspects of Fletcherean comedy and tragicomedy. But in order to assess this, I will also briefly trace the narrative forward into the eighteenth century. As with *Cardenio, The Custom of the Country* was adapted for the early-eighteenth-century stage; Colley Cibber's *Love Makes a Man* (1700) and Charles Johnson's *The Country Lasses* (1715) make some use of Fletcher and Massinger's play. In tracing the way in which relationships between men, and forms of ideal masculinity, alter through this textual history—from Cervantean romance to Fletcherean comedy to eighteenth-century adaptation—further light will be shone on what was at stake when eighteenth-century adaptors confronted outmoded ways of being a man.

Fletcher and Beaumont's *The Coxcomb* has, as a potential source, the "History of the Curious Impertinent" from *Don Quixote*. B. W. Ife has argued that a potential source for this embedded *novela* from *Don Quixote* can be found in Herodotus' story of Gyges and Candaules in the *Histories*. He indicates that Cervantes' motivations in adapting Herodotus for the "Curious Impertinent" are, in part, to increase the emphasis on the potentially homoerotic content of the narrative of an ideal male friendship that is tested by the presence of a wife.[4] The two friends Anselmo and Lothario are at the start of the "History," described as different but complementary, engaged in "reciprocall amity":

> True it is that Anselmo was somewhat more inclined to amorous dalliance then Lothario, who was altogether addicted to hunting. But when occasion exacted it, Anselmo would omit his owne pleasures to satisfie his friends, and Lothario likewise his, to please Anselmo. And by this meanes both their wils were so correspondent, as no clocke could be better ordred then were their desires.[5]

In some Fletcher plays (*The Coxcomb, The Elder Brother, The Custom of the Country*), these kinds of programmatic difference between otherwise comparable young men (brothers or friends)—where one is a hunter and one is a lover, or one is a courtier and the other is a scholar, or one is chaste and one is "lusty"—are played off against each other in order to provide a platform for an examination of different kinds of masculine identity. Here, in the Cervantes story, the differences between Anselmo and Lothario are used as a pretext for insisting that their "wils" are nevertheless "correspondent" and their desires "ordred" together. As Ife points out, in the opening stages of this story "their equivalence is stressed" (677). More than this, however, the description invites a reading of their friendship as marked by the erotic. Although it is easy to see how Anselmo might capitulate to his friend's wish to go hunting for the day, it is less clear how Lothario would help Anselmo with his "amorous dalliance." However, in the opening scenes of Fletcher and Beaumont's *The Coxcomb*, the relationship between the equivalent characters, Mercury and Antonio, could not be presented more differently. Antonio is embarrassingly keen on Mercury, supposing him to be his partner in a classicized, heroic friendship. But the feeling is not reciprocated. Mercury, in the opening scene of the play, is very eager to drop Antonio as a travelling companion. He asks for "leave/ To take mine owne ways now" (I.i.41–2). Antonio won't hear of it and draws a picture, albeit highly satirical, of the kind of male companionship that can be seen in the Cervantes original:

> Must we that have so long time, beene as one,
> Seene Cityes, Countryes, Kingdomes, and their wonders,
> Beene bedfellows, and in our various journey
> Mixt all our observations, part (as if
> We were two Carriers at two severall ways,
> And as the foreshore guides, cry God be with you)
> Without or complement, or ceremony? (45–51)

Antonio betrays class-related anxieties attached to his supposed friendship with Mercury (are these "bedfellows" nothing but "carriers"?); his attachment to Mercury is mocked both in his own idiotically loquacious speeches and in Mercury's sardonic asides to the audience that punctuate their dialogue: "'Tis this tires me" (56), "Is there no way to scape this Inundation?" (74), and finally:

> Patience helpe me,
> And heaven grant his folly be not catching:
> If it be, the townes undone; I now would give
> A reasonable sum of gold to any sherriff,
> That would lay an execution on me,
> And free me from his company; while he was abroad,
> His want of witt and language kept him dumbe:
> But *Balaam's* Asse will speak now without spurring. (79–86)[6]

The homoerotically charged relationship of "The Curious Impertinent" is, in *The Coxcomb*, ridiculed in a parody of idealized love between male friends. As the narrative of the play progresses, the sense of tragic pathos that shadows the final pages of its source, where Anselmo dies of a broken heart, is entirely absent. It is translated into the somewhat awkward farce of the play's narrative in which Antonio tries to make his devotion to his friend an example of famous self-sacrificing love by engineering a situation in which his wife sleeps with his friend. Within *Don Quixote*, the Curate, who has been reading the story, closes by commenting on it. He says that it might be "prettie" but that it is hardly believable. He might have believed it, he says, if it had featured a man who tested the virtue of his *mistress* by letting his friend seduce her but, "being betweene man and *wife*, it containes somewhat that is impossible and unlikely" (*DQ* 4.8.398–9; my italics). The Curate's interpretation belies the power of the embedded story that he has just read, but it is precisely this skepticism that is picked up on in the Fletcher and Beaumont play; their character of Antonio is revealed as almost a Quixote-like fantasist, attaching himself to aristocratic ideals of filial love between men that are not sustainable in the bourgeois world of "man and wife." Here, at least, as Cervantean romance is adapted to the demands of Beaumont-and-Fletcherean comedy, it is not just that the ideals of male friendship are sidelined in favor of other kinds of emotional ties but that the homoerotically homosocial is understood as potentially ridiculous.[7] It is, I think, important to note that Hoy assigns the First Act of *The Coxcomb*, in which the discourse of ideal male friendship is satirized, to the middle-class Fletcher rather than the aristocratic Beaumont.[8]

The Custom of the Country offers a slightly different Fletcherean adaptation of Cervantean romance. As T. L. Darby has demonstrated, while the main protagonists of the play, Arnoldo and Zenocia, are based on Ladislao and Transila from *Persiles and Sigismunda*, they are also presented as embodiments of the virtue of chastity that, in Cervantes, characterizes the eponymous main protagonists.[9] In addition, and as a means to underline his role as embodiment of chaste virtue, Arnoldo is provided with a brother in *The Custom of the Country*: Rutillio. Characteristically for a Fletcher play, Rutillio represents the exact opposite values to his brotherly counterpart.[10] Where Arnoldo is chaste and loyal, Rutillio is "lusty" and fickle. Rutillio begins the play, as his name suggests, with a powerful sexual appetite. Arnoldo plans to marry, and Rutillio responds:

> …to marry is as damn'd a custome
> As any in the world; for looke you brother,
> Woo'd any man, stand plucking for the Ace of Harts,
> With one packe of cards all dayes on's life? (I.i.22–5)

Arnoldo, however, is anxious over a different "damned Custome": that of *droit de seigneur*, a custom which means that his fiancée, Zenocia, will be obliged to sleep with Count Clodio, the local governor. On first hearing about this, Rutillio heartily approves:

> How might a man achieve that place? a rare custome!
> An admirable rare custome: and none excepted? (I.i.33–4)

Arnoldo complains that this sentiment lacks a certain amount of brotherly support, and Rutillio comes round to an equivocal promise that he will help Zenocia and his brother resist the demands of the imperious aristocrat. It is only in the subsequent narrative, however, that Rutillio fully reforms. The two brothers escape to Lisbon where, separated, Rutillio finds himself put to work as a male prostitute, attending the pleasures of the aristocratic women of Lisbon, in the male stews. Cured of his sexual appetite by the end of the play, he is set to marry Guiomar the widow:

> ...though I once despair'd of women, now,
> I finde they relish much of Scorpions,
> For both have stings, and both can hurt, and cure too; (V.v.201–3)

He may not end the play as the model of chaste virtue, the values of which are the chief moral lesson of the play and which are embodied by both his brother, Arnoldo, and by his future sister-in-law, Zenocia, but he is brought round to an acknowledgment of the illegitimacy of his earlier attitudes to women, sex, family, and marriage.

The Custom of the Country offers a number of different versions of masculinity, besides Arnoldo and Rutillio as the two ends of a spectrum of chastity. Count Clodio embodies an aristocratic rapaciousness, making imperious sexual demands on his subjects and Duarte, the widow Guiomar's son, described in the list of "Persons" as "a Gentleman well qualified but vain glorious" is hopelessly proud and too quick to draw his sword. Rutillio, Clodio, and Duarte all have to reform by the end of the play through their recognition of the virtues of Arnoldo and his beloved, Zenocia. As an adaptation from Cervantes' *Persiles and Sigismunda*, however, one thing that is particularly striking is a marked shift of attitude shown toward male virtue and male sexuality. As Fletcher and Massinger manage the convoluted romance narrative into a Jacobean tragicomedy, they also recodify concepts of ideal masculinity. While the protection of chastity is important in the Cervantes text, it is very much more clearly the dominant focus of the play, notwithstanding some very bawdy scenes. In the play, masculine virtue is secured with reference to remaining true to one woman and not attempting to seduce the wives of others. But, in Cervantes, masculine virtue is more often framed by recognition of male beauty, a beauty primarily recognized by other men.

The equivalent character to Arnoldo in the story from *Persiles and Sigismunda* is Ladislao, but Arnoldo is also supposed, in the play, to carry the burden of ideal male behavior. The equivalent for this in the Cervantes text is Persiles himself, in disguise as Periander at the start of the book. A description of Periander/Persiles opens the first chapter of the first book of Cervantes' text. He is in the deep dungeons of Corcicurbo, being drawn up by a rope in preparation for his execution:

> foure Barbarians drew up a young man tied by the same [a rope] under his
> armes, who shewed to be about nineteene or twenty yeares of age, apparelled in

course cloth like a mariner, but more beautifull then could be well expressed. The first act of these Savages, was to looke upon the manacles and cords which he had on his hands; and then shaking his haire (that covered his head like small rings of spun gold) they made cleane his face, which likewise was full of dust: whereupon they discovered such an admirable beauty, that it mollified the hearts even of the executioners themselves that led him unto death.[11]

His physical beauty persuades the barbarians not to execute him but to let him loose on a raft from which he is picked up by a ship, captained by Arnaldo, the heir to the king of Denmark. The sailors find Periander to be "no lesse faire then disfigured" (4) from his ordeal and this promotes their pity. Their admiring gazes are reciprocated by Periander who, we are told, looked "upon the Captaine whose courtesie and rich attire drew his sight that way" (4). The equivalent to the ideally chaste Zenocia in Cervantes is Sigismunda, disguised at the start of the book as Periander's sister, Auristela. As the story progresses, it turns out that both Periander and Arnaldo are rivals for her affections.[12] Periander claims to be her brother and a plan is hatched to recover her from the barbarians who have captured her, and who may be planning to rape her. It involves dressing Periander in women's clothes and, again, this produces an admiration of his beauty from the captain of the ship who, "if he had not thought this had been *Auristelas* brother, the consideration of his sexe had pearced his heart with a thousand prickes of jealousie" (11). The sense of this ambiguous sentence is not easy to grasp, chiefly because at the same time as ostensibly describing the possibility of jealousy on Arnaldo's part—that Auristela might also find him attractive—it is a jealousy promoted by Arnaldo's own attraction to Periander's physical beauty.

In these two plays from the Fletcher canon, both homoerotic homosociality and tyrannical rapaciousness are identified as in opposition to the "quiet harbour" (V.v.231) of marriage. The threat of aggressive patriarchal and aristocratic sexual possessiveness is given more weight by identifying it with the more plausible figure of Count Clodio. At the same time and unlike Cervantes, the noble virtue of those men placed in opposition to the predatory incursions of patriarchal aggression is not associated with the homoerotically marked discourse of idealized male friendship. *The Coxcomb* turns to farce instead of the pathos of a betrayed friendship.

This, I think, has consequences for how we think about the collaborative text of Fletcher and Shakespeare's *Cardenio*. One fairly simple question to ask is whether, as in a number of Shakespeare plays, the values of male friendship would be a source of intense emotional power, albeit often tinged with melancholic regret, or whether, as in (collaborative) Fletcherean adaptations of romance, these values would be no longer afforded the same power but may even be seen as one aspect of a discredited sex-gender system, associated with other forms of oppression. Of course, given that *Cardenio* would have been a collaborative text, and that *Double Falsehood* is, as are all dramatic texts, a kind of palimpsest containing the traces of multiple hands, these different and potentially opposing attitudes toward male friendship could well occupy the same script or performance, in dialogue with each other.

Theatrical adaptations and the palimpsestic texts of early modern drama are privileged locations in which to examine equally palimpsestic formations of gender codes; the writers and performers have, in some way, to confront, adapt, and account for older ideas. Fletcher has to look across to his collaborators, including the older Shakespeare, adopting, adapting, and altering what he finds in a process that involves both identification and rejection. This process occurs both in specific acts of collaboration and across the multiple relationships through the extended life cycles of these plays. The eighteenth-century adaptations of *The Custom of the Country* make some interesting interventions into their inherited story. Cibber's *Love Makes a Man* (1700) substitutes the initial *droit de seigneur* plot of the Fletcher and Massinger play with the initial plot of another Fletcher play, *The Elder Brother*. In this play, and in Cibber's rewriting of it as a prologue to his version of *The Custom of the Country*, the two brothers are characterized as opposites: one is a scholar, addicted to his books, and the other is associated with the court. In Cibber's hands, this latter becomes an archetypal fop, addicted to pleasure, to material goods, and to clothing. Unlike Fletcher's Eustace, the courtier-brother from *The Elder Brother*, Cibber's Clodio has explicitly been visiting the French court where, he tells us, it is the fashion for men to kiss each other: "I love to kiss a Man, in *Paris*, we kiss nothing else."[13] In borrowing Clodio as the name for its fop from Fletcher's rapacious tyrant in *The Custom of the Country*, the eighteenth-century play downgrades the threat posed by "residual pederasty," turning him into the object of amused, but contemptuous ridicule.

Despite its subtitle, *The Custom of the Manor*, Johnson's *Country Lasses* borrows much less from *The Custom of the Country*. Here the threatening impetus behind the narrative—the sexual demands made by a patriarch that he has a right to sleep with any new bride over whom he has power—is translated into a practical joke that is played at the expense of gullible townspeople who stumble into the world of Freehold, a staunchly anti-court landowner. This reduction of the threat posed by certain forms of male sexuality is of a piece with similar processes at work in *Love Makes a Man*. Johnson's play, though, does contain some intriguing moments, particularly around the character of Sir John English. Sir John is supposed to represent the fading values of "good old English Hospitality."[14] However, he is also characterized, throughout the play, by a passionate attraction to young aristocratic men. As Freehold says: "He is particularly Civil to a Page; he has a wonderful Veneration for a Squire o'the Body; a Knight gives him great Joy, and he is Ravish'd with a Lord" (15). The cross-temporal identifications and disavowals of different forms of masculine behavior are, here, particularly difficult to untangle. But that is, of course, the point. In these palimpsestic performances, such disentanglement may be impossible, as older forms get rewritten and reused. What appears to be happening, in this case, is that Freehold is attempting to satirize his neighbor's predilection for young courtiers as being old-fashioned but that the play, itself, treats Sir John with a degree of nostalgic affection.

These complex textual exchanges and adaptations raise, however, two sets of questions: one local and the other more general. The local concern is, I hope, fairly clear. In *Double Falsehood*, Henriquez is associated both with a vicious assumption of aristocratic privilege in his rape of Violante and is also accused of having a sexual interest in his "page"—actually, Violante in cross-dressed disguise, but described as "a little boy" (*DF* 5.2.114). What is missing is any substantial sense that the friendship between the two rivals for Leonora's hand (Julio and Henriquez) is to be valued. A question remains then: Would an original *Cardenio* play have done the same? Would it have been more Fletcher-like in its distrust of affective ties between men or more Shakespeare-like in its continuing valuation of such ties? Would it have identified erotic chaos with patriarchal tyrant in the manner of a Fletcher play, or with the metamorphic (Petrarchan and Ovidian) incursions of desire itself, in the manner of Shakespeare and, to an extent, of Cervantes? Or, perhaps more interestingly, would it have played out this conflict in the narrative upon which Fletcher and Shakespeare collaborated: the younger Fletcher rejecting the advances of the older Shakespeare and rewriting his two male companions, not as potential idealized friends, but as inevitable rivals? Jeffrey Masten writes that the 1634 Quarto of *The Two Noble Kinsmen* retrospectively establishes "a correspondence between its two noble kinsmen and the two gentle playwrights" by bracketing their names with the word "Gent." on the title page. But, as he goes on to argue, the conjunction of collaborative gentlemanly friendship in the plot of the play and on the title page should not be seen in a "straightforward relation of cause and effect."[15] Inserting the story of *Cardenio* into this relation would interrupt this conjunction as the two male characters, like Shakespeare and Fletcher themselves, would have had different class identifications. Their several couplings (either Cardenio and his master, or Fletcher and his playwright forerunner) through reference to the textualized ideal of male *philia*, were always going to make for more contentious relationships than Arcite and Palamon's friendship at the start of *The Two Noble Kinsmen*, relationships that might contain as much rejection as they did identification.

The commonly accepted understanding of who wrote what in the seventeenth-century play that lies behind *Double Falsehood* is that Shakespeare dominates the first half and Fletcher the second. And this is the framework within which Gary Taylor has worked in order to produce his reconstruction of *Cardenio*. In the 2012 Indianapolis performance of the Taylor script, directed by Terri Bourus, this resulted in a clear distinction between the earlier part of the play in which the actors playing Cardenio and Don Fernando were demonstrative in their physical affection (figure 8.1) and the concluding scenes of the play in which they were not. This marked a difference from an earlier production of the play at Victoria University, Wellington (New Zealand), in 2009, in which the relationship between the two ostensible male leads was not rendered in any particularly emphatic way. Between

Figure 8.1 Intimate "friends": Cardenio (Thomas Cardwell, left) and Fernando (Tyrone van Tatenhove, right) together at court (*THOC* 2.1), photograph by Emily Schwank.

the earlier performance and the more recent one, Taylor had substantially altered the script in order to include a more properly Shakespearian emphasis on the homoerotic potential of male friendship in the early scenes, dropping this emphasis when the play becomes more Fletcherean in its closing sequences and when the narrative itself veers away from a distinctive concern with Cardenio and Don Fernando's friendship. In performance, this resulted in a certain awkwardness that was, nevertheless, poignant and helpful, particularly in Tyrone van Tatenhove's performance as Don Fernando. The air of affected and imperious lasciviousness that characterized his performance from the start looked increasingly out of place in the new worlds being created by the reconciliations at the end of the play; by the end, his archly exaggerated performance seemed already anachronistic.

Authorial distribution is understood quite differently in *The Two Noble Kinsmen*. In that play, Shakespeare appears responsible both for the early scenes of the play that set up the passionate friendship between the two men and for the final act in which the disastrous consequences of their rivalry are played out. Fletcher's contributions are in the middle of the play, where we get the story of their rivalry.[16] While, of course, it is not possible to cordon off one scene from another in quite this programmatic way in any act of collaboration, it does appear that these different distributions do correspond to different ways of writing and rewriting attitudes to the central male friendships of the two plays.

The wider questions are, of course, much more complex and extend well beyond a consideration of these texts. How do we think about the interplay between performed or textualized masculinities and histories of gender and sexuality? In the last few years, there have been some attempts to detach encounters with early modern texts from the Foucauldian frameworks within which histories of sexuality have been working for some time. In Queer Shakespeare studies, Madhavi Menon and Jonathan Goldberg have proposed what they call an "unhistoricism" that allows for cross-temporal kinds of identification, "open to the possibility of anachronism."[17] This would work in a way counter to Foucauldian genealogies prominent in new historicist accounts of early modern sexuality that, rather, work through an acknowledgment of discontinuity between sexual behaviors and identities across time.[18] Beyond Shakespeare studies, Carla Freccero has advocated an account of early modern sexualities that works against the pieties of this historicism, constructing queer conjunctions across period divisions through what she calls a "prolepsis of queer" that interrupts conventional conceptions of the early modern.[19] Concerns with anachronism and the possibilities of identification across period are what motivate these debates. In what I have called the palimpsestic processes of theatrical adaptation and collaboration, these concerns can be seen as already at work in the identifications and rejections that inform glances both across period and between different kinds of collaborator. John Fletcher and Francis Beaumont may be posthumously apotheosized in the 1647 Folio as "Gentlemen," renamed "FRANCIS-FLETCHER, or JOHN-BEAUMONT," and celebrated as "one Poet in a paire of friends"[20] but this is already a kind of romantic nostalgia. The two writers came from very different backgrounds and their friendship will have cut across class boundaries, even as they set up together in their house on Bankside. As Finkelpearl writes, so different were they, "that friendship, much less harmonious collaboration, might well have been impossible."[21] Fletcher's collaborations seem often to be romanticized as forms of idealized male friendship, including of course the supposed love of Massinger for Fletcher that continued into the tomb. As I quoted earlier, Masten has also identified this idealization occurring in the contiguities between the frontispiece of *The Two Noble Kinsmen* and the workings out of the play's narrative with its investment in the virtues of homoerotic *philia*. But some of Fletcher's own work resists this kind of valuation and the complex relationship between Shakespeare as a non-University educated senior partner to Fletcher, the University-educated apprentice, undercuts the idealization of them as a pair of gentlemen. It is, perhaps, in the absent text of *Cardenio* that this complex process of identification and rejection took place. That we only have the belated testimony of *Double Falsehood*, which enacts its own cross-temporal processes of adaptation, identification, love, and rejection, is part of theater's testimony to the palimpsestic text of early modern male sexuality. My title, "Shall I Never See a Lusty Man Againe?" (III.iii.1) comes from *The Custom of the Country* and from the wonderfully demanding Sulpitia, mistress of the male stews, who puts the very lusty Rutillio to work as a male prostitute. The question she asks, "…never…againe" echoes these processes of rejection and identification with forms of male identity, sexuality, and behavior that are only supposedly outmoded but which can always be reactivated in new circumstances.

NOTES

1. "The Friend in *Cardenio, Double Falsehood*, and *Don Quixote*," in *Quest*, 239–55. The essay was written for a 2009 symposium.

2. Thomas King, *The Gendering of Men 1600–1750*, 2 vols (Madison: University of Wisconsin Press, 2004–2008), I: *The English Phallus* (2004), 6 and passim.

3. Jeffrey Masten, *Textual Intercourse: Collaboration, Authorship, and Sexualities in Renaissance Drama* (Cambridge: Cambridge University Press, 1997), 9.

4. B. W. Ife, "Cervantes, Herodotus, and the Eternal Triangle: Sources of *El Curioso Impertinente*," *Bulleting of Hispanic Studies* 82 (2005): 671–81.

5. *DQ*, 343.

6. I don't think that any precise allegorical relation is intended by the reference here to the story of Balaam and the Ass, but the association of Antonio with both an ass and with Balaam, the betrayer of Israel, underlines the witty Mercury's contempt for the coxcomb, Antonio.

7. There is a related disavowal of the emotive force of passionate love between men in Fletcher's play *The Humorous Lieutenant*. In that play, the lieutenant of the title, as the result of mistakenly taking a potion, falls in love with his king, wishing that he "had been a wench of fifteene for" him (V.ii.21). This is part of a process of gulling the lieutenant and, during these scenes, the doting of one man on another is treated as effeminizing, and as a topic for ridicule. For an argument that reads the complex position of the lieutenant in this play as a subtle critique of Jacobean military and gender politics, see Vimala Pasupathi, "The King's Privates: Sex and the Soldier's Place in John Fletcher's *The Humorous Lieutenant*," *Research Opportunities in Medieval and Renaissance Drama* 47 (2008): 25–50.

8. Cyrus Hoy, "The Shares of Fletcher and His Collaborators in the Beaumont and Fletcher Canon (III)," *Studies in Bibliography* 11 (1957). I will discuss the relevance of remarking on their class disparity below.

9. T. L. Darby, "Resistance to Rape in *Persiles y Sigismunda* and *The Custom of the Country*," *The Modern Language Review* 90.2 (1995): 273–84. Darby provides a very helpful table of correspondences between the narratives and characters of the two texts, illustrating the complexity of Fletcher and Massinger's borrowing and adaptation.

10. It is notable that, according to Cyrus Hoy's assignment of authorship in *The Custom of the Country*, Fletcher is given the whole of the opening act, the act in which the sharp distinctions between the male protagonists are established. Cyrus Hoy, "The Shares of Fletcher and His Collaborators in the Beaumont and Fletcher Canon (II)," *Studies in Bibliography* 9 (1957): 147.

11. Miguel de Cervantes, *The Travels of Persiles and Sigismunda: A Northern History* (London, 1619), 2. Subsequent references are to this anonymous translation.

12. As with Arnoldo, the character of Zenocia is a conflation of one person's narrative (Transila) and the ideals embodied by another (Sigismunda/Auristela).

13. Colley Cibber, *Love Makes a Man, or The Fop's Fortune* (London, 1701), 4.

14. Charles Johnson, *The Country Lasses, or The Custom of the Manor* (London, 1715), 25.

15. Jeffrey Masten, *Textual Intercourse: Collaboration, Authorship, and Sexualities in Renaissance Drama* (Cambridge: Cambridge University Press, 1997), 58.

16. See Jonathan Hope, *The Authorship of Shakespeare's Plays: A Socio-Linguistic Study* (Cambridge: Cambridge University Press, 1994), 83–91.

17. Jonathan Goldberg and Madhavi Menon, "Queering History," *PMLA* 120.5 (October 2005): 1616.

18. See Jonathan Goldberg, *Sodometries: Renaissance Texts, Modern Sexualities* (Stanford: Stanford University Press, 1992), Jeffrey Masten, *Textual Intercourse*, Valerie Traub, *The Renaissance of Lesbianism in Early Modern England* (Cambridge: Cambridge University Press, 2002), and David Halperin, *How to Do the History of Homosexuality* (Chicago: University of Chicago Press, 2002).

19. Carla Freccero, *Queer/Early/Modern* (Durham: Duke University Press, 2006).

20. Francis Beaumont and John Fletcher, *Comedies and Tragedies* (London, 1647), sig. b1r; sig. d1v.

21. Philip J. Finkelpearl, *Court and Country Politics in the Plays of Beaumont and Fletcher* (Princeton: Princeton University Press, 1990), 8.

9

SHAKESPEARE, THEOBALD, AND THE PROSE PROBLEM IN *DOUBLE FALSEHOOD*

John V. Nance

Most critics agree that there's not much uncontaminated Shakespearian verse in *Double Falsehood*. Some then leap to the conclusion that Shakespeare had nothing to do with the play. This line of reasoning assumes that dramatic prose is unimportant, or that Shakespeare's prose is indistinguishable from anyone else's. The following analysis seeks to explore these unsubstantiated generalizations by analyzing the unique characteristics of the prose in 1.2.179–224 of *Double Falsehood*. This essay is admittedly partial (36 lines, 334 words), but it provides new evidence to challenge Tiffany Stern's 2011 claim that *Double Falsehood* is a forgery. An analysis of the distinctive dramatic function and vocabulary of these prose lines strongly suggests the presence of Shakespeare more than any other author. In addition, this study confronts Stern's adamant disavowal of stylometric evidence in *Double Falsehood* by illuminating the methods and goals of stylometry as a reliable tool to record evidence of the play's authorship.

An increasing sensitivity to *Double Falsehood*'s textual line of descent has developed many convincing arguments for the play's early-seventeenth-century origins. Extensive stylistic analysis of the verse—expertly discussed in *The Quest for Cardenio* by Gary Taylor, MacDonald P. Jackson, and Richard Proudfoot—supports the opinion that elements of Shakespeare's style and Fletcher's are present in Theobald's eighteenth-century adaptation. However, as Jackson himself admits, focusing on the verse "we may have missed more persuasive evidence from the prose."[1] Of a total of 314 prose lines (2,592 words) in *Double Falsehood*—17 percent of the play—only 19 lines (167 words; 6.4 percent of the prose) have been subjected to comprehensive analysis.[2]

Before I present the results of my own stylometric investigations, it is first necessary to explore authorial attitudes about prose in the canons of *Double Falsehood*'s likeliest originators: John Fletcher, William Shakespeare, and Lewis Theobald. Writing alone in 1608–1618, Fletcher used prose sparingly. The only prose in his eight solo dramatic works in that period is a nine-line

letter split up into four and five-line passages in 2.2 of *Bonduca* and brief
exchanges in 1.3 of *The Tamer Tamed* totaling 58 lines.[3] So in a large sample
size of 18,390 lines, there are only 67 lines of prose (0.3 percent). None of
these prose speeches extend for more than 7 lines. *The Chances* uses a prose
story from Cervantes' *Novelas* as source material, but Fletcher's play contains
no prose. By contrast, Shakespeare, writing alone in 1607–1613, put 2,375
lines of prose in only five plays.[4] The average distribution per play is roughly
20 percent prose, much of it in lengthy passages of more than seven lines.
These figures demonstrate that Shakespeare was more likely than Fletcher to
be writing dramatic prose—especially long, extended prose speeches—just
before and after *Cardenio* was written.

The overwhelming majority of the prose in Fletcher's dramatic canon
comes from coauthored plays. Therefore, if Fletcher did have a hand in writing
Cardenio, he was likely working with a collaborator. The only seventeenth-
century attribution of the play (Moseley's in 1653) identified it as collaborative, and so have recent attribution studies. Tabulating shares of prose
from the collaborative works in the Fletcher canon written in 1608–1618,
I have calculated that Fletcher is responsible for 1,381 of the 4,628 prose lines
(30 percent). When Fletcher was working with a collaborator prone to prose
(like Beaumont, Field, or Shakespeare), he wrote more prose himself. Philip
Massinger, his major collaborator, never wrote prose in his own plays except
for conventional letters, proclamations, and satirized jargon.[5] Massinger may
have later revised or adapted Beaumont and Fletcher's early play *The Coxcomb*,
which contains many prose speeches, but "Hoy finds nothing that points to
the distinctive work of Massinger."[6] Malone suggested Massinger as the original sole author of the manuscript behind *Double Falsehood*, but the presence of
sustained prose in the text makes Massinger an unlikely candidate.[7] The sheer
quantity of prose in *Double Falsehood* suggests that it cannot have been a play
written solely by John Fletcher. Only two known Fletcher collaborators wrote
substantial dramatic prose for the King's Men around 1612–1613: Beaumont
and Shakespeare. Moreover, both Beaumont and Shakespeare have—for reasons entirely independent of their prose—been suggested as potential coau-
thors of the lost *Cardenio*. In order to provide the best possible identification
of Fletcher's probable seventeenth-century collaborator, we must first address
Lewis Theobald and his complex approaches to dramatic prose as both an
adapter and dramatist.

To accept for a moment that Theobald did not forge *Double Falsehood*
and instead truly "Revised and Adapted" a play "Written Originally by
W. Shakespeare," understanding his treatment of prose when adapting early
modern drama for Georgian audiences is essential.[8] *Richard II* has no prose to
revise or adapt, but Webster's *The Duchess of Malfi* does. For *The Fatal Secret*,
Theobald thoroughly eviscerated all 331 lines of Webster's prose, adding only
an innocuous five-line letter in 5.1. David Carnegie points out that Theobald
attempted to "regularize what he called the 'strong and impetuous Genius'
of Webster'" and the final product suggests that prose was not, for Theobald,
part of that "Genius."[9] The presence of significant prose in *Double Falsehood*

seems to conflict with Theobald's treatment of Webster's tragedy. But there are signs of erasure in *Double Falsehood* that agree with Theobald's policies of expurgation. Taylor and Nance show that the eight prose lines spoken by Fabian and Lopez in 2.1 are likely residual fragments of an excised subplot removed by Theobald to protect the integrity of the main action and "to prevent it from looking like 'a direct competitor with an established low-comedy musical,' Thomas D'Urfey's *Comical History of Don Quixote*."[10] These prose lines also contain an abundance of Shakespearian parallels weighted toward the late plays.[11] While we will never know the full extent of Fabian's and Lopez's role in the original play, their sole appearance in 2.1 while speaking low, creatural prose may be suggestive of additional prose passages not retained for the Georgian stage. Vickers finds prose to be "the typical medium for the subplot," and the eighteenth-century stage often shunned Shakespeare's subplots because "they devoted considerable space to characters of a lower class than the principles."[12] The abbreviated Fabian and Lopez of 2.1 replicate patterns of Shakespearian subplots—low characters speaking low prose—and their subsequent evacuation from the narrative is in line with the Georgian imperative to diminish early modern subplots. In his analysis of the prose exchanges in 1.2.1–62 of *Double Falsehood*—additional prose speeches that strongly suggest the presence of Shakespeare—Jackson notes "we would expect him [Theobald] to have been much more concerned to impose his own bland eighteenth-century verse upon Shakespeare's poetic intricacies than to tinker with Shakespeare's relatively straightforward prose."[13] This is not to say that Theobald is completely absent in *Double Falsehood's* prose, but instead that his interventions are *less likely* to be found in the prose than in the verse.[14] When adapting seventeenth-century texts, Theobald is more likely to reduce the role of prose or eject it completely. The surviving prose lines in *Double Falsehood* suggest an appreciation of Shakespeare's comic prose not conferred on Webster's tragic prose. When regularizing Shakespeare's "genius," Theobald retained some—but certainly not all—of the prose present in *Double Falsehood's* antecedent.

As a dramatist, Theobald used dramatic prose only three times, and only when working with classical sources. *The Clouds* and *Plutus* (published together in 1715) are prose translations of Aristophanes that were never performed.[15] Since translation is a different category than original dramatic prose, the 181 prose lines of Theobald's *Orestes* (1731), his own play based on the classical myth, offer more convincing evidence of his style. These lines are also an invaluable specimen of Theobald emulating Shakespeare. Jones recounts that in a letter to Warburton, Theobald admits to "imitating Shakespeare in the play, especially *Macbeth* and *Lear*," and Sutherland notes that "the most interesting signs of Shakespearian influence are to be found in the two comic scenes of the shipwrecked sailors."[16] Those scenes contain the entirety of *Orestes's* dramatic prose.

Theobald's dramatic prose differs from Shakespeare's and from the prose at the end of 1.2 in *Double Falsehood* more specifically. The prose in *Orestes* accounts for only about 8 percent of the play's 2,166 lines. This is clearly indicative of Theobald's inability to sustain early modern syntax and it speaks to his obvious discomfort with dramatic prose more generally. Indeed, Theobald is so inexperienced in early modern prose imitation that he recycles elements of the sailors' trifling conversations within the two scenes (1.4, 3.3): "Recovery of our Ship," "your Native Country," "Casks of Wine, floating to the Shore," in 1.4 becomes "refitting our Vessels," "One Country is as good as another," "would I were well supply'd with Drink," "The Sea will be damnable drunk with our Wine" in 3.3.[17] Akin to the low-prose of shipwrecked Stephano and Trinculo in 2.2 and 3.2 of *The Tempest*, the sailors' conversations are restricted to relaxed concerns over their shipwreck, finding and drinking wine and new nationhood.[18] Nothing is developed or resolved between the sailors, and after 3.3, we never hear from them again.

The dramatic context of Theobald's prose accentuates its triviality. Isolated in two scenes that have nothing to do with the rest of the play and spoken by useless characters that have no interaction with the major roles, Theobald's prose is marooned from the plot. In the early eighteenth century, to mix genres was a violation of decorum (or regularity), one of the rules of neoclassical unity that the Georgian stage considered a veritable theatrical obligation.[19] The normative contextual envelope for prose shifted in accordance with an increasingly strict trend toward genre standardization. Simply put, prose was normally and normatively (though not invariably) reserved for comedy, verse for tragedy. Theobald takes this division quite literally in *Orestes*. The mariners' "comic" prose scenes are intended to alleviate the tragic mood and by necessity they exist in a seemingly alternate universe. Theobald's prose scenes could be completely removed and nothing in the play would change. Shakespeare's prose is never as deliberately quarantined as it is in *Orestes*. Shakespeare often has central characters speaking prose, and prose lines assigned to auxiliary roles are usually embroiled in actions that mirror or intersect with the main plot. In fact, Shakespeare's fluidity with verse/prose transitions is, according to Brian Vickers, one of the defining elements of his dramatic style.[20] *Double Falsehood* has major characters speaking prose, often in scenes mixed with verse speeches.[21]

In a play that he admitted was a Shakespearian imitation, Theobald uses little prose, carelessly repeats it, isolates it completely from the essential dramatic action, and does nothing to prove that he can develop narrative momentum while emulating an early modern style. But what about the lexical units Theobald employs in his imitation? Is he capable of patching together a convincing pastiche of Shakespearian language outside of his larger, structural failures? I have checked all 181 lines of Theobald's prose from *Orestes* in *Early English Books Online* and *Literature Online* for parallels in English Drama from 1576 to 1642.[22] For Theobald parallels, I have supplemented *Literature Online* with *Eighteenth Century Collections Online, Editions and Adaptations of Shakespeare*, and an expanded database containing all of his available works.[23] The databases identify only one unique parallel from Shakespeare: "rest her soul" from *Hamlet* (the play that Theobald knew best, since it was the chief topic of his *Shakespeare Restored*). By contrast, the prose in *Orestes* contains seven unique parallels for Theobald (fourteen links) and forty-six unique parallels from the work of thirty-two other playwrights writing from 1576 to 1642. Of these thirty-two playwrights, eight have more unique parallels than Shakespeare: Fletcher (four with four links), Chapman (three with three links), Killigrew (three with three links), Dekker (two with two links), Jonson (two with two links), Middleton (two with two links), Heywood (two with two links), and Rutter (two with two links).[24] Theobald has more unique parallels than any other playwright on this list and as many links as the top four combined. When Theobald says or believes that he is imitating Shakespeare, in terms of vocabulary he uses unique Shakespearian idioms only 2 percent (1 of 47) of the time. He is also echoing himself: 13 percent (7 of 53) of the unique parallels are found elsewhere in Theobald's canon. The statistics suggest that the majority of Theobald's linguistic profile in 1.4 and 3.3 of *Orestes* comes from the early modern period more generally (85 percent of the unique parallels), not Shakespeare in particular. They also demonstrate that Theobald uses seven times more unique parallels from his own canon than from Shakespeare's when writing original dramatic prose.

Now that we have a sense of Shakespeare's, Fletcher's, and Theobald's prose, we can analyze the prose lines from 1.2 (179–224) of *Double Falsehood*. I quote them here, omitting the intervening verse passages by Julio:

> DON BERNARD What, Julio, in publick? This Wooeing is too
> urgent. Is your Father yet mov'd in the Suit who must   180
> be the prime Unfolder of this Business?
>   *
>
> DON BERNARD Chase! Let Chase alone. No Matter for That.   185
> You may halt after her, whom you profess to pursue, and
> catch her too; Marry, not unless your Father let you slip.
> Briefly, I desire you, (for she tells me my Instructions
> shall be both Eyes and Feet to her;) no farther to insist
> in your Requiring 'till, as I have formerly said, Camillo   190
> make known to Me, that his good liking goes along with
> Us, which but once breath'd, all is done; 'till when, the
> Business has no Life, and cannot find a Beginning.
>   *
>
> DON BERNARD His Father is as unsettled as he is wayward,   200
> in his Disposition. If I thought young Julio's Temper
> were not mended by the Mettal of his Mother, I should
> be something crazy in giving my Consent to this Match:
> And, to tell you true, if my Eyes might be the Directors
> to your Mind, I could in this Town look upon Twenty   205
> Men of more delicate Choice. I speak not This altogether
> to unbend your Affections to him: But the Meaning of
> what I say is, that you set such Price upon yourself to
> him, as many, and much his Betters, would buy you at;
> (and reckon those Virtues in you at the rate of their   210
> Scarcity;) to which if he come not up, you remain for a
> better Mart.

LEONORA My Obedience, Sir, is chain'd to your Advice.

DON BERNARD 'Tis well said, and wisely. I fear, your Lover
is a little Folly-tainted; which, shortly after it proves so,   215
you will repent.

LEONORA Sir, I confess I approve him of all the Men I
know; but that Approbation is nothing, 'till season'd by your Consent.

DON BERNARD We shall hear soon what his Father will do,   220
and so proceed accordingly. I have no great Heart
to the Business, neither will I with any Violence oppose it: But
leave it to that Power which rules in these Conjunctions,
and there's an End. Come; haste We homeward, Girl.

Vickers notes that Shakespeare's prose is usually an intentional deviation
from the norm of blank verse, often used to generate maximum dramatic
meaning through stylistic difference (6–7). Don Bernard's entry at 1.2
(179) is an abrupt theatrical and stylistic disruption of the earnest congress between Julio and Leonora in the verse lines from 1.2 (74–178). His
subsequent castigation of Julio in prose registers a shift in dramatic form
(verse to prose) and it depresses the dramatic mood (love to rebuke) in
accordance with Shakespearian conventions. These deliberate alternations
effectively match "style to character and mood" (Vickers 15), a distinctive
element of Shakespeare's prose. Here, a controlling and unreliable father
deflates the elevated temperament of young love. Don Bernard's prose is an
interruption, and this linguistic feature defines his characterization more
generally throughout the play. Beyond 1.2, Don Bernard continually interrupts Julio's courtship of Leonora by dismissing Camillo's suit in 2.3 (an
exchange between fathers also written in prose) and forcing Leonora to
marry Henriquez in order to improve his social standing (an interference
with his daughter's affections that leads to the play's more notable dramatic
achievements). The presence of two verse speeches by Julio (1.2.182–4 and
1.2.194–9) alongside Don Bernard's prose speeches in 1.2.179–224 suggests further connections to Shakespeare's use of verse/prose transitions.
Despite the energy of reproach in Don Bernard's prose, Julio continues to
speak in normative verse. His retention of verse uses prose "as a springboard,
from which verse attains greater power and resonance" (Vickers 11). This is
a typical Shakespearian maneuver and an attribute of *Double Falsehood* that
highlights a shrewd oscillation between the two forms. Julio resists lowering
his language to the level of Don Bernard's prose—effectively upstaging the
older man's discourse and accentuating the separation of his affections from
the directives of a flawed patriarch. When Theobald imitates Shakespeare,
he does not write prose lines for principal characters, and he does not permit
prose to contaminate the major events of the play. Theobald also proves incapable of mimicking the unique mannerisms of verse/prose transitions. In
fact, he doesn't even attempt it once. His 181 lines in *Orestes* are confined to
scenes written exclusively in prose. In contrast to Don Bernard's lines in 1.2

of *Double Falsehood*, Theobald's prose is radically separate and categorically isolated from the heightened realm of verse.

These prose passages in *Double Falsehood* also contain a sequence of images linked to hunting. "Urgent" (1.2.180) is moved to "chase" (1.2.185, 186), to "halt" (1.2.186), to "pursue" (1.2.186), to "catch" (1.2.187), to "slip" (1.2.187), to "feet" (1.2.189). Caroline Spurgeon indicates: "Next to the river, the most constant outdoor background in Shakespeare's mind is hunting of various kinds" and "by far the larger number of what may be grouped under his hunting and woodcraft similes are concerned with the habits and behavior of the deer and the eager skill of the questing hounds."[25] The concentrated cluster of these images effectively replicates the narrative of a hunt (from the spotting of prey to the chase and attempted capture) with an emphasis on coursing: "chase," "slip," "feet." The "hunt" functions here as a metaphor for courting, aligning Julio with the hound and Leonora with the game (deer, dear). In accordance with what Clemen considers to be a unique characteristic of Shakespeare's dramatic style, the imagery also references the main plot of the play: Julio chases Leonora, he fails to catch her and she slips away.[26] As a result, Don Bernard's linked imagery "points beyond the scene in which it stands to preceding or following acts," and it "lends enhanced expression to the feeling of the character concerned" (Clemen 3). Don Bernard's use of hunting imagery deepens his connection to Leonora's "slipping" by prefiguring his active role in ensuring Julio's failure in the chase.

To supplement these observations, I will turn now to the verbal features of the prose at the end of 1.2 of *Double Falsehood*. I have checked *EEBO* and *Literature Online* for parallels within the canons of Shakespeare and Fletcher.[27] For Theobald, I have used the same supplementary databases used to analyze the prose in *Orestes*. To address recent criticisms that previous stylometric attributions of *Double Falsehood* are unreliable because they have been based on a small portion of Theobald's works (Stern 2011, 586), this investigation uses a much larger sample size of Theobald as a control. It includes all of his currently available dramatic and nondramatic works and his editions of Shakespeare, and Beaumont and Fletcher. Increasing Theobald's sample balances the disparate size of the three canons ensuring the most comprehensive search possible. I list below all parallels found in one of the three canons. All parallels unique to one canon that do not appear elsewhere in dramatic texts of 1576 to 1642 are indicated with an asterisk:

> **of this business**] *MM, WT, Tem* (2 instances), *H8* (3 instances); 10 times elsewhere. This trigram appears once in 2.2 (a scene usually attributed to Fletcher, but Hoy considers it Shakespearian with Fletcherian interpolation) and twice in 2.4 (a scene attributed to Shakespeare). Shakespeare uses this phrase more often than any other playwright; six of only seventeen instances in drama from 1576 to 1642.
> ***halt after**] *AC*
> ***not unless your**] *Philaster* (2.1); 0 instances elsewhere. Hoy attributes 2.1 to Beaumont.

*Briefly, I desire] *Much Ado*

my instructions shall] *AYLI*: "my instruction shall," 3 times elsewhere.

*insist in your] Theobald: *Perfidious, Orestes*

I have formerly] Theobald: *Plato, Le Clerc*, Preface to *Works of Shakespeare*, n.4 to *2HVI*; 2 times elsewhere.

known to me] *MWW*; 11 times elsewhere.

that his good] *All's Well*; 2 times elsewhere.

cannot find a] Theobald: *Perfidious, Restored*; 9 times elsewhere.

mended by] *Scornful Lady* (1.1); 4 times elsewhere. Hoy assigns 1.1 to Beaumont.[28]

the mettal (/ mettle) of] "mettle": *KJ, H5, AYLI, TN;* 4 times elsewhere. *TN* ("the mettle of your sex") also has a male character speaking of a woman's "mettle."

*mettal (/mettle) of his] *MoV* ("a breed for barren metal of his friend"). Like *DF*, the context of this phrase in *MoV* associates "metal" with the womb ("breed," "barren"). Following Mahood, Jackson notes that the double punning of "mettle/metal" in *DF* likely has a Shakespearian origin.[29]

to this match] *Cym*; 10 times elsewhere.

twenty men] *RJ, AC*; 9 times elsewhere.

*unbend your] *Mac* (2.1)

that you set] *Rollo* (3.1.402); 9 times elsewhere. Jowett and Taylor believe this part of 3.1 was written by Field, and Hoy attributes it to Chapman.[30] Williams considers that the authorship of *Rollo* "is one of the most vexed of all such questions in the canon," but there is a consensus that Fletcher did not write 3.1.357–420.[31]

*would buy you] *TNK* (1.1). Shakespeare is the only playwright to use this phrase with the pronoun "you" functioning as a direct object. Jonson's *Sejanus* has "would buy, you said . . ." in an interrupted speech that makes "A Tribune place" the direct object in the following line as opposed to "you."

if he come not] *Dream*; 5 times elsewhere.

you remain] *Tem*; 12 times elsewhere.

by your consent] *Dream, MWW, TC*; 8 times elsewhere.

*father will do] *1H4*

*and so proceed accordingly] *AC*

In a small sample size of only thirty-six lines (334 words), there are seventeen parallels (seven unique) for Shakespeare with twenty-six links to his work and three parallels for Theobald (one unique) with eight links. The statistics alone confirm that prose scenes in *Orestes* and *Double Falsehood* are put together differently. In 20 percent of the quantity of prose in *Orestes*, there are 56 percent more Shakespearian parallels and seven times more unique parallels. Compared to the 113 miscellaneous parallels (forty-six unique) in *Orestes*, the *Double Falsehood* speeches contain only twenty-seven parallels (9 unique) in the works of other early modern playwrights, but not Shakespeare or Fletcher. The author of this passage uses Shakespearian idioms 39 percent of the time (17 of 44) and unique Shakespearian idioms 41 percent (7 of 17) of the time compared to only 10 percent (3 of 30) and 9 percent (1 of 11) respectively for Theobaldian idioms not used by Shakespeare. The only shared expression used in 1.4 and 3.3 of *Orestes* and the prose speeches in 1.2.179–224 of *Double Falsehood* is "have no great," a fragment that occurs thirty-five times in English drama from 1576 to 1642 and twice in Shakespeare (*Henry V, Othello*). If Theobald did forge *Double Falsehood*, his ability to convincingly imitate Shakespearian prose regressed substantially in the years following its first performance in 1727. *Orestes* (1731) postdates *Double Falsehood* by four years and it is demonstrably less Shakespearian than the prose at the end of 1.2. Furthermore, *Orestes* was written at the same time that Theobald was actively preparing his edition of Shakespeare (published in 1733). If Theobald was ever going to demonstrate proficiency in mimicking Shakespeare's prose, *Orestes* should yield the best representative example. Instead, the prose in 1.2 of *Double Falsehood* emerges as the more decisive specimen in terms of its dramatic function and vocabulary.

However, imitation is different from forgery. Theobald admitted to imitating Shakespeare in *Orestes* and claimed Shakespearian provenance for *Double Falsehood*. Though it is unlikely that Theobald was adept enough to write sustained and meaningful dramatic prose in an early modern style, the only way to determine the best candidate for authorship of the prose in 1.2 is to offer a comparative analysis of the verbal data. In addition to the seventeen Shakespeare parallels (seven unique) with twenty-six links and three parallels for Theobald (one unique) with eight links, stylometric evidence for the above passages shows no parallels for Fletcher. The only parallels in the Fletcher canon—"not unless your," "mended by," "that you set"—are from scenes currently attributed to his collaborators. The statistics also demonstrate signs of interference: Theobald's "insist in your," "I have formerly," and "cannot find a" do not occur in works by Shakespeare or Fletcher, suggestive of interventions by Theobald or another post-Restoration reviser. Notably, all three of these parallels are clustered in the same speech.[32] Yet aside from these three ineffectual three-word strings that contribute nothing to the dramatic effect, the rest of the verbal features are indisputably early modern. The data endorses an overwhelming Shakespearian presence in these lines.

The chronology of Shakespeare parallels provides a final and resounding classification for the overall data. Of the seventeen parallels for Shakespeare, eight occur only in plays written after 1605: three three-word strings, four two-word strings, and one four-word string—with twelve links to his work. Four of these parallels are not found elsewhere in English drama from 1576 to 1642. This is 47 percent of the parallels overall and 57 percent of the unique parallels, taken from 25 percent of the Shakespeare canon. Seven of the twelve plays (58 percent) written by Shakespeare from 1605 to 1613 are represented in the above data. As a result, these prose lines participate in a continuity of verbal features used in the majority of Shakespeare's late-plays.

In response to Stern's assertions that "analysts searching for Shakespeare in *Double Falsehood* have found him" (583), I have also kept a record of all parallels not found in Shakespeare, Fletcher, or Theobald to emphasize the uniqueness of the findings:

this wooeing] Rowley, *All's Lost*; Shirley, *Changes*; Marston (and others), *Insatiate*; Lyly, *Mother*; Porter, *Abington*

in the suit] Carlell, *Arviragus*; Daniel, *Cleopatra*; Day, *Gulls*; Massinger, *Florence*; Middleton, *Phoenix*

who must be] Barrow, *Platform*; Bilson, *True Difference*; Brinsley, *Ludus*; Hieron, *Preachers*; Norden, *Surveyor's*; Nowell, *True Report*; Rainolds, *summe*; Henry Shirley, *Martyr'd souldier*; James Shirley, *Wedding*; Walker, *Fisher's*; Wilson, *Commentary*

***whom you profess**] Heywood, *Brazen*

your father let] Anderton, *English Nunne*; Dekker, *Devil*; Heywood, *Golden*

***let you slip**] Thomas a Kempis *Soliloquium animae*

eyes and feet] Heywood, *Pleasant*; Massinger, *Virgin*

***make known to me**] Middleton, *Puritan*

his good liking] Thomas Bell, *Antepast*; Barrow, *Examinations*

***which but once**] Massinger, *Unnatural*

***find a beginning**] William Laud, *Relation*

in his disposition] Chapman (and others), *Eastward*; Jonson, *Every Man in*; Massinger, *Emperor of the East*

***my eyes might**] Anon. *Swetnam*

I could in this] Hales, *Ordinary Complaints*; Pierre La Primaudaye, *Academy*; Webster, *Monuments*

your affections to] Ford, *Broken*; Massinger, *Duke of Florence*; Randolph, *Amyntas*

***but the meaning of what**] Brome, *Northern Lass*

him as many] Boyd, *Last Battell*; Pierre La Primaudaye, *Academy* (2); Marlowe, *E2*; Nashe, *Have with you*; Rowley, *Shoemaker*

***reckon those**] Peter Lowe, whole course of Chirurgerie

those virtues in] Nabbes, *Unfortunate mother*; Richards, *Messallina*

is chain'd] Affinati, *Divine Speaker*; Boyd, *Last Battel*; Dekker, *If It Be Not Good*

shortly after it] Francke, *Cabinet*; Richard Johnson, *Pleasant Walkes*

men I know] Chapman, *Teares of Peace*; Downe, *Treatises*; Wilson, *Coblers Prophesie*

what his father] Middleton, *Revengers*; Marmion, *Fine*

***with any violence**] Chapman, *Caesar and Pompey*

to that power] Calderwood, *Cosmophilus and Theophilus*; Dent, *Plaine Mans*; Downe, *Treatises*; Habington, *Queen*; Killigrew, *Princess*

these conjunctions] Brinsley, *Ludus*; Stubbes, *Anatomie*

Allowing for overlaps in parallels (i.e. "this Wooeing" appears five times in English drama 1576–1642, so it is considered to be a parallel for Rowley, Shirley, Marston, Lyly, and Porter respectively), the data shows six playwrights with more parallels than Fletcher or Theobald.[33] Massinger (six, one unique) has more parallels than any playwright but Shakespeare. However, no playwright but Shakespeare has more than one unique parallel. Of the King's Men playwrights active in 1612–1613, only Middleton (three, one unique) Jonson (one, not unique), and Webster (one, not unique) appear in the above data. Stern's allegations suppose that by "looking" for Shakespeare—and, by extension, looking for any playwright—we will find him. However, what if we chose to "look" for Massinger and not Shakespeare? We would still need to log Shakespeare's parallels (just as we would need to log Fletcher's, and Theobald's) to provide comparative evidence and isolate the exceptionality of Massinger's vocabulary. The only parallel in the prose from 1.2. (179–224) used by both Massinger and Shakespeare is "twenty men." Removing that parallel from consideration and looking for parallels found in only one canon among the works of Shakespeare, Fletcher, Theobald, and Massinger would still give Shakespeare, who has sixteen parallels to Massinger's five, and seven unique parallels to Massinger's one, the decisive upper hand.

In light of comparative stylometrics, the search for authorship of the prose in 1.2.179–224 of *Double Falsehood* shifts back to the seventeenth century and the verbal habits of an author who was working with the King's Men, writing substantial dramatic prose, and collaborating with John Fletcher around the time of the lost *Cardenio*. The only two authors known to satisfy these criteria are Francis Beaumont and William Shakespeare. In the prose passages searched above, there are two parallels for Francis Beaumont ("not unless your," "mended by") compared to seventeen for Shakespeare. Given the results of the various tests used throughout this study, Shakespeare surfaces as the only candidate likely to have written the prose speeches from 1.2 (179–224).

In stylometric analysis, one does not look for a particular author. Instead, the analyst looks for every author that has used the search phrase within a specified range. Identifying how many times that phrase is used and by whom is the primary objective. The stylometrist records these instances and observes patterns (if any) within the data. Taking into consideration any available external evidence (which in the case of *Double Falsehood* involves the use of prose, Fletcher, The King's Men, and Theobald), stylometric studies help eliminate candidates and they can establish a generally accepted attribution through "an accumulation of verbal parallels, each of which is mathematically rare."[34] I did not "look for Shakespeare" in these prose passages from *Double Falsehood*, I simply found an unusually high accumulation of rare parallels from his works within the substantial field of English drama written between 1576 and 1642.

This method of determining authorship is effective because it relies on evidence to make assertions. For this reason, it is more convincing than Kahan's and Stern's blind attribution of *The Adventures on the Black Mountains* (an anonymous "translation" of the Cardenio narrative published in 1729) to

Theobald. Following Kahan, Stern supports the notion that "the author of *Double Falsehood* and the translator of *Adventures* were probably one and the same" because *Adventures* replicates certain deviations from *Quixote* found in *Double Falsehood*.[35]

However, a stylometric study of the passages quoted in her article shows that *Adventures* and the Shelton translation are 72 percent (seventy words) identical. Using the same databases employed throughout this study, I found that in the remaining 28 percent (twenty-seven words) not found in Shelton, there are no parallels for Theobald. I have also searched that passage in *Literature Online* for parallels in all of English literature in 1700–1770. Samuel Richardson (two, none unique) has more parallels than any other author. Although she finds fault with decades of detailed linguistic and stylistic analysis that have linked *Double Falsehood* to Shakespeare and Fletcher, arguing that those studies were insufficiently rigorous, Stern provides absolutely no linguistic or stylistic analysis to justify her own attribution of *Adventures*. In place of substantial, verifiable evidence linking Theobald's vocabulary to *Adventures*, Stern chooses to attribute the novella to Theobald because it suits her larger argument that *Double Falsehood* is a forgery.

Moreover, Stern neglects to address the most obvious characteristic of *Adventures*: how closely it follows Shelton's translation. This is not true of *Double Falsehood*, in its prose or elsewhere. The verbal parallels between *Double Falsehood* and Shelton are widely scattered.[36] You cannot use a disputed and unsubstantiated attribution of *Adventures* to Theobald, in order to "prove" that Theobald owned and used a copy of Shelton. Because the sample size (twenty-seven words) in the current analysis is so small, it is impossible to make a confident attribution to any author, especially Theobald (no parallels). In order to determine a proper and verifiable attribution for *Adventures*, the whole narrative needs to be checked against Shelton's translation, first, and then whatever does not derive from Shelton must be tested against databases of the first half of the eighteenth century (including but not limited to Theobald). For the moment, what we can say with confidence is that Shakespeare's authorship of most of the prose at the end of 1.2 of *Double Falsehood* is much better substantiated than Theobald's authorship of any part of *Adventures*.

Checking every prose speech in *Double Falsehood* in the way that I have demonstrated here is beyond the scope of this essay. However, I hope to have established a research agenda that considers the problem of prose in *Double Falsehood* more closely. Including the current results, only 55 of the 334 prose lines (501 words or 19 percent) in *Double Falsehood* have been comprehensively analyzed. Because this material from 1.2 is not based on Cervantes, we can already conclude that Shakespeare added elements of the play's expanded father–child relationship.[37] Second, Don Bernard speaks prose in 1.2 (a scene normally attributed to Shakespeare) but verse in 3.3 and 5.2 (scenes normally attributed to Fletcher); this is what we would expect, if the traditional attributions are correct. Further research of this type promises to help us achieve a grounded scholarly consensus about who wrote which parts of *Double Falsehood*.

NOTES

1. MacDonald P. Jackson, "Looking for Shakespeare in *Double Falsehood*: Stylistic Evidence," in *Quest*, 151.
2. Gary Taylor and John V. Nance, "Four Characters in Search of a Subplot: Quixote, Sancho and *Cardenio*" in *Quest*, 192–214.
3. For Fletcher's chronology, I have followed: McMullan, Appendix 2. These figures and the ones that follow are based on the lineation and attributions in *Fletcher*. 1.3 of *The Tamer Tamed* has the most concentrated amount of prose in Fletcher's solo plays, but modern editors tend to reduce the number of prose lines in this scene. Daileader and Taylor restore 46 lines of verse (leaving only 12 lines of prose) to 1.3 in their 2006 Revels Student edition. See: *The Tamer Tamed; or, The Woman's Prize*, Celia Daileader and Gary Taylor, eds., (Manchester: Manchester University Press, 2006).
4. 157 in *Antony and Cleopatra*, 697 in *Coriolanus*, 770 in *The Winter's Tale*, 322 in *Cymbeline*, and 429 in *The Tempest*.
5. John Jowett and Gary Taylor indicate that in solo plays, Massinger uses prose sparingly and only in short passages: "'With New Additions': Theatrical Interpolation in Measure for Measure," in their *Shakespeare Reshaped 1606–1623* (Oxford: Clarendon Press, 1993), 231. In collaborative plays, prose "never occurs in passages assigned to Massinger, except in *Love's Cure* 1.2 and 2.2.158–64, where Massinger may have touched up scenes originally written by someone else."
6. *Fletcher*, I:264.
7. On Malone's attribution to Massinger, see Ivan Lupic, "Malone's *Double Falsehood*," in *Quest*, 108–13. Taylor ("History," 24–6) provides other reasons for doubting Massinger's involvement in the play of 1612–1613.
8. From the title page of the first edition of *Double Falsehood* (London: 1728).
9. David Carnegie, "Theobald's Pattern of Adaptation: *The Duchess of Malfi and Richard II*," in *Quest*, 181.
10. Taylor and Nance, in *Quest*, 193.
11. For verbal statistics, see: Taylor and Nance, in *Quest*, 202–207.
12. Brian Vickers, *The Artistry of Shakespeare's Prose* (New York: Methuen, 1979), 5–18; Taylor and Nance in *Quest*, 193.
13. Jackson, in *Quest*, 159.
14. See Taylor and Nance, in *Quest*, 204 for evidence of Theobald's minimal interventions in the prose speeches of Fabian and Lopez in 2.1.
15. Richard Foster Jones, *Lewis Theobald, His Contribution to English Scholarship* (New York: Columbia University Press, 1919), 9.
16. Jones, *Theobald*, 151; James R. Sutherland, "Shakespeare's Imitators in the Eighteenth Century," *PMLA* 28.1 (1933): 29–30.
17. Lewis Theobald, *Orestes: A Dramatic Opera* (London: 1731), 15, 41.
18. *Orestes*, like Shadwell's (oft revived) adaptation of *The Tempest*, was performed for John Rich at Drury Lane. During the early eighteenth century, *The Tempest* was very popular in its operatic form.
19. Carnegie, "Theobald's Pattern of Adaptation," 181.
20. See Vickers, *Shakespeare's Prose*, 4–18.
21. 1.2, 2.1, 2.2, 2.3, 4.1, and 5.2 all contain speeches in both verse and prose.
22. For the purposes of this study, a "parallel" is defined as a word or string of words appearing in one canon and less than ten times elsewhere (+/2). A "unique

parallel" is found in one canon but does not occur anywhere else in English drama from 1576 to 1642.

23. For more on this expanded database, see Taylor and Nance in *Quest*, 201–2, and sla.iupui.edu/Shakespeare (which also gives full details of all the data summarized in this essay). Together, these commercial and private databases account for all of the dramatic texts, all of the verse, and most of the prose in Theobald's canon.

24. The data also shows thirty-three non-unique parallels for Shakespeare, twenty-five non-unique parallels for Theobald (from his other works), and 113 non-unique parallels not used once in the Shakespearian canon. As a result, the prose in *Orestes* uses Shakespearian idioms 23 percent (33 of 146) of the time and Theobaldian idioms 21 percent (29 of 138) of the time. Of the nonunique parallels not used by Shakespeare or Theobald, only Chapman (four), Crowly (two), Dekker (seven), Fletcher (fourteen) Gough (two), Heywood (seven), Lyly (two), Marlowe (two), Rowley (three), and Rutter (two) have two or more parallels.

25. Caroline F. E. Spurgeon, *Shakespeare's Imagery and What It Tells Us* (Cambridge: Cambridge University Press, 1952), 101.

26. W. H. Clemen, *The Development of Shakespeare's Imagery* (Cambridge: Harvard University Press, 1951), 3.

27. In the event that different results appear in *LION* and *EEBO* with the same search, I use the results provided by *EEBO*. In this way, *EEBO* searches serve as independent controls for the *LION* data, since the two databases find different things.

28. Cyrus Hoy, "The Shares of Fletcher and His Collaborators in the Beaumont and Fletcher Canon (III)," *Studies in Bibliography* XI (1958), 96.

29. See Jackson in *Quest*, 155.

30. *Fletcher*, 10:158.

31. Ibid., 10:158.

32. As a result of three consecutive Theobald parallels here, Gary Taylor has altered DF 1.2.189–93 in his own reconstruction (THOC 1.4) based on the assumption that: (a) "Theobald replaced Shakespeare's tautologous, idiomatic 'as I say' with a more logical, legalistic 'as I have formerly said,'" and (b) that "Theobald censored a more explicitly sexual, Shakespearian continuation of what Hammond calls 'the somewhat unsavoury hunting metaphor' (203), substituting abstract verbs and nouns for concrete Shakespearian puns (spend your mouth, my deer, nose, arrow, prick, mark)." Theobald's intervention in 1.2.189—beginning with "insist in your"—also marks the moment in the speech where there is a substantial reduction in hunting imagery. Relatively speaking, they are densely clustered in the lines preceding: 185=1, 186=2, 187=2, 188-0, 189=2, 190=0, 191=0, 192=1, 193=0. Taylor's conjectural alterations suggest why Theobald may have intruded at this point in the original text, while leaving the surrounding prose unscathed. Quotations from Taylor are from private email conversations, June 1, 2013.

33. Massinger (six, one unique), Heywood (four, one unique), Jonson (four, none unique), Chapman (five, one unique), Middleton (three, one unique), and Shirley (three, none unique) Rowley (three, none unique).

34. Taylor, "History," 31.

35. Stern 2011, 582.

36. See Taylor and Wagschal, chapter 2 in this volume. See also Hammond, 81.

37. Jackson's analysis of the beginning of 1.2 is less thorough than my analysis of the end of the scene, because he did not have access to as much of Theobald's work, and because he does not discriminate between authors of collaborative Fletcher plays. But it strongly suggests that Camillo's prose—which again has no equivalent in *Don Quixote*—is also Shakespeare's work. In addition, Vickers notes that in writing *Henry VIII* and *The Two Noble Kinsman*, "Shakespeare invented new and transformed existing material, while Fletcher was content to reproduce what he had read." Brian Vickers, "Incomplete Shakespeare: Or, Denying Coauthorship in *1 Henry VI*," *Shakespeare Quarterly* 58.3 (2007), 323.

10

SLEIGHT OF MIND: COGNITIVE ILLUSIONS AND SHAKESPEARIAN DESIRE

Gary Taylor

> Make not impossible
> That which but seems unlike.
> —*Measure for Measure* (5.1.51–2)

> Beat not the bones of the buried.
> —*Love's Labour's Lost* (5.2.654)

Cardenio believes that Lucinda has betrayed him. He is wrong. Quixote believes that a herd of sheep is an army. He is wrong. Cardenio and Quixote are ethical, educated, eloquent, sympathetic, and undeniably wrong. The intertwined stories of Cardenio and Quixote dramatize, and forgive, the occasional failures of even the best-intentioned human intelligence.[1]

Tiffany Stern believes that Shakespeare had nothing to do with *Cardenio* or *Double Falsehood*.[2] She is wrong. But that's not surprising, or even particularly interesting, in itself. We all make mistakes. What's surprising is to see such mistakes made by an Oxford Professor of Early Modern Drama, the author of two prize-winning books on early modern theatre; even more surprising is that Stern's claim was published by *Shakespeare Quarterly*, which means it persuaded the distinguished editorial board of one of the world's top Shakespeare journals. Super-educated people who love Shakespeare made a serious mistake about him—just as Cardenio, who loves Lucinda, makes a big, bad mistake about her. What is interesting, with Stern and *Shakespeare Quarterly* as with Quixote and Cardenio, is: *why* do such people make such mistakes? (And how can I avoid making them?)

Cardenio and Quixote misinterpret things in front of their faces because the books they love—and one canonical book in particular—have primed them to misinterpret the evidence. The keys of rhetoric unlock the weaknesses of human cognition.[3] Magic depends on sleight of hand; but it also, like polemic and theater, depends on sleight of mind.[4] Quixote and Cardenio believe in magical fictions, not mundane facts. "No doubt," a father tells his daughter, "you have old stories enough to undo you" (*DF* 2.3.121–2).[5] All too often, we see what a good story leads us to expect to see.

Confirmation Bias

"Most critics looking to find evidence of Shakespeare, Fletcher, or Shelton," Stern writes in the first sentence of her essay on *Double Falsehood*, "have found it" (555).[6] Later, beginning her skeptical survey of a century of stylometric evidence, she asserts that "answers always reflect questions," and then asks two rhetorical questions: "*If* analysts searching for Shakespeare in *Double Falsehood* have found him, does that *merely* illustrate what they looked for? What are we to make of *the fact* that, to date, no analyzer has balanced results against a 'control' early modern author to show how unique their findings *actually* are?" (583; my emphasis). Stern's insinuations belittle some great scholars. Nevertheless, she is not alone in suggesting that critical responses to *Cardenio* and *Double Falsehood* are driven by "the critical desire for the authorial hand" and "the desire to *know* Shakespeare."[7] Cognitive psychologists would endorse such suspicions. We are all hardwired with susceptibility to "confirmation bias."[8] Daniel Kahneman—winner of the Noble Prize in Economics for his work on cognitive error—sums it up: "Contrary to the rules of philosophers of science, who advise testing hypotheses by trying to refute them, people (and scientists, quite often) seek data that are likely to be compatible with the beliefs they currently hold."[9]

But is Stern right to claim that such bias pervades all previous studies of this play? No. Her argument contains at least seven significant errors.

1. Look at the shift between her initial statement and her later question: "Shakespeare, Fletcher, or Shelton," then simply "Shakespeare." No serious attribution scholar has ever claimed that Shakespeare wrote everything in *DF*. From 1910 to 2012, they have identified some passages as Shakespeare's, some as Fletcher's, some as Theobald's.[10] Every scholar who provides evidence of Shakespeare has "balanced results against" *at least two* other early modern playwrights, and *at least one* early modern translator. (It is advocates of forgery who have emphasized Shakespeare, ignored Fletcher, and discounted Shelton.[11])

2. Stern dismisses (in advance of its publication) a wide-ranging stylistic study by MacDonald P. Jackson because "he does not look for any other writers" besides Shakespeare, Fletcher, and Theobald (586). Well, you may think, there's no need to read Jackson's essay. But if you do read Jackson's essay you will discover that he specifically and convincingly tests Shakespeare against Francis Beaumont, the most likely alternative author or coauthor of a 1613 pastoral tragicomedy performed by the King's Men.[12] Stern launches a similar preemptive strike (in advance of its publication) against Richard Proudfoot's analysis of polysyllabic words at the end of verse lines, claiming: "He too has not looked for other writers" (586). Another essay you don't need to read? But Proudfoot checked his results against "Beaumont,

Chapman, Day, Dekker, Field, and Middleton."[13] Stern's statements about Jackson and Proudfoot are just not true. Two other essays in *Quest* check parts *of DF* against Theobald and all plays from 1576 to 1642, and find two passages more likely to have been written by Shakespeare than anyone else, and one more likely to have been written by Fletcher than anyone else.[14]

3. Stern does no better when she wades into hard data. To prove that Theobald forged *DF*, she cites, among "many instances where Theobald's hand is visible in the play" (587), seven places where *ere* (meaning "before") is spelled "e'er" (588). Although you may not think that the spelling is important, she quotes Hammond's observation that it is a "secure identifier of [Theobald's] hand" (192). But "hand" did not mean, for Hammond, "authorship." Theobald's Preface publicly declared that he had edited *DF*, and editors have hands. The same unusual spelling occurs nine times in Theobald's 1733 texts of Shakespeare.[15] Likewise, Stern cites (588) Jackson's essay for evidence of "linguistic forms that are used elsewhere by Theobald, but not by Shakespeare or Fletcher" (*Quest*, 142). She omits Jackson's explanation that "eighteenth-century editors of Shakespeare...introduced many metrical elisions," making the presence of those contractions here "not surprising" (142). Theobald's 1733 edition confirms Jackson's explanation. Theobald's Shakespeare uses *can't* nine times, *don't* twice, *to've* five times, and *good heav'ns* twice.[16] Are we therefore to conclude that Theobald forged *The Tempest, Love's Labour's Lost, The Comedy of Errors, All's Well that Ends Well, The Winter's Tale, King John, Richard II, Henry V, Henry VIII, 1 Henry VI, Cymbeline, Coriolanus, Timon of Athens, Othello,* and *Hamlet*? Obviously not. Stern absurdly misrepresents Hammond's and Jackson's evidence.[17]

4. Stern again misrepresents Hammond when she demonstrates that Theobald used four of the "nine lexical items *said to be specific to Shakespeare* in the Arden text" (585, my italics). In the passage she cites, Hammond was listing individual "words used by Shakespeare *but not Fletcher*" (104, my italics). Hammond never claimed that those nine words were unique to Shakespeare, or that they proved *DF*'s authenticity. At that late point in his introduction, having established by other means the play's authenticity, he was trying to identify which playwright wrote which parts. Stern properly eliminates four of those nine words, showing that Theobald's intervention might have disrupted the original collaborative pattern. But that still leaves five words that point to Shakespeare rather than Theobald or Fletcher. Those five words occur in 1.1, 1.2, 1.3, 3.1, and 3.2 (twice)—scenes frequently, on other grounds, attributed to Shakespeare. Stern's correction unintentionally strengthens the case for a stylistic distinction between a Shakespearian first half and a Fletcherian second half.

5. Stern also misunderstands the evidence of linguistic forms. Authors can often be distinguished by their preference for *hath* or *has,* and *doth* or *does.* Attribution scholars have counted the distribution of these two binaries in many plays. Stern asks: "Why does *Double Falsehood* favor *has* (forty times) and *does* (three times), yet occasionally opt for *hath* (ten times) and *doth* (three times)?" (584). Stern frames the question incorrectly: Her words

contradict her numbers. *DF* does not "favor ... *does*" but "occasionally opt" for *doth*; it uses each three times. By contrast, it favors *has* four-to-one over the obsolescent *hath*. To her misleading question, Stern supplies a misleading answer. It is not mathematically true that "this odd tendency is Theobald's" (585). Stern reports that Theobald's *Cave of Poverty* prefers *does* eight times, but "still uses" *doth* once; but the ratios here are not at all comparable (1:1 in *DF*, 8:1 in *Cave*). Likewise, her figures for Theobald's *Orestes* (nineteen *has*, two *hath*) produce a proportion of modern forms more than twice as high for Theobald (9.5:1) as for *DF* (4:1). The fact than an author occasionally used one form is less important than *the ratios of both variants in specific works*. Stern's argument is equivalent to saying that no one won this year's Super Bowl because both teams scored some points. The obsolescent *hath* never occurs in *Cave* (which uses *has* three times); the obsolescent *doth* never occurs in *Orestes* (which uses *does* twenty-three times). If we combine the two binaries, the ratio in *DF* is 3.3 to 1; in *Orestes*, 21 to 1; in *Cave*, 11 to 1. None of Theobald's uncollaborative plays or poems contains both obsolescent forms, or contains so high a proportion of either obsolescent form as *DF*. These ratios alone make it unlikely that Theobald wrote the entirety of *DF*. Moreover, as Jackson demonstrates, the distribution of obsolescent forms within *DF* reinforces the hypothesis of a Shakespearian first half and a Fletcherian second half: Only one of the thirteen obsolescent forms occurs after 3.2.[18]

6. More generally, Stern misrepresents all the attribution scholars she condemns. E. H. C. Oliphant's claim that Shakespeare wrote some parts of *DF* was published in a book on the Beaumont and Fletcher canon, where he analyzed stylistic differences between Beaumont, Fletcher, Massinger, Rowley, Shirley, Shakespeare, Daborne, Field, Jonson, Middleton, Davenant, Brome, Ford, Tourneur and Webster.[19] Jackson's first book identified stylistic features that distinguish Middleton from Dekker, Fletcher, Rowley, Tourneur, Shakespeare, Webster, and others, drawing on a data pool of over one hundred plays. His subsequent voluminous and varied scholarship has demonstrated that Samuel Rowley (rather than Shakespeare) wrote the anonymous play *Thomas of Woodstock*, and that scenes in other plays normally attributed to Shakespeare were written by Fletcher (*Henry VIII*), Middleton (*Timon of Athens*), Peele (*Titus Andronicus*), and Wilkins (*Pericles*).[20] Even more specifically, Jackson proved that Eric Rasmussen was wrong to attribute to Shakespeare parts of Middleton's *Second Maiden's Tragedy* (a.k.a. *The Lady's Tragedy*); Jackson thereby argued *against* a connection between Shakespeare and Cervantes in 1611.[21] Jonathan Hope provides data on Dekker, Fletcher, Marlowe, Massinger, Middleton, Peele, and Wilkins; his study of the apocrypha rules out Shakespeare more often than he rules him in.[22] No one can reasonably claim that these scholars, or these methods, simply find Shakespeare wherever they look.

7. To invalidate the evidence that Shakespeare wrote some passages of *DF*, Stern insinuates that confirmation bias invalidates *all* attribution scholarship. She claims that scholars "learning of the *Cardenio* ascription have

therefore been 'prompted...to wonder if Fletcher had also been involved in *Henry VIII*'"; she then objects that "concluding that both men were involved in *Henry VIII* in order to reaffirm the two men's involvement in *Cardenio* is circular logic" (559). Her objection to circularity would be justified if this is what scholars had actually done. But Stern misrepresents the scholar she quotes; indeed, she misrepresents the entire scholarly tradition. What "prompted scholars," according to Gordon McMullan, was "external evidence that Shakespeare worked with John Fletcher on at least two plays" about the same time that *Henry VIII* was written: *Two Noble Kinsmen* and *Cardenio*.[23] McMullan—who acknowledges Fletcher's coauthorship of *Henry VIII* on the title page of his Arden Shakespeare edition—does not confine the prompting to *Cardenio*, does not make any claims about *DF*, does not address stylometric evidence. The identification of Fletcher's hand in *Henry VIII* has never depended on the *Cardenio* attribution. As early as 1758, scholars noticed major metrical differences between *Henry VIII* and the rest of the plays in the Shakespeare First Folio; James Spedding's historic attribution of specific scenes of the play to Fletcher, in 1850, preceded by sixty years the first brief defense of Shakespeare's coauthorship of *DF*. In the intervening decades Spedding's conclusion had been repeatedly tested and endorsed.[24] Shakespeare's coauthorship of *Cardenio* was not endorsed by a major Shakespeare editor until 1960, when Kenneth Muir published *Shakespeare as Collaborator*. Stern misrepresents the chronology of attribution scholarship by more than 110 years.

The studies that identify Shakespeare and Fletcher in passages of *DF* may be inadequate, but Stern's accusations of systematic confirmation bias are not credible. Her account is riddled with misrepresentations and factual errors. I want to emphasize that I am not playing the popular academic game of ruin-a-rival. Stern's essay does not criticize me, and she has often declared that my early work inspired her own academic career.[25] I have often praised her scholarship.[26] The mystery is: why does such a good scholar make such bad mistakes?

Bias Blind Spot

Stern is not an attribution scholar; this is her first venture into the field. We might therefore charitably assume that, like any of us venturing into the interdisciplinary thicket, she has simply wandered into error, as newcomers often honestly do. But Stern made her reputation as a theater historian, so her command of such evidence should be unassailable. It is not. Again, we can count the errors.

8. In 1613 the King's Men were paid for a performance before King James of "Cardenno" and for a later performance of "Cardenna" before the ambassador(s) of Savoy.[27] Any early modern theater historian, accustomed to working with such primary documents, should recognize that court financial records, transcribed by accountants, often make small mistakes with play

titles.[28] But rather than accepting the probability of paleographical error, Stern conjectures that these records, less than a month apart, refer to "two separate plays" (559). She gives no example of two early modern plays performed by the same company with titles identical except for one vowel.

9. She also speculates that the title "refers to the place 'Cardena'"—but the huge available databases yield her only one reference to that obscure locality, in a Franco-Spanish treaty of 1659 (556–7). She cites no instance of an Elizabethan or Jacobean play with only an unremarkable foreign place-name as a title. Plays were marketed by their titles, and what commercial theater company would base its advertising on an incomprehensible geographical allusion?

10. Stern claims that Richard Farmer in 1767 "thought that Theobald had found a play marked 'W.Sh.' and revised it, failing to realize that William Shirley was the author" (590). Farmer does indeed speculate that "perhaps the mistake arose from an *abbreviation* of the name," and does propose "Shirley" as the author.[29] But there was no seventeenth-century playwright named William Shirley. Farmer's discussion makes it clear that he was referring to the prolific *James* Shirley. Stern's mistake makes Farmer's conjecture sound more plausible than it was, thereby contributing to her larger claim that there are many plausible alternatives to the Shakespeare attribution.[30]

11. Stern notes the name "Cardenes" in *A Very Woman*, a play by Phillip Massinger licensed in 1634, and she recycles an old conjecture that it might be the lost play of 1613. This conjecture requires her to dismiss "current guesses" about the original date of composition of *A Very Woman* (556). What is the evidence for those "guesses"? Massinger's Cardenes story is based on the 1619 English translation of Cervantes's *Persiles y Sigismunda*, published posthumously in 1617.[31] Without a time machine, no "Cardenes" based on *Persiles* can have been performed in 1613.

12. Stern's argument requires her to discredit Massinger scholarship (and the great theater historian G. E. Bentley), as well as attribution scholarship. It also forces her to insist that the title of the 1613 play "is a three-syllable name" (556, 559)—in contrast to "Cardenio" (the title recorded in 1653), which is a "four-syllable" name (559, 588). This distinction assumes that the scribes responsible for financial accounts were working from oral memories of the name, rather than mis-transcribing a manuscript. Moreover, Stern admits that "Julio" is "nearly always" treated as a two-syllable name (588), with the common (then as now) elision of "-io" to "yo." If "Julio" can be two syllables, "Cardenio" can be three, with the same accentuation as "Cardenno." Theater history should be grounded on something more than ambiguous pronunciation.

13. When Theobald writes, in 1729, that he had "now a Benefit [performance] upon the anvil, the solicitation of which breaks a little upon" his editing of Shakespeare's works,[32] Stern interprets this excuse as a confession that *DF* was "taking him *away* from Shakespeare" (562). But Theobald's work on *DF*—whether he was forging it, or editing and adapting it—was finished in 1727. In April 1729 he was drumming up an audience for a

performance that would directly improve his financial situation. As anyone who has worked in the theater knows, marketing a play is an exhausting business that bears no relationship to writing a script or rehearsing a performance. In this case, Theobald was talking about a revival, where marketing is even more removed from dramaturgical work.

14. Stern claims that Theobald forged *DF* as part of his "ambitious three-year campaign to win the right to be a Shakespeare editor himself" (559, 574). But she is misled here by what psychologists call "hindsight bias."[33] Stern knows that *DF* was "a considerable success" onstage (Hammond, 15). But a new play is always a risk. More plays fail than succeed. Theobald had learned this from bitter personal experience. Theobald's credentials as an editor had been established by *Shakespeare Restored*; if he wanted to strengthen those credentials, he need only have continued hammering at the weaknesses of Pope's first or second edition, examining Pope's treatment of other plays with the same acidic thoroughness that had discredited Pope's *Hamlet*. He knew that he could beat Pope at that game. By contrast, he did not know that *DF* would succeed any better than his adaptation of *Richard II*. If it had flopped, it would have *undermined* his Shakespearian reputation, not enhanced it.

15. In December 1727 Theobald claimed, unambiguously, that he owned a manuscript "of above sixty years standing, in the handwriting of Mr Downes, the famous old prompter; and, as I am credibly informed, was early in the possession of the celebrated Mr Betterton" (*DF*, Pre.12–15). The statement about Downes could easily have been verified or discredited by many people in the London theater who were familiar with the handwriting of the long-time prompter. It very precisely locates the origin of Theobald's manuscript between 1661 and 1667 (not long after 1653, when bookseller Humphrey Moseley recorded his possession of a play called "The History of Cardenio"). Stern admits "there are many reasons why" the prompter John Downes, actor Thomas Betterton, and theater manager Sir William Davenant (who employed both men in the mid-1660s) might have owned such a play. But she finds it "difficult to explain why it was not performed" (564, 565). That "not performed" leads her first to conjecture that "they had the play but did not think it was Shakespeare's" (565), and finally to conclude that no such manuscript ever existed, "total forgery" being a "more likely possibility" (590, 592).

Stern's premise does not acknowledge that "modern understanding of the Restoration repertoire is extremely incomplete."[34] The leading documentary historian of Restoration drama, Robert D. Hume, concludes that we have evidence for no more than about 7 per cent of the performances that were given between 1660 and 1700.[35] Given these skimpy records, how can any modern theater historian be sure that *Cardenio*, or *Double Falsehood*, was never performed in the 1660s? Stern's only evidence for its unperformance is—Lewis Theobald, the very man whose reliability she systematically denies. Perhaps plans were disrupted by the Great Plague of 1665, or the Great Fire of 1666. Or perhaps the play was performed only once in the 1660s, because it failed on its first night. Would Theobald, in promoting his adaptation, want to acknowledge that failure, even if he knew about it? Scholars ignore Theobald's assertion that the play had never been performed in Shakespeare's lifetime because the payment records of 1613 provide evidence of what seems to have been the same play. If we do not believe Theobald's negation of a Jacobean performance, why should we believe his negation of a Restoration one? After reporting the hearsay claim that Betterton "designed to have...ushered [the play] into the world," Theobald confesses, "What accident prevented this purpose of his, I do not pretend to know; or through what hands it had successively passed before that period of time" (Pre.16–18). Like a good theater historian, Theobald confesses the limits of his knowledge. Stern does not.

16. But let's assume for the moment that Theobald is telling the truth, and the play in the handwriting of Downes was never performed. How does Stern get from "was not performed" to "did not exist"? She asserts that Downes, Betterton, and Davenant *would* have performed a Shakespeare play if they had possessed it, because all three men "shared a Shakespeare obsession" (564). Clinical diagnosis of the dead is a tricky business. Downes recorded, pragmatically, that nine Shakespeare plays were good box office. That is less than a quarter of the core canon. Is that proof of obsession? Davenant never revived all Shakespeare's plays; neither did Betterton, though he remained active in the theater for half a century. Britain's Royal Shakespeare Company, Canada's Stratford Festival, and other modern bardathon enterprises feel an obligation to perform all Shakespeare's plays, but no such obsessive-compulsive comprehensiveness-complex existed, in the theater, before the twentieth century. Stern's premise anachronistically projects modern stage practice onto the Restoration.

As these nine examples illustrate, Stern ignores, dismisses, or misrepresents evidence we would expect a theater historian to recognize. So her seven failures as an attribution scholar are not simply the innocent mistakes of a novice; some more systematic tilt must be distorting her reasoning here. Confirmation bias, after all, can work *on both sides of an argument*. Each polemicist seeks evidence to confirm their own conviction. That's why confirmation bias is sometimes called "myside bias."[36] Stern never considers or acknowledges that she, too, like every other Shakespearian, has desires, which might affect her own interpretation of the evidence. Stern's double standard illustrates what cognitive scientists have long identified as the "bias blind spot": the pan-human ability to see clearly other people's biases, while remaining happily oblivious to our own. Unfortunately for academics like Stern, myself, and (I presume) most readers of this essay, the bias blind spot actually increases with intelligence and education.[37] The smarter we are, the better we become at finding reasons to believe our own pet theories. That is "Why Most Published Research Findings Are False"—even in what we call hard science.[38]

Rather than simply set Stern's pit bull against my own, it might be more profitable to reframe the debate about *DF* in terms of Anthony Grafton's account of the historical dialectic between forgery and scholarship. Suspicions of forgery have often led to the development of new intellectual tools.[39] Stern's campaign against Theobald exposes some hitherto-unexamined assumptions, and thereby enables more sophisticated approaches to the *Cardenio* problem—and to the larger problems of attribution and cognitive error.

PRIMING

Stern's personal bias will not explain her ability to persuade anonymous peer reviewers, a distinguished editorial board, and some readers of her published essay.[40] How did bad evidence fool so many experts? The answer lies in the relationship between rhetoric (what we study in English departments and law schools) and cognitive illusion (what we study in psychology departments).

The first words of Stern's title are "The Forgery of Some Modern Author." That title primes us to suspect forgery, even before we see any evidence. Indeed, the title itself seems to provide important evidence: those six words are placed in quotation marks, identifying them not as Stern's private opinion but as testimony, the accusation of a presumably reliable witness. Stern does not identify that witness until essay's end, when she states matter-of-factly that the accuser was "Theobald himself, or one of his friends" (593). That makes the testimony particularly damning. By that point, after thirty-eight pages of attacks on Theobald, few readers seem to have noticed that

- the quoted accuser was anonymous, writing under the pseudonym "Philo-Shakespeare";
- it is Stern herself who (in footnote 25 on page 561) identifies him as Theobald or his friend: an attribution made on the basis of no technical or historical evidence, and despite the fact that Theobald, notoriously, had very few friends: only one person attended his funeral;
- the fore-grounded phrase was preceded by an "if" (not quoted in the title).

By contrast to this anonymous and ambiguous testimony, consider Alexander Pope. Pope, who had the strongest possible motive to defame Theobald, nevertheless accepted that *DF* was Theobald's adaptation of a pre-Restoration play.[41] Richard Farmer, who mocked and refuted Theobald's claim that Shakespeare read fluently and widely in Greek, Latin, French, Italian, and Spanish literature, nevertheless accepted that *DF* was Theobald's adaptation of a pre-Restoration play.[42] Edmond Malone, who quickly exposed *Vortigern* as a forgery, angrily marked up his copy of *DF* with criticisms of Theobald—but he, too, accepted that Theobald adapted a pre-Restoration play.[43] All these major eighteenth-century Shakespeare scholars disliked Theobald. But none of them accused him of forgery. Eighteenth-century expert testimony does not support Stern's hypothesis.

Why does Stern foreground, instead, the weak testimony of "Philo-Shakespeare"? Because—as psychologists have demonstrated, repeatedly and irrefutably, and as prosecuting attorneys have known for millennia—all human beings are prone to priming error. The first thing we see, or hear, disproportionately affects our evaluation of whatever follows.[44] Stern's title, of course, is in larger and bolder type than the rest of her essay, and—as advertising executives have always understood—larger and bolder type makes readers prone to believe that a statement is true and important.[45] The title is also the part of Stern's essay most often repeated, beginning with the enquiry sent to potential peer reviewers, asking them to evaluate it, then continuing in print with the table of contents of the journal and the running title that looms over the pages of the essay itself, then duplicated in print and online by every bibliographical citation of it. Such repetitions contribute to "the mere exposure effect" and "the illusion-of-truth effect": the more often we are exposed to something, the more we like it, and the more times we encounter a statement, the more likely we are to believe it.[46]

Stern is not alone in recognizing or exploiting the rhetorical importance of priming. Everyone knows that "you don't get a second chance to make a first impression." Forgers, too, know this. Stern claims that Theobald was capable of forging every line of DF because he "wrote comfortably" in "imitation Shakespeare" (577). "In fact," she claims, "the more directly a passage recalls Shakespeare, the more likely it is to be an imitation" (583). In other words: evidence of authenticity is evidence of forgery. Would anyone believe such an extraordinary claim if they had not already been primed to see forgery?

Nevertheless, Stern's exaggerations and omissions should not prevent us from investigating, objectively, the possibility of imitation. And perhaps we should be especially suspicious that the first seven lines of DF have been identified as Shakespearian by many critics. Could the strong start just be evidence that the forger recognized the importance of first impressions? We can test this hypothesis by examining Theobald's *The Cave of Poverty, A Poem. Written in Imitation of Shakespeare* (1715). Its first seven lines should represent the imitator's best effort to prime his reader to recognize Theobald's facility in writing Shakespearian verse.

> In barren Soil, and damp unwholsome Air,
> Where weeping Clouds Eternal Dew distill'd;
> Where no gay Sun-shine did the Morning chear,
> Or Mid-day Fires the dark Meridian gild;
>   A Cave there stood; whose vaulted Sides were spread,
>   When Nature first rear'd her Created Head.
> Ten Thousand Doors, like Flaws in mouldring Earth

For every phrase ("in barren," "soil and") and collocation ("thousand...flaws") in this speech, I have searched for parallels in databases of the work of

Shakespeare and Theobald. The results can be divided into two categories. A *type* is one phrase or collocation that provides evidence for one author or another: "soil and" counts as one Theobald type, because it occurs in Theobald's work, but not Shakespeare's. A *token* is an individual example of a parallel: for instance, "soil and" counts as five Theobald tokens, because he uses it five times elsewhere (*Electra, Persian, Odyssey,* and twice in *Plato*). We can also then test all the types, turned up by the initial comparison of Shakespeare and Theobald, to determine whether they are rare or common. An "unparalleled" type (which I distinguish with an asterisk) is a phrase or collocation that I cannot find anywhere else in the Literature Online database of English drama, 1576–1642.

This technique does not depend on loose "parallels" or debatable paraphrases. Instead, it focuses on collocations: repetitions of vocabulary, which can be objectively identified, searched for, counted, and verified by others. It combines two kinds of evidence. The exact phrasal sequences include combinations of function words (in, and) with nouns, adjectives, verbs, and adverbs (barren, soil). Function words represent only about one one-thousandth of the types in your total vocabulary, but they constitute about 60 percent of the tokens.[47] Although individuals differ in the frequency of their use of function words, such differences can be detected only by analyzing very large samples.[48] However, exact juxtapositions of a function word with a substantive word are rare enough to reflect the particular neural pathways in an individual mind. Collocations of two or more substantive words are rarer and more interesting. Comparisons of one writer to another help differentiate them from each other; examination of the semantic field of all early modern drama helps differentiate each writer from the entire set of early modern playwrights.[49]

A summary of the data for the first seven lines of *Cave of Poverty* can be found in table 10.1(a). This passage contains two Shakespearian types that I have found nowhere else in the available Theobald databases: the commonplace "weeping clouds" (*2 Henry IV*) and the unusual *"thousand...flaws" (*Lear*). By contrast, Theobald's other works yield eight types found nowhere in Shakespeare ("in barren," "soil and," *"damp unwholesome air," "gay...morning," *"sun-shine...gild," "a [noun] there stood," "rear'd her," *"rear'd...head"). This "Imitation of Shakespeare" reeks of Theobald. The first line consists entirely of unShakespearian Theobaldian phrases. Even the single unique Shakespeare parallel loses its luster when we realize that the passage also contains one unique parallel with Thomas Heywood (clouds eternal), one with John Tatham (dew distill'd), one with John Ford (nature first...created), and one with John Fletcher (when nature...created). Random scatter will explain the distribution of rare parallels to pre-1643 drama in these seven lines.

So much for Theobald's alleged ability to create a convincing first impression of Shakespeare's style. But did Theobald perhaps imitate Shakespeare's plays better than his poems? or get better at Shakespearian imitation with the

Table 10.1   Parallels with Shakespeare or Theobald (but not both) in (a) the first seven lines of *The Cave of Poverty*, (b) *Orestes* 1.1.1–7, and (c) *DF* 1.1.1–7

(a)

Types: LT 8, WS 2
Tokens: LT 13, WS 2
Works with tokens: LT 11, WS 2
Works with more than one token: LT 2, WS 0
Work with most tokens: *Plato* and *Orestes* (two each)
Types unparalleled in drama 1576–1642: LT 3, WS 0

(b)

Types: LT 9, WS 7
Tokens: LT 13, WS 7
Works with tokens: LT 8, WS 7
Works with more than one token: LT 3, WS 0
Work with most tokens: *Orestes* and *Fatal* (three each)
Types unparalleled in drama 1576–1642: LT 2, WS 2

(c)

Types: LT 0, WS 13
Tokens: LT 0, WS 29
Works with tokens: LT 0, WS 21
Works with more than one token: LT 0, WS 7
Work with most tokens: *Ado* (three)
Types unparalleled in drama 1576–1642: LT 0, WS 6

passage of time? We can test those conjectures by fast-forwarding sixteen years to examine the first seven lines of Theobald's *Orestes* (1731), a play Theobald confessed himself "arrogant enough to fancy a little Shakespearesque."[50]

> Remembrance cannot match th'unquiet Night,
> So loud this Tempest: In my Walk of Guard,
> I thought the ruffian Wind would from their Roots
> Have torn the sturdiest Trees; with such Convulsions
> They shook, and groan'd, and bow'd their Tops to Earth.
>
> Our Shores felt most its Rage; and still the Sea
> Runs Mountain-high; If those tall lab'ring Barks

This is more plausible (table 10.1(b)). It contains seven Shakespeare idioms I have not found in Theobald (*"remembrance cannot," "th'unquiet," *"the ruffian" [used of wind], "the...wind...the sea...mountain" [compared to waves], "shook and," "bow'd their tops," "our shores"). Nevertheless, Theobald still dominates, with nine collocations not found in Shakespeare ("loud...tempest," "in my walk," *"from their roots have torn," "roots...trees," "with...convulsions...shook," "and bow'd...to earth," "felt most," "its rage," *"those tall"). Theobald's smaller canon provides more types and tokens than Shakespeare's, and Fletcher's canon contains as many unique parallels as Shakespeare's or Theobald's.[51] Although there are differences in these two Theobald imitations, Fisher's Exact Text nevertheless identifies them as statistically homogenous: even if we knew nothing else about them, we could, on the basis of these two passages, conclude that they probably belong to the same population.[52] Even in small bursts, Theobald cannot produce unadulterated Shakespeare.

Stern implies that *DF* followed *Orestes*.[53] In fact, *Orestes* was written four years later. During those four years Theobald spent most of his time editing thirty-six Shakespeare plays. So if *DF* were a forgery, we should expect its first seven lines to be a less successful imitation of Shakespeare than the opening of the later *Orestes*. What do you think?

> My gracious Father, this unwonted Strain
> Visits my heart with Sadness.
> > > > Why, my son?
> Making my Death familiar to my Tongue
> Digs not my Grave one Jot before the Date.
> I've worn the Garland of my Honours long,
> And would not leave it wither'd to thy Brow,
> But flourishing and green; worthy the Man

These seven lines contain thirteen Shakespeare types for which we have found no equivalents in Theobald, including six unparalleled elsewhere in the drama of 1576–1642: "my gracious father," *"this unwonted," *"visits my heart with sadness," *"death familiar," "familiar to my," "to my tongue," "digs...my grave," "one jot," *"I've worn the garland," "the garland of," *"the garland...wither'd," *"would not leave it," "worthy the."[54] By contrast, we have not found a single type that links the passage to Theobald rather than Shakespeare. Nor have we found any other dramatist whose works contain more than one unique parallel. The contrast between the two Theobald imitations and *DF* could hardly be clearer (table 10.1(c)). Statistically, there is less than one chance in seventy-eight thousand that the opening of *DF* belongs to the same population as the opening of *Cave of Poverty* and *Orestes*.[55] Theobald's two imitations begin with literary descriptions of landscapes; these seven lines, by contrast, immediately establish an emotional relationship between parent and child (not found in Cervantes, but central to Shakespeare's late romances and to the plot of *Double Falsehood*). Moreover, this added interest in father-child relationships also shows up in the prose at the end of *DF* 1.2, which John Nance has convincingly attributed to Shakespeare (in chapter nine of this volume).[56] Neither Stern, nor any other critic in the last century, has detected evidence of Theobald in these seven lines. I can find no way to *prove* that Theobald wrote this passage, or to *disprove* its attribution to Shakespeare.

Stern's exaggerated estimate of Theobald's capacity to duplicate Shakespeare's style arises from a simple but entirely understandable category error. Stern assumes that Theobald's productive vocabulary (as a writer) equaled his receptive vocabulary (as an accomplished life-long reader of Shakespeare). But linguists know that our active idiolect is always a subset of our ability to recognize a much larger sociolect.[57] Reading Shakespeare is easier than writing Shakespeare. Theobald's other imitations, before and after *DF*, give us no reason to believe that he could write such convincingly Shakespearian verse, even for seven lines at a time, even the seven lines most critical to priming readers' responses.

But although Stern's claims about imitation do not stand up to objective assessment, we should not reject one priming effect only to succumb to another. The fact that the first seven lines of *DF* are much more Shakespearian than the first seven lines of Theobald's Shakespeare imitations does not prove that Shakespeare wrote *the whole play.*

THE CONJUNCTION FALLACY AND
BASE RATE NEGLECT

The 1653 entry for *The History of Cardenio* attributes it to both Fletcher and Shakespeare. From 1727 to 2012, critics have discerned stylistic evidence of Fletcher in *DF*. But Stern dismisses the 1653 entry, and all those critics, and all that stylistic evidence. Theobald, it seems, could imitate Fletcher as convincingly as he imitated Shakespeare: "Were Theobald to have forged a play from scratch, it would probably have come from *Don Quixote,* resembled Shakespeare and Fletcher in style, and contained fragments of Shelton's translation" (592).

I'll return to the claim about Fletcher later, but first let us examine the form of Stern's sentence. This is one of seven uses of the word "probably" in her essay; the synonym "likely" (or antonym "unlikely") occurs twenty-two times. Probability is a mathematical concept, but Stern's twenty-nine invocations of it are rhetorical, not mathematical. "For laypeople," Kahneman realizes, probability "is a vague notion, related to uncertainty, propensity, plausibility, and surprise" (150). Stern's sentence yokes "probably" to two instances of the conjunction "and"; a third conjunction is elided (between "*Quixote*" and "resembled"). The sentence thus constitutes a perfect example of what Kahneman and Avos Tversky christened "the conjunction fallacy."[58]

Those of us who make a living trying to correct the wayward grammar of student papers recognize the importance of conjunctions. But most people are easily misled by the logical consequences of the innocuous word "and." The more conjunctions you add to a proposition, the less likely it becomes. "She is a feminist" is more probable than "she is a feminist and she works for a bank," because the second clause imposes an additional condition, and that second condition will inevitably narrow the pool of candidates. I know a feminist economist who works for the Federal Reserve Bank, so such combinations are possible and interesting; but there are many more feminists who do not work in banks, and many more bankers who are not feminists. Stern's forgery hypothesis requires the simultaneous conjunction of four different claims: one about *Don Quixote,* and another about Shakespeare, and another about Fletcher, and another about Shelton. *If any one of those claims is false, Stern's forgery hypothesis cannot be true.*

Stern's first claim is that any play forged by Theobald "would probably have come from *Don Quixote*." How can we judge the probability of that hypothesis? We have to exclude *DF* itself because that is the problem we are trying to solve. Instead, we must use Theobald's other dramatic works to establish an independent "base rate" or "prior probability." Stern does not do that; indeed, she fails to establish a base rate for any of her claims. That is not surprising. Even statisticians are sometimes guilty of "base rate neglect," and it's endemic among the rest of us.[59]

Quixote is indeed the source of one of Theobald's other works (*Happy Captive*, 1741). But sixteen others use some other source. That gives us a base rate of 1/17, or 6 percent. By contrast, ten of the seventeen derive from classical sources (60 percent). Theobald is thus ten times more likely to use classical materials. Since Shakespeare got at least nine of his plots from ancient Mediterranean stories, "were Theobald to have forged a play from scratch" it would probably have dramatized a classical narrative—like, for instance, the life of Hannibal, the subject of the only play that Theobald publicly declared to be an imitation of Shakespeare. Moreover, this assessment of probabilities takes no account of chronology. Theobald's only Cervantean play was written more than a decade after *DF* was performed; it could easily have been inspired by *DF*'s theatrical success. If we limit our base rate to Theobald's work before 1727, there would be no Cervantes parallels. A 1727 Shakespeare forgery based on Cervantes is theoretically possible, but by no means *probable*.

Base rate neglect also undermines Stern's claim that such a forgery would "probably have...contained fragments of Shelton's translation." This is even less likely, because—aside from *DF* itself—"fragments of Shelton's translation" have not been found in any work assigned to Theobald in his lifetime, or by modern eighteenth-century attribution specialists. Theobald never refers to the Shelton translation, but he does quote the Spanish text twice elsewhere, and does mention Spanish editions of 1605 and 1611. *Happy Captive* is based on the Spanish text, and does not contain a single Shelton fragment.[60] The base rate for "fragments of Shelton's translation" in Theobald is zero.

The required combination of the *Don Quixote* hypothesis *and* the Shelton hypothesis already makes Stern's forgery claim very unlikely. Her third hypothesis requires Theobald to have imitated Shakespeare's style well enough to bamboozle such influential Shakespearians as Alfred Harbage, Kenneth Muir, and Jonathan Bate, and such major attribution scholars as Oliphant, Jackson, Hope, and Proudfoot. No other forgery or imitation of Shakespeare has been so successful for so long, or become more successful over time. The base rate, again, is zero. I have shown above that the first lines of Theobald's two professed imitations of Shakespeare strikingly differ from the first lines of *DF*:

	LT parallels	WS parallels
LT imitations	17	9
DF	0	13

The zero here (like the zero for Shelton fragments) does not encourage confidence in the probability of Stern's hypothesis. Neither Stern nor anyone else has discovered a passage in Theobald's work that imitates Shakespeare as perfectly as some passages in the first half of *DF*.

Elsewhere I have tested *DF* 3.1.13–26 for parallels in the Theobald database and in all extant plays performed between 1576 and 1727 ("History," 57–8). I found no unique Theobald parallels. (Another zero.) In 1289 plays from that period, I found eighteen unique parallels to the passage. On the basis of random scatter, we would expect the 1,249 non-Shakespearian plays to contain more than fourteen of those fifteen collocations, and expect the forty plays wholly or partly written by Shakespeare to contain less than one-half of one collocation. Instead, the non-Shakespeare plays produce just seven (from seven different dramatists). The Shakespeare plays, by contrast, contain eight: more than seventeen times the expected number.[61]

Stern's fourth proposition, her claim that Theobald could successfully imitate Fletcher's style, suffers from the same logical weakness as her claim about Theobald imitating Shakespeare. She asserts that Theobald, "working phrase by phrase through Fletcher to emend him, had absorbed much of that poet's style, too" (584). She again equates reading with writing, reception with production; she offers no proof of the skill or accuracy of Theobald's mimicry of Fletcher. But her Fletcher claim is even weaker than her Shakespeare claim. Theobald imitated Shakespeare in extant works of 1715 and 1731, and in his lost tragedy *Hannibal*; he adapted *Richard II* in 1719; he published a monograph on Shakespeare in 1726. But Theobald never announced any intention to imitate Fletcher, never adapted him, and never wrote about him at any length. Even scholars sympathetic to the possibility of forgery find Stern's argument about Fletcher unconvincing.[62]

The signs of Fletcher's style in *DF* cannot all be echoes of Theobald's reading, because they include six unique links between *DF* 4.2 and the Fletcher scenes of a manuscript play *Sir John Van Olden Barnavelt*, which was lost from 1619 to 1851.[63] Stern's forgery hypothesis thus requires two more subsidiary claims: that Theobald was the only person in those 232 years who read *Barnavelt*, and that he concealed his knowledge of it, even though it would have established his credentials as an editor of Fletcher. Unless all six of these unlikely propositions is *simultaneously true*, Stern's forgery hypothesis collapses.

But we do not need *Barnavelt*'s smoking gun to kill claims about Theobald's "native Fletcherisms" (592). Stern slides silently from Theobald's acquaintance with "Beaumont and Fletcher" (578, 579, 580) to claims about Theobald's ability to imitate "Fletcher," specifically (584, 586, 587, 591, 592). But "Beaumont and Fletcher," as understood by Theobald and his contemporaries, meant all "Fifty Famous Plays" published in the 1679 folio edition. Modern scholarship has established that Fletcher wrote only fifteen of these plays singlehanded; the rest include writing by Beaumont, Field, Ford, Massinger, Middleton, Rowley, Shakespeare, Shirley, and Webster (and possibly Chapman and Jonson, too).[64] Stern's definitions of Fletcher's style depend on modern scholarship's identification of what distinguishes Fletcher from his many collaborators. Theobald had no such knowledge.

Stern does nothing to undermine the great variety of evidence, assembled and evaluated by Jackson, that Fletcher wrote most of the last half of *DF*. Instead, she calls the effort to differentiate one author's verse from another's "a mild form of collective insanity."[65] She then quotes the opening speech of *Perfidious Brother* to show that Theobald could write successive lines with feminine endings (586–7), and quotes one example from *Fatal Secret* and another from *Perfidious Brother* to show that Theobald occasionally wrote "feminine endings composed of two monosyllabic words" (587). But this anecdotal evidence misrepresents the nature of metrical analysis. No one ever claimed that Fletcher had a monopoly on feminine endings, with or without double monosyllables. Fletcher differs from other playwrights in the *frequency* of those features. Stern correctly states that Theobald "increasingly favored feminine endings" (586), but she does not acknowledge that his highest recorded frequency (22.6 percent in 1731, in *Orestes*) is far lower than the 38.1 percent in the 1,447 blank verse lines of *DF* (four years earlier)—or that the *Orestes* proportion is only just over half of the 44.2 percent in the 754 blank verse lines of the scenes attributed to Fletcher. Stern's two examples (from different plays) of double-monosyllable feminine endings do not stand comparison with the 137 examples in *DF*, or the 21 in that play which end with "sir" or "not."[66]

Why would Theobald deliberately imitate Fletcher in a forgery that he was trying to pass off as a play by Shakespeare? One explanation is that he knew about the 1653 Stationers' Register entry (or the 1719 transfer) of "The History of Cardenio. By Mr. Fletcher. & Shakespeare." This explanation, of course, requires another conjunction, and therefore another necessary subsidiary hypothesis. Again, the base-rate for this explanation is zero, because Theobald nowhere else made reference to the Stationers' Register. So, as with *Barnavelt*, this explanation entails two additional conjectures: that Theobald knew the importance of the Stationers' Register, *and* that he concealed that knowledge throughout his life—even though it would have given him new ammunition against Pope and would have considerably enhanced the authority of his Shakespeare edition. Stern's forgery hypothesis now requires the simultaneous conjunction of at least eight different subsidiary claims. Each of those subsidiary claims is itself intrinsically unlikely, making their combination fantastically improbable.

Since Theobald never claimed to imitate Fletcher, we cannot test particular passages of his other works against corresponding passages in *DF*. Any passage I choose might be dismissed as "not a good example of Theobald trying to imitate Fletcher." We can, however, look at different passages in scenes attributed to Fletcher in *DF* itself. Attribution scholars have given Fletcher most, but not all, of the final scene. One speech there has been singled out by the Royal Shakespeare Company's Gregory Doran, but identified as Theobald's work by Oliphant and Hammond.[67] If Stern is right,

then we should not be able to determine whether this speech was written by
Fletcher or by Theobald.

> *Leon.* The righteous Pow'rs at length have crown'd our Loves.
> Think, *Julio*, from the Storm that's now o'erblown,
> Tho' sour Affliction combat Hope awhile,
> When Lovers swear true Faith, the list'ning Angels
> Stand on the golden Battlements of Heav'n,
> And waft their Vows to the eternal Throne.
> Such were our Vows, and so are they repaid. (5.2.251–7)

Examine table 10.2(a) and you will see that, in every category, Theobald
saturates the language of these seven lines. And it is not hard to explain why
Theobald might have added this speech to his adaptation of a Jacobean play.
It gave a big moment at the end of the play to the company's leading actress.
It also provided a satisfactorily conventional, ethical, and religious "lesson"
to be drawn from the play's primarily unethical actions. Restoration and
eighteenth-century theatrical adaptations of Fletcher (and Shakespeare) routinely make just such changes.

Another speech by Leonora belongs to an entirely different stylistic
register.

> *Leon.* For such sad Rites must be perform'd, my Lord,
> E'er I can love again. Maids, that have lov'd,
> If they be worth that noble Testimony,
> Wear their Loves here, my Lord; here, in their Hearts;
> Deep, deep within; not in their Eyes, or Accents;
> Such may be slip'd away; or with two Tears
> Wash'd out of all Remembrance: Mine, no Physick,
> But Time, or Death, can cure. (5.2.94–101)

Table 10.2 Parallels with Fletcher or Theobald (but not both) in (a) DF 5.2.251–7 and
(b) 5.2.94–101

(a)

Types: LT 18, JF 2
Tokens: LT 37, JF 5
Works with tokens: LT 19, JF 5
Works with more than one token: LT 10, JF 0
Work with most tokens: LT's *Richard II* (four)
Types unparalleled in drama 1576–1642: LT 7, JF 0

(b)

Types: LT 0, JF 23
Tokens: LT 0, JF 43
Works with tokens: LT 0, JF 22
Works with more than one token: LT 0, JF 13
Work with most tokens: JF's *Faithful Shepherdess* (six)
Types unparalleled in drama 1576–1642: LT 0, JF 4

Unlike the "righteous Pow'rs" speech, this one actually contributes to the plot: After the initial happy reunion of parents and children, it establishes an emotional obstacle, which prevents a premature reconciliation between her and Henriquez/Fernando, which in turn allows time for the reappearance of Violante and then Julio/Cardenio, and the final proper alignment of the two couples. When we compare this speech with the canons of Fletcher and Theobald, the parallels point overwhelmingly to Fletcher (table 10.2(b)). He is immeasurably more likely than Theobald to have written it; indeed, he is more likely than any other playwright. In English drama 1576–1642, I have found only ten unique parallels. Fletcher has four. No other playwright has more than one.[68] How could Theobald, who could not distinguish Fletcher from his collaborators, achieve such a perfect imitation? If Theobald could not provide, or did not attempt to provide, anything remotely resembling Fletcher's style in the other speech, how could he have imitated Fletcher so convincingly in this speech by the same character in the same scene? There are only about three chances in a billion that these two speeches belong to the same stylistic population, or were written by the same writer in the same historical period.[69] After all, Theobald was not even trying to imitate Fletcher.

Neither of these two speeches can be attributed to Shakespeare. Shakespeare resembles Fletcher, historically and sociolinguistically, more than either of them resembles Theobald.[70] But in the "sad rites" speech (5.2.94–101, table 10.3(a)), Fletcher shuts out Shakespeare in fifteen collocation-types (including four unique ones). By contrast, only three collocations link the speech to Shakespeare, rather than Fletcher; only one is unique— and it comes from the exceptionally popular, often-quoted, early *Romeo and Juliet*.[71] It thus resembles Fletcher's own allusions to, or imitations of, Shakespeare.[72] Even when Fletcher is imitating, echoing, or collaborating with Shakespeare, his style dominates the speeches he wrote himself.

Table 10.3   (a) Parallels with Shakespeare or Fletcher (but not both) in DF 5.2.94–101 and (b) parallels with Shakespeare or Theobald (but not both) in DF 5.2.251–7

(a)

Types: JF 15, WS 3
Tokens: JF 32, WS 5
Works with tokens: JF 20, WS 5
Works with more than one token: JF 9, WS 0
Work with most tokens: JF's *Faithful Shepherdess* (four)
Types unparalleled in drama 1576–1642: JF 4, WS 1

(b)

Types: LT 13, WS 5
Tokens: LT 24, WS 9
Works with tokens: LT 14, WS 8
Works with more than one token: LT 7, WS 1
Work with most tokens: LT's *Richard II* and *Happy Captive* (three each)
Types unparalleled in drama 1576–1642: LT 7, WS 1

In the "righteous Pow'rs" speech (5.2.251–7, table 10.3(b)), Theobald shuts out both Shakespeare and Fletcher in twelve collocation-types, including six where he shuts out all early modern dramatists.[73] By contrast, the larger Shakespeare canon contains only three collocation-types that appear in neither Theobald nor Fletcher; only one of those three is unique.[74] That makes Shakespeare just one of three pre-1642 playwrights with a single unique link to the speech.[75] If we restrict our comparison to Shakespeare and Theobald (ignoring Fletcher altogether), Theobald still dominates every category.[76] Moreover, although this speech cannot belong to either the Shakespeare or the Fletcher canon, there are three chances in four that it belongs to the same population as the passages we have analyzed from Theobald's two Shakespeare imitations.[77] You don't need to be a statistician to understand that three chances out of four (the probability that 5.2.251–7 is by Theobald) is a more credible hypothesis than three chances in one billion (the probability that Stern is right, and Theobald wrote both these speeches in 5.2).

Both Fletcher and Theobald occasionally echo Shakespeare, so a single Shakespeare parallel proves nothing (and proves less than nothing if it comes from Shakespeare's early work). But even in passages this short, we can easily distinguish both Fletcher and Theobald from Shakespeare, if we examine vocabulary systematically and attend to *concentrations of collocations*. We can also easily distinguish Theobald from Fletcher. Stern's claim about Theobald imitating Shakespeare may have seemed plausible to her readers, but only because most Shakespearians do not know Theobald's style at all, and no one nowadays knows Fletcher's style as well as Shakespeare's. But the imitation hypothesis does not stand up to empirical testing. Each of Stern's linked propositions is improbable in itself, and more improbable when linked (as it must be) to every one of its improbable siblings.

Stern herself seems to recognize the weakness of her argument that Theobald had "internalized many Fletcherian habits" (587). Her conclusion admits the possibility that "Theobald had a play of some kind" (590), then claims that the "most likely" option is "Theobald's possession of a corrupt text of some kind" (592), then imagines Theobald "writing a Shakespeare play onto a text by someone else—or from scratch" (592). Nevertheless, she still insists that "forgery is [a] more likely possibility than has been conceded" (592). But unless Theobald could convincingly imitate Fletcher, forgery is not likely at all, and if Theobald possessed any manuscript, then her thirty pages of arguments for forgery must be wrong. This jumble of contradictory hypotheses, all in one paragraph, is held together by only one thing: the desire to relieve Shakespeare of any responsibility for the play performed and published in 1727.

AFFECTIVE BIAS AND THE HALO EFFECT

Theobald claimed that the play he was adapting had been written entirely by Shakespeare. He was wrong. That's not surprising, or even particularly interesting, in itself. We all make mistakes. Theobald was the best Shakespeare editor of his time, but (like most modern editors) he was not an attribution specialist. Indeed, in 1727 there were no such experts. Moreover, Theobald admitted that he was biased: "my partiality for Shakespeare makes me wish that everything which is good or pleasing in our tongue had been owing to his pen" (*DF*, Ded. 40–2). Theobald is the granddaddy of all "Shakespearians," the first intellectual to have written a scholarly monograph on Shakespeare and to have dedicated much of his professional life to Shakespeare. The original Shakespearian here confesses to a desire, a "wish," that critics would now recognize as a symptom of bardolatry. Theobald's affective attachment to Shakespeare weakened his ability to make rational judgments about attribution. Theobald is not the only Shakespearian to have succumbed to such weakness. Indeed, bardolatry is a tiny subset of the panhuman bias that psychologists call the "halo effect."[78]

But Stern proposes a more sinister explanation for Theobald's mistake. Her title primes us with a readily recognizable frame of reference. "Forgery" is a crime that requires a criminal agent ("Some Modern Author"), who is then immediately named ("Theobald") and linked to his victim ("Shakespeare").

Our emotional reaction to a crime depends in part on how we feel about the perpetrator. Most modern readers have never heard of Theobald, or encountered any of his work. Textual editors recognize his importance to the history of their discipline, but editing itself has been for millennia the target of suspicion and ridicule.[79] Stern plays to this anti-editorial prejudice, writing that Theobald "emended his way through Shakespeare's complete works" and then linking editing to forgery with the assertion that "conjecture can easily turn into rewriting, and thence to writing afresh" (578). Her title's reference to "Theobald's Shakespeare" in fact quotes an anonymous attack on Theobald's edition.[80] Throughout, Stern repeats, and amplifies, *ad hominem* attacks on Theobald. For instance, she tells us that, because he was not very accomplished at creating original dramatic plots, Theobald "would batten on the structures of other plays and novels" (575). Even without the echo of Hamlet's derisive "batten on this moor," Stern's verb makes Theobald's behavior seem predatory and contemptible. Shakespeare also borrowed almost all his plots, but we do not usually describe *him* as a parasite, or compare him to the fratricidal usurper Claudius.

Our emotional reaction to a crime depends, even more strongly, on how we feel about the victim. In this case, the victim will elicit maximum sympathy from any reader or editor of *Shakespeare Quarterly*. Indeed, people who care for poetry at all are more likely to say that they "love" it, not just "like" it, so we might as well admit that Shakespearians *love* Shakespeare, and that our awareness of that love is sharpest when we feel that something precious is "in danger of being lost."[81] As Stern tells us in her first paragraph, her attack was explicitly motivated by the publication, in March 2010, of the Arden *Double Falsehood*. Arden effectively, for the first time, elevated Theobald's text into the Shakespeare canon, and made it widely available in a cheap but prestigious paperback. Within months, the play was produced twice in London and once in New York, and in April 2011 a widely publicized adaptation of it was performed by the RSC in Stratford-upon-Avon. More people than ever before read and/or saw *DF*. Almost all of them were disappointed and incredulous. Some, including particularly those most invested in Shakespeare's reputation, were as outraged as Pope, Farmer, and Malone had been, and for the same reason: *DF* is an insult to Shakespeare.

The play as a whole will strike any Shakespearian as "disappointingly lacking in wit, vigour or bite."[82] Unlike Shakespeare, unlike Cervantes, *DF* fails to supply what C. Stephen Jaegar calls the "enchantment" of "charismatic art," an art that conveys "the sense of living a heightened form of life" and promises "to transport the viewer into that world." Jaegar contrasts normative Aristotelian "mimesis" with a "hypermimesis," associated with Longinus, in works that "violate the mimetic and ignore or subordinate realism and the real."[83] Sublime art need not represent humans at all, but charisma is a specifically human quality, and Shakespeare's plays have enchanted audiences for more than four centuries by combining the personal magnetism of star actors with the sublime emotional stimulus of hyperarticulate poetry. Great roles, great words. In the "secular magic" of "synthetic experience" in the seventeenth-century theater, what Joseph Roach calls "abnormally interesting people" speak abnormally interesting English sentences.[84] *DF* does not supply much magic. This failure is particularly embarrassing because it juxtaposes a seemingly inept Shakespeare with Cervantes at his most magnificent. Shakespearians may desire to connect the great English writer with his great Spanish contemporary—but not if the resulting match-up lets Spain win the literary World Cup.

If I am told that the only two choices available are (a) to defame Shakespeare, or (b) to defame Theobald, I will believe any story that blames Theobald. Wouldn't you? Stern's story saves Shakespeare from responsibility for an embarrassing failure—and relieves Shakespearians of any need to pay attention to *DF*. After all, if previous attribution scholarship was based on inadequate databases, Stern could have championed research to produce more accurate, comprehensive, searchable digital texts of Theobald's work. By contrast, her forgery hypothesis discourages any further investment in *Double Falsehood*, by making it appear that we already know the answer to the only question that matters.

But do we have to accuse Theobald of forgery in order to satisfy our emotional allegiance to Shakespeare? Theobald's "Preface by the Editor" identifies him as the editor of *DF*, but the title page of the same book declares that the text has been "Revised and Adapted to the Stage / By MR. THEOBALD." Was Theobald the editor or adapter? Stern considers this ambiguity suspicious. But M. J. Kidnie argues that all editing is adaptation, and that, in particular, the editorial modernization and standardization of a play cannot be logically distinguished from its adaptation in performance.[85] All Restoration and eighteenth-century theatrical adaptations of Shakespeare's plays are, by our standards, acts of desecration. Theobald's adaptation of *Richard II* insults Shakespeare, his adaptation of *The Duchess of Malfi* insults Webster.[86] Nevertheless, those poetically and theatrically inert adaptations do not undermine anyone's confidence that Shakespeare wrote the Elizabethan *Richard II,* or that Webster wrote the Jacobean *Duchess of Malfi.*

Consider the following thought experiment. We now know that *Timon of Athens* was added to the canonical 1623 folio of Shakespeare's *Comedies, Histories, and Tragedies* to replace *Troilus and Cressida.* If the printing of *Troilus* had not been suspended (probably because of copyright problems), *Timon* might never have been included.[87] Most editors and attribution experts now accept that Thomas Middleton wrote about a third of *Timon,* and the play's collaborative authorship might explain the uncertainty about its inclusion. Suppose it had not been included; suppose the manuscript of *Timon* had survived until the Restoration, but subsequently disappeared. Would we then believe that Thomas Shadwell's *The History of Timon of Athens, the man-hater* (1678) contains "the inimitable hand of *Shakespeare* in it" (sig. A2v–A3)? Shadwell's text begins with a soliloquy by Timon's steward, Demetrius.

> How strange it is to see my Riotous Lord
> With careless Luxury betray himself!
> To feast and revel all his hours away;
> Without account how fast his Treasure ebbs,
> How slowly flows, and when I warn'd him of
> His following dangers, with his rigorous frowns
> He nipt my growing honesty i'th' Bud,
> And kill'd it quite; and well for me he did so.
> It was a barren Stock would yield no Fruit:
> But now like Evil Councellours I comply,
> And lull him in his soft Lethargick life.

You would be right to object that this does not sound like Shakespeare— but wrong to leap to the conclusion that Shadwell forged the entire play. And could you distinguish Shadwell from Middleton? Or would you instead assume that the unShakespearian lines were all written by Shadwell? Once you had subtracted Middleton-Shadwell, would enough Shakespeare be left to satisfy your expectations of sustained dramatic and poetic genius?

Within a few months of Stern's essay, Arthur Phillips published a satirical novel about forgery and scholarly attribution. "Once you know it isn't Shakespeare," Phillips concludes, "none of it sounds like Shakespeare."[88] But adaptation creates a different, more complicated problem than forgery or imitation. Since *some of it* is not Shakespeare, it's easy to leap to Stern's conclusion that *none of it* is Shakespeare. And once *you've decided* it's a forgery, "none of it sounds like Shakespeare."

Stern alleges that Theobald had motives to commit forgery: he needed the money, and *DF* was part of his "ambitious three-year campaign" to get a contract to edit Shakespeare. But who does not have a motive for forgery?

Who does not, at some point, want to make money, or get famous, or discredit a rival? Does that mean that everyone is a forger or liar? No. Proving that someone had a motive is irrelevant, unless we first establish that a crime has occurred.

"Except by Theobald's friends," Stern asserts, "*Double Falsehood* was assumed to be some kind of forgery" (589). This claim is circular: Stern defines as "Theobald's friend" anyone who praised his work.[89] And what does "some kind of" mean? A forgery is a forgery, or not. Certainly there were, and are, honest critics who rejected Theobald's attribution to Shakespeare. But Grafton insists, correctly, that "Forgery does not include all works wrongly attributed to authors," because "works have been misattributed for many reasons, some of them quite innocent."[90] Consider the base rate of forgery versus misattribution (ignoring *DF* itself). In the two centuries between 1590 and 1790, there are no examples of forgery of a play by Shakespeare. In the same period, at least twenty plays of which he wrote nothing, or only a part, are misidentified as the work of Shakespeare alone.[91] Base rate: misattribution 20, forgery 0.

Writing an author's name on a manuscript and then pretending that the name had been there originally, or that it was the author's signature, would be forgery *of the name* but not of the play. But Shakespeare's name had been attached to a manuscript of such a play (rightly or wrongly) as early as 1653.[92] Theobald might be accused of suppressing Fletcher's name from the title page, but his Preface acknowledges the possibility of Fletcher's presence. Foregrounding Shakespeare's name for marketing purposes is still done routinely by people we do not call forgers. Is Hammond's edition "some kind of forgery" because the front cover proclaims "The Arden Shakespeare" but does not mention Fletcher? Is the RSC's adaptation "some kind of forgery" because the front cover and the subtitle (*Shakespeare's "Lost Play" Re-Imagined*) does not mention Fletcher, or anyone else?

A theatrical adaptation is a "kind of forgery" because it blurs the distinction between present and past, author and adapter. Like many nondramatic examples described by Grafton, it mixes a genuine original with entirely new material "more to the taste of modern readers…than the real antiquity" provided by technically rigorous historicism (18–26). The frustration of scholars, when confronted with such hybrid texts, is articulated in Hammond's complaint about the RSC's *Cardenio*: "who actually wrote those lines…Shakespeare? Fletcher? Theobald? Shelton? Doran and Álamo? Should it be so difficult to know?"[93] When some of Theobald's enemies objected that he was passing off his own writing as Shakespeare's, they were voicing the same complaint made by Hammond and innumerable other critics of theatrical adaptation.

Stern labels adaptation "a forgery on top of a real manuscript" (590). Theobald was a lawyer, and he would have recognized that Stern's prejudicial and prosecutorial rhetoric elides a crucial distinction. Theatrical adaptation was an entirely legal, ethical, and normal activity in Theobald's world. Forgery was not.

The Planning Fallacy and Anti-Knowledge

Stern's primary evidence for the hypothesis of criminal activity is an absence of evidence. Where are the manuscripts that Theobald claimed to possess? Why did he never publish a transcript of them? Why did he never publish the "dissertation" he promised, defending Shakespeare's authorship of the original play?

We should remind ourselves, again, of the base rate for such phenomena. Is Theobald the only scholar to have promised us a book that never materialized? Hardly. Any academic can cite contemporary examples, and intellectual historians could cite many more. Mortality overtakes ambition. Our frailty betrays our promises to others and ourselves. Distractions reroute us. Cervantes knew this. So do cognitive psychologists. Kahneman and Tversky called it "the planning fallacy": An innate inclination to make predictions and forecasts based on best-case scenarios that ignore the base rate of failure in other people's best-laid plans.[94]

For Theobald, things did not go as planned. From the perspective of getting tenure in a modern English department, Theobald should have published all his scholarly evidence before his adaptation was performed. But Theobald needed to make a living, needed to recoup the expenses incurred in buying the manuscripts and securing a royal monopoly. There was no publishing precedent for the kind of academic attribution monograph that he proposed to write. His chances of persuading a publisher depended on his ability to arouse public interest by a successful theatrical production, and a successful theatrical production would demand adaptation. *Double Falsehood*'s success might have encouraged him to continue work on his dissertation. On the other hand, for some people the simultaneous applause of hundreds of spectators provides an immediate gratification more rewarding, financially and psychologically, than the scattered sales of a treatise.

Even if Theobald began work on such a monograph, its commercial and intellectual prospects were destroyed by two events early in 1728: the unprecedented and colossal theatrical success of John Gay's *The Beggar's Opera*, which opened on January 29 and ran for 62 successive performances, followed by the unprecedented and colossal print phenomenon of Alexander Pope's *The Dunciad*, published on May 18. Gay and Pope were friends. Both despised Theobald for political, religious, and aesthetic reasons. In this transformed landscape, Theobald could not hope that a necessarily difficult and dull attribution treatise would get a fair hearing.

It made more sense, financially and strategically, for Theobald to concentrate on his Shakespeare edition. He knew he could out-edit Pope. Why then, the skeptics cry, did Theobald not include *Double Falsehood*, or *Cardenio*, in his 1733 edition? From the perspective of the publisher or author, inclusion of either in the *Works* would have been a strategic disaster. It would have provided Theobald's detractors with an easy satirical target, to the detriment of everything else in the edition. Even without the added play, publication was repeatedly postponed; including *DF* would require a long defense of its authenticity, which would make the edition bigger and more expensive, and further delay its completion. Was Theobald, or Tonson, so deluded as to believe that any argument, however rational, however well-substantiated, would satisfy Pope and Co., or persuade them to sheathe their acidic pens? Even after a century of determinedly scholarly arguments for Shakespeare's part-authorship of *Double Falsehood*, self-appointed "Shakespeare cop" Ron Rosenbaum mocked Hammond for including the play in the Arden Shakespeare.[95] Compared to Pope and Gay, Rosenbaum is an impotent teddy bear.

And after 1733? Theobald by then was forty-five, and *Double Falsehood* was six years behind him. It's hard to return to old projects. It's especially hard when you are living hand-to-mouth, when you have every reason to believe that returning will not make you enough money to justify the time required to complete the project, when returning is guaranteed to provoke more wounding mockery. Why would Theobald want to do something that risked unraveling whatever respect he had earned from his *magnum opus*? From the relative security of our professorships, surrounded by an immense research infrastructure, it is easy to insist that Theobald *should* have written that book. But from the perspective of the fragile economies of eighteenth-century untenured freelance scholarship without a landed or inherited income, it is hard to imagine how Theobald could ever have done so. Placed in the long history of unpublished or uncompleted scholarship, Theobald's failure to deliver needs no explanation. Poor Theobald! (literally). We cannot know with absolute certainly exactly why he never published his dissertation, but we do not need to know, because it does not matter.

Nassim Nicholas Taleb calls what we do not know "anti-knowledge." Our ignorance of other people's motives belongs to this much larger category of silent evidence, called (depending on the discipline) "anthropic bias," or "survivorship bias," or "wrong reference class."[96] Our failure to take account of such unknowns distorts our judgment of what we do know, just as dark matter in the universe affects visible matter. Kahneman calls this bias "What You See Is All There Is" (or "WYSIATI").

This bias bears an obvious relationship to the problem of lost texts. Moseley's manuscript of *The History of Cardenio* is lost. The only question is whether it disappeared before or after 1727. Stern and other skeptics find the manuscript's absence suspicious. But an online database (www.lostplays.org) lists 643 lost plays for the period before 1643; for the same period Literature Online contains texts of 644 extant plays. G. E. Bentley's "conservative" estimate was that "between 1590 and 1642" alone "there probably were written as many as 500 plays of which we know not even the titles." From this global perspective, for every single early modern play that survives there were probably two others that have disappeared.

We generally overlook the scale of these extinctions because our research, teaching, and funding focus on Shakespeare, who is exceptionally well-preserved. Shakespeare wrote some or all of at least thirty-nine plays and three books of poetry. But none of his manuscripts survive. Shall we join the Holy Order of Paranoia and declare that those manuscripts were destroyed in order to conceal the author's true identity? Or shall we simply accept that most manuscripts perish? Printing produced hundreds of copies, but most printed copies of early modern plays have also disappeared. A comedy called *Love's Labour's Won* was attributed to Shakespeare, by a normally reliable source, in 1598, and a book with that title had been printed by 1602. That work has disappeared. Rather than admit that anything by Shakespeare has been lost, most Shakespearians apparently prefer to believe that *Love's Labour's Won* is an alternative title for some other, extant play. But even those who swear allegiance to this face-saving conjecture must still accept that the printed edition of the play, consisting probably of 500 copies, is lost. So are the manuscripts of Theobald's *Hannibal* and his biography of Lope de Vega. Why should we be astonished by the disappearance of other manuscripts that Theobald possessed? *Cardenio* is one drop in a long, deep, widening river of loss.

Or perhaps three drops. Theobald claimed to possess at least three manuscripts. Like other skeptics before her, Stern objects to this plurality, and feels that it makes the disappearance of the original play much more unlikely. But why be incredulous at the disappearance of three texts of *Cardenio,* when five hundred copies of *Love's Labour's Won* disappeared? Once Theobald collected the three manuscripts, they could be destroyed by a single event—just as all the copies of the 1623 folio now collected in the Folger Library could be destroyed by a single nuclear blast or meteorite. By collecting texts, or anything else, in one place, or in the hands of one person, we multiply the risk of their extinction. Among biologists, "geographic range is perhaps the most widely cited determinant of extinction risk."[97] The more scattered an organism, the more likely its survival. Whether or not Theobald himself was responsible for the destruction of the manuscripts, merely by collecting them he unintentionally (like Henry Clay Folger) endangered them. Doran has no trouble documenting five different incendiary scenarios that would account for the post-Theobald loss of the manuscripts.[98]

Stern tries to prove that Theobald never had a manuscript by using Theobald's own words against him. This is like cross-examining a dead witness, who cannot speak up to clarify ambiguities, provide explanations, or rebut insinuations. The prosecution ends its summation with the title of the play, which is interpreted as a confession. Stern's final sentence tells us that "the drama entitled *Double Falsehood,* by a man professionally obsessed with wordplay, may finally have lived up to its name" (593). Stern's essay in *Quest* ends with a similar assertion: "*Double Falsehood* appears to have been, on several levels at least, aptly named" (130). A forgery is obviously a falsehood. But in what sense is it a *double* falsehood? The 1727 title aptly describes the story that Cervantes tells: Fernando betrays both his friend and his fiancé, Dorotea is betrayed by her fiancé and by her master. In *Don Quixote,* falsehoods double. But that story also offers another possible meaning to the doubling: Cardenio falsely believes that Luscinda is false, and those two falsehoods (like a grammatical double negative) produce a truth, because Luscinda remains true to her vows. As both verb and adjective, *double* could refer to deceit, so the title is indeed a pun, but Shakespeare and Fletcher were actually much more "professionally obsessed" with wordplay than Theobald. "Double Falsehood" could not have been the main title of the King's Men's play, but it could have been somewhere in the script, in a passage that Theobald removed; it would be characteristic of his practice as an adapter to pick out and transfer a phrase he liked to some other place in the text. But wherever the title comes from, it describes the plot of *Double Falsehood* much more "aptly" than it describes forgery.

Stern also discerns a damning contradiction between Theobald's claim to possess several manuscripts and the advertisements for *DF*, which "repeatedly stressed the single Shakespeare manuscript in Theobald's hands" (560). But Stern's attack assumes that the singular "Play" is equivalent to the singular "manuscript." Even today, honest editors and critics refer to the singular "play" *A Game at Chess* (which survives in five manuscripts and two independent editions) or the singular "play" *Hamlet* (which survives in three independent editions). When Theobald refers to a particular line "in *Shakespeare's* old Copy," the word "Copy" does indicate a particular manuscript. But the singular there distinguishes one manuscript ("Shakespeare's old") from the other manuscripts, "which may not, perhaps, be quite as old as the former" (*DF*, Pre. 24–5). Or it distinguishes Theobald's printed adaptation from the older manuscript play. Theobald does not contradict himself.

Stern complains that "Philo-Shakespeare," who defended *DF*'s derivation from a Shakespearian source, "does not address the manuscript's age, quality, appearance, or handwriting" (561). But this demands that a literary critic in 1727 should follow the protocols of modern bibliographers. It does not prove that "Philo-Shakespeare" never saw an original manuscript. When Theobald refers to a manuscript, Stern asserts, he "*must* have been referring to his own play" (561) rather than the seventeenth-century original, but of course the verb that she italicizes cannot be proven.

Theobald, she claims, "repeatedly, and contradictorily, maintained in his scholarly work that no such manuscript existed" (561). This would indeed be a damning contradiction. But again Stern misrepresents the evidence. In writing about the problems encountered by an editor of the thirty-six canonical Shakespeare plays—the plays contained in the folios of 1623 and 1632, and in the edition by Pope, which he was discussing—Theobald lamented "the want of *Manuscripts*" and the "Want of *Originals*" and the fact that "the Assistance of Manuscripts is wanting."[99] For the plays Pope had edited, and which Theobald was discussing in 1726, there were no manuscripts. When Theobald said in 1733 that "where the Assistance of Manuscripts is wanting to set an Author's Meaning right...many Passages must be...past a Cure," he was introducing an edition of those same plays.[100] Such statements do not constitute proof that "throughout his scholarly life...Theobald was reconciled to there being no extant Shakespeare manuscripts" (Stern 562). Theobald simply states the obvious truth that there were then, and are now, no manuscripts of the thirty-six Shakespeare plays printed in the 1623 folio.

Throughout his correspondence with Warburton, "Theobald did not mention having any manuscript early modern plays, let alone a Shakespeare one" (562). But again, there were no manuscripts for the plays they were discussing. Theobald does refer to "contraction in the written copies and the current hand of those times."[101] Theobald does not specify *dramatic* manuscripts, because the issue at question concerns handwriting, not the conventions of theatrical annotation.

There is thus no contradiction between (a) Theobald's scholarly statements about Shakespeare's canonical plays and (b) Theobald's claim to possess manuscripts of an uncanonical Shakespeare play based on *Don Quixote*. Theobald's description of those manuscripts is ambiguous, and has been interpreted by different readers to refer either to four, or to three. That ambiguity would be intolerable in the Introduction to a twenty-first-century Malone Society reprint of an early dramatic manuscript. But we cannot hold Theobald in 1727 to the academic protocols of 2013. By the standards of his time, Theobald's account is exceptionally detailed. The ambiguity does not prove that Theobald was a forger.

In any case, skeptics do not care whether the correct number is three or four, because they object to either number. Stern echoes Kahan, asking "why have we never heard of the sale" of these manuscripts, and "why were they (secretly) sold to [Theobald] and not Pope?" and "why did none of the sellers later identify themselves when the play was successfully performed or afterward when it was regularly greeted as a hoax?"[102] These rhetorical questions are a typical tactic of prosecuting attorneys and show trials. They take the absence of evidence as proof of guilt. These insinuations suggest that there can have been no manuscript because there is something extraordinarily irregular about the fact that we do not know the seller's identity. But anyone who has attempted to trace the history of the provenance of an early manuscript knows that it is normal to find gaps in the history of its movement from one owner to another. Those gaps increase as we move backward in time. Perhaps the seller or sellers hated Pope, because of his politics or his religion, or because he had mocked them in his satirical poems. Perhaps they were impressed by *Shakespeare Restored*. We just do not know. The historical record is irritatingly reticent about the motives of the dead.

Recognizing that her forgery hypothesis depends upon an "unlikely" conjunction of coincidences, Stern claims that forgery is "no more unlikely than that Theobald, careful editor of Shakespeare, had an early modern play in manuscript...and destroyed it (or them) in pique at realizing that Fletcher—his other favorite English writer—could also be seen there" (592). When confronted with a difficult question, "we often answer an easier one instead, usually without noticing the substitution."[103] We should be asking whether forgery is likelier than *any of the possible alternatives*. Instead, Stern asks a more restricted question, which we feel more confident about answering. Is it likely that a modern editor of Fletcher (or Stern, or any reader of *Shakespeare Quarterly*) would destroy the manuscript(s) of *Cardenio* because they realized that the play was partly or wholly by Fletcher? No. That scenario, we can all agree, is extremely unlikely. But Theobald did not belong to a global community of academic early modernists. His fragile reputation was heavily invested in Shakespeare's authorship of the play. Did his own reputation matter more to him than Fletcher's? How can we know? It certainly mattered more to his livelihood.

The one alternative scenario that Stern offers us is, like her forgery hypothesis, based on the conjunction fallacy: it presumes that Theobald (a) only subsequently realized that Fletcher was coauthor (b) *and* then destroyed the manuscript (c) *for* that reason. Stern therefore offers us a choice between two improbably complicated options. But the manuscripts might have disappeared for other reasons. They might have accidentally perished during Theobald's lifetime, or after his death; his wife might have sold them to buy food for the children, or he might have sold them to buy books that he needed for his Shakespeare edition; or he, or someone else, might have destroyed them for reasons we can only guess. History records too many warped motives for destruction: jealousy, megalomania, envy, patriotism, righteousness.

Maybe righteousness considered the original *Cardenio* disgusting, and wanted to suppress it. Theobald's version does not contain anything particularly objectionable, let alone shocking. But we know that Moseley and his heirs possessed a manuscript of the play, but did not publish it. Theobald says that Betterton possessed a manuscript of the play, but did not perform it. Even more significantly, in 1719 Charles Gildon reported that a play written by "*Beaumont* and *Fletcher*, and the immortal *Shakespear*, in the Maturity of his Judgment...cannot make its way to the Stage," and he identified Colley Cibber as the obstacle to its performance.[104] Cibber prided himself on "keeping the Stage clear of those loose Liberties it had formerly too justly been charged with."[105] Gildon may or may not be right about the authorship of the manuscript play or about Cibber's motives, but Cibber was part of the management at Drury Lane, which eight years later performed *Double Falsehood*. Three separate sources tell us that between 1653 and 1719 Moseley, Betterton, and Cibber all had access to the manuscript, but did not make it public. Then in 1727 Theobald's adaptation was successfully performed and printed. This sequence of events suggests that Theobald's adaptation removed whatever in the story or style had troubled Moseley, Betterton, and Cibber.

Stern throws a paragraphful of hostile questions at Gildon's testimony (565–6), but she never addresses or acknowledges its incompatibility with her forgery hypothesis. If Gildon's friend possessed a manuscript of *Cardenio* in 1719, then Theobald could not have forged it in 1727.[106] If Gildon's friend possessed something else, then that manuscript disappeared without subsequent trace, and all Stern's objections to the improbability of such a loss apply to it, and cannot be cited as evidence of Theobaldian forgery. Moreover, if Gildon's friend possessed something else, then we have to suppose that Theobald forged a late Shakespeare play containing elements that suggested Fletcher, despite the fact that a manuscript of a late Shakespeare-Fletcher play had recently circulated in the London theaters, and could be brought forward at any moment to contrast with his forgery. The simplest and most probable scenario is that Gildon's friend possessed the same play that Moseley registered, Downes copied, Betterton possessed, and Theobald adapted.

In adapting the play to make it acceptable to Drury Lane's management and to Georgian mainstream taste, Theobald would also have removed from the script the very evidence that might explain the suppression or destruction of the Jacobean original. As a result, we can only guess what that objectionable material might have been. Theobald's adaptation is blandly heterosexual, but the original might have been more daring in its representation of Shakespearian desire. The initial intimate friendship between Cardenio and Fernando, described by Cervantes, might have been portrayed by Shakespeare, in the first half of the play, in a way that provoked homophobic anxiety or disgust.[107] My own reconstruction of *The History of Cardenio* imagines that the Jacobean play transformed Cervantes to produce a drama of interracial desire. That transformation could have included elements of the cross-cultural romance described by Cervantes in Zoraida's tale, and it would have satisfied English prejudices about Spanish racial mixture, picking up on Shelton's marginal comment that "Here the Author taxeth some one cunningly to be descended of a Moorish race" (*DQ* 2.2.125). But it would also have required audiences to accept an interracial marriage as a happy ending. That would certainly have disturbed or disgusted many English readers and spectators.

The preceding sentences are necessarily conjectural. We do not know, and cannot know, what Theobald removed from the original play. But such conjectures demonstrate that Moseley's and Betterton's hesitation, and the eventual disappearance of the manuscripts, *could* be due to racist or homophobic hysteria. The desire of Shakespeare's readers and audiences for a straight white bard *could* have left us with nothing but the blandness of *Double Falsehood*. Remember: Davenant, Pope, Theobald, and other adapters and editors of Shakespeare in the late seventeenth and eighteenth centuries believed that they were improving Shakespeare. In that climate, preserving the improved version, and throwing away its inferior prototype, would be no more surprising that trading in your first-generation iPad for its successor.

"Theobald had long wished to muddy the distinction between himself and Shakespeare," Stern asserts, preternaturally reading a dead man's mind; "In *Double Falshood* he did that" (589). But if the play were a forgery, it would be all Theobald. On the other hand, an adaptation would do what Theobald did elsewhere, in his *Richard II* and *Shakespeare Restored* and 1733 edition: mix Theobald with genuine Shakespeare. If Theobald had printed a transcript of the original manuscript(s), we could easily do what we do to all other adaptations: compare the adaptation with the original, and praise Shakespeare by disdaining his adapter. It is not forgery or adaptation but the disappearance of the manuscripts that muddies the distinction between Theobald and Shakespeare.

What happened to the manuscripts after 1727? I do not know. The possibilities are literally infinite.

THE NARRATIVE FALLACY

"It is easy to be overimpressed by research that involves mathematics or a computer," Stern warns. "In particular, stylometric analysis is often treated as though it has a rigor that mere human judgment does not" (583). Instead of numbers, Stern tells us, and tells herself, an appealingly simple story. It can be summarized in one sentence: A bad man named Theobald wrote *DF* and then sold it as the work of Shakespeare. Everything happened at Theobald's desk in 1727. One of my students praised Stern's essay as "a detective story."

Stern's contrast between overrated numbers and the human judgment articulated in a good story uncannily echoes the battle between statisticians and conservative pundits at the end of the 2012 presidential election campaign. The statisticians combined many different polls (just as the attribution scholars have combined many different stylistic tests). The numbers, whether analyzed by Nate Silver or the Princeton Election Consortium, showed a probability of more than 90 percent that Obama would win. But the pundits accused the statisticians of bias, and appealed instead to their "gut feeling," their years of political experience, their judgments about momentum, and the nation's emotional landscape. Numbers beat "mere human judgment."

In my experience, most members of English departments are anything but "overimpressed" by mathematics. Indeed, many of us chose literature, rather than science, because we hated math. The magic of theater to a considerable degree depends on confirmation bias and other cognitive illusions.[108] But we cannot escape what the Elizabethans called "numbers" or "measures," what we call meter. Repetition and rhythm (which means, frequencies) are the spine of poetry, song, dance, theater. The audience cannot see the stage manager keeping track of the number of minutes in a performance in relation to the burning time of candles; cannot see the producer measuring the capacity of an auditorium, counting the number of actors, calculating what they will cost, estimating ticket revenue; cannot hear rehearsing dancers, or actors in scenes of stage combat, counting out loud ("one, two, *three!*"). Early modern theater requires architecture, economics, acoustics, and music—and all of those are mathematical.

Stories with simple, identifiable agents and familiar plots are easier for the human mind to absorb than numbing numbers and abstract data. Taleb calls this "the narrative fallacy." Naturally, those of us who dedicate our lives to literature believe in the value of stories. We would agree that human beings "favor *the narrated*." We recognize "narrativity's simplification of the world around us," its ability to "reduce dimensionality." We brag that "abstract statistical information does not sway us as much as the anecdote." We revel in the fact that stories, unlike raw data, are "sensational" and "emotional." Nevertheless, we will admit that "narrative can be lethal when used in the wrong places" (or by the wrong people). We want doctors, engineers, physicists, and chemists to "denarrate," and "spot the difference between the empirical and the sensational."[109] We should expect the same of attribution scholarship.

But, you may object, I have been telling stories too: about Theobald's career, about accidental loss, about possible motives for the deliberate destruction of manuscripts. I plead guilty. We cannot escape narrative. The origin of stories is the origin of our species.[110] But my narratives differ from Stern's. Mine are compatible with the statistical data. Stern's are not. Mine describe possibilities, without pretending that I know which actually happened. Stern instead treats her chosen narrative as proof. My stories expand the range of the imaginable possible. Stern narrows it.

To solve the problem of *Cardenio*, we do not need to speculate about past, irrecoverable human motives. Like the bones discovered under a parking lot in 2012, the 1727 edition of *DF* is an object, a fragment of the past that has survived into the present, where it can be objectively described, probed, and analyzed.

Let me end, then, with a fragment, part of the surviving skeleton of a play. I have already analyzed two speeches by Leonora, one apparently written by Theobald (5.2.251–7), the other apparently written by Fletcher (5.2.94–101). Here is a third. Because it is shorter than the other two, for symmetry's sake I include the lines by Julio that cue her speech.

> —No Impediment
> Shall bar my Wishes, but such grave Delays
> As Reason presses Patience with; which blunt not
> But rather whet our Loves. Be patient, Sweet.
>
> *Leon.* Patient! What else? My Flames are in the Flint.
>   Haply, to lose a Husband I may weep;
>   Never, to get One: When I cry for Bondage,
>   Let Freedom quit me. (1.2.109–16)

This earlier scene, like most of the earlier part of the play, has been repeatedly attributed to Shakespeare-revised-by-Theobald, so I will initially limit myself to comparing those two authors. The results (table 10.4(a)) strikingly differ from Leonora's speech in 5.2.251–7 (table 10.2(a), 10.3(b)) and from Theobald's Shakespeare's imitations (table 10.1(a) and (b)). Everything here points to Shakespeare; nothing suggests Theobald. Statistically, setting Shakespeare parallels against Theobald parallels, there is only about one chance in 350,000 that this passage belongs to the same population as the two Theobald imitations, and only one in six million that *DF* 1.2.109–16 and 5.2.251–7 ("The righteous Pow'rs") have the same origin. By contrast, the probability that 1.2.109–16 has the same origin as 1.1.1–7 is 100%.[111] Finally, since 5.2.251–7 apparently belongs to the same population as Theobald's two Shakespeare imitations, and since the two passages we have examined in 1.1 and 1.2 of *Double Falsehood* also apparently belong to a homogenous set, we can statistically compare those two composite populations. The chances that *Cave of Poverty* 1–7, *Orestes* 1.1.1–7, and *DF* 5.2.251–7 (three examples of Theobald imitating Shakespeare) have the same origin as *DF* 1.1.1–7 and 1.2.109–16 (as Stern's forgery hypothesis would force us to believe) is less than one in twenty-four *billion*.[112]

Table 10.4   (a) Parallels with Shakespeare or Theobald (but not both) in DF 1.1.109–16, (b) parallels with Theobald or with Shakespeare's last sixteen plays (but not both) in DF 1.1.109–16, and (c) parallels with Shakespeare or Fletcher (but not both) in DF 1.1.109–16

(a)

Types: WS 26, LT 0
Tokens: WS 43, LT 0
Works with tokens: WS 26, LT 0
Works with more than one token: WS 10, LT 0
Work with most tokens: *Ado* (four)
Tokens unparalleled in drama 1627–1642: WS 11, LT 0

(b)

Types: Late WS 13, LT 0
Tokens: Late WS 17, LT 0
Works with tokens: Late WS 11, LT 0
Works with more than one token: Late WS 3, LT 0
Works with most tokens: *Twelfth Night* and *King Lear* (three each)
Tokens unparalleled in drama 1576–1642 (tokens): Late WS 4, LT 0

(c)

Types: WS 20, JF 1
Tokens: WS 31, JF 1
Works with tokens: WS 20, JF 1
Works with more than one token: WS 8, JF 0
Work with most tokens: *Richard III* and *Hamlet* (three each)
Tokens unparalleled in drama 1576–1642: WS 11, JF 0

Stern objects that such comparisons are intrinsically biased, because "Shakespeare's theatrical output is almost ten times the size of Theobald's in terms of word count" (586). But the Theobald databases I am using are much larger: in them, Shakespeare is not 10 : 1, but only 3 : 2.[113] However, we can even the odds by restricting our search to Shakespeare's last sixteen plays. That eliminates the four works that Theobald knew best: *Hamlet* (to which he devoted most of *Shakespeare Restored*), *Richard II* (which he adapted), and the narrative poems (which he imitated in *The Cave of Poverty*, and to which he alluded in the dedication of *DF*).[114] The resulting late dramatic Shakespeare canon contains only 312,703 words.[115] Our Theobald sample is more than half again as large as this "Late Shakespeare" sample. So if there is any bias, it now favors Theobald. But even this reduced Shakespeare canon still overwhelmingly dominates the language of this passage (table 10.4(b)). Indeed, in 1.1.1–7 and 1.2.109–16 there are twenty parallels (types) with late Shakespeare, and none with Theobald; by contrast, in Theobald's three passages imitating Shakespeare, there are only seven parallels (types) with late Shakespeare, and forty-three with Theobald. Using only this chronologically reduced Shakespeare sample, the probability that the two passages in Act I of *Double Falsehood* belong to the same population as the three Theobald imitations (as Stern's forgery hypothesis requires) is still less than one in eighteen *billion*.[116]

Nor is Fletcher a candidate. Fletcher shares more language patterns with his contemporary Shakespeare than does Theobald, but a direct comparison makes it perfectly clear which of the two King's Men playwrights wrote these seven lines (table 10.4(c)). The verbal pattern here differs fundamentally from the pattern in 5.2.94–101 (table 10.3(a)). In 1.2.109–16, Fletcher's work provides only a single parallel unmatched in Shakespeare or Theobald (table 10.5).[117] There is less than one chance in two hundred thousand that the same person wrote both speeches.[118] Moreover, Shakespeare is not only likelier than Fletcher to have written this speech; he is likelier than any other playwright. Against the eleven Shakespeare parallels otherwise unmatched in drama 1576–1642, there are only four by other playwrights—one each for George Chapman, Thomas Heywood, Lodowick Carlell, and William Strode.[119] Even the reduced Shakespeare sample, with only sixteen plays (four of them collaborative), contains as many unique parallels as all the non-Shakespearian plays 1576–1642, and four times as many as any other individual playwright.

If Theobald could not provide, or did not attempt to provide, anything remotely resembling Shakespeare's style in "The righteous Pow'rs," how could he have imitated Shakespeare so compellingly here? Nevertheless, Harriet Frazier denies Shakespeare's authorship of this passage. As proof that Theobald forged the entire play, she stresses his exceptional familiarity with *Hamlet,* and in this passage she notes the *Hamlet* parallel for the collocation of *blunt* and *whet,* claiming that "in no other canonical play does Shakespeare combine the words *whet* and *blunted* in a single line."[120] Frazier's claim is very carefully phrased. Frazier rules out the collocations, in other canonical plays, of *blunt* and *whetted,* or *whetstone* and *blunt.*[121] Frazier stresses the fact that the collocation appears within a single verse line in *Hamlet*—even though the collocation here does not. Finally, Frazier singles one Shakespeare parallel (and by no means the most unusual one) out of forty-six, and one

Table 10.5 *DF* 1.2.109–16, 5.2.94–101, 5.2.251–7. (a) Parallels otherwise unrecorded in English drama, 1576–1642: types; (b) parallels recorded in only one of these three writers: types; (c) parallels recorded in only one of these three writers: tokens

	LT	JF	WS	All Other Playwrights
(a)				
5.2.251–7	6	0	1	4/4
5.2.94–101	0	4	1	6/6
1.2.109–16	0	0	11	4/4
(b)				
5.2.251–7	12	0	6	
5.2.94–101	0	15	3	
1.2.109–16	0	1	20	
(c)				
5.2.251–7	24	0	7	
5.2.94–101	0	31	3	
1.2.109–16	0	1	27	

work of Shakespeare out of twenty-six linked to these seven lines. The ten
Shakespeare works that boast unique parallels do not include any of the four
Shakespeare texts that Theobald knew best. What is most particular to this
passage is not what most interests Theobald elsewhere.

Jackson records three of the Shakespeare parallels for Leonora's speech, but
objects that her half of this passage reads "more like collages of Shakespearian
scraps than authentic Shakespeare" (*Quest,* 153). But twenty-six parallels in
thirty consecutive words is an extraordinary density of Shakespearian echoes.
The impression of collage is created by a sequence of short, grammatically
unrelated clauses:

> Patient
> What else
> My flames...flint
> Haply...one
> When...me

As John Porter Houston and Russ McDonald have demonstrated, such
disjointedness ("asyndeton") is particularly characteristic of Shakespeare's
late verse style.[122] Moreover, parallels from *Antony and Cleopatra* (Patient!
What else), *Twelfth Night* and *Othello* (Patient! What) and *Tempest* (husband...bondage...freedom) leap across two of the four grammatical dis-
junctions. Notably, all these crossover parallels come from the "reduced" late
canon. The echo of *patient* binds her speech to its cue; *flint* picks up on *whet*
in the preceding line, which itself grows from *blunt* in the line before that;[123]
flames are put out by the implied tears that she may *weep*; the synonyms *weep*
and *cry* link the final two sentences. Within the two longer sentences, binaries (haply/never, lose/get, bondage/freedom) connect the two clauses. More
generally, the clipped style implies metaphors (patience is flint, marriage is
bondage) that are not spoken here, though Shakespeare does elsewhere connect patience to stone (*Twelfth Night*'s "patience on a monument") and marriage to bondage (in the *Tempest* parallel noted above, and elsewhere). The
elisions create an impression of a mind thinking as it speaks, leaping rather
than plodding. Word-associations characteristic of Shakespeare bridge the
syntactic gaps, giving the speech an energy that actresses and audiences alike
love—as I know from having witnessed eight readings and two productions
of my own version, including these lines, and three performances of other
versions that also retained them.

This speech significantly, and dramatically, adds to Cervantes. *Don Quixote*
tells this part of Luscinda's story from Cardenio's perspective. It gives no hint
that Luscinda might have been frustrated by a suitor who twice postpones
their promised marriage by running off to court. The clash between him and
her in these seven lines not only makes the scene psychologically and theatrically interesting. It also prepares us for the possibility that she might lose
faith in him (as she seems to do in her invented soliloquy that begins *DF* 3.2).
And it explains why he might lose faith in her, believing (as he does for most

of the second half of the play) that she has betrayed him. Like the opening seven lines of the play, these seven were written by a dramatic poet capable of dramatically transforming (dare we say improving?) Cervantes.

If Theobald wrote these lines, we must recognize him as one of our greatest dramatic poets, the greatest literary chameleon of all time, and the only forger in history who perfectly copied the style of a writer who had been dead for more than a century. I find it simpler to assume that these lines, and others like them scattered throughout the first half of *DF*, are the remains of Shakespeare's contribution to a play performed by the King's Men in 1613.

LORD, WHAT FOOLS THESE MORTALS BE

Unlike Puck, I am one of those foolish mortals, no more infallible than Tiffany Stern (or Demetrius, or Lysander, or Cardenio, or the Pope). At the age of seventy-seven, Daniel Kahneman concluded: "My intuitive thinking is just as prone to overconfidence, extreme predictions, and the planning fallacy as it was before I made a study of these issues…I have made much more progress in recognizing the errors of others than my own" (417). I have thought long and slowly about *Double Falsehood* and *Cardenio*, but my very familiarity with it undoubtedly blinds me to aspects of the problem that others can see more clearly. I count on you to correct me.

NOTES

1. For help in overcoming the limits of my own intelligence, I am deeply grateful to readers of earlier drafts of this essay: Terri Bourus, Gerald Baker, Meaghan Brown, Gabriel Egan, MacDonald P. Jackson, Kate Lechler, Rory Loughnane, Anna Pruitt and Joe Travis.

2. I focus on Stern's 2011 essay, because it incorporates, endorses, and expands earlier claims about forgery, made by less distinguished scholars. I have already answered, in "History," some of the objections made by earlier skeptics (quoted by Stern), and will not repeat those arguments here.

3. My approach differs fundamentally from that articulated in Raphael Lyne's excellent *Shakespeare, Rhetoric and Cognition* (Cambridge: Cambridge University Press, 2011), which also provides a useful survey of cognitive literary theory (28–67, 251–3).

4. See for instance Stephen L. Macknik, Susana Martinez-Conde, and Sandra Blakeslee, *Sleights of Mind: What the Neuroscience of Magic Reveals about Our Everyday Deceptions* (New York: Picador, 2011).

5. On the "exacting tyranny of old stories" in *DF*, see Frances E. Dolan, *True Relations: Reading, Literature, and Evidence in Seventeenth-Century England* (Philadelphia: University of Pennsylvania Press, 2013), 242–3.

6. On Stern's claims about Shelton, see Nance's essay (chapter 9), and Taylor and Wagschal's (chapter 2), in this volume.

7. Philip Lorenz, "'Absonant Desire': The Question of *Cardenio*," in *Shakesqueer: A Queer Companion to the Complete Works of Shakespeare*, ed. Madhavi Menon (Durham: Duke University Press, 2011), 66, 64.

8. Margit E. Oswald and Stefan Grosjean, "Confirmation Bias," in *Cognitive Illusions: A Handbook on Fallacies and Biases in Thinking, Judgment and Memory,* ed. Rüdier F. Pohl (New York: Psychology Press, 2004), 79–96.

9. Kahneman, *Thinking, Fast and Slow* (New York: Farrar, Straus and Giroux, 2011), 81. Lyne's *Rhetoric and Cognition* does not cite Kahneman, but his distinction between fast and slow reading could be related to Kahneman's between fast System 1 and slow System 2.

10. Gamaliel Bradford, "'The History of Cardenio by Mr. Fletcher and Shakespeare,'" *Modern Language Notes* 25 (1910): 51–6.

11. See Rudolph Schevill, "Theobald's *Double Falsehood* ?" *Modern Philology* 9 (1911): 269–85; Leonard Schwartzstein, "The Text of *The Double Falsehood*," *Notes and Queries* 169 (1954): 471–2; Harriet Frazier, *A Babble of Ancestral Voices: Shakespeare, Cervantes, and Theobald* (The Hague: Mouton, 1974); Jeffrey Kahan, *Shakespeare Imitations, Parodies and Forgeries, 1710–1820,* 3 vols. (London: Taylor and Francis, 2004). Stern cites all these critics approvingly, without objection to their focus on Shakespeare.

12. Jackson, "Looking for Shakespeare in *Double Falsehood*: Stylistic Evidence," *Quest,* 160–1.

13. Proudfoot, "Can Double Falsehood Be Merely a Forgery by Lewis Theobald?" *Quest,* 175, n. 11.

14. See Taylor, "History," 39–58, and Taylor and Nance, *Quest,* 201–11.

15. *The Works of Shakespeare…Collated with the Oldest Copies, and Corrected; with Notes, Explanatory, and Critical: By Mr. Theobald* (1733), 1:32, 1.67, 2.446, 3:248, 3.305, 6.379, 7:354, 7:359.

16. For examples of *can't,* see *Works* 2:174, 3:236, 4:135, 5:30, 5:291, 6:33, 6:112, 7:50, 7:103, 7:419, 7:469; for *don't,* 3:23, 4.74; for *to've,* 2:335, 3.68, 5:81, 6:441, 7:380; for *good heav'ns,* 6:412, 437. Stern does not record Jackson's observation that only "the apostrophe" makes this last example evidence for Theobald's spelling; the oath itself appears twice in Shakespeare, both in *Cymbeline,* a late play written within a few years of *Cardenio.*

17. Of Jackson's listed contractions, only *Look'ee* (at *DF* 2.3.189) does not appear in Theobald's Shakespeare edition. It occurs in pre-1643 drama only in Ford's *Perkin Warbeck* and *Broken Heart,* but became increasingly common after the Restoration, including three examples in Theobald (*Plutus* 54; *Orestes* 15, 41), before and after *DF*. This word was almost certainly written by Theobald. For other evidence of his presence in the vicinity, see Taylor, "History," 41 (*DF* 2.3.213) and Hammond (notes to *DF* 2.3.37, 62,103, 110, 144); Jonathan Hope, *The Authorship of Shakespeare's Plays* (Cambridge: Cambridge University Press, 1994), provides strong statistical evidence (p. 92) that 2.3 cannot have been written in its entirety by the author of 1.2 (who matches Shakespeare); Jackson and Proudfoot provide evidence of Theobald's extensive presence in Act Two. I think 2.3 contains fragments of original Shakespeare, but even if it were entirely Theobald's that would not prove that he wrote the whole play. Rather, the reverse: the fact that so many scholars independently establish Theobald's strong presence in 2.3 indicates that their methods are not biased by a desire to find Shakespeare everywhere.

18. Jackson, "Looking," *Quest,* 140–1. Although she elsewhere cites Jackson's essay, for these linguistic forms Stern (584) acknowledges only the less comprehensive discussion in Stephan Kukowski, "The Hand of John Fletcher in *Double Falsehood*," *Shakespeare Survey* 43 (1991): 88.

19. Oliphant, *The Plays of Beaumont and Fletcher: An Attempt to Determine Their Respective Shares and the Shares of Others* (New Haven: Yale University Press, 1927).

20. Jackson, *Studies in Attribution: Middleton and Shakespeare,* Jacobean Drama Studies, vol. 79 (Salzburg, 1979); *Defining Shakespeare: Pericles as Test Case* (Oxford: Oxford University Press, 2003); "Affirmative Particles in *Henry VIII*," *Notes and Queries* 206 (1962): 372–4; "Phrase Length in *Henry VIII*: Shakespeare and Fletcher," *Notes and Queries* 242 (1997): 75–80; "Stage Directions and Speech Headings in Act I of *Titus Andronicus* Q (1594): Shakespeare or Peele?" *Studies in Bibliography* 49 (1996): 134–48; "Shakespeare's *Richard II* and the Anonymous *Thomas of Woodstock*," in *Medieval and Renaissance Drama in England* 14 (2001): 17–65; "The Date and Authorship of *Thomas of Woodstock*: Evidence and Its Interpretation," *Research Opportunities in Medieval and Renaissance Drama* 46 (2007): 67–100; "Some Comments on Michael Egan's 'Slurs, Nasal Rhymes and Amputations,'" *The Oxfordian* 12 (2010): 94–8.

21. Jackson, "The Additions to *The Second Maiden's Tragedy*: Shakespeare or Middleton?" *Shakespeare Quarterly* 41 (1990): 402–5.

22. Hope, *Authorship,* eliminates *Cromwell, Oldcastle, Puritan, Yorkshire Tragedy,* and *Birth of Merlin,* and also dismisses *Henry VIII, Kinsmen, Timon, Pericles, London Prodigal,* and *Arden* as works of Shakespeare's sole authorship.

23. William Shakespeare and John Fletcher, *King Henry VIII (All Is True),* ed. McMullan (London: Thomson, 2000), 185.

24. For a useful historical survey of attribution scholarship, see Brian Vickers, *Shakespeare, Co-Author* (Oxford: Oxford University Press, 2002), 333–43 (*Henry VIII*), 403–16 (*Kinsmen*).

25. Indeed, she does not even identify me as coeditor of *Quest* (570, n. 62), perhaps out of an unconscious desire to protect me from any responsibility for the essays there that she criticizes.

26. In 2005 I named her one of the six most promising scholars under forty in the field of Renaissance drama studies; in 2009 I asked her to be on the advisory board for the New Oxford Shakespeare; in 2011 she gave me access to her transcripts of several rare Theobald texts, to add to my database; in the same year I asked her advice on several details of my account of the King's Men's performance of "Cardenna" on June 8, 1613, hosted by Lord Mayor Swinnerton. As an anonymous outside reader for Cambridge University Press, I recommended publication of Stern's *Documents of Early Modern Performance.*

27. Photographically reproduced (10) and transcribed (105–6) in Hammond.

28. For examples see Taylor, "History," 22–4.

29. Farmer, *An Essay on the Learning of Shakespeare,* second edition (Cambridge, 1767), 29.

30. James Shirley cannot have been the author: see Taylor, "History," 25.

31. Phillip Massinger, *Plays and Poems,* ed. Philip Edwards and Colin Gibson (Oxford: Clarendon Press, 1976), IV, 204.

32. Lewis Theobald to William Warburton, April 8, 1729, in John Nichols, *Illustrations of the Literary History of the Eighteenth Century,* 2 vols. (London, 1817), 2:212 (quoted by Stern, 562).

33. Pohl, "Hindsight Bias," in Pohl, *Cognitive Illusions,* 363–78; Kahneman, *Thinking,* 201–4.

34. Kathleen Menzie Lesko, "Evidence of Restoration Performances: Duke Ferdinand Albrecht's Annotated Playtexts from 1664–5," *Philological Quarterly* 79 (2000): 45.

35. Hume, "Before the Bard: 'Shakespeare' in Early Eighteenth-Century London," *ELH* 64 (1997): 74.

36. Keith E. Stanovich and Richard F. West," On the Failure of Cognitive Ability to Predict Myside and One Side Thinking Biases," *Thinking & Reasoning* 14 (2008): 129–67.

37. Richard F. West, Russell J. Meserve, and Keith E. Stanovich, "Cognitive Sophistication Does Not Attenuate the Bias Blind Spot," *Journal of Personality and Social Psychology* 103 (2012): 506–19.

38. John P. A. Ioannidis, "Why Most Published Research Findings Are False," *PLOS Medicine*, 2, e124, August 2005, www.plosmedicine.org/article/info:doi/10.137/journal.pmed.0020124.

39. Grafton, *Forgers and Critics: Creativity and Duplicity in Western Scholarship* (Princeton: Princeton University Press, 1990), esp. pp. 6, 124–7. Schevill's claim of forgery led to further investigation of *DF*'s sources by Graham and Freehafer; Frazier's claim led to Kukowski's demonstration of Fletcher's presence.

40. For Stern's impact, see for instance Michael P. Jensen, "Talking Books with Tiffany Stern," *Shakespeare Newsletter* 62.1 (Spring/Summer 2012): 9 ("It convinced me") and Lois Potter, *The Life of William Shakespeare: A Critical Biography* (Malden, MA: Wiley-Blackwell, 2012), 392 ("convincing").

41. *The Correspondence of Alexander Pope,* ed. George Sherburn, 6 vols. (Oxford: Clarendon Press, 1956), 4:102.

42. Farmer, *Essay*, 29; see also Taylor, "History," 25, 38–9.

43. See Ivan Lupić, "Malone's *Double Falsehood*," in *Quest*, 95–114.

44. Kahneman, *Thinking*, 51–8; Thomas Mussweiler, Birte Englich, and Fritz Strack, "Anchoring Effect," in Pohl, *Cognitive Illusions*, 181–200.

45. Kahneman, *Thinking*, 63.

46. Robert B. Zajonc, ""Attitudinal Effects of Mere Exposure," *Journal of Personality and Social Psychology* 9 (1968): 1–27; Robert F. Bornstein and Catherine Craver-Lemley, "Mere Exposure Effect," in Pohl, *Cognitive Illusions*, 215–34; David M. Eagleman, *Incognito: The Secret Lives of the Brain* (New York: Vintage, 2011), 64–5; Dan Gardner, *Risk: The Science and Politics of Fear* (London: Virgin, 2008), 89.

47. James W. Pennebaker, *The Secret Life of Pronouns: What Our Words Say about Us* (New York: Bloomsbury, 2011), ix.

48. See Hugh Craig and Arthur Kinney, eds., *Shakespeare, Computers, and the Mystery of Authorship* (Cambridge University Press, 2009).

49. Although *Cave of Poverty* is a poem, I have checked it against early modern drama in order to make the results comparable to those for all the other passages analyzed here.

50. Nichols, 2:577, 284, 377 (cited by Stern, 577).

51. Again, there is a random scattering of unique parallels with other dramatists (one each for Wilson, Middleton, Rowley, Daborne, and J.R.'s *The Cid* 1).

52. Fisher's Exact Test gives $p = 0.3989$, or about a two-in-five chance, that the two samples are homogenous. By comparison, $p = 0.01$ (one in 100) is usually taken as indicating statistical significance. Unlike the chi-square test, Fisher's works well in cases where one set of observations is less than five, so

long as the total number of observations in a 2×2 continency table is more than eight; here, there are twenty-six. For help in using and interpreting this test, I am deeply grateful to Mac Jackson. Calculations are based on the free public website http://research.microsoft.com/en-us/um/redmond/projects /MSCompBio/FisherExactTest/ (accessed June 4, 2013). Here and throughout, I cite the two-sided probability value, which is generally considered most useful.

53. "From 1715 onward... *Cave of Poverty*... His adaptation of *Richard II*... *Orestes* followed... then came *Double Falsehood*" (Stern, 577). The dates of these four works are 1715, 1720, 1731, and 1727.

54. Jackson included these seven lines in his summary of results for three passages Oliphant had attributed to Shakespeare, but did not consider them separately (*Quest*, 145). His detailed data does separate 1.1.1–8: see http://liberal arts.iupui.edu/shakespeare/research. But Jackson checks all phrases against Fletcher as well as Shakespeare, whereas I am here making a binary comparison between Shakespeare and Theobald. Moreover, Jackson's Theobald results derive solely from Literature Online; mine are based on searches of a much larger Theobald database (for which see Nance's essay, chapter 9, in this volume). To protect against my own bias, I have had these results independently double-checked by Meaghan Brown.

55. Fisher's Exact Test $p = 0.00007829$. If we compare *DF* with *Poverty* alone, $p = 0.00009178$ (less than one in ten thousand). Even if we compare *DF* with the later *Orestes* alone, $p = 0.001214$ (about one in a thousand).

56. Nance's stylometric tests resemble mine, but he cross-checks all authors in both Literature Online and EEBO, while I focus on playwrights; he also confines his results to material which is relatively rare in both databases. Moreover, he limits himself to exact word strings, and does not include collocations. We have not homogenized our methods, because it seems worthwhile to demonstrate that different methods produce the same results.

57. Francine Melka, "Receptive vs. Productive Aspects of Vocabulary," in *Vocabulary: Description, Acquisition and Pedagogy*, ed. Norbert Schmitt and Michael McCarthy (Cambridge: Cambridge University Press, 1998), 84–102; I. S. P. Nation, *Learning Vocabulary in Another Language* (Cambridge: Cambridge University Press, 2011), 23–59.

58. Tversky and Kahneman, "Extensional Versus Intuitive Reasoning: The Conjunction Fallacy in Probability Judgment," *Psychological Review* 90 (1983): 293–315.

59. Kahneman, *Thinking*, 88, 152, 166–73. For "prior probability" (a.k.a. "base rate"), its relationship to Bayesian statistical reasoning, and its neglect by most people, see Nate Silver, *The Signal and the Noise* (New York: Penguin, 2012), 242–60.

60. For Theobald, Cervantes, and Shelton, see Nance (chapter 9), and Taylor and Wagschal (chapter 2), in this volume.

61. For Shakespeare I include the thirty-six Folio plays, *Pericles, Kinsmen, Edward III*, and the 1603 edition of *Hamlet* (which differs so substantially as to constitute another work). Exclusion of 1603 *Hamlet* and its single parallel would not affect the results. I treat Shakespeare's collaborative plays as entirely his, thereby overestimating his proportion of the database, which if anything should have the effect of *underestimating* the statistical contrast. To calculate expected ratios I have used www.quantpsy.org/chisq/chisq.htm.

62. See Robert Folkenflik, "'Shakespearesque': The Arden *Double Falsehood*," *Huntington Library Quarterly* 75 (2012): 131–43 (esp. 138). Folkenflik's review essay was published before *Quest*.

63. Taylor, "History," 46–7.

64. *Fletcher*, 10:751–2.

65. Stern 586, citing Paul Bertram, *Shakespeare and "The Two Noble Kinsmen"* (New Brunswick: Rutgers University Press, 1965), 186. Bertram's argument against Shakespeare collaborating with Fletcher on *DF* is part of an attempt to prove that Shakespeare wrote the entirety of *Kinsmen,* an argument discredited by overwhelming historical and stylistic evidence. Here as elsewhere Stern's case against *DF* entails a rejection of massively substantiated scholarship about the rest of the Shakespeare canon.

66. Walter Graham, "The *Cardenio-Double Falsehood* Problem," *Modern Philology* 14 (1916): 275–6.

67. Doran, *Lost,* 131: quoting "When lovers swear...eternal throne," he compares the image to El Greco, and calls it "one of my favorite lines" (actually, three of his favorite lines).

68. The six others are: can love again] Carlell, *1 Passionate Lover*; Maids that have] Lording Barry, *Family of Love;* love...in their hearts...eyes] Shakespeare, *Romeo*; hearts...deep within] Randolph, *Amyntas* (deep within my heart); no physic but] Dekker, *Wonder*; time or death can] *Merry Devil of Edmonton* (anonymous).

69. Fisher Exact Test website defines p as 3.123E-010 (or a probability of 0.0000000003123). For a color-coded visualization of the data in these two "Leonora" speeches in 5.2, and a third in 1.2 (discussed below), see *CSI Shakespeare*.

70. Eight of the collocation-types that link 5.2.94–101 to Fletcher rather than Theobald can also be found in Shakespeare (rites performed, Ere I can, If they be, here my lord, my lord here, their eyes or; no...can cure, physic...time).

71. love...in their hearts/...not in their eyes] love then lies/ Not truly in their hearts, but in their eyes *Romeo*; physic...death] *Othello, Coriolanus, H8* 3.2a; physic...cure] Sonnet 147.

72. D. M. McKeithan, *The Debt to Shakespeare in the Beaumont and Fletcher Plays* (New York: Collier, 1938); David L. Frost, *The School of Shakespeare* (Cambridge University Press, 1968), 237–45.

73. Of the eighteen collocation-types linking the speech to Theobald, four can also be found in Shakespeare, and a fifth fits Shakespeare better: at length have *R2*, the storm...o'erblown *Tempest*, sour affliction (exact match *2H6*), true faith *R2, AYLI, JC*, so...repaid *Shrew*.

74. lovers swear] *Troilus*; stand on...battlements] stand securely on their battlements *John*; Such were our] Such were our faults, or then we thought them none *AWW* (unique).

75. The other two are: have crown'd our] Heywood, *Golden Age*; hope awhile] May, *Old Couple*.

76. More than half the Shakespeare parallels here come from before 1598; the only indisputably late parallel echoes *Coriolanus*. That makes no sense for a speech written in 1612–1613. But it fits Theobald, who preferred Shakespeare's early style.

77. Comparing Theobald parallels and Shakespeare parallels in 5.2.251–7 and the first seven lines of *Cave* and *Orestes* (combined), Fisher's p = 0.7477.

78. Kahneman, *Thinking,* 82–5.
79. On the anti-editorial prejudice, see Gary Taylor, *Cultural Selection* (New York: Basic Books, 1996), 121–42, and "What is an Author [not]?" *Critical Survey* 7 (1995): 241–55.
80. *Grub Street Journal,* March 14, 1734 (Stern 555, 578).
81. David Orr, *Beautiful and Pointless: A Guide to Modern Poetry* (New York: HarperCollins, 2011), 185–8.
82. Julia Briggs, "Tears at the Wedding: Shakespeare's Last Phase," in *Shakespeare's Late Plays: New Readings,* ed. Jennifer Richards and James Knowles (Edinburgh: Edinburgh University Press, 1999), 221.
83. Jaegar, *Enchantment: On Charisma and the Sublime in the Arts of the West* (Philadelphia: University of Pennsylvania Press, 2012), 3, 38. Pope's *Peri Bathous* (to which he confined *DF*) explicitly contrasts with the *Peri Hypsous* of Longinus.
84. Roach, *It* (Ann Arbor: University of Michigan Press, 2007). Roach focuses on the Restoration, but (except for actresses) most of the elements of "It-culture" that he analyzes originate in the "synthetic experience" of Elizabethan and Jacobean theater. He admits that "the most popular actors in Shakespeare's time enjoyed robust celebrity status" (30). Royal patronage of the theater began with Elizabeth's creation of the Queen's Men; the first influential formal ritual of "public intimacy" was the Elizabethan soliloquy; Alleyn, Burbage, and Nathan Field inaugurate the circulation of portraits of sexy leading actors; Tamburlaine's conquest of audiences depended on "hypermasculine…sartorial splendor" (84) and the recycling of aristocratic clothing on common stages; "the glorification of romance" (61) is more conspicuous in Shakespeare than in Etherege or Wycherley.
85. Kidnie, *Shakespeare and the Problem of Adaptation* (New York: Routledge, 2009), 140–64.
86. See David Carnegie, "Theobald's Pattern of Adaptation: *The Duchess of Malfi* and *Richard II*," in *Quest,* 180–91.
87. Peter W. M. Blayney, *The First Folio of Shakespeare* (Washington, DC: Folger Library, 1991), 17, 21–4.
88. *The Tragedy of Arthur* (New York: Random House, 2011), 204.
89. "It is likely that Philo-Shakespeare was Theobald himself" (564). Stern's only evidence for this claim is the fact that Philo-Shakespeare endorsed Theobald's attack on Pope. By such reasoning, almost every reader of *Shakespeare Restored* who was not a friend of Pope, and every subsequent editor of Shakespeare, could be identified as "Philo-Shakespeare." Such claims do not encourage much faith in Stern's credentials as an attribution scholar.
90. Grafton, *Forgers and Critics,* 5, 24.
91. Shakespeare did not write *The Arraignment of Paris, The Troublesome Reign of John, Fair Em, Edward II, Edward IV, Sir John Oldcastle, Thomas Lord Cromwell, The Merry Devil of Edmonton, The London Prodigal, A Yorkshire Tragedy, The Puritan, Mucedorus,* or *The Birth of Merlin,* and wrote only a part of seven plays attributed to him alone (*Titus, 1 Henry VI, Timon, Pericles, All Is True, Edward III, Arden of Faversham*). *Henry VI, Parts Two and Three* should also probably be added to this list.
92. For a rebuttal of Stern's attack on Moseley (557–8) see Taylor, "History," 12–13, 17, 20.
93. Hammond, "After Arden," in *Quest,* 78.

94. Kahneman and Tversky, "Intuitive Prediction: Biases and Corrective Procedures," *Management Science* 12 (1979): 313–27. My children, who have often seen this fallacy in operation, call it "the Japanese war plan" (referring to the fact that Japan's military leaders in 1941 knew that they could defeat the United States *only if everything went exactly as they hoped*).

95. www.slate.com/articles/life/the_spectator/2010/05/the_double_false-hood_of_double_falsehood.html

96. Taleb, *The Black Swan: The Impact of the Highly Improbable* (New York: Random House, 2007), xxi, 102, 318.

97. Gerald Eades Bentley, *The Profession of Dramatist in Shakespeare's Time, 1590–1642* (Princeton: Princeton University Press, 1971), 16 (lost plays); Jonathan L. Payne and Seth Finnegan, "The Effect of Geographic Range on Extinction Risk During Background and Mass Extinction," *Proceedings of the National Academy of Sciences of the United States of America* 104.25 (2007): 10506–11. For a survey of the scientific literature see David Jablonski, "Origination Patterns and Multilevel Processes in Macroevolution," in *Evolution: The Extended Synthesis*, ed. M. Pigliucci and G. B. Müller (Cambridge: MIT Press, 2010), 335–54. For application of such biological models to the extinction of human artifacts, see Taylor, *Cultural Selection*.

98. Luffenham Hall (*Lost*, 82), Warburton's cook (108), the Earls of Orrery (172–3), Covent Garden (235–7), and Stradone House (249). He also reminds us of other lost works of art, and their occasional rediscovery (251–3).

99. Theobald, *Shakespeare Restored* (1726), ii, 133 (cited by Stern, 561).

100. Theobald, ed., *Works,* 1:xli.

101. Nichols, *Illustrations*, 2:249.

102. Kahan, *Imitations*, 1:160, quoted by Stern, 563–4.

103. Kahneman. *Thinking*, 12.

104. Gildon, *The Postman Robb'd of His Mail* (1719), 267–8, quoted and discussed by Hammond, 84–6.

105. *An Apology for the Life of Mr. Colley Cibber, Written by Himself,* ed. Robert W. Lowe, 2 vols. (London: Nimmo, 1889), 2:233, 248.

106. Theoretically, Theobald could have forged it earlier than 1715, then anonymously sold it, then bought it back from its new owner and adapted it. But this improbable scenario would entail several more conjunctions. In any case, Stern's thesis heavily depends on the 1727 date.

107. See Huw Griffiths, "The Friend in *Cardenio, Double Falsehood,* and *Don Quixote,*" in *Quest*, 239–55, and Bourus, "Stages," 399.

108. Raphael Lyne, "Recognition in *Cymbeline*," in *Late Shakespeare, 1608–1613,* ed. Andrew J. Power and Rory Loughnane (Cambridge University Press, 2012), 56–70.

109. Taleb, *Black Swan*, 132, 64, 79, 83, 80, 133; Kahneman, *Thinking*, 199–200.

110. See particularly Brian Boyd, *On the Origin of Stories: Evolution, Cognition, and Fiction* (Cambridge: Harvard University Press, 2009).

111. Fisher p = 2.848E-007 (or 0.0000002848), comparing it with Theobald's Shakespeare's imitations; p = 1.650E-007 (or 0.000000165) comparing it to Theobald's added speech in 5.2.

112. The two passages in the first two scenes of *DF* have zero Theobald parallels, but thirty-seven from Shakespeare; Theobald's two Shakespeare imitations plus 5.2.251–7 have thirty Theobald parallels, and only fourteen from Shakespeare: Fisher p = 8.280E-012 (or 0.00000000000828).

113. Taylor and Nance, *Quest,* 211: Theobald 513,828 words (without counting words in the 1,356 notes in his 1733 edition); Shakespeare (with collaborator scenes removed), 784,717.
114. *DF* Ded.13 ("his own Southampton" alluding to the dedications of *Venus and Adonis* and *Lucrece*). The paratext alludes to no other works by Shakespeare.
115. The plays included are *TN, Troilus, MM, Othello, Lear, Timon* (collaborative), *Macbeth, Antony, AWW, Pericles* (collaborative), *Coriolanus, WT, Cymbeline, Tempest, AIT/H8* (collaborative), and *Kinsmen* (collaborative). For collaborative plays I have counted, and searched, only the scenes attributed to Shakespeare. The counts for *Macbeth* and *Measure* probably slightly overestimate the Shakespeare total, since they include short passages that have been attributed by myself and some (but not all) other scholars to Middleton's adaptation; none of the parallels come from those passages.
116. Fisher p = 5.486E-012 (or 0.000000000005486).
117. I cry for] *Scornful Lady* 4.1.
118. Fisher p = 4.585E-007 (or 0.0000004585). The difference in magnitude between the Fletcher improbability and the Theobald improbability is what we would expect: Fletcher was Shakespeare's contemporary and collaborator, whereas Theobald was writing more than a century after Shakespeare's death.
119. The four are: bar...wishes] Carlell, *2 Passionate Lover;* flames are in] Strode, *Floating Island;* in the flint] Heywood, *If You Know Not Me, Part I* ("in the flint-bosoms"); husband I may] Chapman, *Beggar.* Neither Carlell nor Strode could not have written the *Cardenio* performed in 1613.
120. Frazier, *Babble,* 132; quoted by Hammond, without objection (197).
121. For *DF*'s "blunt not," Jackson records a parallel in *Macbeth,* but overlooks "whetstone" in the preceding line ("Be this the whetstone of your sword, let grief Convert to wrath: blunt not the heart").
122. Houston, *Shakespearean Sentences: A Study in Style and Syntax* (Baton Rouge: Louisiana State University Press, 1988), 199–201; McDonald, *Shakespeare's Late Style* (Cambridge: Cambridge University Press, 2006), 88–90.
123. Compare *2H4* 4.3.27–33, where "blunt not his love" is followed, six lines later, by "he is flint."

11

The "Unscene" and Unstaged in *Double Falsehood*, *Cardenio*, and Shakespeare's Romances

Lori Leigh

Onstage in both the first and last scene of Gary Taylor's *The History of Cardenio*, an emblematic coffin bookends the action of the play. A coffin, which simultaneously (and paradoxically) evokes "presence" and "absence"—the presence of a body and the absence of a life—seems an appropriate prop for Shakespeare and Fletcher's lost play *Cardenio*.

Dramatic techniques that rely on presence and absence occur within *Double Falsehood* as well as the various adaptations and recreations of *Double Falsehood/Cardenio*. There are events in the play present through language or sounds, but absent onstage and to the eyes of the audience. This essay will analyze how these scenes function in performance, and relate them to offstage action in elliptical late Shakespeare. This dramaturgical and performative approach clarifies the relationship among *Double Falsehood*, the lost *Cardenio*, and Shakespeare's romances.[1]

Offstage action can be viewed as a kind of ellipsis, a characteristic feature of late Shakespeare. Many critics have discussed the "elliptical nature" of Shakespearian romances. Russ McDonald, for example, writes: "The unexpected juxtapositions, surprising turns of plot, and temporal shifts characteristic of the action represent a mode of storytelling that might be called narrative asyndeton." McDonald summarizes critics on late Shakespeare by stating: "These accounts capture the widely shared sense that the language of the last plays is veiled and ineffable, that it points to something beyond itself but frustrates every effort to apprehend that something directly."[2] Likewise, Majorie Garber says: "As we should expect, the most 'ineffable' moments in Shakespeare come in the later plays, the final tragedies and romances, where the content of the plays themselves seems frequently to demand a dramatic technique that goes beyond the limits of the quotidian and the expressible."[3] One such dramatic technique is a particular type of offstage action, what she labels an "unscene": "deflected or unseen scenes that take place offstage and are reported by an observer" (43), which allow Shakespeare to "bring to life, by narrative, events that take place offstage."[4] This essay will employ Garber's concept of the "unscene" as one means to understand the offstage action in *Double Falsehood* and *Cardenio(s)*.

Dramatically Offstage

The most notorious unscene in *Double Falsehood* is also one of the most discussed parts of the play.[5] Therefore, it will not be the focus here, but it should be mentioned in any discussion of offstage action in *Double Falsehood*. In 2.1, Henriquez enters raving about having raped Violante. Though Cervantes devotes several detailed passages to the equivalent scene (*DQ* 4.1.289–94), Henriquez here provides little information about the event. The audience knows only that he made some oath of marriage to Violante. The 1767 edition of *Double Falsehood* added to the end of 1.3 the lines "She's gone:—No matter! I have brib'd her Woman,/ And soon shall gain Admittance!", presumably to clarify that Henriquez invades Violante's chamber and what permits him to do so.[6] In *Cymbeline*, Cloten aims to use similar means to gain access to Innogen's bedchamber, "I know her women are about her; what/ If I do line one of their hands? 'Tis gold/ Which buys admittance" (2.3.64–6). The 1767 interpolation may have had Cloten in mind. All recent productions of *Double Falsehood/ Cardenio* have transformed Theobald's unscene here into a scene. Even the Classic Stage Company's 2011 production of *Double Falsehood*, whose intention was to "stage the Theobald adaptation with no interpolations," staged the rape.[7] Productions can make the rape clear, graphic, and disturbing (Bernard Richards's *Cardenio*), or they can transform it into a forced seduction scene closer to the one found in *Don Quixote* (*THOC* 1.5).[8] They can put the sex onstage (Mokita Grit) or they can have the characters exit to engage in the act (Taylor, and Doran's RSC production).[9]

In *Double Falsehood*, Theobald's unscene develops the action in a different way than do these choices to bring it onstage. When Henriquez relates the rape, he reveals himself as what in novelistic terms would be called "an unreliable narrator." The audience witnesses Henriquez give conflicting versions of the event and essentially lie to himself. In the hands of Theobald, this becomes a scene not primarily about rape, but one about a master deceiver and his falsehoods. This is reinforced by Henriquez's abrupt shift from Violante to Leonora, Julio's beloved, describing how he has already violated the laws of friendship by deceptively removing Julio so he can pursue Leonora. A final and related effect of the elimination of Violante's rape is that such distancing of the event from the audience, emotionally and spatially—they do not see her immediately before, during, or after—lessens the impact of the crime. The audience receives it secondhand from the attacker, not the victim. Even the presence of the eavesdroppers, Lopez and Fabian, works to achieve this distancing effect: "Fabian and Lopez...do not object to the rape he describes, or morally condemn him."[10] Such distancing was no doubt desirable and intentional on Theobald's part.

Often linked with the rape of Violante and referred to as "the other missing scene" is a piece of offstage action involving the other heroine in *Double Falsehood*, Leonora. After a lengthy absence from each other, Henriquez and his brother Roderick are reunited in the fourth act when Henriquez seeks Roderick's help because he has "lost a mistress" (Leonora). Because Leonora is living in a cloister, Roderick devises a plan,

> We must pretend we do transport a body
> As s'twere to's funeral; and coming late by,
> Crave a night's leave to rest the hearse i'th' convent.
> That be our course, for to such charity
> Strict zeal and custom of the house give way. (4.1.236–40)

Conveniently, moments later, a vacant hearse passes (offstage). At the opening of Act Five, Leonora is with Henriquez and his brother Roderick's train. How this occurred exactly is left rather ambiguous. In 4.1, Roderick says "the means of her conveyance/ By safe and secret force with ease we'll compass" (4.1.244–5). As Hammond notes in the Arden edition: "It is not entirely clear what kind of *force* is meant here" (4.1.245n.). Later, Roderick apologizes to Leonora for a "course of violence" and says she was "surpris'd" or captured. It should be noted that this is not an unscene, strictly speaking, because no sustained or detailed recounting of Leonora's abduction ever finds its way into the text. Rather, it is a piece of offstage action, referred to in vague terms. It is even more open for interpolation by adaptors than the rape/seduction of Violante because there is not much information in *Don Quixote* to fill the gaps. Shelton's translation describes it thus:

> [Ferdinando/Henriquez] choosing those three Gentlemen for his associates, he came to the place where she [Luscinda/Leonora] was, but would not speak to her, fearing lest that as soon as they knew of his being there they would increase the guards of the Monastery, and therefore expected until he found on a day the gates of the Monastery open; and leaving two of his fellows to keep the door, he with the other entered the Abbey in Luscinda's search, who they found talking to a Nunne in the Cloyster, and snatching her away er'e she could retire her self, they brought her to a certain village, where they disguised themselves in that sort they were; for so it was requisite for to bring her away. (*DQ* 4.9.409–10)

This short account constitutes the entire scene, and there is no coffin, no brother, no funeral, and again no clear description of how Luscinda (Leonora) was snatched.

Both Gregory Doran's RSC production and Bernard Richards's Cambridge BATS production of *Cardenio* added substantial scenes showing Henriquez abducting Leonora (Luscinda) from the nunnery. Richards says the scene "seemed" to be missing. Calling the offstage action in *Double Falsehood* "very mysterious, and unsatisfactory," he connects it to another late Shakespearian scene where an intruder invades a woman's private quarters through means of a large container: "The original must, I feel, have spelt it all out. Perhaps Henriquez hid in the hearse, as Iachimo hides in the trunk in *Cymbeline*, and climbed out once inside the nunnery. Did he then drug Leonora and put her in the hearse?"[11] Late Shakespeare rarely spells it all out. Doran is firmer in his position about Leonora's abduction scene, calling Theobald's play "unperformable" without it. Doran connects the scene to Fletcher's sensibilities, however, in writing: "I cannot think that Fletcher would have missed the opportunity to supply another variation on the coffin trick, in the scene where Henriquez/Don Fernando abducts Leonora/Luscinda from the convent. There are plenty of precedents. The scene in *The Knight of the Burning Pestle*, when Jasper jumps out of the coffin to be reunited with Luce, could almost have been inspired by *Cardenio*."[12] For both the RSC and Cambridge BATS, these scenes seem to have worked well in performance. The scene in the RSC production left such an impression on Paul Taylor of the *Independent* that he begins his review evoking it:

> "Where am I?" cries the terrified beautiful heroine, who has latterly taken the veil. She's in a state because she's just been bundled in an imposing coffin and ferried by men in pointy black Ku Klux Klan-like hats to this unknown address. "Not in a nunnery," proclaims the bug-eyed villain of the piece, in one of the many moments in *Cardenio*, exhilaratingly assembled and directed for the RSC by Greg Doran, that is precariously poised on the cusp between consciously camp and inadvertent humour.[13]

On the other hand, that the scene is theatrical (and successful in performance) seems to be the only argument Richards and Doran are able to make for staging Leonora's abduction from the nunnery (and that Theobald's text here is sketchy—but almost the entire play is so). While it certainly could be true that a scene is missing, if we are examining late Shakespeare and offstage action, the opposite is just as likely. If we had plays such as *The Winter's Tale* and *The Two Noble Kinsmen* in fragments, one might say positively that Shakespeare would not have left moments as theatrically appealing as the reunion of Leontes and Perdita or the Palamon and Arcite battle unstaged.

Perhaps a more productive approach is to investigate the dramaturgical function of such a scene. It is not necessary to understand the narrative. The story of Leonora's abduction from the nunnery can be told in scenes surrounding the event (as Theobald and Taylor do). It is also not required to depict Henriquez as a villain. This has already been accomplished earlier in the play where twice he has forced the heroines into actions against their will (i.e. Violante's rape and the wedding scene of Henriquez and Leonora). Additionally, it would not have the same effect as Giacomo in Innogen's bedchamber. The scene in *Cymbeline* works dramatically because it is fraught with danger and titillation. The audience invades Innogen's privacy with Giacomo, and there is always the possibility, enhanced by the text's multiple suggestions, that he will do more than look, that he will physically violate her as he examines her exposed body parts. This is conjured by many details in the text such as Innogen reading in her book about the rape of Philomel and her attending woman being named "Helen." Roger Warren discusses how productions have placed this threat of rape onstage "by having him straddle her, and even pull the bedclothes completely away from her."[14] The same is not true for Leonora's abduction from the nunnery, simply due to the presence of Henriquez's honorable older brother, Roderick. As Roderick reassures Leonora, "nothing shall betide you/ But fair and noble usage" (5.1.1–2). Under the supervision of Roderick, Henriquez's power to do evil or cause harm weakens substantially. The audience will not fear for Leonora's safety with Roderick chaperoning the scheme.

To this list, Gary Taylor adds two other reasons for not staging the abduction of Leonora. First, he believes that it foregrounds religion in a way that would have been difficult for a court audience divided on religious lines, and Richards acknowledges that his use of the Eucharist in the abduction scene would have been prohibited in 1613.[15] More importantly, for Taylor, dramatizing the abduction scene shifts focus from Cardenio (Julio) and places it on Fernando (Henriquez).[16] Indeed, as it stands, Henriquez shares an equal, if not greater, part of the action in *Double Falsehood*. For a play that names its protagonist in the title, one would expect more action to revolve around Cardenio (Julio) than Fernando (Henriquez). *Don Quixote* substantiates such a reading. From the wedding onward in *Don Quixote*, Fernando is remarkably silent.[17] Thus, Taylor's *History of Cardenio* leaves the scene unseen but fills in Theobald's lack of details. Taylor adds a short scene showing Roderick coaxing Fernando (Henriquez) into the coffin to feign a corpse while attendants put on the disguise of friars' robes. By nailing Fernando (Henriquez) into a claustrophobic coffin, Taylor makes sense of Roderick's ambiguous reference in *Double Falsehood* to serving his brother to "save his honour" (4.1.233). Just as in *Double Falsehood,* when next the audience sees the brothers' train Lucinda is with them. Only now, in Taylor's version, she emerges from the coffin drugged. One logical way to take Leonora from the nunnery would be to conceal her in the coffin. The suggestion that she is disoriented comes from Theobald's text (hence, prompting Richards to question if she has been drugged). She asks "Where am I?" as if just realizing she is no longer in the convent; Roderick replies "Not in the nunnery" (5.1.5–6). Therefore, Taylor reveals some of what Theobald leaves vague and "unsatisfactory," but like Theobald, leaves the abduction to the audience's imagination. No review, audience member, or actor, to my knowledge, of either the Wellington or the IUPUI production questioned or missed Lucinda's abduction from the nunnery.

In *The History of Cardenio*, Taylor also takes scenes from *Double Falsehood* and transforms them into unscenes. One such scene also involved Leonora. Theobald both scenes and unscenes the moment. In 2.4, after it has become apparent that Leonora will be forced into a marriage with Henriquez, she waits at a window, hoping to spy an honest messenger below to deliver a letter, detailing Henriquez's treachery, to Julio.[18] She secures a Citizen to convey the letter. In the following scene (3.1), the same Citizen seems to "unscene" what we just saw, describing it to Julio:

> When from the window she did bow and call,
> Her passions shook her voice, and from her eyes
> Mistemper and distraction, with strange wildness,
> Bespoke concern above a common sorrow. (3.1.1–4)

The extreme emotional state described here is typical of an unscene. Taylor retains only the scene between Cardenio (Julio) and the Citizen. This cut is logical from a plot perspective. The audience does not need the information that Leonora has given her letter to a Citizen if we see the Citizen recount as much while delivering the letter to Julio. But the scene parallels two others. Leonora shares a scene with the Citizen (2.4) and immediately afterward Julio converses with the Citizen (3.1). The Citizen has "no character" and is not seen elsewhere in *Double Falsehood*. His entire function is as mediator between Leonora and Julio. Having two scenes, each featuring a lover with the Citizen, allows the audience to embody the characterless Citizen, and to understand the effects of Henriquez's betrayal on both Leonora and Julio. Lucinda's scene at the window (2.4) also parallels Violante's scene at the window (1.3). Both scenes precede a heroine being forced to submit to Henriquez's will, and both center on a woman's mistrust of men, and specifically Henriquez.

Additionally, the scene functions to foreground Leonora's entrapment and her divided self. Both here and in her soliloquy before the wedding, sole focus is given to Leonora. We, as the audience, are allowed access to her private world. In the following scene, she is with Julio and afterward amid attendants, her father, Henriquez, and a priest at the nuptial. Celia R. Daileader discusses how window or balcony scenes can function in this way: "In early modern drama, the balcony tends to further voyeuristic purposes. Balcony scenes create the sense of a visual boundary breached; they create an opening into the private world of the characters; they create, in effect, a stage-within-the stage, whereon we can glimpse an even 'truer' narrative."[19] Leonora is at the window drawn to the outside world, where Julio is, but pulled back into the interior by the offstage (heard, but unseen) voice of her father "*within*." Twice in the scene, Don Bernard shouts calling her inside with "Leonora" and "Why, daughter" reminiscent of the Nurse calling Juliet at her window with Romeo, summoning her back into the Capulet house. Leonora's internal conflict is externalized: duty and obedience to her father or love and promise to Julio (Cardenio). Furthermore, such scenes in performance add an element of danger and intense dramatic timing. Not only is Leonora running out of time as a maid, at any moment her attempts for help may be thwarted.

Taylor takes these two key elements—Leonora (Lucinda) at the window, and the offstage voice of Don Bernard—and transposes them to the scene between Julio (Cardenio) and Leonora (Lucinda) directly before the wedding (*THOC* 2.9). The Wellington production revealed a problem in this staging, and a desirable solution. Lucinda had little time (less than thirteen lines) to get from the upstage gallery (where the window is located) to the stage level for the wedding scene. In the end, as performance demonstrated, this timing was advantageous with Don Bernard, Fernando, the friar, the entire wedding party, and the audience awaiting Lucinda's entrance. From here, we added the business of Don Bernard exiting to retrieve Lucinda, and Taylor transposed from later in the scene Don Bernard's threat to Lucinda, "Nay, no dragging back but with my curses" (3.2.120–1), allowing Lucinda to physicalize her reluctance to participate in the nuptial.[20]

Lyrically Offstage: "Wonder And Woe"

Theobald's unscenes do not have the same detail, depth, and imagery as do those in Shakespeare. The witness of Cordelia in *King Lear* when she hears of her father's treatment at the hands of her sisters describes the tears coming from her eyes "as pearls from diamonds dropped." Likewise, the Third Gentleman in *The Winter's Tale* describes Perdita at the reunion, "she did, with an 'Alas,'—I would fain say—bleed tears; for I am sure my heart wept blood. Who was the most marble there changed color; some swooned, all sorrowed" (5.2.86–8). Unscenes gain power due to the strong imagery involved in the retelling. Garber writes, "Significantly, the subjects of unscenes are almost without exception moments of extreme emotion, and frequently conflicted emotions: joy and fear, love and grief or anger. Their content, like their mode of expression, is ineffable."[21] Henriquez certainly has conflicted emotion (joy and shame) in his narration of the rape of Violante, but it is nowhere near the depth and length of Shakespearian unscenes. A comparison as well could be made between these unscenes and the Citizen's description of Leonora at the window, though his description is a mere four lines. As mentioned above, unscenes are fitting to the romance plays because they contain the most ineffable moments in Shakespeare. Garber writes: "The stylistic form of these episodes is in a way closer to the language of romance than to that of tragedy; they are more lyric than dramatic" (46). In late Shakespeare, the narration of the offstage event hinges around the concept of "woe or wonder," wonder being a particularly apt descriptor of the events of romance plays.[22] Unscenes of wonder include Cleomenes and Dion's description of the temple at Delphos (3.1.1–11), the reunion of Leontes and Perdita and of Leontes and Camillo (5.2.42–57; 5.2.10–19), and Antigonus's description, both woeful and wonderful, of Hermione's specter (3.3.15–36) in *The Winter's Tale*. Descriptions of woe often include grief, near death, or death (which is often equivalent to a theatrical exit) such as Cornelius's narration of the Queen's confessions and death in *Cymbeline*, the final battle between Arcite and Palamon, and the Wooer's account of the Jailer's Daughter at the water's side in *The Two Noble Kinsmen*. Though *Double Falsehood* contains none of the onstage or offstage wonder and miracles of the late plays, there are two moments—both focusing on the "death and resurrection" of

Julio—that seem to evoke "wonder and woe," and both feature a form of offstage action.

In the fourth act of *Double Falsehood*, Julio is attended by two unnamed gentlemen who try to persuade him to abandon the wild mountains and his equally wild state of mind. Suddenly a lute is heard offstage. Julio calls the noise "a sound from heav'n," but the Gentlemen are perplexed by the music. "Here's no inhabitant," says the Gentleman, adding "This is a strange place to hear music in" (4.2.9, 11). Julio endows the "sweet airs" as "The spirit of some hapless man that died/ And left his love hid in a faithless woman" who "haunts" the mountains (4.2.13–15). Interestingly, because the voice has no (onstage) body, Julio casts the voice as himself. He is the unfortunate man who believes his lover has betrayed him. (Later the exact word "hapless" will be used to describe Julio.) This is behavior characteristic of Julio's madness. Earlier in the fourth act, he casts the Second Shepherd as Henriquez, before pouncing on him, pulling his nose, and bashing him in the mouth. Likewise, he places Violante as the wronged virgin he must avenge (though she is dressed as a boy). In his speeches and role-playing alike, Julio's mad world revolves around himself, his betrayal by Henriquez and seeming betrayal by Leonora (the "Double Falsehood" of Theobald's title).

Moments after the lute music, Violante, "within," sings. Like the reference to the haunting spirit, placing the singing offstage further loads the entire episode with a supernatural quality of wonder. Often in early modern stage directions that specify "within" the offstage space represents an interior conjured by the world of the play, such as the example above of Don Bernard calling Leonora from within. He is inside the house. In 4.2 however, as the Gentleman remarks, it is unclear from where the sound is coming, because they are in the mountains. After Violante sings, all the while offstage, Julio says:

> The heav'nly sound
> Diffuses a sweet peace through all my soul.
> But yet I wonder what new, sad companion
> Grief has brought hither to out-bid my sorrows. (4.2.33–6)

The restorative power of music in the Shakespearian romances is a common theme,[23] and Hammond compares the passage to Pericles hearing the music of the spheres (4.2.33–4n.). After Violante's singing, Julio's madness disappears, and remarkably he becomes as invested in Violante's grief as in his own. The voice is no longer "him," but a "new, sad companion" whose grief he does not know. When Violante finally appears, Julio says she is "heav'nly," stops her from suicide (when earlier he had advised it), and swears never to leave her. The audience sees Julio's internalized, isolated, self-involved, self-loathing madness transformed into compassion, empathy, connection, and companionship with another, all via the healing properties of music. It is therefore essential that the music be wonder-full, express something other than and greater than mere words (thus the juxtaposition with the Gentleman whom Julio refuses to engage with), and appear to be from "heav'n."

The multiple references to "heav'n" or "heav'nly" throughout this scene make it tempting to imagine the music coming from above or the upper gallery, if we place it in a Jacobean playhouse (a Fletcher and Shakespeare *Cardenio*). Mariko Ichikawa discusses *Pericles'* "Musicke of the Spheres" by stating: "Although there is no stage direction for the music, and although no other onstage characters can hear it, 'Most heauenly Muscike' (I1v; 5.1.233) might have been shared by the audience. I think it possible that when the play was performed at the Globe around 1608, the celestial music came from the upper tiring house."[24] It was probably common practice for musicians to be located above in a music room, and Ichikawa points to several stage directions including "within" that refer to the upper floor, mostly involving noise or sound (314–35). Furthermore, she states, "Fletcher's and his colleagues' plays contain references to characters' presence on the upper level as '*within*.' *The Chances*, a Blackfriars play by Fletcher provides an interesting example. When in 2.2 'Lute sounds within' (F1, 3A4r), the offstage music is described in the dialogue as being performed 'Above in my Masters chamber' (3A4r)" (323).[25] In *The Knight of the Burning Pestle*, Old Merry-thought is directed to be "within" but the dialogue and song suggest he is on the upper level. Ichikawa argues it would have been preferable to have Old Merry-thought visible for his song and speech, and she conjectures that "within" may allow characters to remain visible (320). But it is clear here that Violante is not visible; Julio exclaims "it appears" when she enters. In the 2009 Wellington production of Taylor's *History of Cardenio*, we placed Violante on the upper gallery in this scene for "Woods, Rocks, and Mountains" (the Robert Johnson song several contemporary productions use to replace "Fond Echo"). We soon discovered an inherent problem with this staging. There is minimal dialogue between the music ending and Violante's appearance at stage level: only seven lines. Several times in rehearsal, the actress playing Violante in our production missed her entrance cue as she was unable to descend backstage from the upper level to the stage in time. We were never able to perfect the timing and therefore gave Cardenio a repeat of Violante's last phrase ("miserable I/ Still weeping my fortunes, drop-drop-drop a tear and die") to afford time for Violante's entrance. In the end, serendipity created one of the most touching moments in the production. Though it was no longer necessary for timing, the IUPUI production retained the repeat, and Taylor has written it into his script (*THOC* 4.3). If the original *Cardenio* had a lengthier sequence, such as we created, between the end of the song and Violante's entrance, then the upper level might have been used.

Another scenario would be if Violante was positioned behind the arras at stage level to sing within. There are other early modern stage directions where music comes from behind the arras. Ichikawa cites an anticipatory stage direction from a Massinger play, performed by the King's Men, that calls for music behind the arras. The manuscript playbook of *The City Madam* has the annotation *"Musicians come down to make ready for the song at Aras"* (324). For *Cardenio* not only would the area behind the stage hangings provide better audibility (than either of the two doors) but the "discovery space" behind the arras was full of connotations of "wonder." (Two ready examples are Ferdinand and Miranda playing chess in *The Tempest* and likely Hermione's statue in *The Winter's Tale*.) And this is the key factor in the offstage singing—that it evokes wonder.

In the Wellington production of *The History of Cardenio* not only was Violante on the upper level but she was also onstage. In that version of Taylor's script, the stage direction read "VIOLANTE enters above, on a rock." Furthermore, from a contemporary perspective, it did not occur to us that offstage singing was particularly appealing theatrically. It seemed that the upper level provided enough spatial distance between Violante and Cardenio and his friends to mystify them—at least at first—as to the origin of the music. While this was true, Cardenio quickly saw Violante and the mystery was short-lived. Additionally, this choice did not consider the audience, who could see Violante from the very first note. Finally and cumulatively, though it was emotionally moving, her presence from the beginning destroyed any air of the supernatural. Conversely, the 2012 IUPUI production had Violenta (Violante) sing the entire "Woods, Rocks, and Mountains" offstage. Bourus considers this "emotionally, the single most important scene in the play," but accepts Taylor's new evidence that the directive to place the music offstage is "the single most authoritative stage direction in the entire play."[26] Taylor's script now has the stage direction, *"VIOLENTA sings, unseen, within,"* and under Bourus's direction in the IUPUI production the music gained an eerie beauty and a quality of wonder.[27] Additionally, it became clear that Violante's absence onstage at this point allows sole focus to be on the *effect* of the music on Cardenio, rather than competing expressions of grief. Once Violante enters, she drives the scene with her soliloquies about Fernando and her impending death.

The piece of offstage action is unique. What connects it to the other offstage action investigated thus far is that the audience experiences it primarily through auditory means and reactions of onstage listeners rather than through an onstage body, but it is also very different in that, temporally, it is happening in the "now" of an onstage moment, even if the business is offstage. Other offstage action or unscenes are situated temporally in the past and reported. If offstage, we can only access Violante's rape through Henriquez's account, or Leonora's abduction through the snippets of dialogue before, but mostly, after the event. Therefore, a strong temporal and spatial separation exists. Here the audience has direct access to the action but is distanced from it not temporally, but only spatially. This spatial gap, I believe, serves the specific purposes described above.

Though the heavenly music's restorative properties soothe Julio/Cardenio's madness, he does not abandon his extreme grief. In the next scene, Violante reveals herself to Roderick as another maid Henriquez has betrayed. When Roderick asks her how she came to the mountains, Violante replies:

That as we pass, an't please you, I'll discover.
I will assure you, sir, these barren mountains
Hold many wonders of your brother's making.
Here wanders hapless Julio (5.1.67–70)

Julio/Cardenio as a "wonder" is significant here. Roderick is so stunned at the mention of Julio/Cardenio that he asks Violante to repeat the name, and then urges her to take him to Julio directly. They exit, and the next entrances are three fathers (Camillo, Duke, Don Bernard), anticipating the return of their children. Roderick's discovery of Julio/Cardenio occurs offstage and unseen. In *The History of Cardenio*, Taylor transforms this discovery into an unscene, the effect of which heightens the dramatic tension and sense of wonder and woe in the final scene.

The entrances of the fathers begin the last scene of *Double Falsehood*, which includes the moments more thematically relevant to late Shakespeare than any others in the play. The entire scene, played out in a series of theatrical disguises and discoveries, includes no less than six reunions. Forgiveness, between lovers, fathers and children, and friends, is paramount. Redemption and reunions abound in the endings of late Shakespeare. *Cymbeline*, *Pericles*, *The Winter's Tale*, and *The Tempest* all close this way, though *Double Falsehood* fails to achieve a real sense of wonder, or the miraculous nature of such events. The miracles pivot on resurrection, and likewise, resurrections hinge on a death or, more pertinently, the illusion of death. In *Cymbeline*, Innogen has clutched what she believes is the headless body of Posthumus. In *Pericles*, the title character is convinced his wife and child are dead. Likewise, in *The Winter's Tale*, Leontes sent Perdita to her death and saw the dead body of Hermione. In *The Tempest*, Alonso and Ferdinand each believe the other drowned in a shipwreck. The audience delights in seeing loved ones resurrected and brought into one another's presence, and in most of the scenarios the reunions happen after years of absence. Of these reunions, perhaps the most spectacular is that of Leontes and Hermione, not only for its stagecraft (Paulina's masterful choreographic teasing with the curtains, the music, the silence, the statue come to life) but also because unlike most of the other reunions the audience can also believe Hermione is dead. Therefore, she comes to life not only for Leontes but also for the audience.

Similarly, in *Double Falsehood*, doubt is placed as to Julio's life, enhanced by offstaging Roderick's discovery of him. When last the audience sees Julio, he is directing Violante to join him at "the Cave of Death/ And in a sigh give up our latest breath" (4.2.115–16). Violante describes Julio to Roderick as sleeping, "Sleep weigh'd down his eyelids,/ Oppress'd with watching, just as you approach'd us" (4.2.72–3). (The connection in the early modern period between sleep and death does not need elaborating here.) Then in the final scene there is a theatrical ellipsis and the description of a hearse in Roderick's offstage train. The coffin and Roderick's train remain ambiguously offstage. Since the coffin is not included in any stage directions in *Double Falsehood*, it likely did not appear onstage. The mention of a coffin prompts Camillo to exclaim: "'Tis my poor Julio" (5.2.37). Later in the scene, Julio will be referred to as "kill'd" and "murder'd." Just as the audience of *The Winter's Tale* can engage with the possibility of Hermione's death, the audience in this final scene is given the illusion that they will not see Julio again, that his life is absent, his body lying in an offstage coffin.

Though some other alterations are made in the final scene, both Richards and Doran have Julio/Cardenio exit the stage in the fourth act (possibly to die) and reenter, resurrected, in the final scene. In these stage versions, the same attention is given to Cardenio's death as in *Double Falsehood*. It is sig-nified by characters' presumptions about an offstage hearse. A less desirable offstage moment is also enveloped in these stagings. Because the hearse is already with Roderick, Henriquez, and Leonora, it is assumed that Henriquez, but more importantly, Leonora, has been led to believe offstage that Julio is in the coffin. Therefore, the audience does not view Leonora's immediate reaction to the revelation of Julio's death. Her grief is staged *in medias res*, as indicated by Don Bernard's "these tears distract me" (5.2.71).

Taylor's reconstruction strengthens dramatically Cardenio's "death" by clearly bringing the coffin onstage and presenting it after the entrance of Lucinda (Leonora) and Fernando (Henriquez) with the stage direction: "*Enter Friars carrying a coffin in solemn procession, set it down. Exeunt.*"[28] This orchestration of entrances gives the reunions of Lucinda and Fernando with their respective fathers weight and time before registering the absence of Cardenio. What follows is Taylor's addition of the unscene delivered by Roderick narrating his discovery of Cardenio in the cave (*THOC* 5.2). With its description of the ineffable conflicting state of Cardenio, both weak and strong, sick and sound, this is very reminiscent of a Shakespearian unscene, and it reinforces the ambiguity of Cardenio's "death" offstage. Teasingly, Roderick reports that Cardenio "spoke no more" leaving both Lucinda and the audience to accept that he is dead. Presence becomes palpable through speech. It is the final test and testament to onstage-ness, to life. After the touchingly ineffable silent reunion of Leontes and Hermione, Camillo says: "If she pertain to life, let her speak too!" (5.3.112). When Cardenio is pre-sented to Lucinda in *The History of Cardenio* as in *Double Falsehood*, she says: "Would he would speak!" (*DF* 5.2.237). In both of these versions, Cardenio shatters the illusion of his death, his "speaking no more," by answering his lover's request that he live, that he speak, with his first resurrected word, her name. Wonder.

Like the contents of the coffin, offstage action remains just beyond the sight of the audience, who must imagine what lies there. What is left unseen and unscene in *Double Falsehood* will remain ambiguous, with contemporary productions of *Cardenio* teasing out which bits are elisions at the hands of Theobald and which moments fulfill the "ineffability topos" or a drama-turgical function by remaining temporally and/or spatially distanced from the audience. These decisions of staging or unstaging should go deeper than assumption. Each performative option renders a significantly different version of the action. Whether they are interpreted as "missing scenes" or offstage action, how these episodes, such as Violante's rape and Leonora's abduction, are staged either brings them closer to or distances them from late Shakespearian dramaturgy. Furthermore, the framing of such action, or the choice to remove the action from the stage entirely, affects audience reception and the meaningful experience of such moments—and, perhaps, the meaning of the entire play.

NOTES

1. Many of the late Shakespearean moments referred to in this essay are discussed at length in my unpublished dissertation, "The Dramaturgy of Female Gender in Early Modern English Theatre: An Investigation of the Theatrical Expression of Gender in Selected Jacobean Plays, Their Restoration/Early Eighteenth-Century Adaptations, and Their Original and Contemporary Staging" (Victoria University of Wellington, 2011).

2. *Shakespeare's Late Style* (Cambridge: Cambridge University Press, 2006), 38, 77–8.

3. Garber, "'The Rest Is Silence': Ineffability and the 'Unscene' in Shakespeare's Plays," in *Ineffability, Naming the Unnameable from Dante to Beckett*, ed. Peter S. Hawkins and Anne Howland Schotter (New York: AMS Press, 1983), 36.

4. Marjorie Garber, *Shakespeare after All* (New York: Anchor Books, 2005), 112.

5. See Leigh, "'Tis no such killing matter: Rape in Fletcher and Shakespeare's *Cardenio* and in Lewis Theobald's *Double Falsehood*," *Shakespeare* 7:3 (2011): 284–96, and "Transvestism, Transformation, and Text: Cross-Dressing and Gender Roles in *Double Falsehood/The History of Cardenio*," *Quest*, 258–66. The discussion of the rape is extensive in *Quest*: see Taylor, "History," 40–4; Hammond, 76–7; Taylor and Nance, 198–9, 213; Richards, 345–6; Proudfoot, 354; Doran, 361; Carnegie and Leigh, 374–6. Peter Kirwan also writes about the rape at length in his blog: http://blogs.warwick.ac.uk/pkirwan/entry/cardenio_rsc_the_1/.

6. See *DF* 1.3.63n.

7. Hammond, "After Arden," *Quest*, 76 (noting that the costumes allowed "Violante's rape to happen on the floor protected from sight by a raised carpet").

8. Proudfoot describes Violante's rape in Richards's Cardenio as "graphic." See "Will the Real *Cardenio* Please Stand Up?" *Quest*, 354. Peter Kirwan's blog discusses in detail the handling of the rape in the RSC *Cardenio*. Kirwan, rightfully, is disturbed at the textual changes attempting to construct a "less serious form of rape" in order to make for a "family-friendly" production.

9. Onstage sexual acts were forbidden in both Shakespeare's and Theobald's theaters.

10. Taylor and Nance, "Subplot," *Quest*, 199.

11. Richards, "Reimagining *Cardenio*," *Quest*, 346.

12. Doran, "Restoring *Double Falsehood* to the Perpendicular for the RSC," *Quest*, 360, 361. (Performed in 1607, *The Knight of the Burning Pestle* precedes *Cardenio*. Likewise, Doran does not acknowledge here that modern scholars attribute the work to Beaumont, not Fletcher.)

13. See "Shakespeare with a Spanish Twist," May 2, 2011, *The Independent*. Online at www.independent.co.uk/arts-entertainment/theatre-dance/reviews/cardenio-swan-theatre-stratforduponavon-2277636.html.

14. *Shakespeare in Performance: Cymbeline* (Manchester: Manchester University Press, 1989), 13. In Bill Alexander's 1987 production, Giacomo kissed Innogen and undid her top buttons to expose her breast. Next, he undid a few bottom buttons, clearly contemplating rape before deciding against it (105).

15. See Richards, "Reimagining *Cardenio*," *Quest*, 346–7. On the religious issues, see Taylor, "*Cardenio* Performed in 1613," *Quest*, 258–66.

16. Taylor's reasons for keeping Lucinda's (Leonora) abduction offstage were given to me in private correspondence.

17. Taylor's post-Wellington revisions duplicate this effect from *Don Quixote*, by removing the Henriquez/Fernando character from 4.1 and from *DF* 5.1 (*THOC* 4.4).

18. The Arden edition notes here that scenes in which letters are posted by immured heroines from windows are common in Elizabethan and Jacobean plays.

19. *Eroticism on the Renaissance Stage: Transcendence, Desire, and the Limits of the Visible* (Cambridge: Cambridge University Press, 1998), 40.

20. The IUPUI production retained this discovery (including Bernard's line), but also inserted a Robert Johnson wedding song after Cardenio's exit. Fernando and his party waited impatiently for Lucinda during the short song. Taylor's post-Indianapolis script, printed in this volume, removes the Johnson song (because the lyric does not seem to be written by Shakespeare or Fletcher) and instead places an act-break between Lucinda's balcony scene (2.9) and the wedding (3.1).

21. "'The Rest is Silence,'" 43–4.

22. This commonplace phrase is taken from J. V. Cunningham's book *Woe or Wonder: The Emotional Effect of Shakespearean Tragedy* (Denver: Alan Swallow, 1960).

23. G. Wilson Knight is the source of this now commonplace idea.

24. "'*Music Within*' and '*Music Above*,'" *The Shakespeare International Yearbook*, 5 (Surrey: Ashgate, 2005), 328.

25. This is the very scene and stage direction that Taylor cites as a unique parallel with *DF* (Taylor, "History," 45).

26. See Bourus's essay, chapter 13, in this volume, for a detailed discussion of her staging of this moment.

27. For more information on this staging, see Taylor's discussion of Edmund Gayton, as a possible eyewitness to Shakespeare and Fletcher's *Cardenio*, in Taylor, "History," 34–6.

28. In the post-Indianapolis revision of Taylor's script included in this volume, the "Friars" are converted to "soldiers" (more appropriately under the command of Roderick).

12

PERFORMING SPANISH CULTURE THROUGH FLAMENCO: AURALITY AND EMBODIMENT IN THE ROYAL SHAKESPEARE COMPANY'S *CARDENIO*

Carla Della Gatta

The Royal Shakespeare Company's 2011 production of *Cardenio* presented a performance of Spanish culture constructed from a variety of cultural and temporal sources. The nature of this "lost play re-imagined" was collaborative, and the title page of *Cardenio* credits eleven men spanning five centuries whose stories, ideas, and in some cases, actual written words, all contributed to what appeared on the stage, and it further states that the production "was developed in rehearsal by the original cast." Despite these numerous contributors, the RSC most emphasized the authorial roles of Shakespeare and Cervantes in their marketing and program information, but the audience's experience with *hispanidad* had little to do with Cervantes's novel, and the script relied heavily on the dialogue of *Double Falsehood*.

In production, *Cardenio* drew on aural features and visual exotica to evoke a Spanish setting. The foreign ambiance was constructed outside of the text of the script through the use of flamenco dance and music, simultaneous markers of both a cultural authenticity and an imagined exoticism. Unlike prior RSC productions of Spanish Golden Age plays, *Cardenio* relegated the sounds of the Spanish language and music to the periphery, marginalizing the representation of *hispanidad* by invoking it primarily through an un-integrated aural landscape. I contend that the spatial and aural distinctions between Spanish flamenco and other cultural signifiers produced a cross-cultural, cross-temporal image of foreignness that resulted in an exoticized portrayal of *hispanidad*. A close look at how *hispanidad* was constructed illuminates the impact of embodiment and eclecticism on Doran's desire for an authentic Andalucía.

Director Gregory Doran's production did not establish its Spanish setting through the use of Spanish words or immediately announce the locale in the dialogue. The only Spanish words in the production were the use of the word "fiesta" to describe the party scene, and the use of the word "Signor" twice in the last scene when Pedro refers to Don Camillo (93–4). Along with this limited use of Spanish words, the Spanish location of the action of the play was initially obscured. In the first scene, Pedro states: "This Cardenio he encountered first in France" (10), establishing the location as "not France," but not necessarily Spain. Unlike most of the RSC's previous Spanish Golden Age translations/adaptations that announced their locations immediately within the dialogue, *Cardenio* at first proclaimed its location through this opposition. Only in the third scene, after another reference to not being in France, does Don Camillo reveal that they are in Andalucía.

If the dialogue did not clearly establish a Spanish setting, casting choices did less to evoke a more specific culture. Patrick Carnegy of the *Independent* writes: "Lucy Briggs-Owen's Luscinda [was] too blondly British and commonly spoken to be convincing in a Spanish context"[1]—though Doran describes the actor portraying Cardenio, Oliver Rix, as having an "almost Mediterranean look" (Doran and Álamo, 155). Rather than through dialogue or casting choices, *hispanidad* was alluded to through props and staging, such as dark costuming, obscured lighting at the Catholic convent, references to horsemanship, and the baroque gates that dominated the stage in key scenes. Critic Ian Shuttleworth claims it was both the Spanish costuming and score that "add[ed] an air of authenticity that is geographical rather than dramatic."[2] The mixture of sources that contributed to these "Spanish" elements complicates Shuttleworth's reading of an "authentic" Spanish mise-en-scène.

Doran sought an "authentic sense of the Iberian world of seventeenth-century Andalucía" (144), as illustrated through his writing on his experience with Spanish culture. He wrote thirty-eight blog entries over five months about his inspiration from his travels to Spain, collaboration with other practicioners, and his theatre research and production process that appear on the RSC website; he included these entries in his 250-page book about his relationship to the production of *Cardenio* published the following year. Doran felt so strongly about his dramaturgical research that he was comfortable challenging the conclusions drawn by the very resources he sought as authoritative. For example, he reflects that Britain's Victoria and Albert Museum holds "this collection of Masquerade costumes, suggest[ing] that the man pictured [in an engraving] is stirring a pot" but instead decided that "we think he's playing a zambomba" (183). Doran based his conclusion on the post–World War II account of daily rural Spanish life by the British expatriate Gerald Brenan in which Brenan describes the zambomba as "an instrument that still featured in Andalucían festivities in the 1950s" (183). By prioritizing the twentieth-century account of Brenan over the historical analysis of the highly regarded V&A, Doran emphasized a more recent personal narrative of Spanish culture over the rigorous archival research of the V&A and concluded: "This sounds like a great noise for our fiesta" (183). When negotiating divergent resources for the production, Doran prioritized those that led to an aural landscape for the production, and specifically, one that he felt would contribute to the creation of a Spanish setting that would resonate with audience members.

Music was the primary element that reinforced the Spanish setting, and it was key throughout, with nineteen pieces of original music by Paul Englishby to unite the script. The flamenco musicians consisted of singer Javier Macías, originally from Cadiz, a Spanish guitarist, a guitarist who regularly plays for the RSC, and a percussionist. Aurality figured prominently in the mood that would signal not just a Spanish setting, but also a Spanish feeling. Doran recollected the emotion that live flamenco singing produced in the preview performance, and wrote singer "Javier [Macías] opens his lungs and sings the final song, filling the air with dark sounds of *Duende*" (234). "*Duende*" signifies the passion of flamenco music, dance, and sound, and encompasses the entire feeling of the rhythm and spirit. In a 1933 lecture given in Buenos Aires, Federico García Lorca described *duende* as "a power, not a work; it is a struggle, not a thought."[3] *Duende* is not static, not something that can be captured on the page. Like theater, it is fluid and never fixed. Although the term dates back to the sixteenth century, when it indicated the spirits of the deceased that embodied a house or space, it became popularized with the emergence of flamenco dance and music in southern Spain in the first half of the nineteenth century.[4] Lorca states: "All arts are capable of the *duende*, but where it finds greatest range, naturally, is in music, dance, and spoken poetry, for these arts require a living body to interpret them, being forms that are born, die, and open their contours against an exact present" (47). It is this force, this spirit, through which the production sought to establish Spanish culture.

The flamenco leitmotif culminated when the cast performed a choreographed flamenco dance number after the close of the story as the production's finale. Reminiscent of the jig at the end of the play at the Globe, and akin to the tradition of a fin de fiesta at the end of Spanish Golden Age plays that left the audience in a festive mood, the finale was in stark contrast to the RSC's more traditional curtain call. Doran's entire cast took flamenco lessons, to prepare, and he writes:

> The entire acting company have been taking flamenco classes (even the *Macbeth* and *Merchant* company, for whom it is not directly relevant)...so they are learning about how to concentrate and focus a passion that seems to rise from the ground....But even after one session last week, the company all seem taller. (Doran and Álamo, 198)

Doran perceived that one week of dance training produced a literal physical alteration in the bodies of cast members, and figuratively, that it gave them an embodied spirit of *hispanidad*. While doubtful that it produced a physical growth spurt within one week, this emphasis on a uniform embodied alteration in stature was evident in the staging of the egalitarian dance number. The dance was an attempt for the actors, or perhaps their characters, to embody *duende*. But interplay between people, especially between genders, is essential to this formulation, and it could not exist in this unison dance that strayed from the principles of flamenco. Anthropologist William Washabaugh describes the flamenco style as one that "plays with seminal but elusive moments of sociality, one male-centered, the other female-centered."[5] Without the interplay of male and female dancers, the gender dynamic that shapes flamenco performance was not invoked. The actors-turned-dancers appeared initially stiff though enthusiastic, all facing the audience and not feeding off each other's rhythm as they danced. Despite the commencing reserve of the actors, the finale intended to shift the embodiment of *duende* from a few select musicians to the experience of the entire cast.

This attempt for the cast to embody *hispanidad* through movement occurred after the play ended, resulting in a choreographed segment that amplified the lack of integration between flamenco and the storyline of the play. When the actors danced, Macías joined them onstage, and it created a moment of his embodiment of *duende* crossing into the space of the narrative that it had not inhabited throughout the entire play. After the actors finished their dance and took their bows, *hispanidad* was returned to the musicians who performed a vocal and instrumental number, again from an elevated balcony above the stage, as the audience remained seated. Flamenco, and more importantly *duende*, was returned to its distant location away from the actors and suggested that *hispanidad* was cast as a kind of performance that could not fully be realized by the primarily Anglo actors, or through the words of the collaborative script. Instead, the spatial striation of flamenco resulted in dismantling the idea of an authentic representation of Spain, which the collaborative nature of the play itself declared from the outset.

Duende, even though temporally and spatially situated outside the play and modified in form, succeeded in rousing, to some extent, what Lorca describes as the "almost religious enthusiasm" (46) that its arrival produces. In the flamenco finale, Susan L. Fischer writes: "The audience exited exhilarated, to the sound of animated flamenco strumming" (666). I too can attest to being surrounded by audience members who were ecstatic about the flamenco music and dance. It is this zeal that marked a shift in the phenomenological experience of *Cardenio* versus other RSC productions that end with traditional bows. The affective response, of energy, applause, and enthusiasm for the flamenco finale was *Cardenio's* distinguishing impression. George Revill writes: "A good classical performance is measured by the stillness and intensity of the audience's mental concentration. A good rock concert, by contrast, is measured by the audience's physical response."[6] If many of the RSC's productions retain the deference of spectatorship that has come to be a hallmark in most modern Western theaters, *Cardenio*, through *duende*, not dialogue, evoked a contrasting affective response. Tiffany Stern notes that "as trained and responsible spectators, moreover, we tend to sit quietly and keep ourselves to ourselves: we do not physically or vocally take part in the action, so that the separation of actor from audience is complete."[7] *Cardenio* in its final moments achieved a performance of Spanish *duende* through a fin de fiesta. *Duende* shifted from the musicians to the audience, aurally from flamenco music to the vocal response and applause of the audience. Stephen Di Benedetto claims that "to reach larger audiences we have to reach the lowest common denominator between cultures—that which is visceral,"[8] and the finale's appeal to embodied emotion successfully roused the passion of the spectators.

The flamenco music in *Cardenio* was spatially staged in accordance to Jacobean theatrical practice but served a dissimilar function in conveying plot and theme. In Jacobean theater, there were no spotlights, mood lighting, or advanced special effects, and music was typically specified in stage directions and motivated and explained by the plot. The spatial relationship between the flamenco musicians, the actors, and the audience further enervated the rhythm that is developed from personal interaction and proximity of flamenco musicians with each other and with their audience. Staging in the RSC's new Swan Theater was reminiscent of staging at the Globe, with the musicians placed on a high balcony above the stage. For most of the production, the musicians performed their music from different parts of the balconies, keeping the Spanish music separated from the Shakespearianesque dialogue below. The sounds of Spain were not only physically distanced from the actors and narrative, but also not performed for them. Macías directed his song to the audience, not the characters, performing as part of the theatrical entertainment, seemingly not integrated with the action onstage.

Spatially isolated as it may have been, the thematic qualities of the music made a more lasting impression on some critics than the dialogue. For example, Susan L. Fischer's seven-page theater review for *Shakespeare Bulletin* is almost entirely composed of details of the music in the production and offers David Johnston's English translations for the flamenco lyrics sung in Spanish. She notes moments when the music complemented the actors' emotional state, such as "the first verse from a traditional *seguidilla* (a poem with four to seven lines used in popular songs) from nineteenth-century flamenco signaled Fernando's anticlimactic attempt to stab a swooning Luscinda."[9] But she also exposes how the lyrics reinforced the action onstage. She writes: "The human emotion underlying Luscinda's distress in conveying to Cardenio news of her forced wedding was captured by the flamenco verses Macías chanted on high" (662). In the printed music in the archived prompt book, the specific instructions for the Shepherd's Song instruct both guitarists to "play gently and echo Dorotea's lines." Fischer explains this coordination between the Spanish lyrics and the English dialogue that would be imperceptible to monolingual audience members.

In Jacobean theater, music did not override dialogue, and its inclusion clearly reinforced a character's feelings or contributed to the plot. Yet the timing of *Cardenio's* flamenco music obfuscated the verbal text at the end of some of the scenes. Doran effectively replaced some of those endings by beginning the between-scene music before a scene ended, overriding the spoken text. For example, after receiving Fernando's letter, Dorotea laments her fallen status with: "What must I do?...The way I go,/ As yet I know not. Sorrow be my guide" (*DF* 2.2.45–6; Doran and Álamo, 36). This entire scene ends when "A sorrowful Dorotea exited to sad guitar strums."[10] Later, at the close of Act Four (Doran and Álamo, 87), when Fernando shockingly jumps out of the coffin and forces Luscinda into it as he abducts her, Macías' singing overshadowed the rhyming stanza that would have otherwise resulted in a weak ending to the scene. Doran's script ends with Fernando's lines:

> Come, "sister," this is all as it may be
> Devoutly witness, pray, my holy vow.
> I too beg converse with divinity:
> Divine Luscinda. Have I found thee now.

But these lines, and the subsequent staging of the abduction, were dwarfed by Macias' lyrics:

> Remedio
> No se alcanza, por otras sino por vos
> Remedio
> No se alcanza, reina y madre de Dios.[11]

It is through the use of flamenco music that scene and act closures were given resolution, allowing for transitions to the next geographical and emotional locales. Although "mood music or atmospheric sound,...is often critically belittled as though it is somehow cosmetic to the drama,"[12] here I am suggesting that Doran effectively utilized it not only to enhance the spoken words and the staging, but at times to supersede the dialogue onstage. Whether the music overshadowed dialogue by Shakespeare, Theobald, Doran, or any of the other authors whose words contributed to the script, Doran chose to invoke a Spanish mood over prioritizing the English dialogue.

The Spanish musical interludes do not appear in the published script, giving readers a profoundly different understanding of the setting than spectators received. In fact, the only lyrics published are found on the last page of the published script for a song called "Wood, Rocks, and Mountains." This song was composed by Robert Johnson, who was "the King's lutenist, and composer for some of Shakespeare's late plays" (Doran and Álamo, 15). Doran and Álamo printed the words to this song but explained that they used Theobald's "Fond Echo" instead because Johnson's setting "did not suit our heightened Spanish setting" (115). The published script, without any of the song lyrics from the production, does not convey the Spanish setting or feeling of the production. The Spanish locale was constructed mostly through music and vocals, but the RSC audience was not filled entirely, or most likely even mostly, with bilingual patrons who could have deciphered such lyrics while at the performance. In Shakespearian drama, "Shakespeare frequently supplies words for the songs that occur in his plays...The presence of the words to the songs shows that the actual substance of the texts was important" (Stern, 111). Fischer's review offers an excellent clarification of the music's role in reinforcing the plot enacted on the stage below by translating the lyrics into English for the reader, but this was not necessarily the experience of the theatergoer.

Theories of sound suggest the ability to cognitively make connections without a conscious understanding of the words. Philosopher Don Ihde writes that "the foreign tongue is first a kind of music before it becomes a language; it is first pregnant with meaning before the meaning is delivered to me."[13] Ihde's contention that there is an awareness of meaning that precedes the knowledge of textual content suggests that the presentation of foreign lyrics contributed to the phenomenological understanding of what was being spoken onstage. Indeed, Di Benedetto's work on the senses concludes that performances that engage aurality to communicate are effective because "we do not need to understand the words being spoken to get a sense of what is meant" (144). Whether or not the audience consciously understood the words that Macías sang, they could perceive that they stood in for a sentiment of *hispanidad*, as well as accentuated the ambiance that the dialogue sought to establish.

The musicians' exceptional skill captured a portion of the sonic quality of flamenco, but the required consistency needed for a season at the RSC did not allow for the spontaneous interplay typically involved in flamenco performance. Doran recalls how Macías was nervous to be part of the show because "he openly admits he is unused to repeating himself. As a flamenco singer, no two performances are the same. He must be moved in the moment to express what he feels...But we all think it is worth the risk" (224). Having an improvisational artist adhere to a script allowed for consistency across performances, but did not stylistically represent the interpersonal and improvisational nature inherent to flamenco. Ron Picard writes: "Like highly trained athletic teams, flamenco singers, guitarists, and dancers play off of one another's improvisations. Their performance is a work in process as they continuously call and respond to each other."[14] Only during the finale, after the actors' bows, were the musicians instructed to ad lib, distancing the improvisational nature of flamenco from the music within the production. Yet the finale's success in invoking *duende* occurred after the play's varied presentation of Spanish culture throughout. The authenticity that Doran sought onstage was founded in international resources from various time periods, and although Fischer celebrates *Cardenio* as "a theatrical *tour de force* of intertextuality, interlingualism, and interculturality" (666), in at least two key aural moments the means of integrating multitudinous sources led to misrepresentations of the very Spanish culture the production wished to celebrate.

Doran's *Cardenio* opened the possibility for an exoticized portrayal of *hispanidad* because of the wide-ranging sources for Spanish culture, the spatial separation of the key aural signifier, and the cast's attempt to embody flamenco outside the frame of the play. Timothy D. Taylor, in *Beyond Exoticism*, a seminal work in ethnomusicology that applies new historicism to the study of musical influences in history, explores the notion of exoticism in music as "manifestations of an awareness of racial, ethnic, and cultural Others captured in sound."[15] Doran's production embraced the depiction of the exotic Other, of Spanish culture, through these various applications of aural expression. In both the fiesta and mountain scenes, the international and cross-temporal sources of aural sounds crafted a non-British, but not necessarily Spanish, locale. In fact, they destabilized the depiction of Spain that the flamenco music had established throughout.

The first is the one dance number staged within the play itself. The fiesta scene was inspired by a heterogeneous group of resources and ultimately produced a risqué scene attributed to Spanish culture. Staging of the fiesta scene was inspired by photographs of Spanish festivals by a contemporary photographer, Brenan's accounts, an early-nineteenth-century Goya paint-ing, and the writing of a sixteenth-century Bavarian theologian. The scene's depiction became a striking display of actors on stilts, bawdy blocking, and "unspeakable acts" that Doran concluded might "earn the show an X cer-tificate" (185). Inspired by the scene in Strindberg's *Miss Julie* in which Miss Julie and Jean have sex while the peasants perform a dance, Doran wanted to create a "dangerous chaotic riot, during which the masked revelers [sic] echo what is happening in Dorotea's room." He succeeded, but "the trashy frippery and glistering apparel" (185) that was incorporated to entertain a modern British audience did not produce a seventeenth-century Andalucían festival, but rather an exotic fiesta constructed of elements from Bavarian counter-reformation thinking, Swedish theater, British early anthropology, and a painting from the Spanish Romantic period, which were meant to conjure a Spanish fiesta.

The second involved a scene in which a conflation of European pastoral culture and various animal sounds attempted to shape a specific Spanish culture. In the mountain scene, Silbo, an ancient means of communication between shepherds, coincided with British dialogue and Dorotea's song in Spanish. Yet Silbo, the lingua franca of call and response from the period that is akin in sound to yodeling, is not composed of Spanish words or spe-cific to Spain, causing the established aural frame to be disrupted. Although Dorotea sang in Spanish, gesturing to the Spanish setting, in order to embel-lish the aural landscape, Doran wrote in his blog: "We add some dog barks, I bring in some copper sheep bells I bought on my travels somewhere (which have been hanging in my study so long I can't remember where I got them!), the actors refine their Silbo technique, and the Sierra Mountains begin to emerge in our imaginations."[16] These diverse, exotic sonic qualities created an indistinct mountain ambience that Doran concluded would depict the Spanish Sierra Mountains. Although historically accurate to the period and dramaturgically useful in distinguishing the shift in location from court to country, the specificity of the location was not enhanced or reflected by the auditory choices, a marked distinction from the use of aurality throughout most of the production.

Exoticism was heightened further in the staging of the finale dance. Fischer notes that the order of the dancers' entrance into participation of the finale dance was in reverse hierarchy of the character's status, "first a servant's solo, then in prescribed order shepherds, maids, lovers, fathers, and the flamenco singer" (666). Fischer gives the singer a higher status than the characters. Yet the servant who started the dance number was the only black actor in the cast, and although his steps, aided by the music, became quickly identifiable as flamenco, the flamenco dance became a striking outside element to the play that had just been viewed. The entire cast stood behind him, watching, and it resonated as a misplaced racially marked moment. Only when the remainder of the cast joined the dance, and all of the bodies moved in unison, did the embodiment of a foreign dance begin to become integrated across the characters and actors onstage. In this final moment when flamenco music and dance were generated from the first-floor stage, the audience gained intimate access to embodied *duende*.

Cardenio's use of flamenco differed from prior RSC Spanish Golden Age productions, though flamenco music and dance have historically functioned as key cultural signifiers for the RSC's depiction of *hispanidad*. The RSC produced three Golden Age plays between 1990 and 2001, all of which depended on flamenco music and dance as markers of their Spanish settings. Danny Boyle's 1990–1991 production of Tirso de Molina's *The Last Days of Don Juan*, Laurence Boswell's 1995–1996 production of Calderón's *The Painter of Dishonour*, and Jonathan Munby's 2001 production of Lope de Vega's *Madness in Valencia* all integrated flamenco dance movements and music into the productions and did not relegate them to the periphery. In *The Last Days of Don Juan*, flamenco stances and gestures enhanced the sexualized *hispanidad* of the Marquis de Mota. Spanish dialogue aligned the Spanish language with lower-class characters and the pastoral when actors ad-libbed Spanish phrases in a wedding scene of country peasants. In Boswell's and Munby's productions, the casts performed flamenco dances as part of the action within the plot, and the casts also sang in Spanish.[17] While Spanish language and dance were used for both sexualized and lower characters, they were also integrated into the larger worlds of the productions and established more cohesive Spanish settings.

Following these separate productions, the RSC's 2004–2005 Spanish Golden Age Season included four productions of full-length plays and one radio-style staged reading. Unlike Doran's re-imagining seven years later, these adaptation/translations used Spanish phrases and flamenco dance within the plays to nod to their own theatricality, signaling a self-awareness of the performance of the exotic through Spanish music, dance, and language. In Boswell's production of Lope's *The Dog in the Manger* it was Tristan's performance of a dance to flamenco guitar music, with a resounding "¡Ole!" at the end that was performed for the audience, not another character onstage. In Nancy Meckler's production of Sor Juana Inés De La Cruz's *The House of Desires,* Leonor constantly used the phrase "¡Dios Mio!" as a comedic expression in an aside to the audience and to acknowledge plot turns. Likewise, Spanish flamenco music played as Castaño waved to the audience and said "¡Hola!" during a slapstick cross-dressing number. In these two shows, these colloquial Spanish phrases were incorporated into the performances to break the fourth wall in humorous scenes, aligning Spanish with comedy and a break from the narrative.

In Simon Usher's production of Tirso de Molina's *Tamar's Revenge*, there were no overtly Spanish tropes as the story is set in the biblical House of David. But in the large countryside musical numbers, the two men who had been seated onstage throughout the show joined the production as actors and singers.[18] Music facilitated their transition from observers/stage crew to actors/singers, thus highlighting their roles both inside and outside the play. Similarly, in Mike Alfreds' production of Cervantes' *Pedro, the Great Pretender*, the largest musical number gestured to the play's theatricality. Actors cried, "¡Ole!" and "Aye, yai, yai" during the number. When cleaning the stage after the musical number, actor John Ramm as Pedro joked, "Health and safety," to the audience. It was only in this moment that he stepped outside his direct addresses as narrator of the story to that of theater employee. In all four of these plays, Spanish sounds and dance served the dual function of characterization and breaking the narrative construct as points of humor.

In the 2004–2005 season, music as cultural signifier was used not only inside the adaptations but also reinforced outside the productions through marketing for the celebration of Spanish culture. *Duende* became the connective tissue for the casts to embody *hispanidad*, and an invitation extended to the audience as well. In an effort to foster an inclusive multicultural experience, the RSC combined Siglo de Oro plays and Latino culture into a homogenizing fiesta. They advertised:

> A weekend of passionate possibility…Get into the Spanish spirit over three days of music, dance and cultural infusion at The Other Place. Feel the flamenco beat, entwine yourself in Tango, and sweat it out to Salsa! (Programme, 2004)

Music and dance were the points of entrance into this conflated Latino culture, combining Spanish flamenco, Argentine tango, and Cuban salsa into one weekend of "Spanishness." These embodied characteristics of a conflated Spanish culture even extended to Artistic Director Laurence Boswell, whom the *Independent* described as having "an appropriate bit of a Latin streak."[19] Further, they were sensualized, as the RSC advertised: "Get into the Spanish Spirit, feel lively and Latino…*Fiesta* is where the fun is. It's time to click those castanets!" (www.rsc.org.uk), playing into cultural stereotypes of Latino and Spanish passion and the idea that it could be embodied by clicking castanets. But the emphasis on embodiment and aurality to deliver a version of *hispanidad* to the audience and patrons has a long-standing tradition at the RSC.

By contrast, in Gary Taylor's 2012 *The History of Cardenio* directed by Terri Bourus, flamenco music was employed as part of an onstage ambiance. Two musicians remained onstage throughout the production, singing and playing guitar in front of a large poster with a female flamenco dancer on it, and the musicians did not exit during intermission. When Fernando said: "Strike up, my masters" (*THOC*, 1.3), the musicians responded with music, showing an integration of flamenco into characterization that was not part of Doran's *Cardenio*. Costuming reinforced the Spanish music as Luscinda appeared in a red, ruffled flamenco dress, and later her wedding dress was a black and gold flamenco-style dress. Notably, "Wood, Rocks, and Mountains" (4.3) was sung from offstage, the voice amplified by the auditorium sound-system, displacing this temporally appropriate and Shakespeare-associated song and re-centering the onstage flamenco musicians (who accompanied the offstage voice) in their direct contact role with the action and characterization. Further, a modern dance number was performed to flamenco guitar music (5.2), revealing Taylor and Bourus's emphasis on storytelling rather than offering a presentation of a specific culture. With an ethnically diverse cast and minimal props, the production did not exoticize any particular culture. In fact, Taylor's Don Quixot and Sancho were both portrayed by African American actors, short-circuiting any association of their characters with Spanish stereotypes. Unlike Doran's production, Taylor and Bourus subverted expectations of *hispanidad* rather than attempting to reproduce them, and contrary to prior RSC productions, they did not exploit cultural clichès to break the fourth wall or as a source of humor.

What distinguished the RSC's *Cardenio* in its use of flamenco is that the music was spatially and culturally distinct from the onstage story. Despite the production's heavy reliance on music to convey culture, other aural Spanish signifiers such as the use of the Spanish language or a cohesive Spanish soundscape were not integrated into the performance. As a result, the foreign elements created an amalgamated unBritish culture that was put forth as a portrait of seventeenth-century Spain. Although it offered an exoticized version of *hispanidad*, *Cardenio's* transference of *duende* from the flamenco musicians to the audience was central to its affective impact. *Cardenio* did not achieve any accurate, complex, or provocative representation of Spanish culture through its script or its staging, but the production's professional Spanish musicians did allow audiences to experience what they believed was a feeling of *hispanidad*.

NOTES

1. Patrick Carnegy, "Double Toil and Trouble," *The Spectator*, Spectator.co.uk, May 1, 2011.
2. Ian Shuttleworth, "Cardenio, Swan Theatre, Stratford-upon-Avon," *Financial Times*, Ft.com, April 28, 2011.
3. Federico García Lorca, "Play and Theory of the *Duende*," *Deep Song and Other Prose*, ed. and trans. Christopher Maurer (New York: New Directions Books, 1980), 43.
4. For a detailed account of conflicting histories of the origin of flamenco see William Washabaugh, "Ironies in the History of Flamenco," *Theory Culture*

Society 12 (1995): 133–55. In summary, the style of flamenco known today was developed and professionalized in the nineteenth century, though Washabaugh claims there are three dominant and conflicting theories of its origin. The first is that flamenco was popularized as an Andalucían song style in the nineteenth and twentieth centuries, the second more substantially credits its Gitano origins from that developed during their persecution between the late fifteenth and eighteenth centuries, and the third that it served as voice of resistance across ethnicities and cultures since the late fifteenth-century (135–8).

5. William Washabaugh, *Passion, Politics and Popular Culture* (Oxford: Berg, 1996), 1.
6. George Revill, "Music and the Politics of Sound: Nationalism, Citizenship, and Auditory Space," *Environment and Planning D: Society and Space* 18 (2000): 604.
7. Tiffany Stern, *Making Shakespeare: The Pressures of Stage and Page* (New York: Routledge, 2004), 26.
8. Stephen Di Benedetto, *The Provocation of the Senses in Contemporary Theatre* (New York: Routledge, 2010), 165.
9. Susan L. Fischer, "Cardenio," *Shakespeare Bulletin*.29.4 (Winter 2011): 663.
10. Ibid., 662.
11. Ibid., 665. Fischer offers the following translation, "Remedy,/ There is none, other than through you./ Remedy/ There is none, Queen of Heaven, Mother of God."
12. Ross Brown, *Sound: A Reader in Theatre Practice* (New York: Palgrave Macmillan, 2010), 143.
13. Don Ihde, *Listening and Voice: A Phenomenology of Sound* (Athens: Ohio University Press, 1976), 160.
14. Ron Picard, "Dancing with the Bulls: Engendering Competition in Hemingway's *The Sun Also Rises* and Silko's *Ceremony*," *Upon Further Review: Sports in American Literature*, ed. Michael Cocchiarale and Scott D. Emmert (Westport: Praeger, 2004), 150.
15. Timothy D. Taylor, *Beyond Exoticism: Western Music and the World* (Durham: Duke University Press, 2007), 2.
16. Greg Doran, "Stage Shepherds Can Be Hard to Do," www.rsc.org.uk, Blog, March 18, 2011. This detailed description is not included in Doran's book and is summarized as "sporadic research" (207).
17. To note, in Boswell's production, the musicians sang a song in English that the cast repeated in Spanish. This allowed the audience to clearly understand the meaning while the actors embodied a Spanish aurality.
18. These two men were seated onstage during the performance when performed in Madrid. In the British production, these two stage-hands did not sit onstage throughout the show, but appeared as needed to assist the characters and move props.
19. Paul Taylor, "Laurence Boswell: A Director for All Seasons," *The Independent*, Independent.co.uk, April 22, 2004.

13

PONER EN ESCENA
THE HISTORY OF CARDENIO

Terri Bourus

the *Actor* is the *Center*

—John Webster (1615)[1]

Thus we move, because by the passion thus wee are mooved.

—Thomas Wright (1604)[2]

The story of Cardenio began in a book. That story contained, as Roger Chartier recognizes, "a dramatic plot full of secret meetings, soliloquies of cadenced verses and scenes of a spectacular nature" (Chartier 44). But unlike Cervantes, a director must *poner en escena,* put onstage, that narrative. Directors place people and objects in an artificial space, in spatial relationships to one another and to spectators. Long before I became a scholar or director, I was an actor. But before I became an actor, I danced, and dance is all about the movement of bodies through space (figure 13.1). I think of actors as dancers who speak. In Shakespeare and Fletcher, the actors are poets too, dancers who speak words that dance, words that move rhythmically, like music.

"Acting Shakespeare is," as Peter Hall says, "a physical, rhythmical and often musical discipline."[3] But it is also a research discipline. We often say that drama is meant to be performed, but in universities that segregate science from the arts we do not always recognize that the same verb describes performing a play and performing an experiment. Experiments, like plays, test an abstract verbal hypothesis by putting it into a particular space, governed by measurable material properties, in a timed sequence of events observed by multiple spectators. The experiment is run not just once, but multiple times, to test whether the results change or hold. The research protocols first formulated by Francis Bacon, a contemporary of both Shakespeare and Fletcher, emphasized the importance of observation and inductive reasoning, moving from material particulars ("accidents") to abstract theorems (Platonic "forms").[4] Like book history, theatre is a profoundly materialist form of literary research, because it literally grounds our speculations in

Figure 13.1   Movement: Quixot (Jonah Winston) rushes at the bowlers Don Bernard, Camillo, Barber, Curate (Michael Hosp, Kevin Burgun, Ben Asaykwee, Glenn Clifton), *THOC* 1.6, photograph by Emily Schwank.

material objects and physical practices that combine at a particular moment in a specific place.

PLACE

You can read *Don Quijote* anywhere, or as you move from one where to another. You can watch Mikhail Baryshnikov and Cynthia Harvey in the Minkus ballet of *Don Quixote*, or Peter O'Toole and Sophia Loren in the film of *Man of La Mancha,* or the unfinished Orson Welles' film of *Don Quixote* simply by downloading a file, at home, on an airplane, or wherever. But a theater has an address, a geography, a demographic. The building is local, and so is the audience. A place you know fills up with people you know.

Indianapolis is not Madrid, or Stratford-upon-Avon, or Wellington, New Zealand. In 2012, it was the twelfth-largest city in the United States, and like other American cities it has a significantly mixed demographic: 59 percent white, 27 percent black, 9 percent Hispanic, Latino, or Spanish. Indiana University/Purdue University Indianapolis (IUPUI) is an urban university, located downtown, in what was, fifty years ago, a culturally rich African American neighborhood.[5] The historic church on the east side of campus was once part of the Underground Railway.

The History of Cardenio performed in Indianapolis was inevitably going to reflect that demographic in casting, costuming, and interpretation. Even before the audition call, I invited an actress of Hispanic descent, Maria Souza-Eglen, to play Lucinda. I worked with Spanish-language faculty to encourage Hispanic students to audition, and I was able to cast Fernando Aké and Alex Carrico in small roles; Andrew Morales joined the crew as voice coach. None of these people are Spanish—but they are Hispanic. In the United States there are now more than fifty million Latinos; the culture of Latin America is far more familiar to American audiences than the Spain of Cervantes. Gregory Doran, working in Europe, naturally traveled to Spain to research his RSC *Cardenio*; audiences in Stratford-upon-Avon are tourists, and Andalusia and the Sierra mountains are now tourist destinations. But *Don Quixote* emigrated, within the first years of its publication, to the Spanish New World, where it has remained canonical ever since. So are we part of that world—I was born in San Diego and am familiar with the Spanish culture of the American Southwest. For this production I traveled to Mexico, and in particular to the desert mountain landscape of Baja Sud. Baja means more to my audiences, is more recognizable, than Andalusia, and I knew from traveling across the mountainous spine of the peninsula that it is not a Disneyfied, user-friendly place. It's much more like the Sierra Morena that Cervantes knew, four centuries ago. The painting of a flamenco dancer that dominated publicity for the show, and the stage, is by a Baja artist, Ivan Hernandez Olivera; that's also where I found the ponchos and serape for the shepherd scene, the black necklace for Marcela, the brilliantly colorful festival dress for the Princess of Micomicon. Traveling through Baja inspired Gary Taylor to return to *Don Quixote,* and incorporate into his script Cervantes's description of the dead mule, the scavenger crows, and the sense of poverty, hunger, and death in the mountains (*THOC* 3.3).

SPACE

Performances are shaped by the stubborn three-dimensional material reality of a particular playing space. *The History of Cardenio* would have been designed for spaces very different from the one I was given. As Lori Leigh remarked about the production she codirected in Wellington, her Sancho could easily step off the low thrust stage, pick up a program from a spectator, and announce: "'Tis better to behold a tragedy, than act in it" (*THOC* 4.1).[6] Atop my proscenium stage, my Sancho could not do that. My Curate could not enter as a magician, in the final scene, "above," as he did in Wellington—because my theatre, located in a basement, had no upper stage, and I had no budget to build a two-story set. The Curate joined everyone else on the already-crowded main stage. My space deprived the character of his elevated prominence in that final sequence, and deprived the audience of the visual variety of vertical as well as horizontal motion in that scene.[7] On the other hand, my theater had a raised alcove between columns in the auditorium, allowing my crazed Cardenio to jump down from the alcove, run forward and then up the steps to the stage, and then exit upstage left (3.3), creating an up-and-down movement that suggested rocky terrain in a way that the Wellington stage could not.

In my conspicuously modern space, I could not use original performance practices, or conduct the kind of archeological experiment Carnegie and Leigh undertook in Wellington. Instead, I had to test whether the play worked for modern audiences in a modern multipurpose auditorium, the way that Shakespeare's undisputed plays can still succeed in such circumstances. What we call "stage directions" imply a stage, and directions that work on one stage will not work on another. Taylor told us all that the stage directions in his script were (with one exception) conjectural elements of the text, and that we should feel free to find better ways to use our space.

Since our theater had wings to the right and left of the stage, I used them in the bowling scene (*THOC* 1.6). My characters actually rolled their bowls offstage, and retrieved them, and the scene mixed the physical movements of the game with the verbal competition between its players. I consciously modeled the rhythms of intersecting sport and talk on my experience of stable golf foursomes that have been playing together for decades.

Although the width of the stage was often a challenge, its great advantage was that it could accommodate the play's final scene, which requires virtually the entire cast to share the platform with a coffin (*THOC* 5.2). The intimate Wellington space had been overwhelmed by that grand finale, and the unavoidable overcrowding had made it difficult for audiences to follow clearly the complex choreography that binds together and resolves the play's multiple stories. Moreover, Cardenio and Quixot—the protagonists of main plot and subplot—require "big acting." Their outsized ambitions and extravagant emotional turns look disproportionate and a bit silly in a small room. They both need worlds to conquer, and large spaces to fill.

Bodies

The script contains twenty-six speaking characters, and also calls for at least three devils, six friars, and musicians.[8] All those performers have bodies, and all have to move (plate 13.1). "Acting is achieved not by thinking or talking or planning," Di Trevis insists, "but by doing things."[9] In any imaginable staging, there's a lot to do in *The History of Cardenio*; unlike *Double Falsehood*, Taylor's re-creation is physically demanding.

Its huge cast can be divided into two groups, based on age. I had seen the unavailability of older actors in Wellington unbalance the show, but I had also seen the dominance of older actors at the Globe reading unbalance it.[10] In Wellington the best performers were all playing the young characters, and as a result the play felt like just another adolescent boy-meets-girl romantic comedy, the kind of thing Shakespeare wrote at the start of his career, but was no longer doing at its end. *The Two Gentlemen of Verona* rather than *The Two Noble Kinsmen*. In director Wilson Milam's reading at the reconstructed Globe in 2011, on the other hand, as in *The Best Exotic Marigold Hotel* (2011), the stand-out performances all came from beloved veterans, and as a result the story of the young lovers seemed a distraction from the accomplished character actors in the older roles. To work well, *The History of Cardenio* needs young actors capable of holding their own in a play-long contest with powerful, confident older ones. Indeed, with the Quixot sub-plot included, the play fits perfectly into the circumstances of the King's Men in 1611–1613, when the shrinking remainders of the original company (led by Burbage) expertly played "old men characters" alongside an upcoming group of younger actors.[11]

To avoid Milam's problem at the Globe, I cast my Cardenio and Lucinda even before auditions, securing commitments from two talented young actors who had played Hamlet and Ofelia in my *Young Hamlet* (the 1603 text) in 2011. To avoid the Wellington problem, my audition call optimistically specified "five or six men over forty." I didn't get them, and their absence diminished the *gravitas* that only biological age can bring to a performance.[12] But I did get one multilingual white-haired actor in his sixties, who captured the emotional authority of the Duke's first speech on "death's dark vast and thousand-gated castle" on a first reading. For the rest, I found well-trained and experienced actors in their mid-twenties to thirties, who made me realize that the symmetry of the play depends on a balance of performative power, not just age.[13]

At least one young role in the play requires a very specific body. The script several times refers to Violenta's skin-color from the "midnight hand" of her first appearance (*DF* 1.3.27; *THOC* 1.3) to the "clay more browner" of Fernando's final speech to her (*THOC* 5.2). The character claims:

> Stronger am
> I than I seem. We country maids milk cows,
> Fetch full pails too. (*THOC* 1.5)

She must be young enough to pass for a boy, physically strong enough for farm work, vulnerable enough to be the target of attempted rape, emotionally fragile enough to break down and verge on suicide. She has to sing well enough to stop a scene in its tracks, twice. The script does not say that she has about her a certain luminosity, but that is how I always imagined the character, perhaps because she enters the play with lantern in hand, compared to dawn—"Day breaks sudden from her window" (*DF* 1.3.26, *THOC* 1.3)—just before she is compared to "midnight." And I suppose I think of her as luminous, too, because she is the play's most sympathetic, most transparent character. Alys Dickerson was all that, and when she walked into auditions I knew that I had a chance to demonstrate that Violenta is the play's female lead.

By contrast with Violenta, the script does not demand anything specific, physically, for the older roles of Camillo and Don Barnard. But they play a *pas de deux*; as do the Barber and Curate; as do Quixot and Sancho. Indeed, those three male pairs spend more time "dancing" with each other than do the play's romantic couples. Consequently, you need to cast three pairs, not six individuals. Michael Hosp's tall authority as Don Barnard against Kevin Burgun's short, stocky, *resentido* Camillo. The dark, ascetic, repressed

Curate of Glenn Clifton against Ben Asaykwee's fashionable, flamboyant, colorful Barber, who whenever he was standing still posed perfectly in a dancer's first position, toes out, heels together, à la Mary Poppins: those feet never broke character, and they were specific to his embodiment of this role. Asaykwee's magical Barber gradually transforms the physically awkward Curate, like a black-and-white movie suddenly blooming into transgressive color (plate 13.2).

And then there's the most famous male couple in world literature, Don Quixote and his squire Sancho. Directors enter rehearsals with an idea of which bodies they want, based on their study of the script, but they also have to be willing to be surprised by the bodies that walk into the room. I had imagined Quixot and Sancho as everyone does, I suppose, whether or not you've read Cervantes: Picasso's angular Quixote on his emaciated horse against short round Sancho on his squat burro. Tim McInerney, who read Quixot at the reconstructed Globe in 2012, perfectly embodied that image. But then Jonah D. Winston walked into the room to audition for Quixot: an actor whose body was as big as his voice and his imagination, as big as Quixot's ambition. I realized that what matters most about Quixot (the play's character, not the novel's) is that his body should immediately, undeniably contradict his aspiration to be a knight in shining armor. The character is the epitome of bad casting, because an ordinary man (Quesada) has cast himself in an extraordinary role (Quixot) that no director on earth would give him. He does not have to be ancient, or stick-thin, or weak. He just has to be *wrong*. And Jonah was perfectly rightly wrong. It is a wrongness that every actor encounters at some point in a career: there are roles you know you will never get, however much you want them, just because of your body. That is what lends so much poignancy to Quixot's exit from the play. He knows he won't get the call-back. (And then, of course, Taylor gives it to him, and to us, by bringing him back for the Epilogue.)

I had planned to cast Sancho with another talented actor from my *Young Hamlet*, Frankie Bolda. I knew from the Wellington production that Taylor's adolescent Sancho could be played convincingly by a young woman, and I wanted more opportunities for actresses in the show—which, like all Shakespeare or Fletcher plays, is dominated by males. Frankie in fact understudied Sancho, and would have been splendid if she'd ever had to go on. But my Sancho had to fit my Quixot, and Brandon Merriweather did. The high school senior's young tenor complemented Jonah's big booming bass baritone. Giant Quixot and his diminutive page, like Falstaff and his page ("like a sow that hath overwhelmed all her litter but one"). And the fact that they were both African American meant that color did not come between them, or differentiate them. Instead, it bound them together against all the other pairs onstage (plate 13.3). Moreover, as in the early modern theatrical apprentice system, Jonah mentored Brandon as an actor: in rehearsal and backstage, he really was the older teacher that his character claimed to be.

Quixot's and Sancho's bodies at once established, for spectators and themselves, that the play's characters were not the novel's. That difference gave the actors permission to discover possibilities on their own: Sancho's attempts to mimic his master physically, or temporarily appropriate his helmet, Quixot's world-conquering around-the-compass "doing, doing, doing" followed by his under-the-table obscene gesture and lowered voice with the fourth "doing" (*THOC* 5.1), Quixot and Sancho's pre-game bonding-warrior warm-up as they anticipate the Princess of Micomicon (5.1), Quixot and Camillo's chest-to-barreled-chest face-off (1.6). They never sacrificed, and sometimes improved, the precision of the language; but they did embody it in ways that no one had ever imagined before.

OBJECTS

The bodies of actors carry costumes and props *en escena*. Those objects primarily function to clarify the story. For that reason, modern playwrights typically specify how characters are costumed. Aunt Judy's "dress is a plain brown frock, with a woolen pelerine of black and aniline mauve over her shoulder, all very trim," for instance, and Krapp wears "rusty black narrow trousers too short for him. Rusty black sleeveless waistcoat, four capacious pockets. Grimy white shirt open at neck, no collar. Surprising pair of dirty white boots, size ten at least, very narrow and pointed."[14] Renaissance plays instead usually specify only a character's position in the social hierarchy, because that is what matters to the story. In order to costume *The History of Cardenio*, I needed to know more about its characters' social identity than Taylor provided. For instance, the initial rehearsal script treated "*Don* Camillo," "*Don* Bernard," "*Don* Fernando," and "*Don* Roderick" as socially identical. I had not noticed this as a problem in any of the readings from 2008 to 2011, but when I started planning my own production that homogenized status seemed wrong to me; it didn't fit the actual dialogue. So before the table reading I asked Taylor to provide me and the actors with notes on each character. This led him to restore details from *Double Falsehood* that he had eliminated in his very earliest work on the reconstruction. "Don Bernard" is socially superior to "good Camillo" (without any honorific), but he clearly belongs below the elevated world of "Lord Fernando" and "Lord Roderick." These changes, in turn, led to further discoveries in rehearsal. For example, Cardenio, having formed a friendship with Lord Fernando at university, is now embarrassed by his father's "dusty" house, dirty hands, and not-new *serape*. Don Bernard, on the other hand, relishes his social superiority over Camillo partly because Camillo has a son, and he does not—a biological fact that Camillo makes a point of rubbing in, whenever he gets the chance.

Quixot had a different problem. For most of the play, he aspires, sartorially, to knight errant status. In his second scene, we watch him dressing up in that new self. But in the initial rehearsal script, "Quesada" began the play with no social identity whatsoever, no costume that he could later abandon. "Who is Quesada?" I wanted to know; "What does he do for a living? Why is he bowling with these men? What is his status in relation to theirs?" Taylor then came up with the idea that Quesada was a schoolmaster. That explained his bookishness in the first scene, and deepened his relationship with his boy Sancho, who now became "pupil" as well as "servant." It also gave Quixot a longer, more pathetic exit from the final scene, when an extra quatrain of the song sent him "home to ordinary school."

In plays designed for theaters without sets or lighting plots, costumes and props also provide most of the visual pleasure of a show.[15] One of the first things I was asked, six months before *Cardenio* opened, was whether I would use "period costumes." My affirmative delighted even the predictable naysayers who would have preferred that I open the new theater with *The Miracle Worker* or *Diary of Anne Frank*. Vaguely Renaissance costumes are, for many spectators, a kind of comfort food. I have actually never before used period costume (except for the play within the play in *Hamlet*); in general I don't like it, and prefer to emphasize the present tense of performance. But unlike Greenblatt and Mea's *Cardenio,* Taylor's reconstruction is an experiment dedicated to the historical circumstances of the original text, and the seeming authenticity of the costumes enabled a "willing suspension of disbelief" in the possibility that the spectators were watching something first performed 400 years ago. Filling the first scene with monastic vestments and generic Renaissance court accoutrements immediately reassured audiences.[16] It also satisfied a hunger that I share with Shakespeare and Fletcher: for the exotic, for the extraordinary, for color and beauty.

If actors are dancers who speak, then their costumes serve choreographic functions. In Shakespeare and Fletcher's multimedia art form, text and texture have to complement each other, providing a color palette as rich as a Titian, Caravaggio, or Van Dyke, something that matches the verbal richness of the script. Antithesis and parallelism are as central to the aesthetics of costume as they are to Renaissance rhetoric. Both work temporally as well as spatially. Lucinda's red dress, at the beginning of the play, matched the flamenco dress of the onstage painting (plate 13.4), its fabric flowing and swirling around her. Her wedding dress mirrored the flounced flamenco, but was black and gold, not the red and white of her earlier, youthful, sexual self-confidence ("women must instruct the men to kiss," *THOC* 1.4). The black also defied our and Fernando's expectations for a wedding ("funeral-nuptial fashion," 3.1)—but then became shockingly appropriate when the wedding turned violent. When we next saw Lucinda, she was wearing a very plain black postulant's habit (4.4). Her expensive dresses in the first half had also contrasted with Violenta's village wench (figure 14.2) early in the play, and again in the final scene Lucinda's repressed, sheltered Catholic uniform emphasized Violenta's extravagantly colorful, hypertextured, sexily slipping-off-the-shoulder Micomicon festival dress (plate 13.2).

The History of Cardenio is partly the history of Cardenio's costume changes. He goes from the casually dressed student of his first scenes (figures 8.1 and 13.2) to courtier (*THOC* 2.1, 2.2, 2.4, 2.8), to courtier-disguised-as-mere-citizen (2.9), to mountain madman (3.3), gradually deteriorating to rags and near-nakedness (4.1, 4.3), while his body grows progressively darker, dirtier, more unkempt (figure 13.3). And then the coffin. And then the resurrection.

Figure 13.2 Sane: Cardenio (Thomas Cardwell) reading, with musician (Samuel Lawson) in background, *THOC* 1.2, photograph by Emily Schwank.

Figure 13.3 Mad: Cardenio (Thomas Cardwell) in the wilderness, beating Quixot (Jonah Winston), *THOC* 4.1, photograph by Emily Schwank.

For characters inside it, the coffin is a costume, a cocoon, and like caterpillars they emerge from it transformed. You can follow Cardenio's journey—or Lucinda's, Violenta's, Fernando's, Quixot's—visually, even if you do not understand a word of English.[17]

STILLNESS

The History of Cardenio's most important prop is specified in its first stage direction: a coffin. In Wellington, that coffin was carried onstage by chanting actors costumed as monks, and then carried offstage, later, by the same monks, again chanting. That beginning made the coffin instantly Catholic and Spanish, long ago and far away. In the Royal Shakespeare Company's very different adaptation, the coffin was visible from the outset, but it shared the space with an elaborately Spanish Catholic set and Spanish Catholic music.[18] I had originally imagined a local parish Scola Cantorum beginning the play with "In Paradisum Chant 4." But the fundamentalist Catholic actor I had cast as the Duke dropped out at the last minute, complaining that the play's resurrections mocked Christianity. And with him went the Scola Cantorum (and my whole vision of the first scene). The coffin could still be carried by monks, but they would have to do so without a thrilling Gregorian chant.

Then one day, late in rehearsals, I arrived early to find a technician using the coffin to test the new theater's partially installed lighting system (plate 13.5). For him, the coffin was just a focal object at the center of a big, almost empty stage. And I decided then to keep it there, to have it waiting for the spectators as they entered the auditorium. And it was there, again, at play's end. Taylor's script brings it onstage in the final scene, but there is no direction for its exit, and in that complicated final sequence no obvious opportunity to remove it. So it was still there, after the curtain call. In a performance full of movement, something that does not move, there before we arrive and still there after we exit.

Not foreign, not marked as belonging to any specific kind of person. Just a recognizably real death-box, center-stage, for everyone to connect to their own lives, in any way they chose, or could not help but choose. In early 1613, audiences could not have avoided thinking about the death of their own Prince Henry. I do not know what the coffin meant for all our spectators, but it would resound personally for each one. Not a comment about Spain, or Catholicism, or the Renaissance, but a reminder of death, everyone's death, anyone's death. The Duke's elder son—who begins the play asking his father a question about that coffin—was played by David Zoeller, a young man whose own father died, suddenly, four days before the show opened.

There is nothing as still as death.

MOVEMENT

Even an empty 150-pound coffin cannot be safely carried on and offstage quickly. My first thought, looking at the half-constructed *escena*, was: how can I move the coffin across that space? At one point stage management wanted to put it on wheels—and I had seen that done in the 2011 New York production of *Double Falsehood*—but that anachronism was potentially farcical, like a speeded-up silent movie, and unsafe for three of my actors, who had to get into or out of that unstable, rolling coffin while onstage.

So when it moved, it had to be moved by actors, lifting it, carrying it, lowering it. Slowly. The coffin consequently shaped the tempo and blocking of every scene in which it featured. With or without chanting, dignified monks carrying a coffin would have given the play a slow start. The first short scene packs a lot of exposition: the Duke's expectation of impending death, Roderick as the good son, Fernando as the prodigal, Fernando's intense relationship with Cardenio, the plot to bring Cardenio to court. The writing is compressed, because the audience will get impatient, otherwise. On the early modern stage, the coffin could have been discovered at the beginning of the scene, and then hidden again at the end, without being carried at all. So I dispensed with the chanting and the slow entrance, and—because I had no central discovery space—had the monks silently carry the coffin off in mid-scene, when it ceases to be the center of attention. Then Cardenio began the second scene running up the stairs just as the Duke and Roderick left the stage. The play began with a motionless coffin, and in a little over four minutes was literally running.[19]

The theater had no backstage. Six inches behind the black back curtain was a blank white wall. The small wing stage left and larger wing stage right were connected by a long, cornered hallway, unfit for coffin-transport. So the hearse had to stay put when not in use. It rested stage right throughout the first half, then went right-to-left for the scene when Fernando gets in it (*THOC* 4.2), then came back left-to-right two scenes later when Lucinda emerges from it (4.4). My Quixot was too big to be carried safely, so I played the final scene's first twenty-seven lines in front of a downstage curtain, which opened to "discover" the coffin mid-stage when Roderick said "Enter, tragedy!"

Productions in different spaces would find different solutions, but any production where the coffin is carried will require actors who do not speak. Since I have defined an actor as "a dancer who speaks," actors who do not speak are, by definition, dancers. What matters about them is how they move. To carry the coffin most productions will want a small group of strong men, well-practiced in synchronized activity. In the Indianapolis script, they were friars; in the text published in this volume, they are soldiers. Economically, it makes sense for the same small group of actors-who-do-not-speak to perform as the dancing black spirits in the masque.[20] But however the roles are cast, any production must block the coffin scenes as carefully as the fights or the rape. Those solemn episodes establish a ritual movement that begins in the first scene, and then recurs three times in the final five.

Those are not the only moments when the play decelerates to ritual tempo. Violenta wants the exchange of vows with Fernando to be slow and solemn; he insists on speeding it up, interrupting her sentences, impatient, dismissing the witness, "and now to bed" (*THOC* 1.5). The second exchange of vows was much more formal, with opening lute song and presiding Curate (3.1). But again the woman's desire to slow things down clashes with Lord Fernando's (and Don Barnard's) desire for uncomplicated speed. Lucinda's moment of silence is the scene's—and the play's—heart. After she finally says, reluctantly, "I will," things immediately speed up again. Cardenio runs onstage, now with a sword instead of a book, to stop the wedding and challenge Fernando to a duel. But then Cardenio stops, too. He loses confidence in himself and his ideals, frozen in soliloquy ("How can I hero it, here?"). All the frantic movements of his subsequent madness spring from that moment of stilled indecision. His *Lord Jim* failure of nerve.

Every scene has its own choreography. Scholar-director Ralph Cohen has written beautifully about the difference between big scenes in Shakespeare (which always "focus on main characters or on some central situation") and big scenes in Middleton (which offer audiences instead "a carousel of activity").[21] The wedding scene (3.1) and the bowling scene (1.6) in *The History of Cardenio* both fit the Shakespearian paradigm—that's why different casts all inevitably identify them by the single action of wedding or bowling.[22] By contrast, the play's unShakespearian final and longest scene is what Cohen calls "centrifugal," because the coffin provides a center of gravity for its long multitask action. That is why, without the coffin, the equivalent scene in *Double Falsehood* has no structure and is theatrically very unsatisfying. Indeed, the coffin is the center of gravity in all four of its scenes.

But no dominant character, prop, or action organizes the play's second-longest scene (307 lines), which puts onstage a very complicated sequence of movements. The casual, chatty entrance of the shepherds; the Master separating himself from the others, watching, and especially watching Violenta, now disguised as a boy; Cardenio's crazed entrance, riding an imaginary horse; Violenta's melancholy song, which I had her play sitting on the front edge of the stage, facing the audience, lost in her own thoughts; the intimate private mid-stage conversation between Cardenio and Violenta; his attack on the second shepherd; Violenta running offstage, terrified; Cardenio's crazed exit, riding his imaginary horse; the post-fight chatter and exit of the shepherds; the Master's soliloquy; Violenta's cautious re-entrance; his attempt to rape her; its interruption by Roderick and his attendant Gerald; Violenta running offstage again, again terrified; Roderick's reacting to Fernando's letter; Gerald's *intermezzo*, bridging the two halves of the scene, joking about coffins and actors (and, in my interpretation, picking up the Clint Eastwood cigarillo discarded by the Master as he began groping Violenta); then Quixot's excited entrance, his brief exchange with Gerald, Gerald's exit, Sancho's dragging entrance; then the climactic Quixot–Cardenio duet, which concludes with Cardenio beating Quixot, then beating Sancho, then riding off again on his imaginary horse; Quixot and Sancho flat on the ground; Quixot's exit in search of trees to pluck up, and Sancho again addressing the audience before reluctantly following his boss.

This scene does not fit any of Cohen's paradigms. Instead, it *wanders*. People come and go, turn and re-turn, apparently randomly. More than any other in the play, this scene dramatizes the central activity of the novel: *vagar, errar*. Nevertheless, the movements here are no more random than the novel's. The complexity of this long scene (or series of linked scenes-within-scenes) is artistically structured by two entrances, three fights, and four exits. Cardenio twice enters and twice exits on his imaginary horse; Violenta twice exits, running for her life (figure 13.4). Those repeated *sforzato* movements are the choreographic equivalent of rhyming couplets; they give a sense of order to what might otherwise seem chaotic unrelated activities. The three fights are bigger and more complicated than the entrances and exits. The first (Cardenio vs. Second Shepherd) demonstrates that Cardenio is really crazy, and really dangerous (figure 13.5). The second (Master vs. Violenta) demonstrates, to the audience and to Violenta herself, that the world is too dangerous for an isolated, defenseless young woman (figure 13.6). Her earlier scene with Fernando undoubtedly was coercive, and should make audiences uncomfortable; but Fernando is better than the brutal rural Master, no question. The third fight (Quixot vs. Cardenio) demonstrates that Quixot's dreams of heroic knighthood are dangerous illusions (figure 13.3). Quixot fantasizes about rescuing others, but he cannot even defend himself against an unarmed vagabond, smaller than he is, and his delusion gets Sancho

Figure 13.4 Escape: Violenta (Alys Dickerson) running from attempted rape by her Master (Noah Winston), *THOC* 4.1, *DF* 4.1, photograph by Emily Schwank.

Figure 13.5 Violence: First Shepherd (Fernando Akè) watches as Cardenio (Thomas Cardwell) attacks Second Shepherd (Frankie Bolda), *THOC* 4.1, *DF* 4.1, photograph by Emily Schwank.

Figure 13.6 Sexual assault: Master (Noah Winston) grapples with Violenta (Alys Dickerson), *THOC* 4.1, *DF* 4.1, photograph by Emily Schwank.

beaten, too. The physical contrasts between these three fights, and their very different rhythms, are as important as the repetition of fighting. The first is the quickest, simplest, and least disturbing; the second, the most upsetting; the third, the most complicated and prolonged, the only one that involves three major characters, the only one that is unmistakably definitive. The shepherds worry that Cardenio may return; the Master pursues Violenta; but no one expects a Quixot vs. Cardenio re-match.

VOLTA

Every major character in *The History of Cardenio* has one or more turning points. Academic criticism since Aristotle has given such a turn the foreign, abstract label "peripeteia."[23] But that Greek word περιπέτεια originally had a physical meaning, compounding περί ("round, around, about") with the stem of πίπτω ("to fall"). A complete turn and a fall. And that makes sense, because in the theater such character-turns are almost inevitably physical and, like a dancer's well-executed *volta,* physically exhilarating. Jocasta, for instance, in *Oedipus Tyrannos,* is motionless as she listens to the news that her husband Oedipus is also her son; but her long preparatory stillness makes more emphatic the moment when she turns and silently exits to her death. The stillness is absorption; the turn is action. Imagine stepping forward to pivot on the ball of your right foot, and then completing the turn with a *relevé* (a raising of the body on the points or demi-pointes of the feet).

The play as a whole has two big turns: one from comedy toward tragedy, the other away from chaos toward cosmos. The first is the wedding scene (*DF* 3.2, *THOC* 3.1), which determines the eventual fate of all four lovers and their parents. In its final fifteen lines, Cardenio is dragged offstage, Fernando runs offstage, and the limp, wounded, unconscious Lucinda is carried offstage—by her father, in my production (figure 13.7). Three very different movements, three very different *battements.*[24] This is the first time that more than two of the lovers have been onstage together; they will not all meet again until the final scene. After these three exits, we do not know, we should not know, what will happen to any of them next.

That's where I finally put the intermission. I had originally planned, like other directors, to place it later, after the first Quixot–Cardenio encounter in the mountains; Sancho's "where apple leads, belly follows" is a great curtain line. But that's a much more upbeat ending to the first half; it reassures the audience that they are watching a comedy, and it structurally asserts that Quixot and Sancho constitute the main plot. I got a lot of resistance about my change of plan (from Gary Taylor and others), but the new position worked, as everyone afterward acknowledged.

The second major turn happens when Cardenio meets Violenta in the mountains (*DF* 4.2, *THOC* 4.3). This has always been, to me, the single most important scene in the play, emotionally. Violenta enters it planning to commit suicide—a double suicide, since she will also be killing her unborn baby. Earlier, she had instantly rejected Cardenio's advice that she "commit

Figure 13.7   Tragicomedy: Don Bernard (Michael Hosp) carries his unconscious daughter
Lucinda (Maria Sousa Eglen), *THOC* 3.1, *DF* 3.2, photograph by Emily Schwank.

self-murder" (*DF* 4.1.101, *THOC* 4.1). But in the interim she has been brutally assaulted by her Master. This resounded with the women in the cast
and audience; in Indiana, more than 17 percent of girls are sexually assaulted
before they are old enough to graduate from high school.[25] The semester that
I was casting *Cardenio,* one of my own students was brutally raped. Many
women in the audience immediately understood Violenta's despair; indeed,
my most moving feedback from spectators came from women who had been
raped, or had sisters or daughters who had been raped, and who appreciated
the play's unflinching sensitivity to their predicament. Cardenio, too, is at
his lowest point, having lost even his imaginary horse, and with nothing to
eat but a louse he picks from his own scalp: a kind of self-cannibalism. But
by the scene's end, Violenta and Cardenio have each found a "suff'ring true
companion" (*DF* 4.2.103). They exit together, no longer alone.

What makes this *volta* emotionally convincing is a moment when, literally, nothing happens. To a reader, it might seem undramatic. Three men,
onstage, silently, motionlessly listen to music (figure 13.8). First the haunting
strings, then the haunting solo voice, unseen, singing. A woman's voice—or
a boy's—rises, fills the entire space of the stage and the auditorium. A powerful voice, singing about powerlessness. The offstage voice sings a stanza

Figure 13.8   Stillness: Cardenio (Thomas Cardwell), Barber (Ben Asaykwee), and Curate (Glenn Clifton) listen to a ghostly voice, *THOC* 4.3, *DF* 4.2, photograph by Emily Schwank.

(which ends with the word "die"), then is silent. The onstage men talk briefly. Then the offstage voice sings again, a second stanza, again ending with the word "die." The direction for this music to be played offstage is the single most authoritative stage direction in the entire play.[26] Nevertheless, the otherwise very different Wellington, New York, and Stratford-upon-Avon re-imaginings of this Fletcher scene put the offstage voice onstage, so that the audience could look at Violenta. I had planned to do the same. It seemed a no-brainer. Would it not obviously be more dramatic if we could see Violenta's face, her body, as she sang her suicide-note?

But Fletcher was right. We have already *seen* Violenta sing a sad song, among the shepherds (*THOC* 4.1). What would be gained by repeating that scenario? By placing her offstage, Fletcher made her a ghost, *before* she commits suicide. Cardenio thinks he is listening to a "heavenly" ghost, a "spirit." Emotionally, Violenta is resurrected in this scene, as Cardenio will be in the last. But more importantly, this offstaging, this decision not to *poner en escena*, forces the audience to listen. And they did: the auditorium was more silent, more attentive, more rapt, in that absolutely still musical moment than in any other of the performance.[27] They *heard* the disembodied lyrical lament of a defeated woman. They wanted her to come back to life. They wanted her and Cardenio to meet. And then they got what they wanted. And they believed it, because it was what they wanted to believe. And because they believed it, they were prepared to believe all the subsequent, implausible, theatrical, jazz-handed happiness of the Princess of Micomicon (plate 13.6) and the final reunions.

BALANCE

The play delivers to an audience eventual happiness and many laugh-out-loud moments. But it also contains some disturbingly dark material. Its happy high notes are underlaid by a deep bass, always threatening, occasionally erupting into violent dominance. "No lions, Sancho," Jonah's Quixot confidently reassured his young companion; "Only snakes. And" (stretching the next word into a howl) "wolves" (*THOC* 4.1).

A few spectators obviously wanted, and expected, nothing but comedy; they protested that they had been tricked, or set up, when the story sheered off toward rape and suicide, and into real violence and insanity. A few others protested that the happy ending was unrealistic, after all that had gone before. It's probably impossible, with tragicomedy, to avoid wrong-footing some spectators; the genre was created to disturb powerfully comforting generic expectations. But for actors and for a director, this generic fluidity means making tough decisions, at every point, about tone. Tragicomedy is not just a random mixture of comedy and tragedy; it actually requires more complex emotional precision than either of its parent genres, because it moves back and forth between them, like a dancer. For instance:

"Art thou a pygmy, or an idiot?" (*THOC* 4.1)

Very funny, but immediately preceded and followed by violence against two harmless and sympathetic characters. I wanted a laugh here, and always got it.

"You promised me an island." (*THOC* 5.2)

The running Cervantes joke about Sancho becoming a governor, but in the play, this is the moment when poor Sancho accuses the utterly defeated Quixot of having betrayed him with false promises, just as Fernando had betrayed Violenta and Cardenio. I did not want a laugh here, and did not get it after the first performance.

The problems and opportunities created by the play's mix of comedy and tragedy intersect with its mix of Shakespeare and Fletcher. Six weeks after my production closed, I saw the broadcast film of Christopher Plummer's 2010 production of *The Tempest* on the Stratford, Ontario Festival Stage. The first play Shakespeare worked on after *The Tempest* (played at court in the winter season of 1611–1612) was the original *Cardenio* (played at court in the winter season of 1612–1613). I was struck by how easily that *Tempest* cast could have followed it with a production of *Cardenio*. Prospero is a "schoolmaster" (*Tempest* 1.2.173), and anyone could imagine Plummer's Prospero—or Gielgud's—as Quixot: vocally grandiloquent, physically frail, poetic, but also capable of rage, determined to right the world's wrongs, a veteran actor beloved by audiences, most of his speeches directed to a young, innocent companion, played by a boy actor. His little servant Ariel (Julyana Soelistyo) could easily have morphed into Quixot's little servant Sancho, entranced by the power of magic and language, but sometimes recalcitrant and impatient. Miranda (Trish Lindström) would be a natural, red-headed, feisty Lucinda, paired with Gareth Potter's Ferdinand/Cardenio. Stefano and Trinculo (Geraint Wyn Davies and Bruce Dow) could have reprised their duo act as Curate and Barber. I imagined casting Gonzalo (James Blendick) as the old, basically good-hearted Camillo, pitted against the less sympathetic but higher-ranking Sebastian/Don Barnard. Alonso, King of Naples (Peter Hutt), like the Duke of Andalusia, has little to do but carry authority and worry about his son. The bad brother Antonio could play the bad brother Fernando; the would-be rapist Caliban, the would-be rapist Master. Iris, a singing goddess played by a boy-actor in Prospero's masque, could return as the singing Violenta, a year later. None of these roles are identical; some challenge their actors more than others. But both tragicomedies are shaped by generational difference, betrayal, forgiveness, an old man's magic. The story of *The Tempest* begins with an offstage marriage between a European aristocrat and an African woman; *The History of Cardenio* ends with an onstage marriage between a European aristocrat and a half-African woman. Once you have seen the two shows performed, you can easily imagine them side by side in the repertory of the King's Men, starring Richard Burbage.

But *The History of Cardenio*, unlike *The Tempest*, was written in collaboration. For me, that collaboration produced a hybrid that was, initially, frustrating and confusing. I could not find my footing. I had never directed, or acted in, a Fletcher play before, and at first I made the mistake of trying to direct him as though he were Shakespeare. He is not. His vocabulary, his syntax, and his attitudes are much more modern than Shakespeare's, but his language is not as dense or complex. Fletcher's style resembles, if anything, Restoration comedy, or seventeenth-century French drama. He achieves many of his best effects by repetition: for instance, the emotionally powerful refrain "while miserable I,/ Cursing my fortunes, drop, drop, drop a tear and die" (*THOC* 4.3). But sometimes the repetitions can just feel repetitive, rather than cumulative. In Violenta's only dialogue with her male Servant (*DF* 4.1.129–55, *THOC* 2.7), for instance, she asks essentially the same question twice ("Art thou corrupted?" "Wilt thou be honest?"), tells him to "Take heed" three times, and four times denies that she doubts him. Six of his speeches do nothing but insist on his good intentions. In *Don Quijote* this Servant will later attempt to rape her, but that does not happen in the play. I did not know what to do with this dialogue, and neither did the actors. But then I realized that the whole scene was really about an attractive young woman, alone, talking to a man about changing her clothes. I told the actor, Alex Carrico, to look at her as though he was undressing her. Without that look, that predatory movement of his eyes up and down her body—a movement most women recognize—the scene made absolutely no sense; but that look made it a necessary part of Violenta's trajectory from leaving home to abandoning her social and gender identity completely. This seemingly repetitive Fletcher dialogue is like something by Pinter, but without ellipses and stage directions to make the menace clear to a reader.

This example illustrates the precision that actors and directors must bring to Fletcher's seemingly casual dialogue. Just as I had to discover the subtext (or rather, the physical text) behind Violenta's conversation with the Servant, so I had to recognize the importance of keeping Violenta's body offstage for the song "Woods, rocks, and mountains," to realize that the intermission belonged between the Shakespearian wedding scene and the Fletcherian meeting of Roderick, Camillo, and Don Barnard, and to see that the seeming incoherence of the long scene that begins with the shepherds was actually an artful, scenery-less representation of the unpredictable, always potentially dangerous experience of wandering through the mountains.

By the final performance, watching from the auditorium, I felt that we had found our footing. Fletcher himself discovered a way to take over Shakespeare's tragic characters and lead them through the mountains and back "homeward, whining as pigs do in the wind" (*DF* 5.2.19; *THOC* 5.2), complementing Shakespeare's voice without surrendering his own. The most interesting duet in *The History of Cardenio* may not be old Quixot and young Sancho, but the two poets, old Shakespeare and young Fletcher.

NOTES

The illustrations identified as "Plates" in this essay are color images in the e-book, but black and white in the printed volume. For additional color images and film excerpts of performances and rehearsals, see *CSI Shakespeare* and www.liberalarts. iupui.edu/shakespeare. The website also contains a digital recording of songs from the production.

1. "An excellent Actor," *The Works of John Webster*, ed. David Gunby, David Carnegie and MacDonald P. Jackson, vol. 3 (Cambridge: Cambridge University Press, 2007), 483.
2. Wright, *The Passions of the Mind in General* (London, 1604), 176.
3. Hall, *Shakespeare's Advice to the Players* (New York: Theatre Communications Group, 2003), 207.
4. On the anti-Aristotelian emphasis on particulars rather than generalities, see Elizabeth Spiller, "Shakespeare and the Making of Early Modern Science: Resituating Prospero's Art," *South Central Review*, 26.1 (2009): 24–41.
5. See Thomas Howard Ridley, Jr., *From the Avenue – A Memoir* (CreateSpace, 2012), and C. Nickerson Bolden, *Indiana Avenue: Black Entertainment Boulevard* (AuthorHouse, 2009).
6. Leigh spoke at the IUPUI colloquium. The student production at Victoria University of Wellington in New Zealand is described in Hammond, 156–8, and more extensively in *Quest*, 368–82 (David Carnegie and Lori Leigh), 383–6 (David Laurence review), and 398–402 (Bourus, "Stages").
7. For more on the space, see Gerald Baker's review in chapter 14 in this volume.
8. Some of those roles can be doubled, but because this was a university production—indeed, the first in a new university theater—I needed to give stage-time to as many students as possible.
9. Trevis, *Being a Director: A Life in Theatre* (New York: Routledge, 2012), 84.
10. See Peter Kirwan's blog review of the Globe reading at http://blogs.notting ham.ac.uk/bardathon/tag/cardenio/.

11. See Andrew J. Power, "Late Shakespeare, late Players," in *Late Shakespeare, 1608–1613,* ed. Rory Loughnane and Andrew J. Power (Cambridge: Cambridge University Press, 2012), 172–86.

12. I think this generational deficit contributed to Steven Wagschal's complaint, in *CSI Shakespeare,* that the reconstruction captured the comedy of Quixote but not his seriousness.

13. This was also demonstrated by John Harrell's performance of Quixot in the Staunton reading; see my "Cardenio by Stages," *Quest,* 396.

14. George Bernard Shaw, *John Bull's Other Island,* and Samuel Beckett, *Krapp's Last Tape,* in *Modern and Contemporary Irish Drama,* ed. John P. Harrington, second edition (New York: W. W. Norton, 2009), 40, 247.

15. Tyrone Guthrie famously foregrounded "the costumed and choreographed bodies of the performers…upon the scenery-less platform" of the thrust stages he championed: see Robert Shaughnessy, "Tyrone Guthrie," in *The Routledge Companion to Directors' Shakespeare,* ed. John Russell Brown (New York: Routledge, 2008), 136.

16. Because of the black backdrop curtain, I could not fill the first scene with "Spanish black" costumes, as Taylor's script requested.

17. See Taylor's account of shows performed for foreign ambassadors, in "The Embassy, The City, The Court, The Text: *Cardenio* Performed in 1613," in *Quest,* 292, 306–7.

18. The RSC's opening dumb show is not included in Doran and Àlamo's published text. On the music see Carla della Gatta's essay, chapter 12 in this volume.

19. I tried to keep it running, cutting 252 lines of the text. The final performance lasted only 155 minutes (including one intermission). In his revised script Taylor has restored some of the lines we cut.

20. I could not do this in my production, because I had asked the university dance company to perform the spirits in the masque, and all the dancers they gave me were petite women, who could not have lifted the coffin. In early modern theater, dancers were usually adult males, who could easily have doubled those roles.

21. Introduction to *Your Five Gallants,* Middleton, 394–5.

22. We could not decide whether to call 1.5 the "rape scene" or the "seduction scene". Now that Taylor has added stage directions for an onstage bed, I'm sure this will become "the bed scene"–and that it will be much easier to block.

23. Aristotle, *Poetics,* edited and translated Stephen Halliwell, Loeb Classical Library (Cambridge: Harvard University Press, 1994), 64–5.

24. A *battement* is a beating action of the extended or bent leg; it comes in different varieties, but all supply the energy for a subsequent turn or other large movement. I am describing the exits here as the energizing actions that make possible the larger turns of the story.

25. Carolyn Gregoire, "Rape Statistics: Over 17 Percent of High School-Age Girls in Indiana Experience Sexual Assault," *Huffington Post,* April 9, 2012. In her preshow talk on April 20 ("When Is Sex Legal?"), Professor Jennifer Drobac called attention to this article, as evidence of the continuing relevance of *Cardenio.*

26. For the authenticity of this direction (*DF* 4.2.7), see Taylor, "History," 35–6, 45–8.

27. I like to think that this was one of the "moments of truth and beauty" recognized by an otherwise unsympathetic critic, who also felt that the music did the "heavy lifting" in the show, even in the preview performance he reviewed: www.ibj.com/lou-s-views – no-great-shakes/PARAMS/article/34080.

Plate 13.1 Moving bodies: Don Bernard (Michael Hosp) chases his angry daughter Lucinda (Maria Sousa Eglen), *THOC* 2.5, *DF* 2.3, photograph by Emily Schwank.

Plate 13.2 Transgressive color: Barber disguised as squire (Ben Asaykwee), Violenta disguised as Princess of Micomicon (Alys Dickerson), Curate disguised as governess (Glenn Clifton), *THOC* 5.1, photograph by Emily Schwank.

Plate 13.3 "The most famous male couple in world literature": Quixot (Jonah Winston) and Sancho (Brandon Merriweather) hide to watch the mad Cardenio, with musician Al Hoffmann in background, *THOC* 4.1, photograph by Emily Schwank.

Plate 13.4 Visual rhetoric: Lucinda (Maria Sousa Eglen) in flamenco dress beside onstage bandstand and painting of flamenco dancer (by Ivan Hernandez Olivera), *THOC* 2.5, *DF* 2.3, photograph by Emily Schwank.

Plate 13.5 Focal point: Coffin in spotlight, opening and close of show, *THOC*, photograph by Emily Schwank.

Plate 13.6 "Enchanted": Razzle-dazzle jazz-handed happiness of Quixot (Jonah Winston), Violenta as Princess of Micomicon (Alys Dickerson), Barber as squire (Ben Asaykwee), *THOC* 5.1, photograph by Emily Schwank.

14

TIME BEGETS A WONDER:
THE HISTORY OF CARDENIO AT IUPUI

Gerald Baker

Sometimes in early modern drama a small phrase, made up of simple short words, will hang in the ear and accrete meaning. It's certainly a characteristic of Shakespeare, especially when Time is in question, and it's also a characteristic feature of Gary Taylor's reconstruction of the lost Fletcher/Shakespeare tragicomedy *The History of Cardenio*. "Time may beget a wonder," says Violenta (Alys Dickerson), in shepherd boy disguise, before starting the next stage of her flight into the mountains—a Fletcherian line that comes out of *Double Falsehood* (3.3.128) into this script.[1] On top of its resonance in the play, the line is also an emblem of the story of the script's making and realization: the twenty-years-and-counting of Taylor's work,[2] and its first full staging with (some) professional actors, directed by Terri Bourus.[3]

Watching the show on the last two nights of its IUPUI run, there was no doubt that both audiences were engaging directly and deeply with the script, in a way that seldom happens with a known quantity.[4] While the local elders play bowls, Don Bernard (Michael Hosp) takes from the schoolmaster the book he is reading: he tears out a page. In the audience, someone audibly gasps, in surprise or horror. A small everyday action had generated a spontaneous response that exemplified the degree of engagement Bourus's staging excited in its auditors and spectators.[5] Her account of the script was passionate and diverting by turns, with full effect derived from, and full authority apparent in, the major coups—Quixot (Jonah D. Winston)'s first sword-wielding, the aborted wedding, Cardenio (Thomas Cardwell)'s madness, the various reveals of the coffin's inhabitants, Quixot's last glorious line. The production had great clarity, in both overall arc and individual journeys.

The script is a gift for actors in one respect above all: the lost original was a Fletcher/Shakespeare collaboration and Taylor acknowledges their two different styles in *his* work, so it has a high proportion of Fletcherian smoothness and lucidity, fewer problem and knotty areas for an actor to unravel than undiluted very-late Shakespeare. And it provides several scenes of riveting effectiveness. Don Bernard (Hosp) handing his daughter Lucinda

(Maria Souza-Eglen) to her unwanted bridegroom was another moment eliciting audible horror in the audience. Cardenio (Cardwell)'s crazed mountain dialogue with Winston's Quixot recalls, in different mode and with all allowance for different circumstances, crazed Lear and damaged Gloucester, on the road, comparing *their* worlds (and this echoing seems entirely characteristic of last-phase Shakespeare). In a way it's the heart of the play: two men with one book in common—the romance *Amadis of Gaul*—each driven out of his wits by the kind of love it celebrates: so much alike, it would seem, yet coming to violent blows (played as vigorously in their way as the attempted rape discussed below, and therefore as disturbingly). Their crazinesses are different, though. Cardenio's "realism...unhinged in ways that rightly feel uncomfortable" contrasts with Quixot's "delusionary obliviousness."[6]

The strengths of this production were very much in the principal actors' performances, in Cardwell's trust shattered and hope disintegrated, in Dickerson's luminous resource and courage, in Souza-Eglen's initiative and independence, and in the rich humor of Jonah Winston's Quesada/Quixot and of Brandon Merriweather's Sancho. The writing of this pair and of the characters associated with their plot-thread (including the Barber, successfully anachronistic in Ben Asaykwee's performance) is Taylor's most substantial contribution to the script, and remarkable for two things. First, the couple's scenes are not only funny but very comprehensible at first exposure[7]; and second, these two characters, so iconic or even mythic in modern and postmodern consciousness, do not have that functional domination in the play. They keep proportion: not simply in the script, but in realization too. Sancho is re-imagined as a "boy" rather than Cervantes's guzzling peasant and Merriweather at the time of performance was indeed a high school senior. Quixot begins as the schoolmaster and Winston had nothing of the lean old hidalgo, being in his prime and large-physiqued. He emerged as one from many out of the communal dialogue in his first scene, and his resonant voice combined with Merriweather's fast delivery gave a different yet authoritative dynamic to that one hears in Quixote/Sancho exchanges in the novel. Hence this auditor simply accepted the pair as *the* pair in this version, in their own right and in scale with the play.[8]

Not all of the rest of the company were as strong, even some middling roles lacking differentiation in delivery of expression or in mood from moment to moment.[9] Some really interesting work though was done in minor roles that were played gender-blind, Kelley Ellyse and Meagan Matlock doubling their maids' parts with two gallants and Frankie Bolda playing a shepherd, all of them offering clear, lively identities in each role. This might have caused confusion—Bolda for example played a male in the same scene where Dickerson's Violenta was disguised as a boy—but none in fact occurred. Overall, action was clear, emotions directly expressed, characterizations "broad and vivid" and "in the major roles...consistently brought off."[10]

The production's clarity was much aided by the costumes (designed by Clark Foster), which worked within a convention, locating actors quickly and simply on social and geographic axes. The Duke (Edwin Faunce) and his sons

(David Zoeller and Tyrone van Tatenhove) as well as Cardenio (after he has been taken to Court) wore early-seventeenth-century robes, doublets, and breeches, and in some scenes spurs. Townsmen differed in style and texture from the ducal court, wearing loose muslin shirts and trousers. The disparity between Don Bernard's household and his neighbors was clarified (in addition to the servants attending him) by the costume of his daughter Lucinda (Souza-Eglen), by some degrees a richer material and more decorated design than that of the farm girl, Violenta (Dickerson). Lower down the scale shepherds had rough hoodies (though the Master ran to a serape), while at the bottom of the hierarchy the schoolmaster's boy, Sancho (Merriweather), had tears and holes in the usual shirt-breeches combination. Overall, the costuming's simplicity was successful.

So too was Brian Hartz's soundscape. It instantly indicated change of environment (approaching thunder, bird-caws in the mountains, sheep baa-ing for the flocks scene, running water) in those places where the script requires it. However, the live musical performances of Al Hoffmann, Samuel Lawson, and Ben Michaelis were less helpful, especially at the beginning of the play.[11] Hoffman's cover of a top-of-the-pops break-up song (Gotye's "Someone that I used to know") stood for Prologue, whereas the first scene would be better aided by a somber, religiose introduction to the Duke, as he contemplates his own coffin and his advancing death-date. The scene quickly goes in a different direction, shifting to conversation about his wayward son, and it is therefore perhaps the more necessary that its speakers should initially have a created atmosphere to support them. As it was, the familial and moral concerns of the Duke and his older son in their opening dialogue were severely underemphasized, and thus the first scene seriously missed fire. There was only one other place in the production where one felt similarly disappointed, the final scene's dance of "black spirits." On the one hand a perfectly acceptable piece of choreographed movement for beginning-level dancers, it was on the other essentially undramatic, with this spectator being conscious of *dancers* rather than *persons pretending to be spirits* in a kind of exorcism; the disguised Cardenio had no function when he appeared with them, making his extraction and unmasking as they leave less surprising and revelatory than it might have been. (The spirit-dance is integral to resolving both Cardenio and Quixot plots: if it were simply ornamental, one would say that no dancing would have been better than what the choreographer offered.)[12] Both of these misfired sequences have to this auditor's mind one thing in common: the involvement of departments or personnel from elsewhere in IUPUI. Given the location, there was presumably a desideratum to involve other university elements; but other collaborators, more in tune with the project, might have delivered opening music and climactic choreography more integrated into and appropriate to the action.

This account has so far focused on the achievement of individual shapers, but it's necessary to speak of the way the theatrical space itself shaped the production: it is not the most hospitable for an early modern-esque play (figure 14.1). The stage space is in effect a proscenium arch situation, wide

Figure 14.1 Inhospitable space: IUPUI proscenium stage with (left to right) Sancho (Brandon Merriweather), musician (Lawson), Quixot (Jonah Winston), Violenta as Micomicon (Dickerson), Barber as squire (Asaykwee), and Curate (Clifton), *THOC* 5.1, photograph by Emily Schwank.

(forty-two feet) and shallow (twenty-one feet). At each flank short flights of steps go from auditorium floor-level to stage. Supporting pillars running along the auditorium aisle on the right have bays between them, letting actors appear there and interact with others on the stage proper (figure 14.2). The floor-space between the stage and front row of seats assists too. All of these areas—stairs, pillars, and front aisle—were used by Bourus, giving variety and relief to an unfriendly acting space.

There was no set, simply dark curtains upstage as backdrop. Stage right the two musicians were set in front of the flamenco dancer painting that had been used for publicity. Other than this there was no permanent visual feature. For a realization of a reconstructed early modern script, it was for this writer totally correct. It proved to local commentator Rita Kohn that "you don't need lavish sets to be taken to multiple places."[13] For another local reviewer it was a problem, though, possibly skewing his whole sense of the production: Lou Harry took the fact that "'Cardenio' *[sic]* eschews sets" as evidence of 'the overall amateurism of the exercise."[14] Regina Buccola makes no comment either way, remarking simply that beyond musicians, flamenco painting and the coffin "very little else was provided in the way of set or major props." For Buccola, as a seasoned writer on staging early modern scripts, the absence of set is not an issue, positive or negative. And any early modernist and most theater practitioners will reject Harry's implication here that "professional" theater *requires* sets to demonstrate its credentials.

Figure 14.2   Pillars: Violenta (Dickerson) on her "balcony," in one of the alcoves between pillars in the IUPUI auditorium, looking toward Fernando on the main stage, *THOC* 1.3, *DF* 1.3, photograph by Emily Schwank.

The stage width shaped the show to good and bad effect. It helped the actors maintain a high energy level. *Entering* to an encounter center stage required a fast crossing of the space to avoid undue delay or deadening pauses. Similarly, an *exit* from center allowed for built-up, prolonged effects—especially for several of the Quixot/Sancho exits and for Cardenio's mad "giddy-up" departures, riding a tree-limb as if it were a hobby-horse and lashing it on. The width also greatly facilitated the bowls scene; but was most effective in the scene where the Master (Noah Winston) tries to rape the disguised Violenta. This—the most distressing sequence in the whole production—was played sharply and brutally, with the Master at one point pulling a frantically crawling Violenta back by one ankle. The *distance* over which he pursued her enhanced one's sense of his determination and ruthlessness, as well as demanding energy of both Winston's Master in his rapacity and Dickerson's Violenta in her resistance.

But in other situations the width was less helpful. I missed depth in heavily populated scenes (Lord Fernando's arrival at Don Bernard's, and the final scene) whose people had to be strung in line, and craved more opportunity to shift emphasis by backward-and-forward movement. Similarly,

Taylor reconstructs a tautly written scene for Lord Fernando bribing his way into Violenta's house and forcefully vowing marriage as prelude to sex: and Dickerson and Tatenhove acted it to the hilt. Played across the whole width, though, it lacked an intimacy that would intensify and ultimately justify Violenta's acquiescence. Rather than the fairly uniform wash that was the production's usual state, more selective lighting would have been useful here, to define a space within which the two interacted and outside of which they could not go.[15]

Overall, one would say that where Taylor's script was directly mediated through director and actors it usually had immense impact, and that the less successful elements of the production were those most closely related to the institutional *context* in which it was situated. But the balance of the performance tilted much more to the success side, as one last anecdote demonstrating the degree of audience involvement shows. At the interval, the low point of every character's fortunes, one audience member talking over the play with her party opined: "Someone's got to die." The intensity generated by the script and its actors was making that auditor anticipate tragedy. In the light of part of Fletcher's own description of the tragicomic genre—"it wants deaths…yet brings some neere it"[16]—I was moved by her involvement and openness to how the story might play out, and by how she *thought* she knew what she was dealing with. Twenty years of Taylor's posthumous collaboration have begotten a script that allows auditors to enjoy the delights of surprise in a way that they seldom can now when the overfamiliar name of Shakespeare is in question, and delight was in ample evidence in Hoosier Bard's staging. And that is the true wonder of Taylor and Bourus's *History of Cardenio*.

NOTES

1. The phrase could be seen as encapsulating the script's history: "Time" as the agent of resolution is a very Shakespearian idea; Matthew Wagner's "In This Good Time: *Cardenio* and the Temporal Character of Shakespearian Drama," *Quest*, 267–82, describes the iconography and characterizes the aspects of Time in Shakespeare and goes on to position *The History of Cardenio* in relation to those positive and negative aspects of time and its dramaturgical use. This statement of it however is in a Fletcher passage carried in the medium of Theobald's adaptation, and it is amplified and echoed by Taylor throughout the reconstruction by such additions as bells ringing time and by the watch that passes through several characters' hands.
2. The development of that work is described in Bourus, "Stages."
3. Presented by the Indiana University School of Liberal Arts at IUPUI and Hoosier Bard Productions, April 19–28, 2012, in the IUPUI Campus Center Theater. Cardwell is a UK Equity actor, while trained nonstudents active in small Indianapolis theater groups and venues played other principal roles.
4. Regina Buccola, reviewing the production in *Shakespeare Bulletin* 30.4 (2012): 649–53, notices a similar intensity of response in speaking of the script as "a lively, gripping piece of theatre" and of Bourus's production as "a fast-paced emotional rollercoaster of a production" (652 both).

5. It is entirely appropriate that the damaging of a book should be a high point of the script's realization, since that script itself derives from a series of fragments and is itself an attempt to restore to the book of the play its missing pages.

6. Jay Harvey at www.indystar.com/apps/pbcs.dll/article?AID=2012204270354, accessed May 8, 2012.

7. A measure of Taylor's accuracy in reconstruction: comedy in Fletcher plays still often speaks to an audience directly without the kind of footnoting editors of Shakespeare have to rely on or the diversionary physicality his directors sometimes resort to.

8. Another way in which both Winston and Merriweather vary from expectation is in their ethnicity. I mention it simply to note Bourus's directorial bravery in casting nonwhite actors as two of the European tradition's most conspicuous characters, and to report very happily that for neither of the audiences I joined did this obtrude upon the pleasure and authority of the actors' performances.

9. There was a serious problem with one actor in particular. The Duke in this production lacked authority and melancholy wisdom, because his actor seemed to lack any sense of how his verse moved or even how the grammar worked. Both first and final scenes therefore badly lacked a tonal dimension.

10. Harvey, www.indystar.com/apps/pbcs.dll/article?AID=2012204270354.

11. Recordings of all the live music from the show, except the opening cover, can be found at http://liberalarts.iupui.edu/shakespeare/research/.

12. I should say that my sense of missed possibilities in the first scene and with the dancers and the Cardenio revelation may be due to prior knowledge of the material, having not only attended the Globe Education reading and having been privileged to access the script by Gary Taylor, but also having directed a rehearsed reading of *Double Falsehood* for the Richmond Shakespeare Society in the United Kingdom (Twickenham and Hampton, April and May 2010).

13. At www.nuvo.net/indianapolis/review-the-history-of-cardenio-at-iupui/Content?oid=2440910, accessed May 8, 2012.

14. At www.ibj.com/lou-s-views—no-great-shakes/PARAMS/article/34080, accessed May 8, 2012.

15. "This was the IUPUI Campus Center Theater's first show," Terri Bourus informed me (email May 15, 2012); "no lighting was available until just before the production opened, and mid-show lighting changes were not possible."

16. "To the Reader," *The Faithfull Shepheardesse*, in *Fletcher*, 3: 497.

15

CARDENIO: SHAKESPEARE'S LOST RACE PLAY?

Ayanna Thompson

The History of Cardenio, Gary Taylor's reconstructed/collaborative performance script, offers something new for the early modern canon, a romance whose central focus is a "mulatta" who marries the "white" son of a duke. For early modern race scholars, this text and future performances of it will provide new avenues for scholarship. Finally, we can theorize more fully about how race functions in the romance genre to balance out the tragedy-/Othello-obsessed focus of much of our research; the play, after all, ends with a double marriage instead of a murder-suicide. In addition, *The History of Cardenio* allows us to discuss the intersectionality of race, class, and gender in a much more comprehensive way, complementing and even challenging the Cleopatra-obsessed focus of much of our work on race and gender in the early modern period.

Yet that is not where I want to begin this essay. Instead, I want to begin with two brief quotations from actors in Terri Bourus's 2012 IUPUI production of *The History of Cardenio*, which was billed as the first full production of the play in North America:

> If the pinnacle is to be in an August Wilson play or a Tyler Perry movie, even though they are great, that is not enough. There are too many other great roles, especially Shakespearean ones. (Jonah Winston, who played Quixot)

> I was excited to play a biracial character, and a Shakespearean one at that, but after I read the script I realized that I was still getting beat, still getting raped. (Alys Dickerson, who played Violenta[1])

In the first statement, William Shakespeare is juxtaposed with the two twentieth/twenty-first-century writers whose theatrical works have employed countless black actors, August Wilson and Tyler Perry, and Shakespeare comes out on top. In the second statement, the assumption is that Shakespeare will offer roles that are meatier for a young, black actress, but instead the actress feels as if Shakespeare is trafficking in the same old stereotypes she was hoping to avoid as a woman and a black woman. In this statement, Shakespeare does not come out on top.

These statements, I think, encapsulate the push and pull actors of color face when they are cast in contemporary productions of classical plays. The desire for meaty, language-driven, capital-rich roles like those by Shakespeare is palpable; and this desire is often accompanied by an espousal of the benefits and virtues of nontraditional casting as a means for enriching contemporary performances. Gerald Baker, whose review of the 2012 IUPUI production appears in this volume, reflects this view. While Baker never mentions race in the body of his review, he praises the use of nontraditional casting in a footnote: "I mention [the 'ethnicity' of two of the actors] simply to note Bourus's directorial bravery in casting non-white actors as two of the European tradition's most conspicuous characters, and to report very happily that for neither of the audiences I joined did this obtrude upon the pleasure and authority of the actors' performances." Statements like the one by Baker make it clear that a colorblind or nontraditional approach is viewed as progress and progressive, and Shakespeare provides an important engine to propel this progression.

Nonetheless, many of us who work closely with actors of color have heard the flipside of this colorblind encomium. Many complain about the unspoken typecasting that occurs in contemporary productions of classical works. To give two easy examples: black actresses are routinely cast as the witches in *Macbeth*, and black actors are routinely cast as Escalus in *Romeo and Juliet*.[2] While the old adage may be true that "there are no small parts, only small actors," many other adages could be created about the small, sexless roles into which black actors are consistently cast when they are not playing Othello.[3] The roles assigned to black actors in *The History of Cardenio* are neither small nor sexless, and that is what will make the play so appealing to early modern race scholars. While there is much to praise and areas to highlight for future research, I am interested in complicating the ways authenticity gets invoked when racial politics are made explicit in performances of classical texts.

The History of Cardenio makes it explicit that Violenta, the young woman who is wooed into bed by the promise of marriage by the Duke's son Fernando, impregnated because of that sexual encounter, sexually assaulted by the Master of the Flocks in the woods, and then married to Fernando in the final scene of unions and reunions, is a "mulatta."[4] In her fascinating account of the theatrical evolution of Taylor's script, Terri Bourus explains that Violenta was not originally conceived as a mixed-race woman; in fact, it was not until after the first full-scale production in 2009, by students in Wellington, New Zealand, that Taylor realized Violenta's character should be of mixed race to "restore the kinds of provocation that would have disturbed Theobald and other [18th century] readers, publishers, and theatrical producers." Bourus goes on to speculate that "*Cardenio* may have disappeared because it was Shakespeare's and Fletcher's most daring play."[5] These accounts make it clear that race played a central and pivotal role in the revisions of the script, and that race became central and pivotal to the plot itself.

The 2012 IUPUI production directed by Bourus, however, walks the typical tightrope of contemporary classical stagings. As many of the actors noted, the production was cast in a colorblind fashion with the exception of Violenta's part and Lucinda's part. Bourus was specifically looking for a biracial actress to play Violenta and a Latina actress to play Lucinda.[6] Thus, the colorblind-cast roles were the comic duo of Quesada/Quixot (Jonah D. Winston) and Sancho (Brandon Merriweather) and the Master of the Flocks (Noah Winston). This casting approach was praised by many for diversifying the cast and making discussions about race irrelevant. For example, Noah Winston stated that the production "had a diverse cast, like most of the productions [he has] been in," and that "the diverse cast gave the play color and made it multi-dimensional." Likewise, many cast members noted that race did not enter their minds during the production because it was not introduced during the rehearsals. For instance, Brandon Merriweather, the young black actor who played Sancho, indicated that he "had not thought that much about race playing a role in Sancho's character" because it was a colorblind production. And Jonah Winston who played Quesada/Quixot explicitly said that "conversations about race never came up during rehearsals" because they were not necessary. Race was not central to his portrayal of Quesada/Quixot because he "relied on the suspension of disbelief" that is always necessary in live theater.

While most of the actors I spoke with expressed praise for the colorblind approach, some expressed uncertainties, misgivings, and/or discomfort with the mixture of content and casting in *The History of Cardenio*. The moments that Bourus so carefully outlines as additions to the plot after the 2009 Wellington production, the moments in which Taylor returned to Cervantes to "simplify the scene's narrative and strengthen its emotional complexity" ("Stages" 401), are precisely the moments the actors mentioned. For instance, Quesada, as the knight Quixot, promises Sancho that he will be an "earl or emperor or potentate" of an island if he remains loyal to him in his quest (*THOC* 2.5). In Taylor's script as in Cervantes's novel, Quesada's friends attempt to cure him of his knight-mare by appearing as "Moors," to which Sancho objects: "When you promised me an island, I never thought it should be in Africa." Quesada, as Quixot, quickly retorts:

> Why, child, you need not live in Africa
> To govern it. You may by deputation,
> As other great conquistadors have done,
> Sell your black subjects into slavery,
> Three thousand, or six thousand, or ten thousand,
> And fear no nightmares, neither, but in peace at home
> Live rich, respected, honored, nay, adored. (*THOC* 5.1)

As Bourus astutely points out, these additions to the script create a coherent racialized subplot that unites Quesada/Quixot's views of Africa with Cardenio's use of blackface to disguise himself during the masque (5.2) and

Violenta's black identity: "The play now ends with two couples: a white man engaged to a black woman, a white woman engaged to a black-face man. Those symmetries provide a kind of closure that mirrors the play's combination of tragedy and comedy" ("Stages" 402). In the 2012 IUPUI production, blackface was not employed by the actor playing Cardenio precisely because there were objections from the actors about the racial implications. Instead, Cardenio covered his face with black mesh that he quickly removed.

Nonetheless at this moment in 5.1, Brandon Merriweather who played Sancho glances at his own black hand, looks over at Quesada/Quixot's black skin, and then gives the audience a perplexed look, which received peals of laughter the night I was in attendance. Merriweather explained that this bit was not originally part of the blocking: "it came late in the rehearsal process." Taylor's performance script diverges from Cervantes' novel by having Quixot instead of Sancho raise the issue of selling slaves, by specifying the race of the slaves as "black," and by allowing Sancho to voice a skeptical response: "What, may I sell a thousand men and women as though they were so many sheep?" While these changes to the text were made long before Bourus cast a black actor to play Sancho, Merriweather indicated the metadramatic blocking occurred very late in the process.

Merriweather and Jonah Winston, who played Quesada/Quixot, both stated that race never came up during their rehearsal process; not even when they approached the lines from 5.1, quoted above. Winston noted that the exchange about the slaves "became a joke" and the only moment when the races of the actors were meant to be apparent because he "thought it was important to make the audience feel okay even as they were uncomfortable with what was being said. Like Dave Chappelle's use of humor, this helps to dispel stereotypes." This moment when Merriweather and Winston broke the fourth wall (which they did throughout the production), however, was also the moment when Merriweather first realized that Quixot and Sancho were characters "not meant for my kind"; the lines made him realize that those roles were explicitly written for white actors. Merriweather went on to explain: "While it is understandable because of the history [of the Renaissance], it stings a bit to realize that usually only one race is allowed to play a starring role." The tension between (1) the text's employment of early modern racial rhetoric (which might be called racist by today's standards), (2) the colorblind approach to casting black actors as the comic duo who employ this rhetoric, and (3) the desire to break the fourth wall to ease the audience into this early modern rhetoric deserves a clear airing. This is not to suggest that Taylor and Bourus were not acutely aware of the tension; they were very aware of it. The tension raises productive (but not easily answered) questions about how to approach race in the rehearsal room; how to frame race for audiences of colorblind productions; and how to frame race in classical, but as yet little-known, productions.

Alys Dickerson also expressed that she had moments of misgivings and discomfort about playing Violenta, which is an incredibly rich role with a large emotional register: the actress who plays Violenta must swing between the giddy highs of young love and the emotional lows that bring one to the brink of suicide. The role is also very physically and vocally demanding: the actress must be physically able to handle an intensely violent attempted-rape scene, and she must have a trained singing voice for two important solos. Dickerson knew the IUPUI team was looking for "a pretty, biracial singer," and, as Bourus explains in this volume, Violenta "requires a very specific body." Dickerson was immediately interested in the prospect of playing a biracial role, instead of the "sassy, mean, stereotypical" black roles into which she had been typecast in acting school.

Yet Dickerson was concerned when she read the script because "there were so many quips throughout the play" about Violenta's color. For instance, when speaking to Violenta, Fernando is stymied by the fact that she is not willing to sleep with him. He muses that no one would believe that a poor, black woman would *not* jump at the chance to sleep with a duke's son (1.5):

> Will ignorance believe it? or your father?
> Will grossness such a brown-bread lass believe
> So proud, that though the heavens at your feet
> Down dukedoms rain, you will not stoop to pick one?
> Good wench, does't not ring false?

Likewise, Cardenio refers to Violenta as a "farm-bred half-black daughter" (2.1). Through the course of the play, Violenta never waivers in her devotion to Fernando and helps the racist-spewing Cardenio and Quesada/Quixot get their grooves back (or at least their sanities); and Dickerson wondered how Violenta was "okay with it; how she was okay with these white men talking about her in these terms?"

Dickerson was also very clear that despite the fact that she and the character are both biracial, her own upbringing made it difficult for her to understand Violenta's motivations; a problem, of course, that stems from the Cervantes source material. Because Dickerson's parents taught her that men should always treat women like "queens," and because she was taught to be proud of her mixed heritage, she "didn't want to be a victim; didn't want to play victimization." She constantly asked Bourus to explain "when do I fall for Fernando?" Eventually, Bourus and Dickerson decided that Violenta was very young, that this is her first love, and that by the end of the play when she is unwed and pregnant (staving off rapists in the woods!) she is merely looking for survival. Thus, Dickerson decided that "Violenta was okay with it" because "she knew it was necessary to be Fernando's servant" in order to survive. Although the character Violenta often frames her difficulties in terms of her gender—in how difficult it is to be a woman in that world, Dickerson framed her difficulties in playing Violenta in terms of her own race—in how important it is to her to be a proud, strong, and independent biracial woman.

Like the tensions expressed by Merriweather and Winston about the slave-selling scene, the tensions Dickerson felt between the text as an historical artifact, the twenty-first-century production she was inhabiting, and her own socio-racial identity are fascinating and fascinatingly rich. Bringing these tensions to light, the actors reveal how productive conversations about Shakespeare, race, and performance can be. While *The History of Cardenio* is enthralling as a collaboration that spans centuries, or as Bourus says a theatrical "*Jurassic Park*, using the DNA of dead playwrights instead of dinosaurs," the collaboration does not end on the page ("Stages" 388). Rather, it is imperative that audiences and scholars be encouraged to think about the collaboration as something that occurs through performance *and* that race is central to the experimental nature of the collaboration. Bourus acknowledges this in an astute fashion in the program notes, writing: "We are testing *The History of Cardenio* in the laboratory where Shakespeare and Fletcher worked for decades: a theater. Audiences are crucial to this kind of experiment. By watching, listening, and responding, you become our collaborators, helping us to test new ideas about what Shakespeare created, how it should be edited and performed, what it means today."[7]

Experiments, however, do not need to aim for authenticity; they can aim for something new (e.g. "what it means today"). While *The History of Cardenio* is billed as a "recreated" script, rhetoric that does not claim exact *recovery*, the 2012 IUPUI production seemed to want to fend off criticism through a reliance on authenticity.[8] For example, the production used "period costuming" in the first scene because, as Bourus explains in chapter 13 this volume, the period costuming "delighted even the predictable naysayers." She continues: "Vaguely Renaissance costumes are, for many spectators, a kind of comfort food...And for this experiment, their seeming authenticity enabled a 'willing suspension of disbelief' in the possibility that the spectators were watching something first performed four hundred years ago." The production also used a type of period-music performance style with musicians onstage throughout the production, playing lutes and guitars. While the music itself was not strictly from the Renaissance, the performance style was. I could not help wondering why the production wanted the audience to eat "comfort food" during this "laboratory" "experiment." I wondered why it was important for the audience to feel as if they were "watching something first performed four hundred years ago." Ultimately, I was puzzled by what I would term a type of performance schizophrenia, in which the authenticity of past performances and the newness of contemporary productions were struggling for dominance. Of course, this is not unique to this production of *The History of Cardenio*; it occurs for many modern performances of classical scripts. Nevertheless, when modern performances employ nontraditional casting, the issues come to the fore in unique ways.

To be clear, I am delighted by the artistic and scholarly doors that are opened by the recreation/reconstruction of *The History of Cardenio*. As I mentioned at the beginning of this essay, I know that early modern race scholars will write about this text and future performances of it. I also think that actresses of color will delight to struggle with Violenta, Shakespeare/

Fletcher/Taylor's meatiest black, female role. My hope, however, is that future productions will shy away from the traps of authenticity and embrace creating something new. As I have written elsewhere, Shakespeare's cultural capital wields a double-edged sword when artists and scholars address issues of race, especially in terms of originality or authenticity.[9] After all, an authentic historic production of *The History of Cardenio* would necessitate a black-face performance of Violenta, played by a young, male, white actor. This may be an experiment some would want to test, but there are just as many who would reject the desire to revisit or recreate that authentic past.

To my way of thinking, *The History of Cardenio* can promise the most by flouting historicism. I am more interested in seeing the ways a production can shed light on contemporary interracial relations. Why not set a production in a contemporary gated community in Scottsdale, Arizona? The complex intersectionality of race, class, gender, and ethnicity may not be exactly the same in twenty-first-century Arizona as in early modern England (or early modern England's idea of Spain), but the socio-historical transposition would allow the theatrical-laboratory experiment to generate knowledge production that is freed of the cultural baggage inherent in historicity. After all, *Jurassic Park* presented a failed experiment of recreation; the revived dinosaurs ran amok. What I hope for is more akin to Spike Jonze's 2002 film *Adaptation*, written by Charlie Kaufman and based on the nonfiction book *The Orchid Thief* by Susan Orlean. That film revels in the complex ways narratives are *adapted* into different genres and different media. But to embrace that approach, *The History of Cardenio* would need to be framed as an adaptation that invites further adaptations.

NOTES

1. Over the course of May 23 and 25, 2012, I interviewed Alys Dickerson, Brandon Merriweather, Jonah D. Winston, and Noah Winston. All quotations attributed to them in this essay are taken from these interviews. I thank them for their time and generosity!

2. Katherine Goodland, the coeditor of *A Directory of Shakespeare in Performance, 1970–2005*, 3 vols. (Basingstoke: Palgrave Macmillan, 2007 and 2011), has created a fascinating spreadsheet that tracks the roles black actors and actresses have performed in League of Resident Theatre (LORT) companies from 1970 to 2005. I want to thank her for generously sharing this data with me.

3. The force of the stereotypes created by Othello is brilliantly documented in Celia Daileader's *Racism, Misogyny, and the* Othello *Myth: Inter-Racial Couples from Shakespeare to Spike Lee* (Cambridge: Cambridge University Press, 2005).

4. The list of "Characters" in the Indianapolis performance script is explicit: "VIOLENTA, a mulatta, courted by Don Fernando." William Shakespeare, John Fletcher, and Gary Taylor, *The History of Cardenio*, script dated January 20, 2012.

5. Bourus, "Stages," 401.

6. Although I am not addressing the casting of Hispanic actors in Spanish roles, this is a rich area that future scholars may wish to take up.

7. Terri Bourus, "Director's Note: A New Play in a New Theatre," *The History of Cardenio*, Playbill (IUPUI 2012), 7.

8. The playbill, for instance, lists the play as "*The History of Cardenio* by William Shakespeare & John Fletcher, Inspired by Cervantes' *Don Quixote*, *Recreated* by Gary Taylor, Directed by Terri Bourus" (emphasis mine).

9. See Ayanna Thompson, *Passing Strange: Shakespeare, Race, and Contemporary America* (Oxford: Oxford University Press, 2011), esp. 97–117.

PART II

THE HISTORY OF CARDENIO, 1612–2012

16

A Posthumous Collaborator's Preface

Gary Taylor

The script that follows is a thought experiment. What would *The History of Cardenio* have looked like, before Theobald turned it into *Double Falsehood*? Can we unadapt Theobald's adaptation?

Like any good experiment, the value of this one depends upon systematically applying certain rules.

1. Anything in *Double Falsehood* that was demonstrably written by Theobald, or demonstrably belongs to the eighteenth century rather than the early seventeenth century, must be eliminated.

2. Anything that is removed, or altered, must also be *explained*. Either the language or the content or the theatrical conventions of the original play, performed by the King's Men in 1613 and based upon *Don Quixote*, must have been unacceptable to Theobald himself, or to his audiences, or to the actors and stage management of Drury Lane theater in 1727. The presumed adaptations must be typical of Theobald's own adapting work elsewhere, or more generally of prevailing modes of theatrical adaptation.

3. Whatever we imagine to have been altered or deleted by Theobald must originally have been written in the style of John Fletcher and William Shakespeare, the two King's Men dramatists who were first identified as the authors of the lost play, and whose presence has been confirmed by the most reliable stylistic analyses.

4. Therefore, whatever we alter, or add, to *Double Falsehood* must be written in the style of Fletcher *or* Shakespeare. Not in a casual amalgam of the two styles (which never occurs in the work of either), but in the style of Fletcher (ca. 1612–1613) in those parts of the play identified by modern attribution scholars as Fletcher's work, or in the style of Shakespeare (ca. 1612–1613) in those parts of the play identified by modern attribution scholars as Shakespeare's work.

5. Any songs must either be written in the style of one of the two drama-tists, or must belong to the extant canon of otherwise-anonymous songs by the lutenist Robert Johnson, who was composer for the King's Men in 1612–1613.

6. By 1612–1613, Shakespeare and Fletcher were both experienced and successful professional playwrights, and the lost play was given two com-mand performances within twelve months of its composition. Therefore, the unadaptation must be theatrically rewarding: it must be a play that actors want to perform and audiences want to watch.

7. The unadaptation must be based on Shelton's 1612 translation of the original (first part of) *Don Quixote*, or on other sources that either Shakespeare or Fletcher is known to have read by early 1613. For exam-ple, Shakespeare had read Florio's translation of Montaigne's *Essays* by November 1611 at the latest.

8. Neither Fletcher nor Shakespeare was ever robotically true to his sources. Therefore, to be faithful to the practices of Shakespeare and Fletcher, and faithful to initial English responses to *Don Quixote* more gener-ally, the unadaptation cannot be entirely faithful to Cervantes. It must instead creatively adapt *Don Quixote*, in ways comparable to Fletcher and Shakespeare's treatment of other narrative sources.

9. Fletcher and Shakespeare very rarely reproduced whole sentences they had used before, and neither ever recycled verbatim whole speeches, or sequences of more than eight or nine words. Therefore, we cannot fill the gaps created by Theobald's abridgement of the original play by pad-ding out *Double Falsehood* with undigested chunks of our favorite lines or speeches from other works by Shakespeare or Fletcher. Instead, we must creatively recombine and adapt vocabulary and imagery and ideas scattered elsewhere in their work.

10. Because we aim to recreate the work of Fletcher specifically and Shakespeare specifically, we cannot use material from scenes in either canon that the latest and most reliable scholarship attributes to a collaborator.

11. Because every play by Shakespeare or Fletcher contains new words and new images, we must presume that the lost play contained some addi-tions to their idiolects. Those additions must either belong to the larger Jacobean sociolect, available to them both, or it must be characteristic of the kinds of neologisms found elsewhere in their work.

12. Because Fletcher and Shakespeare worked for theaters that were (by our standards) visually and musically impoverished, but (by our standards) verbally rich, and because both Fletcher and Shakespeare were celebrated in their own time primarily for their language, the unadaptation must derive most of its theatrical power from its words.

These protocols may seem to contradict themselves. How can a pedantic insistence on historical and grammatical rules cohabit with the playfulness and "flow" necessary to poetic and theatrical creativity? But poetry and the theater have always depended on rules, on material or self-imposed obstacles that may seem to impede creativity, but actually unleash it. If great poetry can be written by a mind pacing in the tiny prison cell of a sonnet, it could, theoretically, also emerge from this set of rules. If Joseph Conrad could write masterpieces in a second language, then a modern playwright could, theoretically, write a masterpiece in the second dialect of Jacobean English. Whether I am that poet, or that playwright, is another question; but I see no intrinsic conflict of interest between rules and creativity.

This experiment forces me to imitate Shakespeare and Fletcher, and therefore in some ways it resembles Theobald's attempts to imitate Shakespeare. But I have the advantage of centuries of Shakespeare scholarship and criticism, twenty years of development, access to many different theater companies, and feedback from life-long Shakespeare scholars. I had edited Shakespeare's works before I even began, and tenure has given me the luxury of not rushing into print.

The rules require command of the full range of modern scholarship, historical, theatrical, editorial, and stylistic. That scholarship is itself continually evolving. When I began work on this project, there were no concordances or databases of Fletcher's canon, or Theobald's, and no intellectual protocols for identifying small-scale adaptation rather than large-scale collaboration. This volume significantly expands, and builds upon, the scholarship contained in *The Quest for Cardenio*, which itself had significantly expanded upon the scholarship available in Hammond's Arden edition of *Double Falsehood*. As scholars improve our understanding of Theobald, *Double Falsehood*, and early modern drama, I will undoubtedly need to revise some features of this script.

These protocols also depend upon what can be learned from theatrical collaboration. Terri Bourus (in "Stages") has described the development of the script through a series of theatrical experiments from 1992 to 2009, and her essay in this volume describes some of the changes made as a result of a 2011 reading at Shakespeare's Globe (London), directed by Wilson Milam. Her own 2012 production had a more profound effect on the theatrical dimension of this script than any of its predecessors; some of those changes were incorporated in the performances, but many more are made here for the first time. I have learned from every director, and from many actors, and I hope to learn from future productions.

This unadaptation is therefore, necessarily, a work in progress. I expect it to continue to change, in response to further theatrical experiments and further scholarly discoveries. But I also expect that it will change in response to the reactions of readers. Indeed, I am publishing it now, not because I think it is finished, but because at this point crowd-sourcing offers my best tool for further development. I need feedback and criticism from "the great variety of readers." I have learned from twenty years of talk-backs with audiences and performers, and I know that many of you will have things to teach me, too.

I have never imagined that this thought experiment would produce a play, or a poem, as good as the one that Shakespeare and Fletcher wrote. I never hoped that I could reconstruct the original play exactly and accurately enough to satisfy an editor of Shakespeare's, or Fletcher's, works. But that is not the purpose of this experiment. Its purpose is three-fold. First, like every other adaptation of *Don Quixote*, this *History of Cardenio* pays tribute to Cervantes, by listening to him and then talking back to him, as creatively as I can. Second, my experiment, like every other adaptation or interpretation or imitation of their work, pays tribute to Fletcher and Shakespeare. A mimic has to watch and listen, first. Fletcher and Shakespeare wrote dialogue, and dialogue is the best way to understand them. Third, this particular dialogue between present and past is designed to enable us to imagine the lost support structure—of character, narrative, ideas, and images—that once surrounded the surviving fragments of unalloyed Shakespeare and unalloyed Fletcher, fragments now scattered, scratched and dulled amid the dust of Theobald's adaptation. The power of a playwright depends upon the cumulative interaction of thousands of words, hundreds of speeches and actions.

"He that tries to recommend him by select quotations," Samuel Johnson said of Shakespeare, "shall succeed like the pedant in Hierocles, who, when he offered his house to sale, carried a brick in his pocket as a specimen." We cannot properly appreciate the theatrical or literary power of the Shakespearian and Fletcherian passages in *Double Falsehood*, unless our awakened imaginations can glimpse, through the fog, the palace to which those blocks of marble once belonged.

17

THE HISTORY OF CARDENIO, 1612–2012

John Fletcher, William Shakespeare, and Gary Taylor

PERSONS IN THE PLAY

DUKE Ricardo of Andalusia
Lord General RODERICK, his eldest son
Lord FERNANDO, his youngest son
CARDENIO, Lord Fernando's friend
Senor CAMILLO, Cardenio's father
LUCINDA, courted by Cardenio
Don BERNARD, Lucinda's father
VIOLENTA, a "half-black" farmer's daughter, courted by Fernando
Senor QUESADA, an old schoolmaster, who becomes a mad knight-errant,
    calling himself "Don QUIXOT"
SANCHO, his boy
Fabian, a BARBER
Lopez, a CURATE
LEONELA, Violenta's maid-servant
MARCELA, Lucinda's maid-servant
Corporal GERALD
Man SERVANT in the household of Violenta's father
MASTER of Violenta, when she is disguised as a shepherd boy
Two SHEPHERDS
Three CITIZENS
Two GALLANTS
Servants, soldiers, musicians, devils

ACT 1, SCENE 1

A coffin. Enter old DUKE *Ricardo (with a book), his son Lord General*
RODERICK, *and soldiers*

RODERICK Whose is this hearse here, sire?

DUKE.   Mine, soon enough, son.
    When we shake off our borrowed wardrobe-greatness
    To lie down naked in a pale cold sheet,

Death lullabies us, then—hush!—snuffs the light:
This little bone-bed, this last habitation,
This is the reason, Roderick, the reason
I commanded thy crusading sword and army
To hasten home to Spain. Dukes too are dust.
—Nay, listen, Roderick. Exceptionless,
Unalterable, all, we die, we die
By accident, disease, assassination,
The unexpected arrow in the eye-ball,
Or down stairs falling, or between the thighs
Of generation, on the throne, the privy,
Mere everywhere everyday death knocks down
Our doors, knocks out our brains, plucks our last heart-string,
And when death knocks, I mean to be prepared,
Booted and spurred, ready to ride, no deed
Unsigned, duty unpaid; therefore this business
Of thy brother must I finish now, before
That plucked string of oblivion summons me
To dust's dark vast and thousand-gated castle.

RODERICK. My gracious father, this unwonted strain
   Visits my heart with sadness.

DUKE.   Why, my son?
   Making my death familiar to my tongue
   Digs not my grave one jot before the date.
   I've worn the garland of mine honours long
   And would not leave it withered to thy brow,
   But flourishing and green, worthy the man
   That with my dukedom's soil my soul inherits.

RODERICK. This praise, which is my pride, spreads me with blushes.

DUKE. Think not I flatter thee, or in the scale
   Let blood o'erpoise my judgment, when in thee
   Age sees reflected fair my early virtues—
   While fond Fernando, thy irregular brother,
   Sets the large credit of my name at stake,
   His taints of wildness foul our nicer honor,
   And call for swift reclaim.

RODERICK.   My brother pranks
   And gambols, but these hot unsaddled 'scapes
   The vantage of cool wisdom will ere while
   Redeem, to court opinion goldenly.

DUKE. Be thou a prophet in that kind preságe!
   But I, by fears weighing his unweighed course,
   Interpret "has been" for "shall be." Thou, though,
   Art inward with him. Why hath he of late
   By importunity o'erstrained petition,
   Wresting our leave t'absent him from our love?

RODERICK. Why he hath pressed this distance, sir, I know not,
     But I have private letters read, wherein
     He praises "delicate Cardenio,"
     Of Andalusia, good Camillo's son,
     Who, as he says, at university first meeting,
     As fire meets gunpowder, in an instant
     Their minds so married, and so hooped their hearts
     In intricate perfection of affection
     That each, half th'other, wishes himself doubled,
     "The more me's him to give."

DUKE. Where tends this story?

RODERICK. Fernando lovingly
     Commends his "friend" Cardenio to my favor
     Wishing I would retain him here i'th' palace.

DUKE. Oh, do it, Rod'rick, and assay to mold him
     Honesty's spy upon thy brother's riots.
     Make us acquainted when the youth arrives:
     He shall from us receive note, he may play
     The instrument to pipe our prodigal
     Again to grace. Grace grant it may be so!—
     Death, pause a little, let me judge th'event.—
     Bring him to court.   *Exeunt severally*

ACT 1, SCENE 2

Enter CARDENIO, *reading a book*

CARDENIO. Book, on your wings transport me, Pegasus
     Me heavenward, into a high dream heave me
     Of heroes, far from roofed and chastened childhood.
     History, take my hand again, and open
     Charm-gated gardens of word-wielding love.   *He reads, apart*

Enter old CAMILLO, *apart, reading a letter*

CAMILLO. How comes the Duke to take such notice of my son?— "Horsemanship"? Cardenio? He'd rather read than ride. I think he can no more but gallop a hackney, unless he practiced mounting at university. I have not heard him speak much of his horsemanship. No matter, though a tired mare would not bear him, all's one, he must bear what lordships the court would thrust upon him, by front gate or back door. Lords may do what they will in anything, save what they cannot do.—O, there you are, son, read this paper. No more ado, but read this. It must not be answered by my hand, nor yours, but in gross, by your person, your whole and person. Read aloud.

CARDENIO. Please you, to let me first o'erlook it, sir.

                              CARDENIO *reads the letter*

CAMILLO. I was this other day in a spleen against your new doublets; I do now think some Fate was the tailor that hath fitted them, for this hour they are for the palace of the duke; your father's house is too dusty.

CARDENIO. [aside] None but Fernando could have compassed this. Fernando, O Fernando, friend Fernando!

CAMILLO. You shall find your horsemanship much praised there. Are you so good a horseman?

CARDENIO. I have been, Ere now, commended for my seat, or mocked.

CAMILLO. Take one commendation with another, every third's a mock. Affect not therefore to be praised. Lord, how the praises fly at court— his divine thing, her heavenly what-ye-call't—and the mocks chase after, and trip up their heels. I am no stranger to court custard, I can tell you. I have seen Duke Ricardo himself many times—two or three times. He called me, I remember, "good Camillo." There I am written "good Camillo" again, am I not? I thought so: "good Camillo" still.

CARDENIO. [aside] No moving of a marriage to him now.

CAMILLO There's no denying. You must go, peremptorily, he enforces that. He rather conjures than importunes.

CARDENIO. [aside] What may Lucinda's father think of me, who expects to be solicited this very night?

CAMILLO. Great fortunes have grown out of less grounds.

CARDENIO. [aside] He will surely think I deal too slightly, or unmannerly, or foolishly indeed—nay, dishonestly, to bear him in hand with my father's consent, who yet hath not been touched with so much as a request to it.

CAMILLO. Well, have you read it over?

CARDENIO. Yes, sir—

CAMILLO. And considered it?

CARDENIO. As I can—

CAMILLO. If you are courted by Lady Fortune, you must o'erleap your modesty, vault into the saddle, and ride.

CARDENIO. So it please you, sir—

CAMILLO. By any means, and tomorrow. Is it not there the limit of his request?

CARDENIO. It is, sir—

CAMILLO. I must bethink me of some necessaries, without which you might be unfurnished. Come to my closet by and by; I would there speak with you.   *Exit*

CARDENIO. I am sued to be Fernando's servant, and

To be Lucinda's too. What fortune ever
My going shall encounter, cannot be
Good fortune; what I part withal unseasons
Any spice of goodness. I'll not go.—And yet,
Why goes Fernando's sweetness 'gainst my stomach?
His hand invites me; her eye asks sharp questions.
How may unworthiness a lover's ear
Earn, but by venturing? The court's the main
Of honor, and (mine author tells me) there, soon,
Into some shape fitter to lip and linger
May I be metamorphosed, more than this
Weed-idle caterpillar keep-at-home.
                    Camillo calls within "Cardenio!"

I come! (Fernando!)—But my farewell first
I must Lucinda tender.   *Exit at another door*

ACT 1, SCENE 3

Enter Lord FERNANDO, *musicians, and servants with lights*

FERNANDO. Strike up, my masters!   *Music*
    Listen, woman!
Scream the weasels, foxes bark,
Howl the wolves in reason's park
Where nine nightmares ride the dark.

Listen! If only you only me kissed
How quick were your darkness dismissed.

    Listen, woman!
Through the roaring of the dark
Rudderless your dreaming barque
Rushes love to rock and shark.

Listen! If only you only me kissed
How quick were your darkness dismissed.

    Listen, woman!—

                    A light appears in the window

FERNANDO. Vanish, gross spirits! Day breaks sudden from her window.
                    Exeunt all but FERNANDO

    VIOLENTA *enters above, holding a taper*

FERNANDO. O taper, gracèd by that midnight hand!

VIOLENTA. Who is't, that woos at this late hour? What are you?

FERNANDO. One who for your dear sake—

VIOLENTA.   —watches the starless night.
    My lord Fernando, or my ear deceives me.
    You've had my answer, and 'tis more than strange
    You'll combat these repulses. Good my lord,

Be friend to your own health, and give me leave,
Securing my poor fame, nothing to pity
What pangs you swear you suffer. 'Tis impossible
To plant your choice affections in my shade—
At least, for them to grow there.

FERNANDO.   Why, Violenta?

VIOLENTA. Alas sir, there are reasons numberless
To bar your aims. Be warned to hours more wholesome,
For these you watch in vain. I have read stories—
I fear, too true ones—how young lords like you
Have thus be-sung mean windows, rhymed their suff'rings
E'en to th'abuse of things divine, set up
Plain girls like me the idols of their worship,
Then left them to bewail their easy faith
And stand the world's contempt.

FERNANDO.   Your memory,
Too faithful to the wrongs of few lost maids,
Makes fear too general. Your particular,
So high-esteemed, o'erleaps the hedge of birth;
State curtsies to your beauty; purposed falsehood
Would to itself be false, and turn to true,
Gazing upon your graces.

VIOLENTA.   Let us be homely,
And let us too be chaste, doing you lords no wrong,
But crediting your oaths with such a spirit
As you profess them; so no party trusted
Shall make a losing bargain. Home, my lord.
What you can say is most unseasonable; what sing,
Most absonant and harsh. Nay, your perfume,
Which I smell hither, cheers not my sense
Like our field-violet's breath.

FERNANDO.   Why, this dismission
Does more invite my staying.

VIOLENTA.   Men of your temper
Make everything their bramble.—But I wrong
That which I am preserving, my maid's name,
To hold so long discourse. Your virtues guide you
T'effect some nobler purpose.   *Exit*

FERNANDO.   Stay, bright shadow!—
She's gone. What am I that am thus contemned?
The second son to th' dukedom. Well, what then?
Dukedoms are not so pleasantly put off.
But can it kiss me? No. Is't usable?
Not in such sort. T'enjoy her, I would give—what?
What would Cardenio counsel? Jealously
He would dissuade me hence. But in his absence

Be opportunity my god, wit bless my suit,
Soon must I have her, though I stoop to do't.   *Exit*

ACT 1, SCENE 4

Enter CARDENIO, *with his book*

CARDENIO. I fear me I'll disturb the house, so late.

He crosses to the other door, and knocks. Enter MARCELA

MARCELA. What mouse doth scratch so soft?

CARDENIO.   'Tis but Cardenio.
  Gentle Marcela, tell your lady, prithee,
  I beg but one short word.

MARCELA.   "No" is one word,
  And short too. Hath your book not words enough?

CARDENIO. I would but speak with her; the thing is urgent.

MARCELA. Ay, every man's thing is urgent. Well, I'll tell her;
  But if she'll come, I cannot tell.   *Exit*

CARDENIO.   Nor I.
  I do not see that fervor in Lucinda
  My book says love should kindle. She consents
  As 'twere to feed without an appetite,
  Tells me she is "content," and plays the cony,
  Like those that subtly make their word their ward,
  Keeping desire from catching. This affection
  Is such a frail reed as will break untouched,
  Die frosty ere't be thawed—while my Fernando,
  Like to the clime beneath Hyperion's eye,
  Burns with one constant zeal, which chides her coldness.

Enter LUCINDA *with* MARCELA

  But O her beauty doth ingem the night!—
  Lucinda, speak, make this place paradise.
  Is heaven silent?

LUCINDA.   Hear you not my heart?
  That claps and dances, leaps, like steeple-bells
  Triumphing, like the laughing girl unguarded
  Who took your boyhood hand, then not yet heeding
  Propriety of distance, or the miles
  'Twixt boy and man, nor could imagine years
  Nor count the many mornings since one lark's alarum
  Child Cupid woke, musk-roses opened, and
  Vowed heart what tongue lacked language to pronounce
  Until tonight—is it night? Happiness
  Eclipses darkness—till this long longed-for star-time

When my Cardenio (name I adore
More than thirst worships water) at the gate
Of my unwillingly-still-virgin garden
Knocks now at last to tell me, for why else knock
So late, if not to tell me?—what says your father?

CARDENIO. I have not moved him yet.

LUCINDA.   Then move him not.

CARDENIO. Not move him? Was it not your own command?

LUCINDA. The moon hath changed.

CARDENIO.   The northern star hath not.
    It stands still, like my love, true.

LUCINDA.   True: it stands still, and
    Doth nothing.

CARDENIO.   Do not rack me with these doubts—

LUCINDA. Besides, as he perchance may say you nay,
    You who are so obedient must discharge me
    Out of your fancy.

CARDENIO. Think not, though in my father rheumy age
    Put out love's flame, it puts his eyes out too,
    Or lames his judgment. You belie your beauties,
    Fearing what cannot be.

LUCINDA.   What cannot be?
    When you dare not do aught without your father
    And, dare you love, you dare not vouch it; must not,
    Though you have eyes, see with 'em; would, but will not.

CARDENIO. You deal unkindly—misbecomingly
    I'm loath to say, for all that waits on you
    Is graced and graces. No impediment
    Shall bar my wishes, but such grave delays
    As reason presses patience with, which blunt not
    But rather whet love's edge. Be patient, sweet.

LUCINDA. Patient! What else? My flames are in the flint.
    Haply, to lose a husband I may weep;
    Never, to get one. When I cry for bondage,
    Let freedom quit me.

CARDENIO.   What spirit hath possessed you?

LUCINDA. 'Twere well, sir, one of us possessed some spirit.

CARDENIO. I now perceive too plain you care not for me.—
    Duke, I obey thy summons, be its tenor
    What fortune will. If war, I come thy soldier—*Going*

LUCINDA. Why talk you of the Duke? Wherefore of war?

CARDENIO. [*showing her the letter*]
How this new note is grown of me, I know not.
Coming to move my father in our business,
I did find him, reading this.

LUCINDA.   To court?
Ay, there you shall, perhaps (rather, past doubt)
Behold some courtesan—

CARDENIO.   Fear no mere female, love.
There lives no woman man enough to challenge
The promise of Lucinda.

LUCINDA.   But when go you?

CARDENIO. Tomorrow, love—so runs the Duke's command,
Stinting our farewell kisses, cutting off
The forms of parting, and the interchange
Of thousand precious vows with haste too rude.
Would I could stop time—

LUCINDA.   'Tis stopped already.
Make not your absence long. Here, take my watch,
Count every absent hour, each minute, stroke
That the court steals from me, I am untimed.

CARDENIO. I am unlanguaged. Here, take my book.
Read this, and you read me: *The History
Of Amadis of Gaul*, mirror of heroes
And passion's pattern unsurpassable.
Let Amadis remember you my promise.—
Why heaved that sigh?

LUCINDA.   Saints!—Can you not interpret?
—'Tis a poor scholar.—What a world is this,
When women must instruct the men to kiss?

MARCELA. Your father.

Enter Don BERNARD

BERNARD. What, Cardenio, so late? This wooing is too urgent. Is your father yet moved in the suit, who must be the prime unfolder of this business?

CARDENIO. I have not, yet, indeed, at full, possessed
My father whom it is my service follows,
But only that I have a wife in chase.

BERNARD. Chase? Let chase alone, no matter for that. You may halt after her you profess to pursue, and catch her too. Marry, not unless your father let you slip. Briefly, I desire you (for she tells me my instructions shall be both eyes and feet to her), no farther to spend your mouth in requiring, nor to snuff after my deer, till, as I say, Camillo make known to me that his good liking goes along with us—which but once breathed, all is done; till when, the hound hath no nose, and the arrow cannot prick the mark.

CARDENIO. Sir, I will know his mind ere I taste sleep.
I take my leave.—Remember, and be faithful.   *Exit*

BERNARD. His father is as unsettled as he is wayward in his disposition. If I thought young Cardenio's temper were not mended by the mettle of his mother I should be something crazy in giving my consent to this match. And, to tell you true, if my eyes might be the directors to your mind, I could in this town look upon twenty men of more delicate choice. I speak not this altogether to unbend your affections to him; but the meaning of what I say is, that you set such price upon yourself to him as many, and much his betters, would buy you at (and reckon those virtues in you at the rate of their scarcity), to which if he come not up, you remain for a better mart.

LUCINDA. My obedience, sir, is chained to your advice.

BERNARD. 'Tis well said, and wisely. I fear your lover is a little folly-tainted; which, shortly after it proves so, you will repent.

LUCINDA. Sir, I confess I approve him of all the men I know; but that approbation is nothing till seasoned by your consent.

BERNARD. We shall hear soon what his father will do, and so proceed accordingly. I have no great heart to the business, neither will I with any violence oppose it, but leave it to that power which rules in these conjunctions, and there's an end.
                     Thunder in the distance
Come, haste we in, girl.   *Exeunt*

ACT 1, SCENE 5

Bed put forth. Enter VIOLENTA *and her maid-servant* LEONELA,
in their night-gowns

VIOLENTA. Would my father were at home this wild night.
The candles tremble and weep wax, as they
Did spy calamity in corners shifting.
Are all the doors shut safe?

LEONELA.   What fear you, madam?

VIOLENTA. Think you Fernando comes again tonight?

LEONELA. You have so thumped him with hard words, I wonder
He will continue wooing your reproaches.
I would not use him so; faith, you'll not pluck
From every tree a man so amorous,
Beauteous, courteous—

VIOLENTA. Nay, spare your ABC, girl. My father means
To some youth of this village, or the next,
To match me soon, to thwart Fernando's wooing.

Mother once told me, men are of a muchness.
I hope 'tis true. One much like him would do,
So finely featured, and demeanoured so.
But him I cannot have, not honestly,
Nor would not have him any fouler way;
So, should not hear him.

LEONELA.   'Tis no sin to listen,
Nor no dishonor, madam, an a man
Thrust music in your ear, so you do not
Sing prick-song with the fiddler.

VIOLENTA.   Leonela, fie!
Where did you borrow such a bawdy tongue?

LEONELA. Faith, of my mother, bless her; she would say,
A woman needs a bawdy tongue and fingers
To play on a man's pipe.

VIOLENTA. *Basta*, for shame.   *Music without*
Listen, lust sounds alarum.
Good Leonela, try the doors again;
I'll close the windows.

LEONELA.   Madam, what you will.

LEONELA, *as she goes out, lets in* FERNANDO, *who pays her*

VIOLENTA. The moon demurely through the dark clouds walks
Like the night-watch, lantern in hand. Look down,
Virgin surveyor, on my smallness cast
Thy calm regard; secure me from night's harm.   *Music plays still*

FERNANDO. Stand not amazed. I am no dragon, nor
Will not devour you. How? turned stone? Blest image,
Let me Pygmalion be, of maiden marble
To make a woman; this cold flesh I'll warm
With chafing, and these lips with kissing.

VIOLENTA.   Nay,
My blood's enough chafed, that you dare break open
My solitude and maiden contemplation.
How came you hither?

FERNANDO.   On a love-song's note,
Unnoted, which into your chamber stole
With an invisible quick nimble air,
Each cranny penetrating; love and music
Not labyrinths can long hold out, nor stone
Withstand.

VIOLENTA. Pretty, and false. More keys hath money
Than music to unlock a poor maid's honor;
You have suborned my servant.

FERNANDO.   I am your servant.

VIOLENTA. The services that you would do me, sir,
    I know full well, and fulsome, it abhors me.
    Are there no drabs at court, that you must venture
    So far abroad to feed your codpiece? Fie!
    And I am not so simple, though a weak
    Unpracticed maiden, to untie my ribbon
    At the first fair word, and take for love
    A little scratching on a gittern, or
    This golden show of changeable attire,
    Nor showers of dropped ducats, cracked sighs and tears
    Cannot blow down my fastness—for what follows?
    Honor goodnight, another broken maid
    Gotten with child by promises. God keep you!

FERNANDO. Urge not suspicions of what cannot be.
    Ever your servant I profess myself,
    And will not blot me with heart-change, for all
    That sea and land inherit.

VIOLENTA.   Easily said.

FERNANDO. What must I do? run mad? milk goats? turn shepherd?
    What turn will serve? The pains I take to serve you
    You take for injuries; these rich vestments, which
    Love dons for ceremony, you think bait
    And armor to betray. What will persuade you
    I speak my naked conscience? Would you have me
    Throw all my gay caparisons aside?

VIOLENTA. 'Tis not your clothes; please you, sir, keep them on.

FERNANDO. Is it my feature then? What part offends you?
    I'll pluck it out.

VIOLENTA.   No part, but that you play.

FERNANDO. So seriously I have never thirsted.
    Fair gypsy—

VIOLENTA.   Nay, no closer! I can crow
    Louder than any cock; I'll wake all Spain.   *Music plays still without*

FERNANDO. Say that you did; the louder that you squeal
    The shriller shall my music play to drown it.
    But if your clamor out the bolted doors
    And shut-fast casements flying, were heard and heeded
    Above the thrumming, which your honest neighbors
    Snore out this night, as last: what then? when throng
    The gossips, gaping, tell your story, how
    A grandee did a farmer's daughter's chamber
    Invade, all uninvited; I'll say nothing,
    But blush, or smile, or sigh; you may sigh too,
    Or not, all's one; what fell, 'twas not your fault.
    Will ignorance believe it? or your father?

Will grossness such a brown-bread lass believe
So proud, that though the heavens at your feet
Down dukedoms rain, you will not stoop to pick one?
Good wench, does't not ring false?

VIOLENTA. My not-good lord,
I am your vassal; I am not your slave.
Be on your way, sir.

FERNANDO. I will not depart,
Nor will you neither, till I have the thing
I came for.

VIOLENTA. Thing? Am I a thing? What thing?

FERNANDO. You know what thing.

VIOLENTA. Are you ashamed to name it,
But not ashamed to take it?

FERNANDO. My great desire
Puts down your little logic.

VIOLENTA. No!

FERNANDO. One "no"
Cannot outwrestle my strong throng of yeses.

VIOLENTA. Then double no, and triple: no! nay! never!

FERNANDO. Must I stop your mouth with kisses? but one kiss.

VIOLENTA. If one would satisfy you, I could spare it,
But will one stop you? No. Mean you to rape me?
O that were precious manly! excellent!
Brag such a conquest, you shall win good fame—
And when men story St. George and the dragon, tell,
Brave knight, how your beast strength and devil cunning
O'er one lone innocent weak virgin triumphed—
And yet, not so weak neither, stronger I
Am than I seem, we country maids milk cows,
Fetch full pails too, ay, and my nails are minded
To write sharp testimonies in your flesh
How fond I liked your wooing.

FERNANDO. I did not dream
Rape would be necessary.

VIOLENTA. Rape—or marriage.
There is no third way to unmaiden me.

FERNANDO. Is that all? I will marry you tomorrow.

VIOLENTA. Tomorrow pays no debts.

FERNANDO. The dukedom pays my debts. Here, take my ring; now,
Give me your ring, we're bound by law as love.
                                        Thunder and rain

VIOLENTA. By law indeed, my lord, by heaven's book,
And dukedom's bench. Look what you do, weigh well
The wrath of your wronged father, when he learns
You have dared match his palace to my porch.
If, as you feign, you love me, leave me free
To roll in mine own sphere. My thoughts yet never
Trespassed beyond this house; pray, do not tempt me
Outside my circle, to be burnt for reaching.
Your father his son's falling may forgive,
But my presumption shall be thunderbolted.

FERNANDO. Girl, we are not the first, nor like to be
The last, matched against manners, and we make
No new world, doing this.

VIOLENTA.   Leonela!—
Forgive me, good my lord, but I would have
On earth one witness to this match, to back
The host in heaven.—Ho, Leonela! quickly.

Enter LEONELA

LEONELA. Why, madam, how came he into the house?

VIOLENTA. How, we'll forget, so you will faithfully
Remember what you witness, in this instant
That shall my future instants all determine.

LEONELA. Mistress, forgive me, on my mother's soul
I will not sell your goodness, but cry truth
I'th' wilderness, and give the lie to th' palace.

VIOLENTA. My Leonela! Bless you!—Now, my lord,
May you unswear your before-vows, heart-high
And hyperbolical; sure, they were writ
In air and error; farewell, the wiser. But
What now you speak, in fire on stone shall truth
Inscribe, and I in my soul hold.

FERNANDO.   Proceed.

VIOLENTA. With this ring that you gave me I here give you
My hand, my heart, in pure-most matrimony.
By the blessed virgin, will your lordship take and keep me
Forsaking every other love—

FERNANDO.   I will.

VIOLENTA. For your lawful wife?

FERNANDO.   Have I not said I will?
He kisses VIOLENTA.

VIOLENTA. Then, by the holy church, we are contracted.
—Be you our witness.

FERNANDO. And be you gone.   *Exit Leonela*
                    And now to bed.

VIOLENTA.   Nay, patience—

FERNANDO. Why, we are married, madam, well enough
    Already; nothing short, save priest and altar,
    Which fashion doth but dress the naked joining
    Souls make and bodies sign. 'Tis time to stamp
    My seal in thy soft wax, and with a deed
    Confirm my title, and my love be fee'd.   *He takes her to the bed.*

VIOLENTA My lord!

FERNANDO Your lord indeed, and master too, and hungry.

                                               The bed drawn in

ACT 1, SCENE 6

Enter QUESADA, *reading, then the other old men: Don* BERNARD,
CAMILLO, *Fabian the* BARBER, *Lopez the* CURATE, *as playing
at bowls*

BARBER. One more, but for fellowship! One more, prithee!

CAMILLO. Nay, master barber, Don Bernard has lost his penniworth
    already.

BERNARD. 'Tis but fortune; 'twill turn.

QUESADA. Yea, so do poets vouch; *Dea Fortuna*
    Stands ever juggling on a turning ball.

BARBER. What's that you say, schoolmaster? That the giddy wench
    "stands ever"?

CURATE. Doth your text not teach that, like other heathen women, she
    sometimes falls?

BARBER. Ay, backward.

CURATE. Verily.

BARBER. Ay, and naked too.

CURATE. As Eve in paradise.

QUESADA. Fortune is, truly, like a game at bowls.

BERNARD. Will you play, or no?

CAMILLO. Hath your physician prescribed a purge of your purse?

QUESADA. This earth, what is't, but a great bowling green?

BERNARD. Bowl, man.

CAMILLO. This is the worst green in the kingdom. Did you mark my
    last cast?

QUESADA. Yea, what is man's life, but a winding quest?

CAMILLO. Did you ever see a more perfect cast?—Achilles himself never bowled better—and at the last so be-bumped and swerved aside by a rub i'th' ground—

QUESADA. Each man's way stopped with rubs, obstructments, hind'rings, To try his genius in the overcoming.

CAMILLO. A pocky uneven villainous ground, made of purpose to rob the cunning, and reward foolishness.

BERNARD. How can a man bowl so short, and talk so long?

CAMILLO. Well, thank me that I do not take so long in my bowling as a certain ancient gentleman, who must handle his ball, weigh his ball, eye his ball, hem at his ball, advance his ball, discharge his ball, and after ply, wring, and twist his body as if he could by such sorcery steer his ball—and to what purpose? he bowls no better than the next man, his great preparation being matched by as little skill.

QUESADA. And each man hath his bias, like each ball.

BERNARD Little skill? Little, sayst thou?

CAMILLO. So said your wife.

BERNARD. Well, if you talk of wives, I'll show you how to kiss the mistress.

CAMILLO. I think he kisses few mistresses at his age.

BARBER. None.

CAMILLO. I have seen him, once or twice, I must confess, creep up to kiss a mistress, but then he stopped, partly for bashfulness, partly having clean forgot what should come next, and while he stood by puckering his dry lips along came another, more impudent, and thrust home between him and his mistress.

QUESADA. Men are balls only.

BERNARD. I cannot bowl, gentlemen, till it be quieter.

He makes as if to bowl

QUESADA. Some cannonballs, some balls of sovereignty, Some footballs, but balls all, and bowled by Fortune.

BERNARD. If you unruly gossips keep to your caterwauling, I will not cast away my skill, nor my money. Bowl, if you will, bowl in this hurricane of huffing, but I will not.

QUESADA. The goddess Fortune bowleth all men's balls: A noble allegory. I wonder Homer Did never think on't.

CURATE. Homer? He's dead, eight year now and more, dead and rotten, bless him. His son's dead too, or gone; the young jacks all are dead or rotten, gone to th' grave, to th' court, to th' new world, gone, all gone or going.

CAMILLO. Fresh pasture makes fat calves.

BERNARD. [*to* QUESADA] Put up your book, prithee, and bowl.

CAMILLO. What is't you read, Senor Quesada?

QUESADA. Never was better book penned, since Apollo,
    Donning his deity, first pricked a poem:
    Supersuperlative, hyperheroical,
    The History of Amadis of Gaul.

CAMILLO. A goodly book; not so manly as *Palmerin of England*, truly, but a choice book enough.

QUESADA. "But choice enough?" Dolt! Amadis of Gaul—

BARBER. Which is to say, "Amadis the Welshman."

CURATE. Indeed, for "Gaul" in the vulgar signifieth "Wales," an ancient heathen superstitious nation—

CAMILLO. Of mountain goats, and goat-cheese, and cheese-eating harp-bards—

BARBER. With goat-beards—

CURATE. Who gabble a goat-language no one else understands.

BARBER. [*to* QUIXOT] Is your book written by a little Welshman?

QUIXOT. The god of poetry, Apollo, wrote it.

CAMILLO. Ay, with his left hand, and left it full of blots, but with his right he penned Palmerin, a right warlike knight. Amadis weeps; Palmerin thwacks.

QUESADA. Flat heresy! What dost thou know of poets?

CAMILLO. I know which please me.

QUESADA. Vile voluptuary!—Excommunicate him,
    Parson, to the Inquisition whip him
    For slanders against letters!—Canst thou read?

BERNARD. Gentlemen, gentlemen, peace. Let me reconcile you: your Palmerin and your Amadis both are equal, for both are nought, and one nought is as good as another. 'Tis but the choice between twin liars. Sure you do not credit these pitiful-gross impossibilities, believed only by children, of lakes of melted metal boiling like pots of porridge, drawbridges of steel, and what not, infinity of iron men with no employment but wooing silk princesses and fighting turbaned giants? Toys and untruths. Have done, and bowl.

QUESADA. Sir, reason instructs us better to consider.
    Have authors no authority? teach they
    No truths? Have books no beauty? beauty, no power

To inspire more-than-mortal virtue?
Is it not written, here, that Amadis
Felled a fell giant? If there be no giants,
Thinkst thou his Christian Majesty the King
Would let such lies be printed? That were monstrous.
What world were this, were there no *veritas* in *verbum*!
Thinkst thou the poet, if there be no giants,
Would be so simple to record *verbatim*
The giant's name, age, birthplace, list his kindred,
The very village note where, on a Wednesday,
Amadis thwacked him, that thou pilgrimage
Mightst make to th' spot, yea, touch his vasty bones,
And ask his neighbors, if there be no giants?
"Giant" is written; look, "giant" is set down.

BERNARD. [*tearing the page*] Now "giant" is torn out.

QUESADA. O outrage! O! Give me my book again.

BERNARD. Nay, I see "giant" looks big on this page, too, and here's
another looms.   *He tears more pages*

CURATE. Bless us, our schoolmaster stares and gapes so, a man would
think now, faith, with every page you tore out his brains by the roots.
Spare the text; give him his book, Don Bernard, for Christian charity.

BERNARD. [*to* QUESADA] Here, sir, is the second edition, much
corrected.

QUESADA. O villain, thou hast—O, I will—I will—

BERNARD. Will what? bowl me to death?

                                    Exit QUESADA with his book

I see we shall never finish this game.

QUESADA. [*within*] O! O!

BARBER. Be there no giants, truly?

CURATE. None, since Goliath.

BARBER. Enchanted towers, neither?

CURATE. None, since Babylon.

BARBER. Even in England?

BERNARD. None certainly in England, which is a paltry, small, crammed,
wet, shrunken country, a floating acorn, look you, where is no room for
enchanted towers; only playhouses and taverns, which drunkards think
enchanted, for therein their purses vanish; nor no fierce giants neither.
Tut! a dwarfish people, and tame.

CAMILLO. What giant lies you tell now! Is it not known of every school-
boy in Spain how some score of English giants waded plashing into the
sea and there sunk the great armada, like so many toys in a tub? I was
there; here the proof is writ, look you, in my flesh.

BERNARD. Ay, the whole parish has seen your scar, sir—which I think, if truth be told, he got it slicing a turnip.

CAMILLO. What's that you mumble, Malice?

BARBER. Look where Senor Schoolmaster comes. I think he means to shave you, Don Bernard.

Enter QUESADA, *with an ancient great sword*

QUESADA. Genius of Amadis, enable me!

BERNARD. Got you that sword of Gogmagog the giant? Pedant, if you would play a knight, return to your school tiring-house and fetch a smaller sword, one you can lift.

QUESADA. Ha! Genius, hast thou heard my prayer? –See!

BERNARD. See? I see you drowned your wits in your inkpot.

QUESADA. Genius, hast thou unblinded only me?

CURATE. Who is it you speak to, Senor Quesada?

QUESADA. Virtue, invisible to imbecility.

BERNARD. Sir, this is not your schoolroom, and we are not your students, to be shamed by your aphorisms, or threatened with your rod. Do you know who I am?

QUESADA. Thy name thou'st torn from out the book of blessing.

BERNARD. Put away your silly sword, man.

QUESADA. Deep-damned decoction of the devil's dung!
Prepare to perish, knave! Thy knell is rung.

BERNARD. Are you mad? Hold, hold!

QUESADA *chases* BERNARD *about the stage*

CAMILLO. [*to* QUESADA] Thwack the villain soundly! Ha ha!—Look at the fat ram run. Ha ha ha!

QUESADA. Out, varlets vile! Foul filthy malefactors!

CAMILLO. [*to* QUESADA] How now, sir?—O!

CURATE *stands between*

CURATE. [*to* QUESADA] Blessed are the peacemakers.

QUESADA. O devil, cit'st thou Scripture? Get thee gone, Satan!

BERNARD, CAMILLO, BARBER *and* CURATE *run off.*

QUESADA. Truth triumphs over numbers.—Dost behold,
Good Genius?—Spoils of war. Leaves of gold.

QUESADA *begins to pick up torn pages*
The boy SANCHO *peers out*

SANCHO. Senor Quesada?

QUESADA. Ha! Who's there? More infidels? Invisible?

He carves the air with his sword

SANCHO. Master? 'Tis I, Sancho, your boy. Is all safe?

QUESADA. As safe as sanctity. I minced the villains.

SANCHO. What, was it robbers, master? Or murderers? How many, sir?

QUESADA. Not many, boy. A million or so.
    Armies are merely cowards, multiplied.
    Valour is ever singular, and unallied.

SANCHO. A mill-i-on? Bless us!—Is that more or less than a dozen?

QUESADA. O ignorance! sea-deep, and strewn with wrecks.

SANCHO. Are the villains departed, master? Are they all gone?

QUESADA. Not gone: dead, disembowelèd, decapitated.

SANCHO. [*coming forth*] Dead? Well, sir. I wish you had left a pair for
    me, or five. You never leave me aught. I'd have peppered the swine,
    and salted 'em too, and hung 'em from the rafters for bacon.—Prithee,
    grandsire, where be the bodies?

QUESADA. Eyes hast thou none, child?—What, vanished? snatched? all?
    How is this possible?—Some wizard's trick:
    They have by whirling demons been wind-quick
    Transported, where the magic five-eyed knife
    And surgeon's engines drag death back to life.

SANCHO. [*aside*] Well, 'tis an ill wind blows nobody good. So am I saved
    the burying a mill-i-on bodies.

QUESADA. So glory waneth,
    And teeth, and hair, and wisdom; nought remaineth.

SANCHO. Nay, they left their bowls behind them.

QUESADA. Bowls?—Cannonballs.

SANCHO. [*aside*] Mercy! Why, they look as innocent as cabbages. How if
    they should leap up again like crows and fly about? I'll stand farther off.

QUESADA. Lo, what lies here, beneath the foot of fortune?

He picks up another torn page

SANCHO. [*aside*] My master will read anything. I have known him chase
    scraps of paper blown in the street, and pore upon a torn scrip dropped
    by a peasant going to market, as it were Scripture.

QUESADA. Eloquent spirit! Finely said; said wisely.

SANCHO. [*aside*] And he talks to himself, too, as if he had two heads.—
    What's that you read, master?

QUESADA. A summons, hidden in a cunning shift,
That the elect alone his sense might sift.
Predestination dropped it in my way.
From forth the suburbs of obscurity
To th' palaces of prowess I must wend.
My genius prompts me, clean to scour this land
Of dragons, and to succor misused maidens.

SANCHO. Alas, master, this news comes too late; hereabouts, I doubt there be left any maidens.

QUESADA. There are as many virgins here as dragons.
Innocence, fetch these cannonballs, we'll fire 'em
Hot down the dragon's throat, and choke him. How
Books fascinate a man's imagination!

Exit with sword and pages

SANCHO. Did he say "fattenate"? His mouth is full of the finest, fattest, heigh-ho-heroical words that ever tickled my ears. "Predigestination!" I know not what it means, but the rumble of it in my lungs gives me the heart and stomach of a don. Predigestination! And is it not glorious to "wend from forth the suburbs of absurdity"? Before, I would have thought myself a mere drudge, lugging left-behind bowls, but now I see leftenant Sancho, carrier of cannonballs!

Exit, marching, with bowls

ACT 2, SCENE 1

Enter four young men, from tennis: Lord FERNANDO, CARDENIO
dressed gallantly, and two GALLANTS

FERNANDO. Nay, winning wearies me. What's else to do?

FIRST GALLANT. I know a wench, sir—

FERNANDO.   Not like mine. O woman!
Though she were darkling born, she is as fair
As nature's richest mold and skill can make her,
Mended with strong imagination.
She drives me into wonder when I sometimes
Hear her discourse. The court, whereof report
And guess alone inform her, she will rail at,
As if she here sev'n reigns had slandered time.
Then when she reasons on her country state,
On beauties true in title, scorning art,
Freedom as well to do, as think, what's good,
Windmills, wine-presses—pretty witty gypsy!
My heart of empty vanity grows sick,
And I a simple villager in wish.

CARDENIO. My lord, you are no simple villager,
Nor can become one. What we are, we are;
Imagination's cup cannot transform us.

FERNANDO. Why? are not you transformed? new-made, shape-shifted?

FIRST GALLANT. My nose smells courtier.

SECOND GALLANT.   His gait speaks courtier.

FIRST GALLANT. He has been dipped in courtier, that no eye
    Can pierce the armor of his courtiership.

SECOND GALLANT. He pisses courtier.

FERNANDO.   Has Love less art than Fortune?
    Had my sunburnt beauty given you to taste
    Her sharp deliciousness, you'd bite your tongue out,
    Rather than doubt love's potency in changing,
    Or the witching and all-ableness of beauty.—
    I think he's jealous now of my Egyptian.

CARDENIO. I know what love is, and what beauty; though
    You be my better, none my love bests.

FIRST GALLANT.   Whoa!

SECOND GALLANT. Love rides his tongue so fast, wit cannot catch him.

FERNANDO. Pretty boy, if you know love, how can you thunder
    So pulpit-high and sullen 'gainst my passion?

CARDENIO. May I speak private?

FERNANDO. [to GALLANTS]   Leave us.

GALLANTS.   Good my lord.
                                   Exeunt GALLANTS

FERNANDO. Well?

CARDENIO. My love, so please you, shall be blessed i'th' church.

FERNANDO. Why, so may mine. If I should wed her—

CARDENIO.   If?
    Why, your great birth forbids you to descend
    To low alliance. Will your proud father
    Smile blessings on a farm-bred half-black daughter?

FERNANDO. Th'obscureness of her birth and her complexion
    Cannot eclipse the luster of her eyes,
    Which makes her all one light! She doth inherit
    Deserts t'outweigh the galleys and their gold.
    Dad hath forgiven worse, and will again.—
    Why frown you so? You're jealous.

CARDENIO.   Good my lord.

FERNANDO. Nay, speak: friendship is free.

CARDENIO.   Then I would say, sir,
    False to a false love is to love's truth true.

FERNANDO. You speak now with my father's tongue, which fits
    His mouth better than yours. False do you bid me be?
    Then I would say, sir, who is false to one
    Cannot be true to others.—Nay, now I pain you,
    And pain should never this fair face disfigure.
    How may I ease you of your conscience? Faith,
    I shall abandon my new country friend
    If you abandon your new friends i'th' court.
    Shall we once more to hound and horse, Adonis?
    Shall we ride twinned again, each to the tune
    O'th' other, hand to hand and hoof to hoof
    Leap hedges, hunt wild boar, and flee forever
    Court gates and lady closets? For a man
    On foot's a peasant, even in a palace,
    But put that man on horseback, he's a centaur,
    Half god, half animal, ungovernable.
    What say you?

CARDENIO.   "Excellent, my lord!" and "when?"

FERNANDO. Now is the only "when" I know or need.

CARDENIO. And where?

FERNANDO.   Your father's house.

CARDENIO.   My father's house?

FERNANDO. I'll see your "fair Lucinda," and decide
    If she, or any woman, 's worthy of
    My fair Cardenio.

CARDENIO.   I'll write straight to my father.

FERNANDO. And I to my blackberry Violenta
    Delaying my return—but on condition
    That you yourself deliver her my letter.
    My fastest horse I gift you, the white jennet.
    We'll exchange mistresses for the perusal,
    And lay bets on their beauty.

CARDENIO.   You will lose, my lord.

FERNANDO. Look to your purse, fond boy. And now I think on't,
    While you to Violenta spur, shall I
    Deliver your Lucinda your love-letter?

CARDENIO. Nay, good my lord, that would be gross unproper:
    The lord do double-labor as the messenger.

FERNANDO. I'll play what parts I please.   *He kisses Cardenio*
                                 Pen-work; quick, quick! *Exeunt*

ACT 2, SCENE 2

VIOLENTA *discovered, alone, writing a letter*

VIOLENTA. O false true husband, thy troth-plight begets
　Untruth in me. Now with my very father
　I equivocate, playing the maid I once was.
　To hearts like mine, suspect is misery.

Enter LEONELA

LEONELA. My lord Fernando—

VIOLENTA.　　　　　　　　Here?

LEONELA.　　　　　　　　　　No, but the bravest horse,
　And braver horseman, panting come from court,
　Fernando's squire, one Cardenio, who—

VIOLENTA. I am no dish, nor cast shirt, to be passed
　From lord to servant.

LEONELA.　　　　　—who brings a letter to you.

VIOLENTA. Bawd, practice your profession, fetch your client.
　　　　　　　　　　　　　　　　Exit LEONELA
　How shall I speak? How look? There's not an eye
　Not pierces to my guilt.

Enter CARDENIO, *booted and spurred, and carrying a letter. He bows
to* VIOLENTA.

VIOLENTA.　　　　　[*aside*] Impudence curtsies.

CARDENIO. [*aside*] She's bashful, as the country girl at court.

VIOLENTA. [*aside*] Why does he smile so?

CARDENIO.　　　　　　　[*aside*] She has been weeping, sure.

VIOLENTA. Your lord's for court, Cardenio, is he not?

CARDENIO. Not so, virgin.

VIOLENTA. [*aside*]　　　Not so virginal,
　I thank his lordship's pleasure.

CARDENIO.　　　　　His business now
　Steers him some other course.

VIOLENTA.　　　　　Whither, I pray you?

CARDENIO. Some two months' progress.

VIOLENTA.　　　　　　　Whither, whither, sir?
　I do beseech you. Did he deliberate this
　Or sprang the business but as then conceived
　When it was born?

CARDENIO.　　　Virgin, when 'twas conceived—

His business, or the message I have borne you—
I know not that, nor is't in the command
I labour under to await delivery
Of your answer. For the perusing
The letter, I commend you to your leisure.   *He bows, departing*
[*aside*] I pity her, but to preserve her honor
Nothing will serve but discontinuance.
Lucinda waits for me; I must spur homeward.   *Exit*

VIOLENTA. Wax, render up thy trust.
    [*Reads*] "Dame Prudence should now teach us to forget what the devil
      Indiscretion forged."
    O wretched and betrayed! Lost Violenta,
    Poisoned with candied language, and bequeathed
    To desperation, now my womb become
    The tomb of my dead honor, a dark mansion
    For maggot infamy to breed in. Come,
    Consuming desolation, to this temple,
    Now fit to be thy spoil. What must I do?
    I will commend to hazard every breath
    That I shall spend hereafter. Farewell, my father,
    Whom I'll no more offend; and men, adieu,
    Whom I'll no more believe; and maids, God buy you,
    Whom I'll no longer shame. The way I go
    As yet I know not. Sorrow, be my shepherd.   *Exit*

ACT 2, SCENE 3

Flourish within. Enter MARCELA, *and two servants*

FIRST SERVANT. What a horse!

MARCELA.   What a rider!

SECOND SERVANT.   Did you see him?

FIRST SERVANT. The trappings of his horse would buy this house.

    Enter DON BERNARD *and* LUCINDA

BERNARD. Be still!

MARCELA.   I swear, his spurs are jeweled.

BERNARD.   Silence!

    Enter Lord Fernando, booted and spurred, with a riding crop,
    carrying a letter. Bernard etc. curtsy.

BERNARD Welcome, my lord!

FERNANDO.   Lucinda?   [*He raises her.*]
                            Who ne'er beheld
    More than a hawthorn shall have leave to say
    The cedar's a tall tree, and scorn the shade
    The loved bush once had lent him.

LUCINDA. Good my lord,
I understand you not.

MARCELA. He talks of trees, madam.

FERNANDO. By my troth, I not understand myself.

BERNARD. What business brings my lord post-haste from court?
That letter?

FERNANDO We can talk of that anon, sir.

He puts the letter up

Yesterday's dust my courser has outgalloped,
I breathe the instant air, I am all future.

BERNARD. Will my lord taste our hospitable thanks?—
Though poor, to a court palate.

FERNANDO. Rich, most rich! *Exeunt*

ACT 2, SCENE 4

Enter QUESADA, *and* SANCHO *following, carrying a heap of rotten armor*

QUESADA. Deliver my proud sword Castilian.

SANCHO *gives* QUESADA *an old sword*

QUESADA. Thou length of death!

SANCHO. I hope, grandsire, you do not mean to commit any murders.
I am loath, while I am still a virgin, to be hanged, for company's sake.

QUESADA. Stirrup and steel have license for employments
Forbidden lesser flesh.—Clap on my spurs,
That I may hear my heels heroical
Jingle upon the floor of chapels royal
And echo in the archduke's antechambers
And prick the sides of—faster, faster, boy,
Fasten mine armor on, make me all metal,
That I may spur ambition into battle,
Whereupon, having armies of black pagans slain,
Thus leaning on this blade, I'll from the fray refrain,
(Fool, this goes there)—and then, like every mighty knight,
Infallibly, my faithful squire, I will thee requite.

SANCHO. Squire? Is not a squire a pimp? Though I would, like a good servant, willingly be the master of your whores, I have no skill in the trade.

QUESADA. Pimp? Didst ever read, in books of knighthood, "pimp"?

SANCHO. Never, truly, sir [*aside*] he has not yet taught me how to read.

QUESADA. The knight doth to his faithful page repair,

(Nay, this!)—and, having emperies to spare,
Makes his brave page the governor of some island—

SANCHO. The governor?

QUESADA. Or earl or emperor or potentate.

SANCHO. I, Sancho Pauncha, governor of an island?

QUESADA. Island, or isle, or demi-continent.

SANCHO. I'll not have Ireland.

QUESADA. What thou wilt, witling.

SANCHO. Or Switzerland.

QUESADA. What isle imagination can conjure, I shall conquer.

SANCHO. Must I be wise, sir, to be governor? Can I not command others
to be wise for me?

QUESADA. Thou mayst get wisdom by contagion, thus:
Do as I tutor thee.

    QUESADA *muses;* SANCHO *muses*

SANCHO. Schoolmaster, now I think on't, is it writ down every knight-
errant's page shall have his own island? Pardon me, sir, but nowadays
great men, when they climb ashore they shake off their servants, their
friends, and their promises as a dog does water. Is it writ down?

QUESADA. Upon eternal parchment in the ink of faith.

SANCHO. Master, I must consider.

    SANCHO *stands aside, and muses.*

Sancho Pauncha, you would be wise now to venture abroad. What's
in this dusty parish? You know every mouse, by name and parentage,
and all the maids too, and the mice are handsomer. Princesses! Palaces!
Pomegranates! To come back perfumed, so becourtiered, the neighbor's dog will bark at me for a stranger, my very mother salute me for a
grandee!—Yet: my master is certainly mad. Yet: what is a hero, but mad,
o' the right side? Yet: cannonballs. Yet: governor! Yet: fear. Yet: hope!—
Master, write me down page.

QUESADA. Advance thy hand, companion.
This fellowship, forever unforsaken,
This bond can nothing cancel, till life crack.

SANCHO. Ay, but your worship, setting forever aside, how soon shall I
have my island?

QUESADA. Six days, or five. But we must trudge tonight.

SANCHO. Ay, your eminence, the sooner the sweeter.

QUESADA. Steal from thy mother's house at midnight, and prepare
My charger Rozinante—

SANCHO. Rosie? The mule?

QUESADA. My great steed Rozinante, dressed and saddled.
  A man is not a man without a horse.
  When I mount Rozinante, I ascend
  To the empyrean of hoof and hero.
  Hand me my hurtless helm.

He dons a rusted barber's basin for a helmet

                              Spur, sword, and helmet,
  Now am I not knight-errant pat, and perfect?

SANCHO. As perfect a knight-errant as ever I saw. But, senor Quesada—

QUIXOT. No, not "Quesada," 'tis too ordinary,
  Like the shop sign of an apothecary.
  Heroes when into knights of steel they change
  Adopt some nomination high and strange,
  Word-monument to where they were begot,
  That sounds like "Camelot," or "Lancelot."   *He muses.*
  Hm.—Ha! Henceforward, page, you must proclaim
  (New-designate by th' filèd quill of fame)
  "Don Quixot de la Mancha" my true name.

SANCHO. Oyez! Don Quick-sot of la Mancha approacheth! Oyez!

QUIXOT. Hush!—Of our adventures shall the hallowed pages
  In untold languages unnumbered ages
  Be read; but now, tell no one. Not thine ass,
  Asses may be enchanted. Hush!—Pass.   *Exit*

SANCHO. All masters are mad, but few pay their wages in islands.
                                                       Exit

ACT 2, SCENE 5

Enter old CAMILLO *with* CARDENIO, *booted and spurred*

CAMILLO. Marriage? Lucinda still? spur'st thou from court on such a
  blind-man's errand? Bernard's brat, sayst thou? Thou sell'st thyself right
  cheap. Better a duke's crumb than a clown's loaf.

CARDENIO. Father, Don Bernard will not let me see her,
  Unless you first assure him your consent.

CAMILLO. [*aside*]Those scattered pieces of virtue which are in him, the
  court will solder together, varnish, and rectify.—Would the Duke had a
  daughter!   *Exit*

CARDENIO. O sweet Lucinda, on what briars sharp
  The roses of devotion grow, and wither.

Enter Lord FERNANDO

FERNANDO. [*apart*] The wager I have lost, and lost my heart, too.

Lucinda's the prime maid. O that a man
Could reason down this fever of the blood.
Then might I be indeed thy friend, Cardenio.—
How now? downcast?

CARDENIO. Her father gives consent, but on condition
My father first should ask him, who—alas!

FERNANDO. Now are you paid for praising fathers. I
Would praise instead your stallions here, you breed
The world's best horses, beasts of pride and fire,
Fit for a king.

CARDENIO.   My lord, what shall I do?

FERNANDO. I have done nothing but admire all,
And envy all, and dream of riding all.

CARDENIO. My father, though—

FERNANDO.   Doth he refuse outright?

CARDENIO. He puts me off, and makes delays denials.

FERNANDO. Don Bernard offers me the non-pareil
Of his own stable, but the price is high,
And I must answer quickly.

CARDENIO.   Good my lord—

FERNANDO. Be you my squire, spur to the court, deliver
This, doth solicit the return of gold   *Gives letter.*
To purchase certain horse that like me well.

CARDENIO. What help were this, my lord?

FERNANDO.   O innocence!—
I in your absence in your saddle sitting
Shall take the reins and in an ear paternal
Pour milky hints till I secure the mare
Your father will not buy you, that you pine for.

CARDENIO. My lord, how shall I e'er repay your love?

FERNANDO. Fut! It pays itself.—I'd not lose my purchase;
Which done, be henceforth Master of my Horse.
Leave your farewells for me to take. Make haste!

CARDENIO. Fear not, my lord, the swiftest wing of time
With double love will labor my return.   *Exit at one door*

FERNANDO. Ay, love doth double, and will steal time's wings.
How else so quickly could Lucinda rule,
Reel, in the streets of my revolted heart?
Is this love, or drunkenness? Or was the other?
Did not Cardenio himself advise me,
"False to a false love is to love's truth true."

Were Violenta's dark intoxications
All nought in her, but a disease in me,
That fancied graces in her?—Soft! mine honor
Begins to sicken in this black reflection.
How can it be that with my honor whole
I should pursue Lucinda for my wife?
That were accumulating injuries
To Violenta first, and now Cardenio,
Perjured to her, to him perfidious,
To mine own self in sorest terms accused
Of pois'ning honor—which once vomited,
My dog's the creature of the nobler kind.
But pleasure runs too strong for reason's curb,
And conscience melts, o'ergreased with heat and sweetness.
Roderick, keep Cardenio at court,
While I here court Lucinda and her father.
I have no choice. Falseness my business now.   *Exit at other door*

Act 2, Scene 6

Enter softly with a stealing pace QUIXOT *in his armor, with a lantern in his hand, followed by* SANCHO *with the laden ass, noisily. Quixot makes signs for Sancho to be silent. Sancho makes signs for the ass to be silent. They pass over the stage and exit.*

Enter Don Bernard, followed by LUCINDA *(carrying the book), and* MARCELA

LUCINDA. Within these two days, married? to a stranger?
     I do beseech you, father, on the edge
     Of your posterity's destruction pause.

BERNARDO. Destruction? 'Tis but the breaking of your maidenhead, which will be the making of my posterity. Prithee, fear neither t'one, nor t'other. I tell thee, girl, there's more fear than danger. For mine own part, as soon as thou art married to this noble lord, my fears are sped.

LUCINDA But my firm-plighted faith by your consent
     Was long since given to Cardenio.

BERNARD. Why then, by my consent e'en take it back again. Thou, like a simple wench, hast given thy affections to a fellow cares not a farthing for them; one that left thee for a jaunt to court, as who should say, "I'll get a place now; 'tis time enough to marry, when I'm turned out of it."

LUCINDA. I heard my mother say a thousand times—

BERNARD. Go to, you're a fool. No doubt you have old stories enough to undo you. Go, go your ways!

MARCELA. Be gentler to her, good master.—Do you weep?

LUCINDA. Would I could weep! For then mine eye would drop
     Upon my heart, and 'suage the fire there.   *Exit* LUCINDA

BERNARD. Go thy ways, contradiction!—Follow her, follow her!

Exit MARCELA

The girl says right. Her mother was just such another. I remember, two of us courted her at once. She loved—neither of us, by my faith, but me she chose merely to spite that surly old blockhead my father-in-law.— Who comes here? Camillo? Now the refusing part will lie on my side.

Enter old CAMILLO

CAMILLO. My worthy neighbor, I have a suit to you.

BERNARD. Please to name it, sir.

CAMILLO. Sir, I have long held you in singular esteem, and what I shall now say will be a proof of it. You know, sir, I have but one son.

BERNARD. Ay, sir.

CAMILLO. And the fortune I am blessed withal, you know pretty well what it is.

BERNARD. 'Tis a fair one, sir.

CAMILLO. Such as it is, the whole reversion is my son's, who, now attending on our master the Duke, ere he left, left with me the secret of his heart. I took a night, indeed, to think upon it, and now am come to bind the contract with half my fortune in present. Ha? What say you to't, Don Bernard?

BERNARD. Why, by Palmerin of England, neighbor—I have heard something of this matter.

CAMILLO. Heard something of it? No doubt you have.

BERNARD. Yes, now I recollect it well.

CAMILLO. Was it so long ago then?

BERNARD. Very long ago, neighbor. On Tuesday last.

CAMILLO. What, am I mocked in this business, Don Bernard?

BERNARD. Not mocked, good Camillo, not mocked. But in love-matters, you know, there are abundances of change in half an hour. Time, time, neighbor, plays tricks on's all.

CAMILLO. Time, sir? What tell you me of time? Come, I see without spectacles how this goes. Can a little time take a man by the shoulder and shake off his honor? Neighbor, it must either be a strong wind, or a very mellow honesty that drops so easily. "Time" quoth'a? Tripe!

BERNARD. O' God's name, Camillo, will you please to put your indignation in your pocket for half a moment while I open the whole matter? My daughter, you must know, has such a tender eye she cannot feelingly see a duke's younger son without falling flat in love with him. Now, you know, neighbor, when greatness rides post after a man of my years, 'tis both prudence and good breeding to let my mare be overtaken. And who can help all this? I profess, it was not my seeking, neighbor.

CAMILLO. I profess, a fox might earth in the hollowness of your heart, neighbor. If I were to give a bad conscience its true likeness it should be drawn after a very near neighbor to a certain poor neighbor of yours. "Neighbor?" With a pox! Nay, a horse would make a better neigh-bor, he is incapable of hypocrisy.

BERNARD. Nay, you are so nimble with me you will hear nothing.

CAMILLO. Sir, if I must speak nothing, I will hear nothing. As for your neighing, it if comes from your heart, 'tis a lie in your throat before it trips over your double tongue. I'll to Lucinda, and if I find her tale like yours, why, I shall turn Turk, and swear by Mahomet your wife was true to you, one night at least, and your daughter is your own.—Fare you well.   *Exit into* BERNARD's *house*

BERNARD. Ay, but two words must go to that bargain.   *Exit, following*

ACT 2, SCENE 7

Enter Violenta, with the letter

VIOLENTA. My servant loiters. Sure he means me well.—
I dare not tell him of Fernando's letter.
What will't avail me, to say I was not willing?
Nothing, but that I publish my dishonor.

Enter Servant. She puts away the letter

O, are you come? What news?

SERVANT.   None but the worst. Your father
Makes mighty offers yonder by a crier
To anyone can bring you home again.
He well describes you: age, apparel, all.   *Looking at her.*

VIOLENTA. Art thou corrupted?

SERVANT.   No.

VIOLENTA.   Wilt thou be honest?

SERVANT. I hope you do not fear me.

VIOLENTA.   Indeed, I do not.
Thou hast an honest face, that means me well,
And such a face, when it deceives, take heed,
Is cursed of all God's creatures.

SERVANT.   I'll hang first.

VIOLENTA. Heav'n bless thee from that rope's end!—I've heard a man
Say more than this, and yet that man was false.
Thou'lt not be so, I hope.

SERVANT.   By my life, mistress—

VIOLENTA. Swear not; I credit thee. But prithee, though:
    Take heed thou dost not fail. I do not doubt thee.
    Yet I have trusted such a serious face
    And been abused too.

SERVANT.   If I fail your trust—

VIOLENTA. My life and death I will put equally
    Into thy hand. First, for apparel:
    Get me a shepherd's habit.

SERVANT.   Well, what else?

VIOLENTA. And wait me in the evening, where I told thee.

SERVANT. But for the rest? Your years, complexion, sex?   *Looking at her*

VIOLENTA. What in a woman makes the blood stand still
    Is in a man invisible as air.
    My face already nature's enough umbered
    To be taken for a sun-tanned shepherd-boy's.—
    Take heed.

SERVANT.   D'ye fear me still?

VIOLENTA.   No, this is only counsel:
    Be honest but for virtue's sake, that's all.

SERVANT. [*looking at her*] He that has such a treasure cannot fall.   *Exit*

VIOLENTA. I do not trust him. I must find a way to lose him.   *Exit*

ACT 2, SCENE 8

Enter CARDENIO *dressed as a courtier, reading a letter, followed
by* FIRST CITIZEN

FIRST CITIZEN. When from the window she did bow and call,
    O there an angel spake! beauty beteared.
    "Know you Cardenio, sir?" she asked—her voice
    By passion shaken, and her eyes expressing
    Mistemper and distraction with strained wildness;
    "Yes, very well", I answered; then she conjured,
    "Sir, if you be, what some but seem, a Christian,
    Convey this paper to him," promising
    I did heav'n service in't.

CARDENIO.   Sainted Lucinda!
    She prays her letter may come safe and sudden
    Unto my hands, ere her good hand be joined
    To his, who handles honesty so ill,
    Damned hand, damned, damned Fernando!

FIRST CITIZEN.   Have patience, sir.

CARDENIO. O my good friend! Methinks I am too patient.
   Roars there a treachery like this base baseness
   Recorded anywhere? It sounds the deepest:
   Nought but itself can be its parallel.
   And from a friend, professed—friendship? Why, 'tis
   A word forever maimed. In human nature
   It was a thing the noblest, e'en 'mong beasts
   It stood not in mean place: things of fierce kind
   Hold amity and concordance. Such monstrosity
   A writer could not put down in his scene
   Without taxation of his auditory
   For fiction most enormous.

FIRST CITIZEN.   These upbraidings
   Cool time while they are vented.

CARDENIO.   A richer hand
   Than mine requite you. You've done much for us
   So gently pressed to't that my need persuades me
   You'll do a little more?

FIRST CITIZEN.   Put me t'employment
   That's honest, though not safe, with my best spirits
   I'll give't accomplishment.

CARDENIO.   No more but this—
   For I must see Lucinda, and to appear
   Cardenio, as I am, might haply spoil
   Some good event ensuing—let me crave
   Th' exchange of habit with you. Some disguise
   May bear me to my love unmarked and seen.

FIRST CITIZEN. You shall not want.

CARDENIO.   Still I thank you, sir.   *Exeunt*

ACT TWO, SCENE 9

Bells toll the hour. Enter LUCINDA *above in her wedding dress and jewels*

LUCINDA. I've hoped to th' latest minute hope can stretch.
   He will not come. H'as not received my letter.
   May be some stranger view has from our home
   Repealed his changed eye, for what business can
   Excuse a tardiness thus willful? None.
   Well then, it is not business—or such business—
   O suggestion, wherefore wilt thou fright me?
   Fernando on Cardenio...prevails.
   Cardenio to Fernando on mere purpose,
   Fore-plotted purpose, yields me up, to barter
   Real bliss for unsure honour, he hath chosen

His master fore his mistress. All presumptions
Make pow'rful to this point:—his own protraction,
Fernando left behind—that strain lacked jealousy,
Therefore lacked love. So sure as life shall empty
Itself in death, this waked surmise of mine
Is a bold certainty. 'Tis plain and naked,
Fernando could not, durst not, thus infringe
The law of friendship, thus provoke a man
That bears a sword and wears his flag of youth
So fresh as he. He durst not. 'Tis contrivance,
Gross daubing 'twixt them twain.

Enter CARDENIO, *booted and spurred and panting,*
disguised, below

—But I'm o'erheard.

CARDENIO. Lucinda, stay!

LUCINDA. Who art thou?

CARDENIO. Dost not know me? So soon hath this thin seeming
  Quite lost me to thy knowledge?

LUCINDA. O Cardenio!
  You are full possessed how things go here?

CARDENIO. Possessed? yes, by that devil who here plots *Shows letter*
  To dispossess me.

LUCINDA. First, welcome heartily.
  Welcome to th'ending of my bliss and summer,
  My lease in 'em's expired.

CARDENIO. Not so, Lucinda.

LUCINDA. E'en so, Cardenio. An everlasting storm
  Is come upon me, which resistless bears me
  Unto this rock. I cannot stay much talk.
  We have lost leisure. Your absence hath giv'n breeding
  To what my letter hath delivered, 'tis
  This instant brought to birth-tide. *Flourish within*
  Hark! the music
  Is now a-tuning, which must celebrate
  This business so discordant.

CARDENIO. Wear I not a sword?
  Ne'er on man's thigh rode better. If I suffer
  That Judas play my part, if I not do
  Manhood and justice honor, let me be deemed
  A tame pale coward, whom the night-owl's hoot
  May turn to aspen leaf.

LUCINDA. Patience, Cardenio.

CARDENIO. I'll kill the traitor!

LUCINDA.   And be hanged for treason?
　　Or hanged for trying? Roaring boys and duels
　　Better our cause no whit.

CARDENIO.   I know not what—
　　Advise me, love.

LUCINDA.   I have forethought the means
　　To disappoint these nuptials.   *Music within*
                              Hark, again!
　　These are the bells that knoll for us.

BERNARD. [*within*]   Lucinda!

LUCINDA. [*to Cardenio*] I have my reasons; you anon shall know them.
　　Whate'er you see, or hear, whate'er shall hap
　　I'th' passages of this night's sacrifice,
　　Remember—

BERNARD. [*within*] Why, daughter!

LUCINDA. [*to Cardenio*]   —that I loved you.

CARDENIO. Stay!   *Exit LUCINDA*
　　Night falls; light flies from me.—What means Lucinda?—
　　This late betrayal, bleeding in me now—
　　I know an entrance; none will note me, so,
　　Amid the sweat and hubbub.   *Exit*

ACT 3, SCENE 1

Music. Enter FERNANDO, *the* CURATE, BARBER, *and servants
with tapers and censers*

FERNANDO. This obstinacy must be cómbated
　　By importunity as obstinate.
　　Passions in women are as short in working
　　As strong in their effect.

                    At the other door enter Don BERNARD, LUCINDA *with
                    a black veil and black ribbons, and* MARCELA

BERNARD. [*to Lucinda*] Nay, no dragging back but with my curses.

FERNANDO. Lucinda, why this funeral-nuptial fashion?
　　What wan displeasure hath subdued that cheek
　　Where love sits throned?

LUCINDA.   My lord Oblivion,
　　I cannot not-remember the rites due
　　To friendship's holy law, to faith reposed,
　　To truth, to honour, to Cardenio.

BERNARD. Fie!

FERNANDO. [*to Lucinda*] By my faith, each hour of growing time

Shall task me to thy service, till by merit
I purchase grace. Blot the low-born Cardenio
From thy fair mind.

LUCINDA.   So I shall make it foul.
This counsel is corrupt.

FERNANDO.   Come, you will change.

LUCINDA. Why would you make a wife of such a moonling,
Who is so apt to change? This foul proceeding
Still speaks against itself, and vilifies
The purest of your judgment. For your birth's sake
I will not dart my hoarded curses at you,
Nor give my meanings language. For the love
Of all good things together, yet take heed
And spurn the tempter back.

BERNARD.   Perverse and foolish!

LUCINDA. How may I be obedient and wise too?
Ungracious, if I not obey a father;
Disgracèd, if I do.—Yet, lord, consider
Or ere too late, or ere that knot be tied
Which may with violence damnable be broken,
No other way dissevered—yet consider
You wed my body, not my heart, my lord,
No ounce of my affection. Sounds it well,
Cardenio's lover is Fernando's wife?

FERNANDO. No shot of reason can come near the place
Where my love's fortified. The day shall come
Wherein you'll chide this backwardness, and bless
Our fervor in this course.

LUCINDA.   No, no, Fernando,
When you shall find what prophet you are proved
You'll prophesy no more.

BERNARD.   Have done this talking.
If you will cleave to your obedience, do't;
If not, unbolt the portal and be gone,
My blessing stay behind you.

LUCINDA. [to CURATE]   Holy father,
I, by an oath, stand fore-bound to another.

CURATE. Nay, but that oath was drunk, pledged in the wine
Of folly, will, pride, disobedience.
The voice of fathers is the voice of heaven,
For to their children they are God's lieftenants,
Made fathers not for nature's uses merely
Of procreation (beasts and birds would be
As noble then as they are), but to steer
The wanton freight of youth through storms and dangers

Which with full sail thou bear'st upon. For this
Are men made fathers, and for this may challenge
Their daughters' duty.

LUCINDA.   O the opposing wind,
Should'ring the tide, makes here a fearful billow;
My poor barque needs must perish.

MARCELA   Why look at me?
Alas, I cannot help you.

LUCINDA. [*kneeling to* BERNARD] I conjure you,
By the chaste love 'twixt you and my dear mother
(O holy saints, that she were living now!)
Forgive and pity me.

BERNARD.   Nay, to the point.

Enter CARDENIO *in disguise, unseen*

LUCINDA. [*to Bernard*] I will not swerve a hair's breadth from my duty.
It shall first cost me dear.

BERNARD. [*raising her*]   Give me your hand.—
My lord, receive my daughter of me.—Come, be brief.

CURATE. Will you, forsaking every other love,
My lord Fernando, take and keep this lady,
Lucinda, for your lawful wife?

FERNANDO.   I will.

CURATE. Will you, forsaking every other love,
Lucinda, take this ring, and take this man,
Fernando, for your lawful lord and husband?

                    LUCINDA *remains silent a long time*

LUCINDA. I will.

CURATE. Then, by the holy church, I now pronounce you—

CARDENIO [*coming forth with his sword*] Hold, sir-priest!
An elder claim craves hearing.

BERNARD.   What are you, sir?

CARDENIO. A wretch that's almost lost to his own knowledge,
Struck through with injuries.

FERNANDO.   Cardenio? Dare you
Steal away unprivileged, and leave
My doing and your duty unaccomplished?

CARDENIO. Ungen'rous lord, the circumstance of things
Should stop the mouth of question. You have wronged me,
Wronged me so basely, in so dear a point
As stains the cheek of honor with a blush,
Cancels the bonds of service, bids allegiance

Throw to the wind all high respects of birth,
Title, and eminence, and in their stead
Fills up the panting heart with hot defiance.
If you have sense of shame or justice, lord,
Forego this bad intent, or with your sword
Answer me like a man, and I shall thank you.
Cardenio dead, Lucinda sells for sixpence,
But, while I live, she is my whore, not yours.   *Lucinda swoons*

FERNANDO. She dies upon me, help!

CURATE   Throng not about her,
Give her air.

FERNANDO. What paper's that? Let's see it.
It is her own handwriting.

BERNARD.   Bow her head.

FERNANDO. [*to Cardenio*]
Vain man, the present hour is fraught with business.
I have no leisure to chastise this boldness.   *He reads the letter*

CARDENIO. Too much love once; too little now; now, none.
My blood stands still, and all my faculties
Are by enchantment dulled, like windmills turning
Into stone. In what book am I bound now?
The characters confound me. Read me my part, pray.
How can I hero it, here? Ha ha ha.
Am I a coward? Am I anything?
Some man take this, give me a distaff for it.   *He lets fall his sword*

BERNARD [*to servants*] My servants, turn this boistrous sworder forth.

CARDENIO *is seized and dragged out by servants*

CURATE. [*to Fernando*] What learn you by that paper, good my lord?

FERNANDO. That she would do that violence to herself
Which nature hath anticipated on her.
Search her well, I pray you.

MARCELA.   Here it is.

MARCELA *discovers a poynard hidden in Lucinda's clothes*

FERNANDO. O double falsehood! when she vowed "I will,"
False first to false Cardenio, and then,
Juggling equivocatress, false again,
And falser, to that vow, and to me falsest,
For bride's blood on my wedding sheets to trade
Her deathbed.—Am I paid with such disdain
That you count consummation crueller
Than stabbing? Kissing worse than killing? Death
Do you desire? Death to wed? Death be it!

Fernando wounds LUCINDA, CURATE *stops him*

CURATE. Rash e'en to madness!   *Exit Fernando*

BERNARD.   My lord, my lord!

MARCELA. My girl, my mistress!

CURATE.   Bear her to her chamber,
    Pray her unnuptialed innocence may yet
    God-brided be.   *Exeunt, carrying* LUCINDA

ACT 3, SCENE 2

Enter Lord RODERICK

RODERICK. Cardenio's parting thus in secret from me
    With the long doubtful absence of my brother
    (Who cannot suffer but my father feels it)
    Have troubled me with strong suspicions
    And dreams that will not let me sleep nor eat,
    But like a whirlwind hither have they snatched me
    Perforce to be resolved.

Enter old CAMILLO
                Old sir, I am glad
    T'have met ye thus. [*aside*] What ails the man?—Camillo?

CAMILLO. Ha?

RODERICK. Is't possible you should forget your friends?

CAMILLO. Friends? What are those?

RODERICK.   Why, those that love you, sir.

CAMILLO. Y'are none of those, sure, if ye be Lord Roderick.

RODERICK. Yes, I am General Roderick, and I lie not
    If I protest I love you passing well.

CAMILLO. You loved my son too passing well, I take it;
    One that believed too suddenly his court-creed.

RODERICK. [*aside*] All is not well.—Good old man, do not rail.

CAMILLO. My lord, my lord, y'ave dealt dishonorably.

RODERICK. Good sir, I am so far from doing wrongs
    Of that base strain, I understand you not.

CAMILLO. Ye understand not neither, o' my conscience,
    How your most virtuous brother, noble Fernando—
    Ye look so like him, lord, you are the worse for't,
    Rots upon such dissemblers!—under color
    Of buying coursers and I know not what,
    Bought my poor boy out of possession
    Ev'n of his plighted faith. Was not this honor?
    And this a constant friend?

RODERICK.　　　　　　　　I dare not say so.

CAMILLO. Now ye have robbed him of his love, take all.
　　Make up your malice and dispatch his life, too.

RODERICK. If you would hear me, sir—

CAMILLO.　　　　　　　　　　Your brave old father
　　Would have been torn in pieces with wild horses
　　Ere he had done this treachery. On my conscience,
　　Had he but dreamt you two durst have committed
　　This base, unmanly crime—

RODERICK.　　　　　　　Why, this is madness.

CAMILLO. I have done. I have eased my heart. Now ye may talk.

RODERICK. Then as I am a gentleman, believe me—
　　For I will lie for no man—I am so far
　　From being guilty of the least suspicion
　　Of sin that way, that fearing the long absence
　　Of your Cardenio and my brother might beget
　　Something to start at, hither have I traveled
　　To know the truth of you.

　　　Enter VIOLENTA *disguised as a shepherd's boy, behind*

VIOLENTA.　　　　　　　I'll step aside
　　And hear what fame is stirring.　　*She stands aside*

RODERICK.　　　　　　　Why this wond'ring?

CAMILLO. Can there be one so near in blood as you are
　　To that Fernando, and an honest man?

RODERICK. While he was good, I do confess my nearness,
　　But since his fall from honour he's to me
　　As a strange face I saw but yesterday,
　　And as soon lost.

CAMILLO.　　　　　I ask your pardon, lord,
　　I was too rash and bold.

RODERICK.　　　　　　No harm done, sir.

CAMILLO. But is it possible ye should not hear
　　The passage 'twixt Lucinda and your brother?

RODERICK. None of all this.

　　　Enter SECOND CITIZEN

CAMILLO.　　　　　　　How now?

SECOND CITIZEN　　　　　　　Hast heard? Quesada,
　　Rusty-armored, madly rides among the mountains,
　　Asking the whereabouts of distressed damsels.　　*Exit*

　　　Enter THIRD CITIZEN

THIRD CITIZEN. Hast heard? My lord Fernando, like a madman,
(Saving your reverence) leapt on his horse
Without a word and rode off, none knows whither.   *Exit*

Enter FIRST CITIZEN

FIRST CITIZEN. I bear ye tidings, sir, which I could wish
Some other tongue delivered.

CAMILLO.   Whence, I pray ye?

FIRST CITIZEN. From your son, sir.

CAMILLO. Prithee, where is he?

FIRST CITIZEN. That's more than I know now, sir.
But this I can assure you, he has left
The city raging mad. God comfort him!
He came from that cursed wedding—the fiends take it!—
And traded his court jennet for a mule,
Saying he would not sell his soul for horseflesh,
And madly spurred the poor mule toward the mountains.

CAMILLO. Prithee, be gone, and bid the bell knoll for me.
I have had one foot in the grave some time.
Nay, go, good friend, thy news deserves no thanks.
                                        Exit FIRST CITIZEN
How does your Lordship?

RODERICK.   That's well said, old man.
I hope all shall be well yet.

CAMILLO.   It had need,
For 'tis a crooked world.—Farewell, poor boy!

Enter Don Bernard, melancholy

BERNARD. This comes of forcing women where they hate.
It was my own sin, and I am rewarded.
Now I am like an agèd oak, alone,
Left for all tempests. I would cry but cannot.
I am dried to death almost with these vexations.
Lord, what a heavy load I have within me.
My heart, my heart, my heart!

CAMILLO.   Has this ill weather
Met with thee too?

BERNARD.   O wench, that I were with thee!

CAMILLO. You do not come to mock at me now?

BERNARD.   Ha?

CAMILLO. Do not dissemble. Thou mayst find a knave
As bad as thou art, to undo thee too.
I hope to see that day before I die yet.

BERNARD. It needeth not, Camillo. I am knave
    Sufficient to myself. If thou wilt rail,
    Do it as bitterly as thou canst think of,
    For I deserve it. I have lost my daughter.—

RODERICK. Dead?

BERNARD.   Stol'n away, and whither gone I know not.

CAMILLO. Sh'as a fair blessing in being from you, sir.
    I was too poor a brother for your greatness.
    You must be grafted into noble stocks
    And have your titles raised. My state was laughed at
    And my alliance scorned. I've lost a son too,
    Which must not be put up so.

                      CAMILLO *offers to draw his weapon*

RODERICK.   Hold, be counseled.
    Y'ave equal losses. Urge no farther anger.
    Heav'n, pleased now by your love, may bring again,
    And no doubt will, your children to your comforts,
    In which adventure my foot shall be foremost—
    And one more will I add, my honoured father,
    Who has a son to grieve for too, though tainted.
    Let your joint sorrow be as balm to heal
    These wounds of adverse fortune.

BERNARD.   Come, Camillo,
    Do not deny your love. For charity.
    I ask it of you. Let this noble lord
    Make brothers of us, whom our own cross fates
    Could never join. What I have been, forget;
    What I intend to be, believe and nourish.
    I do confess my wrongs. Give me your hand.

CAMILLO. God make thee honest. There.

                                They shake hands

RODERICK.   'Tis done like good men.
    Now there rests nought but that we part, and each
    Take sev'ral ways in quest of our lost friends.
    Some of my train o'er the wild rocks shall wait you.
    Our best search ended, here we'll meet again
    And tell the fortunes of our separate travels.

              Exeunt severally CAMILLO, BERNARD, *then* RODERICK

VIOLENTA. [*coming forward*]
    I would your brother had but half your virtue!
    Yet there remains a little spark of hope
    That lights me to some comfort. The match is crossed,
    The parties separate, and I again
    May come to see this man that has betrayed me

And wound his conscience for it. Home again
I will not go, whatever fortune guides me.
No, no, Fernando, I will follow thee
Where there is day. Time may beget a wonder.   *Exit*

ACT 3, SCENE 3

Enter Don QUIXOT *followed by Sancho, panting*

QUIXOT. Of death or dying screech those wheeling crows,
    And either equal meat to feed adventures:
    Death to revenge, or dying to restore.

SANCHO. I shall have, on my island, no mountains.

QUIXOT. Thy mind makes mountains. Thy legs would labor less
    If thou'dst imagine more.

SANCHO. Master, my legs have little imagination.

QUIXOT. Suppose this steep-most summit but a floor
    Planed flatter than a flatness mathematic.
    Now, is't not airier, thy dainty foot?

SANCHO. No your worship, after these weeks of wandering, the air about
    my feet is not so dainty. The mule smells better than I do. She thinks
    better too, she flat refused to climb these rocks. And why did we?

QUIXOT. From this height, should be damsels visible
    In distant miniature distress for me
    To perpetrate some chivalry upon.—
    Ha! What's that? On that rock there? Fetch that something.

SANCHO. I would rather fetch my breath.

QUIXOT. Presently, sirrah, fleetly, sirrah, fly!

SANCHO. Ay, master, I would happily sell my legs for wings.—The first act
    of my governorment shall be a bill for the paving the whole island flat.
                                                                    Exit

QUIXOT. Genius of Amadis, where be these poets?
    When heroes need a poet, none appear.
    Let me see.
    [*Sings*] That doughty knight, Don Quixot hight,
            Did steed bestride, and stirrup ride
            Upon a mountain, where was no fountain—
    Well, I'm a pretty poet. But this savors
    Something of bragging. Knights must modest be.
    I'll hire a balladeer to brag for me.

Enter SANCHO, *dragging a saddle and a portmanteau fast to it*

SANCHO. Whew! this is wondrous heavy. But not so heavy a sight as
    the pitiful-horrible dead beast yonder, near this pack, with his belly

exploded, and stinking worse than the mills, and the poor worms that work in the mines of his entrails, and the crows chattering and chomping like priests on Fat Tuesday, and Master Ass as he is eaten grinning, and his empty eye asking me, am I the next ass come here to become carrion, carrying some other creature's treasure?

QUIXOT. Fear nothing, little pigeon. I will foster thee.
Break ope the wallet, solve this mystery,
Whose was it, what is in it, why he left it? see.

SANCHO. Ay, master. Item, [*he holds up two shirts*] four fine holland shirts, fit for a damsel, or a young courtier; item, tablet, bound very costly;

> SANCHO *tosses the tablet aside. Quixot picks it up, and reads*

item, handkerchief, wherein—O holy mother!—gold, gold!

QUIXOT. Keep thou the trinkets; I these sonnets take.

SANCHO. O most liberalest master!

QUIXOT. These golden poems do remember me of those
Odes amorous I wrote upon my lady's toes.

SANCHO. What, love you a lady, master?

QUIXOT. Am I a knight? Fool, dost thou think me crazy,
To style myself a knight, and lack a lady?

SANCHO. [*aside*] Is it not horrible that this ancient ragged puppet, who cannot lift a cup to his lip but the palsy shakes it half-empty, should offer his dry, stinking, grandfatherly mouth to play at kiss-catch?—Who is your mistress, master?

QUIXOT. Dear dainty famous Dulcinea del Toboso!

SANCHO. [*aside*] Well, I never heard of her. She must not dainty it hereabouts.

QUIXOT. O toes of Dulcinea del Toboso!

SANCHO. [*aside*] I hope her toes are the prettiest thing about her, I would not have this old toad hop after any but an ugly woman.—That tablet you read, master, can it tell you who left this saddle here?

QUIXOT. A courtier-scholar-lover-poet-knight. Attend.

Enter CARDENIO *above on a rock in ragged clothes, and mad*

QUIXOT. [*reads*] "Sweet mistress of my meanings! Love's heart's book!"

CARDENIO. Horsemanship? Whore! Riding shall be abolished.

QUIXOT. Soft, soft you, child. Who comes here? Pray you, slink aside.

CARDENIO. Usurping spurs! Off, off! Turn the barbed steed
Loose to his native wildness, beast too noble
To property man's baseness. What a letter
Wrote he to's brother! What a cavalier was I!
Why, Perseus beneath me, Parthians behind—

O serpent! what a venomous world is this,
When commendations bait us—gyves and fetters
To keep me bolted there, while the false sender
Played out his suit of false hearts!—O Lucinda!
If heav'n had made thee stronger than a woman,
How happy had I been! Loose, verily,
Lucinda, loose and light; her lightness casts me
Into down darkness.

QUIXOT. [*to* SANCHO] Lo you now, for certain
This is the author of these very sonnets.
'Tis the same style. Love, love, luminous love!

CARDENIO. Break, heart, I gave half to each, and they ate up all, not a
shard for me, not a crumb.

SANCHO. Downright love! I see by the foolishness of it.

CARDENIO. Not a crumb to feed a beggar's dream. What scraps are left
me to believe? Not him, not her, not myself, not my book. Burn my
books, burn, Fernando, Lucinda, cinders, cinders, ash for the asking,
ash for answers.

SANCHO. [*to* QUIXOT] What a heap of stuff's this! This fellow's head
would make a good pedlar's pack, grandsire.

CARDENIO. [*sings*]　Lucifer he,
　　　　　　　And Lucy she,
　　　　　　　And me makes three
　　　　　　　　　ding dong damned!
Him I cannot, her I cannot, myself I can, I will, torment.—There, there,
villain, I will teach thee. Coward!—I will run from myself, I will, I will!
Exit above

QUIXOT. This man is reasonable mad.

SANCHO. And may be mischievous. Prithee, your mightiness—

QUIXOT. My peerless chivalry I first shall vent
On this unfortunate itinerant.
There's some moral in his madness. We may profit.
Let's follow him.　　　　　　　　　　　　　　*Exit*

SANCHO. But at some distance, for fear of the worst.—'Tis a rule in philosophy, where one madman leads, there many a fool will follow. But for
myself, masters, I mind no rule but the rule of nature: where apple leads,
belly follows.　　　　　　　　　　　*Exit, munching an apple*

ACT 3, SCENE 4

Enter the CURATE *and* BARBER

BARBER. It can be none but our old friend Quesada.
These carriers describe him perfectly,
How he made war on windmills—

CURATE.   war on sheep—

BARBER. war on innkeepers, shepherds—

CURATE.   war on peace.

BARBER. He's mad, sure.

CURATE.   Those heathen fictions broiled his brains.
   By my tithes, this frenzy that possesses him
   Must be cast out, with prayer cast out, psalms, candles—

BARBER. Bring a man's buttocks to the barber's chair
   Before ye shave his face. Before your learning
   Can cure Quesada, we must catch him.

CURATE. I am no man for swordplay.

BARBER.   No, nor I.
   But if we use and humour his delusion,
   We may entrap him.

CURATE.   Yes, but how?

BARBER.   With a device
   Worthy a barber, as full of wit as hair.
   Now that ye have, and charitably too,
   Locked up Lucinda in that nunnery,
   Under this beard, I shall become a squire, so.
   And, if it please ye, vicar, ye shall be,
   Under this wig, a poor afflicted damsel, so.

CURATE. My dignity would rather play the beard's part.
   In God's name, I could never do a woman.

BARBER. Ay, you must leave out God's name, when you do a woman.
   I have a dress too, fit for a princess,
   Far finer than your cassock.

CURATE.   How shall all these help?

BARBER. I'll tell ye, and we'll plot more, on the way now.   *Exeunt*

ACT 4, SCENE 1

Within, the baaing of sheep, sheep-bells, and sheep-whistling of
SHEPHERDS. *Enter the old* MASTER, *three or four*
SHEPHERDS, *and* VIOLENTA *in boy's clothes*

FIRST SHEPHERD. Well, he's as sweet a man, God comfort him,
   As ever mother looked on.

SECOND SHEPHERD.   Truly, neighbor,
   For a mother may be fond on her first born
   Though he be naked, dirty, crazed, and sunburnt.

MASTER. What drives such a sweet man to these sour mountains?

FIRST SHEPHERD. His melancholy, sir, that's the main devil does it.
  Go to, I fear he has had too much foul play offered him.

MASTER. How gets he meat?

SECOND SHEPHERD. Why, now and then he takes our vittles from us,
  And for a short grace, beats us well and soundly,
  And then falls to.

MASTER. Where lies he?

FIRST SHEPHERD.   Even where the night o'ertakes him.

SECOND SHEPHERD. Hang me, an some fair-snouted skittish woman
  Or other be not at the tail on's madness.

FIRST SHEPHERD. Oh here he comes again.

Enter CARDENIO, [*half*] *naked, sunburnt, mad, as if riding a hobby horse*

MASTER.   Let him alone.
  He wonders strangely at us.

FIRST SHEPHERD.   Not a word, sirs,
  To cross him, as you love your shoulders.

MASTER Boy, sing your ditty. Melody may lull him.

VIOLENTA *sings*
  With endless tears that never cease
    I saw a heart lie bleeding,
  Whose griefs did more and more increase,
    Her pains were so exceeding.
  When dying sighs could not prevail,
    She then would weep amain.
  When flowing tears began to fail,
    She then would sigh again.

  Her sighs like raging winds did blow,
    Some grievous storm foretelling,
  And tides of tears did overflow
    Her cheeks, the rose excelling.
  Confounding thoughts so filled her breast
    She could no more contain,
  But cries aloud, "Hath love no rest?
    No joys, but endless pain?"

CARDENIO. Come hither, child. Shake not, good pretty soul,
  Nor do not fear me.

VIOLENTA. Why do ye look so on me?

CARDENIO.   I have reason,
  I study natural philosophy,
  The rude blast, hot sun, dung and dirt, tears and torrents.
  Ye weep too, do ye not?

VIOLENTA.   Sometimes I do.

CARDENIO. I weep sometimes too. Y'are extremely young.

VIOLENTA. Indeed, I've seen more sorrows far than years.

CARDENIO. Yet all these have not broken your complexion.
    You have a strong heart, and you are the happier.
    I warrant, y'are a very loving woman.

VIOLENTA. A woman, sir? [*aside*] I fear he's found me out.

SECOND SHEPHERD. He takes the boy for a woman! Mad again!

CARDENIO You've met some violation, some foul play
    Has crossed your love. I read it in your face.

VIOLENTA You read a truth then.

CARDENIO   Where can lie the fault?
    Is't in the man?—Ho! Have I hit the nick?

VIOLENTA Y'are not far off.

CARDENIO This world is full of coz'ners, very full.
    Young virgins must be wary in their ways.
    I've known a duke's son do as great a knavery.
    Will you be ruled by me?

VIOLENTA.   Yes.

CARDENIO.   Kill yourself.
    'Twill be a terror to the villain's conscience
    The longest day he lives.

VIOLENTA.   By no means! What?
    Commit self-murder?

CARDENIO.   Yes, I'll have it so!

FIRST SHEPHERD. [*to other Shepherds*]
    Take heed of all hands.—Sir, do ye want anything?

CARDENIO. Thou li'st! Thou canst not hurt me, I am proof
    'Gainst farther wrongs.—Steal close behind me, lady,
    I will avenge thee.

VIOLENTA. [*aside*] Thank the Lord, I'm free.

             CARDENIO *seizes on the* SECOND SHEPHERD.
                       VIOLENTA *runs out*

CARDENIO. O treach'rous base Fernando! Have I caught thee?

SECOND SHEPHERD. Help! help! good neighbors, he will kill me else.

CARDENIO. Faith-breaker! Villain! I'll suck thy life-blood.

FIRST SHEPHERD. Good sir, have patience. This is no Fernando.

             They rescue the SECOND SHEPHERD

CARDENIO. Well, let him slink to court and hide a coward.
  Not all his father's guards shall shield him there,
  Or if he prove too strong for mortal arm
  I will solicit ev'ry saint in heav'n
  To lend me vengeance. I'll about it straight.

Exit as if riding a hobby horse

SECOND SHEPHERD. Go thy ways, and a vengeance go with thee!—
  Pray, feel my nose. Is it fast, neighbors?

FIRST SHEPHERD. 'Tis as well as may be.

SECOND SHEPHERD. He pulled at it, as he would have dragged a bullock backward by the tail. An't had been some men's nose that I know,
  neighbors, who knows where it had been now? He has given me such a
  devilish dash o'er the mouth, that I feel I shall never whistle to my sheep
  again. Then they'll make holiday.

FIRST SHEPHERD. Come, shall we go? For, I fear, if the youth return,
  our second course will go much more against our stomachs.

MASTER. Walk you afore. I will but give my boy
  Some short instructions, and I'll follow straight.
  We'll crash a cup together.

FIRST SHEPHERD.   Pray, do not linger.

MASTER. I will not, sirs.   *Exeunt Shepherds*
          This must not be a boy.
  He but puts on this seeming, and his garb
  Speaks him of such a rank, as well persuades me
  He plays the swain rather to cloak some purpose
  Than forced to't by a need. I've waited long
  To mark the end he has in his disguise,
  But am not perfect in't. The madman's coil
  Has driv'n him shaking hence. These fears betray him.
  If he prove right, I'm happy. O, he's here.

Enter VIOLENTA

Come hither, boy; where did ye leave the flock, child?

VIOLENTA. Grazing below, sir. [*aside*] What does he mean,
  To stroke one o'th' cheek so? I hope I'm not betrayed.

MASTER. Have you learnt the whistle yet, and when to fold?
  And how to make the dog bring in the strayers?

VIOLENTA. Time, sir, will furnish me with all these rules.
  My will is able, but my knowledge weak, sir.

MASTER. That's a good child. [*aside*] 'Tis certainly a woman.

VIOLENTA. [*aside*] Lord! how I tremble.—'Tis unusual to me
  To find such kindness at a master's hand,
  That am a poor boy, ev'ry way unable,

Unless it be in pray'rs, to merit it.
Besides, I've often heard old people say
Too much indulgence makes boys rude and saucy.

MASTER. Are ye so cunning?

VIOLENTA. The ewes want water, sir. Shall I go drive 'em
Down to the cisterns? Shall I make haste, sir?
[aside] Would I were five miles from him. How he grips me!

MASTER. Come, come, all this is not sufficient, child,
To make a fool of me. This is a fine hand,
A delicate fine hand—and a woman's hand.

VIOLENTA. Y'are strangely out. Yet if I were a woman,
I know you are so honest and so good
That though I wore disguises for some ends
Ye would not wrong me.

MASTER.   Come, y'are made for tupping.
Will you comply? I'm madder with this talk.
There's nothing you can say, can take my edge off.

VIOLENTA. Oh, do but quench these foul affections in you
That, like base thieves, have robbed ye of your reason,
And I will be a woman, and begin
So sad a history that if there be aught
Of human in ye, or a soul that's gentle,
Ye cannot choose but pity my lost youth.

MASTER. No stories now.

VIOLENTA.   Kill me directly, sir.
As you have any goodness, take my life.

MASTER. I will take somewhat: not your life; somewhat sweeter.

RODERICK. [within] Ho! Shepherd, will you hear, sir?

MASTER. What bawling rogue is that, i'th' devil's name?

VIOLENTA. Blessings upon him, whatsoe'er he be!   *Runs out*

   Enter Lord RODERICK, *with his Corporal Gerald*

RODERICK. Good ev'n, my friend. I thought ye all had been
A-sleeping in this country.

MASTER.   You had lied then,
For ye were waking when ye thought so.

RODERICK. [taking off his hat] I thank you, sir.

MASTER. I pray, be covered. 'Tis not so much worth, sir.

RODERICK. Was that thy boy ran crying?

MASTER.   Yes. What then?

RODERICK. Why dost thou beat him so?

MASTER.   To make him grow.

GERALD. [*aside*] A pretty medicine!

RODERICK.   Thou canst not tell me
  The way to the next nunnery?

MASTER.   How do you know that?
  Yes, I can tell ye, but the question is,
  Whether I will or no, and indeed I will—not.   *Exit, following Violenta*

RODERICK. What a brute fellow's this! Are they all thus?

GERALD. [*aside*] Yes.
              Roderick takes a letter from his pocket

   RODERICK.   Fernando too, I fear. Is he so hot?

GERALD. [*aside*] Some wenching matter.

RODERICK.   My brother's letter tells me
  Lucinda not far hence takes sanctuary,
  From which he begs me bring her back again.
  But by what means from her close life to win her?—

GERALD. [*aside*]
  I take it, is not mentioned.

RODERICK.   Said he aught else?

GERALD. I never knew him speak so little, sir.
  Mute as a gravestone, with the name erased.

RODERICK. A gravestone?—By the mass, it shall be so.
  I must convince him, now, to feign a corpse.
  And, opportune, my father's summer hunting
  Brings him into these mountains, with that coffin,
  Which now attends him, everywhere and always,
  Like a court favorite. My father's vacant hearse
  Stands ready to receive his living son.
  I'll serve him, be it but to save his honour.   *Exit*

GERALD. This is a plaguy business. Play a corpse?
  I grant ye, it were not too hard a part,
  Any could act it, I could act it to the life,
  For the whole action lies in doing nothing.

Enter QUIXOT, *mad, and beaten*

QUIXOT. Soldier, didst see a madman hereabouts?

GERALD. None but yourself, sir. But I'll look for more.   *Exit*

QUIXOT. I saw him in the cleft of that great rock.
  Knight of the Rock! Spirit of Amadis!

Enter SANCHO, *bedraggled*

SANCHO. [*aside*] We have nothing to eat, but grass and stones, and the stones are not good for a man's kidneys, and as for grass, it makes cows fart poisonously, so you may guess how the wind sits with us.—I see nothing here worth eating.

QUIXOT. See, Sancho: something for thy mind to chew on.

> *Enter* CARDENIO, *half-naked, sunburnt, mad, as if riding a hobby horse*

SANCHO. His rags look as if they had been chewed by lions. Are there lions hereabouts?

QUIXOT. No lions, Sancho. Only snakes. And wolves.
   —Sir, I have sworn never to quit these mountains
   Until I found ye, and could learn directly
   The source of that great grief which sinks your soul.

CARDENIO. Sir, whosoe'er you be—sorrow and salt
   Have so perplexed my eyes, my proper hand I know not,
   Nor you, sir; my wits wander, with my body—
   For your condolement now and courtesy
   I thank ye warmly, wonderingly thank ye;
   Pardon me that my poor thanks are so...bare.

SANCHO. [*aside*] He looks my master up and down, as if he were a horse for sale; sure he shall count his teeth next; and to tell truth, if my master were a horse, I would not buy him.

QUIXOT. Sir, I beseech ye, tell your history,
   How you have come to dwell here among beasts,
   No better than a beast, like mad Orlando
   Burnt brown as an Egyptian, and I vow
   I shall if possible repair your fortunes,
   Or if not possible, help ye lament 'em.

CARDENIO. If you would hear my story, ye must vow, sir,
   Not once to interrupt the doleful file
   Of my narration, not with questions stay me,
   Not comment in the margin, not exclaim,
   Or tug my sleeve, or cry hm! but in silence
   Let the long army of my miseries march past,
   For my afflictions, sir, are legion, legion,
   And to recount my griefs adds to my grief.

QUIXOT. I shall not speak one word. Nor shall my page.

SANCHO. I shall stand, master, like a little puppet, with my mouth sewn shut. [*aside*] May as well be sewn shut, now there's no food to put in't.

QUIXOT. Now, sir, proceed, recount your history.

CARDENIO. The history of who? Who am I? No one.
   Once I was...a book; now, only scattered leaves.
   My name's Cardenio, and I loved Fernando.
   No, my name's Cardenio, and I loved Lucinda,

And she loved me. No, not me, not this self, no,
Some self that she and I conspired to dream.
She seemed a lady legendary heroes
Might have adored, and poets celebrated.
She and I loved especially to read
Of knights and damsels and their misadventures,
Of false Angelica and mad Orlando,
False Guinivere, false Lancelot, fool Arthur;
There, in those books, began my misery;
The History of Amadis of Gaul
I gave her—

QUIXOT. Good sir, if your Lucinda were enamored
On books of chivalry, you need no further
To amplify her wit or worth or wisdom,
For on this evidence of her devotion
To works of knighthood, she is sure, I vouch it,
The most accomplishèd, idëal female extant.
And I beseech ye, pardon this transgression
Of my agreement not to interrupt you,
For speak one syllable of chivalry
And 'tis no more within my tongue's controlment
To hold its peace, than can the sun leave shining;
So pardon me, and prosecute your story.

SANCHO. For want of the discreet ladle of a cool understanding, will this
fellow's brains boil over.

QUIXOT. Hush, sirrah, thou disturb'st him with thy prating.
—You left at "Amadis," or so, sir. Will ye speak, sir?

CARDENIO. I will—kill any book that dares deny it.
I will. Do ye not think—I swear 'tis so—
That good Queen Guinivere had gonorrhea?
A whore, on excellent authority,
A back-door drab, and rotten with the pox,
And served the turn of every servingman
Who served hot sausages at the Round Table.

QUIXOT. O thou vile fool, thou dost belie a lady,
A noble lady, and a virtuous!

CARDENIO. A hot bitch, and would sniff each passing codpiece.

QUIXOT. Oh rogue! Oh modernist! thou speakst profanely.
Look ye, he who slanders one man's mistress slanders
Every man's mistress, and my mistress too,
And shall repent it, soon repent, and dearly,
As I shall champion her chastity
And chop thy head off, that dares house so lewd a tongue,
And take it to the lady on a dish,
A silver dish—

CARDENIO. Thou art an ass.

SANCHO. [*aside*] Right.

QUIXOT. Thou art a madman.

SANCHO. [*aside*] Right.

QUIXOT. If thou wert weaponed, I should carbonado thee.

CARDENIO. Callst thou that toy a weapon?—Turk!   *Strikes him*

QUIXOT.   Jew!   *Strikes him*

CARDENIO.   Convert!

> CARDENIO *beats* QUIXOT, *as* SANCHO *speaks*

SANCHO. [*aside*] My master charged me, I should not rescue him, even were he alone against an army of pagans, for 'tis against the law of arms for a page to thrust in amongst knights.—He pounds him horribly.—But 'tis better to behold a tragedy, than act in it.—I may not fight a dubbed knight, that's certain, but if he be but squire, I think it were lawful my fist should leave half a dozen mementos on his face. I shall enquire.—Good sir, pray you, are ye a knight, or a squire?

CARDENIO. Art thou a pygmy, or an idiot?

> SANCHO *thinks. Then* CARDENIO *beats him.*
> SANCHO *and* Quixot *lie prostrate*

Blessings upon you both, for this good exercise!
Models of Christian manhood! I'll go pray too.
> *Exit, as if riding a hobby horse*

SANCHO. Is this adventures?

QUIXOT. Oh!

SANCHO. Dear Don Quixot, speak again; only, do not say you are dead; I would rather ye never spoke again, rather than say you're dead. Say somewhat poetical.

QUIXOT. Is this Elysium?

SANCHO. I do not think so, master.

QUIXOT. Oh!

SANCHO. Is this how a page becomes a governor? I looked to be anointed with balm; I find I am well basted with cudgels.

QUIXOT. Why, Sancho, to procure a dïamond
Wouldst thou not thrust thy hand once in the fire?

SANCHO. No, master, I would take me a stick and knock the diamond out.

QUIXOT. Talk not, wise child, of knocking.

SANCHO. Why the devil must ye take the part of a woman against a madman?

QUIXOT. Does not a painter, when he learns his art,
　　Follow and imitate the most famed masters?
　　So every knight-apprentice-errant copies
　　Th'original of manhood, Amadis of Gaul,
　　The sun of chivalry, and moon of madness.
　　This mad lad here, would he be mad now, think you,
　　If he had not read *Amadis of Gaul*?
　　Had Amadis not run mad, and Orlando,
　　When their fair mistresses scorned and disdained 'em,
　　Would I fall frantic now, and tear my hair out,
　　And, as I shall do soon, pluck trees up by the roots?
　　Oh lady Dulcinea del Toboso!

SANCHO. What, has your lady of tobacco scorned you?

QUIXOT. No, Sancho, not a whit; therein consists
　　The full perfection of my enterprise.—
　　For hitherto, all heroes who have lost their wits,
　　Look ye, have found some reason for their madness;
　　I shall be perfect mad, without all reason—
　　As if to say, "If I do this for nothing,
　　Imagine then what I would do for something."—
　　Oh Dulcinea! where's a tree to pluck up?　　　*Exit* QUIXOT, *running*

SANCHO. I would rather pluck up a carrot or onion or any root
　　that's eatable. Would I were home.　　　　　　*Exit, following*

ACT 4, SCENE 2

Enter Lord RODERICK, *Lord* FERNANDO, *and soldiers carrying an
empty hearse. They open it, and take out friars' robes, and begin to put
them on*

RODERICK. You're ever in these troubles.

FERNANDO.　　　　　　　　　　　　Noble brother—

RODERICK. You must into the hearse; you will be known else.
　　Ye said ye would make anything to win her.
　　Lucinda's in a cloister, is she not?
　　Within whose walls to enter as we are
　　Will never be. Few men, but friars, come there.
　　We must pretend we do transport a body
　　As 'twere to's funeral, and coming late by,
　　Crave a night's leave to rest the hearse i'th' convent.
　　That's our best course, for to such charity
　　Strict zeal and custom of the house give way.
　　When we're once lodged, the means of her conveyance
　　By safe and secret force with ease we'll compass.
　　But a light coffin will too hollowly
　　Report our practice.

FERNANDO.   This coffin is too small.

RODERICK. Room enough, brother, Caesar had no more.

Fernando climbs into the coffin and lies down

FERNANDO. I cannot move.

RODERICK.   Excellent, ye will toss less.

FERNANDO. Nay, do not drop me. Now I think better on't—

RODERICK. Down, brother, 'tis not far (put on the lid),
    Ye shall not be dead long (knock in the nails),
    Not very long, a good time now to nap
    (Knock 'em in soundly), but a brief rehearsal
    For your last lasting sleep. (Heave him up, sirs.)
    Now a short journey, brother, for your sins,
    Short as a man's life, and as comfortable.   *Bells ring*
    The nuns are at their vespers. 'Tis our cue.
    Now to our plot. We bring the night in with us.

Exeunt, carrying the coffin

ACT 4, SCENE 3

Enter CARDENIO, *followed by* BARBER *and* CURATE

CARDENIO. Courtier louse, why are you struggling vainly?
    Do you aspire to perfect louse-iness?
    Have ye read all the louse-iest philosophers?
    Have you imagined ideal lady lice?
    And did your fantasy betray you? bite you?
    Was she lice-entious? Sucked your friend's blood? Blood-sucker!

He bites the louse, and eats it

BARBER. [*aside to Curate*] Is that not good Camillo's son, Cardenio?

CURATE. 'Twould break his father's heart, to see him thus.

BARBER. He's a torment to a barber to behold.

CURATE. Maybe he can help us find our friend Quesada.—
    [*to Cardenio*] Neighbor, do you not know me?

CARDENIO. [*to Curate*]   Oh Lucinda!

CURATE. These wild and solitary places, sir,
    But feed your pain. Let better reason guide you,
    And quit this forlorn state that yields no comfort.

BARBER And let my scissors guide your wild beard back
    To civilization.

CURATE.   Have you seen hereabouts
    An old schoolmaster, or an old mad knight?

CARDENIO. You have a horse-face, sir, of wondrous wisdom,
    And, as it seems, are traveled deep in knowledge.
    Have you e'er seen the phoenix of the earth,
    The bird of paradise?

CURATE.   In troth, not I, sir.

CARDENIO. I have, and known her haunts, and where she built
    Her spicy nest—till, like a credulous fool,
    I showed the treasure to a friend in trust,
    And he hath robbed me of her.   *Lute music within*
    Ha! hark, a sound from heav'n! Do you hear nothing?

BARBER. Yes, sir, the touch of some sweet instrument.
    Here's no inhabitant.

CARDENIO.   No, no, the better.

CURATE. This is a strange place to hear music in.

CARDENIO. I'm often visited with these sweet airs.
    The spirit of some hapless man that died
    And left his love hid in a faithless woman
    Sure haunts these mountains.

                            VIOLENTA sings, unseen, within

VIOLENTA. Woods, rocks, and mountains,
                        and ye desert places
    Where naught but bitter cold and hunger dwells:
    Hear a poor maid's last will, killed with disgraces.
    Slide softly while I sing, ye silver fountains,
    And let your hollow waters like sad bells
    Ring, ring to my woes, while miserable I,
    Cursing my fortunes, drop, drop, drop a tear and die.

CURATE. [*aside to* BARBER]
    See how his soul strives in him.

CARDENIO.   Excellent sorrow!
    You never loved?

CURATE.   No.

CARDENIO.   Peace, and learn to grieve then.

                            VIOLENTA sings, unseen, within

VIOLENTA. Griefs, woes, and groanings,
                        hopes and all such liars,
    I give to broken hearts that daily weep:
    To all poor maids in love, my lost desires:
    Sleep sweetly while I sing my bitter moanings,
    And list may hollow lovers, that ne'er keep
    Truth, truth in their hearts, while miserable I,
    Still cursing my fortunes, drop, drop, drop a tear and die.

CARDENIO. [*singing*] Miserable I,
   Still cursing my fortunes, drop, drop, drop a tear and die.—
   Is not this heavenly?

CURATE.   I never heard the like, sir.

CARDENIO. I'll tell you, my good friends—but pray, say nothing—
   I'm strangely touched with this. The heav'nly sound
   Diffuses a sweet peace through all my soul.
   But yet I wonder what new sad companion
   Grief has brought hither to outbid my sorrows.
   Stand off, stand off, stand off! Friends, it appears.   *They hide themselves*

   Enter VIOLENTA, *disguised as a shepherd*

CURATE. [*aside*] It is a boy.

                    VIOLENTA takes off her cap, and lets down her hair

BARBER. [*aside*]   Nay, now it is a girl!

CURATE. [*aside*] Boy, girl, it's difficult deciding, sometimes.

                              She begins to wash herself

BARBER. [*aside*] Maybe she's mad, and will run naked too!

VIOLENTA. Sweet water, wash away the scent of man.—
   How much more grateful are these craggy mountains
   And these wild trees than things of nobler natures,
   For these receive my plaints. All good people
   Are fall'n asleep forever. None are left
   That have the sense and touch of tenderness
   For virtue's sake—no, scarce their memory—
   From whom I may expect counsel in fears,
   Ease to complainings, or redress of wrongs.

CARDENIO. [*aside*] This is a moving sorrow. But say nothing.

VIOLENTA. What dangers have I run, and to what insults
   Exposed this ruin of myself? O, mischief
   On that soul-spotted hind, my vicious master!
   Who would have thought that such poor worms as they—
   Whose best feed is coarse bread; whose bev'rage, water—
   Would have so much rank blood. I shake all over
   And blush to think what had become of me
   If that good man had not relieved me from him.

CARDENIO. [*aside*] Since she is not Lucinda, she is heav'nly.
   When she speaks next, listen as seriously
   As women do that have their loves at sea
   What wind blows ev'ry morning.

VIOLENTA. I cannot get this false man's memory
   Out of my mind. You maidens that shall live
   To hear my mournful tale when I am ashes,

Be wise, and to an oath no more give credit,
To tears, to vows (false, both!) or anything
A man shall promise, than to clouds, that now
Wear such a pleasing shape and now are nothing.
For they will cozen (if he may be cozened)
The very God they worship.

CARDENIO. [*aside to* BARBER *and* CURATE]
                          Do not you weep now?
I could drop myself into that fountain for her.

CURATE. She weeps extremely.

CARDENIO.   Let her weep. 'Tis well.
Her heart will break else. Great sorrows live in tears.

VIOLENTA. Oh false Fernando!

CARDENIO. [*rising up*]   Ha?

VIOLENTA.   And O, foul fool,
Forsaken Violenta—whose belief
And childish love have made thee so—go drown
Thy self and sorrows in that cold deep pool.
For there is nothing left thee now to look for
That can bring comfort but a quiet grave.
There all the travails that I long have borne,
And those to come, shall sweetly sleep together.   [*Going*]

                CURATE, BARBER, and CARDENIO come forward

CARDENIO. Stay, lady, stay. Can it be possible
That you are Violenta?

VIOLENTA.   That lost name,
Spoken by one that needs must know my fortunes,
Has taken much fear from me. Who are you, sir?
For, sure, I am that hopeless Violenta.

CARDENIO. And I, as far from any earthly comfort
That I know yet, am the once-courtier
                He bows to Violenta, as before
And messenger Cardenio.

VIOLENTA.   Cardenio?

CARDENIO. I once was thought so. If the cursed Fernando
Had pow'r to change your sex, why, lady, should not
That mischief-maker make me anything,
That have an equal share in all the miseries
His crimes have flung upon us? And pardon me
For any harm I have done you—

VIOLENTA.   No harm, sir.
And pardon me I could not know your virtues
Before your griefs. Methought when last we met

The accent of your voice struck on my ear
Like something I had known, but floods of sorrow
Drowned the remembrance. If you'll please to sit,
Since I have found a suff'ring true companion,
And give me hearing, I will tell you something
Of your Lucinda that may comfort you.

CARDENIO. [*to Violenta*] Talked you of comfort? 'Tis the food of fools,
And we will none on't. Come, feed me fresh sorrows.
—Friends, I have met your madman, and can tell you
Where you may find him. But my soul grows weary.
Come to my cave, where we may sleep together.
Exeunt CARDENIO *and* VIOLENTA

BARBER. [*to* CURATE] She falls out excellently for our purpose.

CURATE.   How?

BARBER. Why, she will make a better princess than you would.
Come, we may help her tame wild Lord Fernando,
While she helps us lead mad Quesada home.

CURATE. Will not a princess need a governess?   *Exeunt*

ACT 4, SCENE 4

Bells and birdsong. Enter Lord RODERICK *and soldiers dressed as friars,
carrying the coffin.*

RODERICK. Set down the coffin; none may spy us here,
But birds, and they are busy at their matins.—
Arise, and death forsake. From your long rest awake,
From your confinement break. Arise, a new life take.

LUCINDA *rises from the coffin, in the habit of a novice*

LUCINDA. Who are you? and what would you? Bless me, heaven!
I think I should stay safer in the grave.

RODERICK. Rest certain, lady, nothing shall betide ye
But fair and noble usage. Pardon me
That hitherto have drugged you in your sleep,
And snatched you from that seat of contemplation
To which you gave your after-life.

LUCINDA.   Where am I?

RODERICK. Not in a nunnery. Never blush nor tremble.
Your honor has as fair a guard as when
Within a cloister. Know then, what is done
(Which I presume ye understand not truly)
Has this use: to permit you to speak freely,
And, if you will, free to the world come back,
And him, who for your sake forsook the world
And laid down in this coffin, as one dead,

Under which color we desired to rest
Our hearse one night within your hallowed walls,
Where we surprised you.

LUCINDA.   Are ye that Lord Rod'rick
So spoken of for virtue and fair life?
And dare you lose these to profanely pander
For such a brother, such a sinful brother,
Such an unfaithful, treach'rous, bloody brother?

RODERICK. This is a fearful charge.

LUCINDA.   Protect me from Fernando,
And I am happy.

RODERICK.   Lady, draw this way.
I am not perfect in your story yet.
Only you must have patience to go with us
To yon small lodge, which meets the sight from hence.
Till when, your griefs shall govern me as much
As nearness and affection to my brother.
Call my companions yours and use them freely,
For as I am a soldïer, no power
Above your own will shall come near your person.

          As they are leaving, enter VIOLENTA *in her shepherd's disguise*

VIOLENTA. [*plucking* RODERICK *by the sleeve*]
Your ear a moment.

RODERICK. [*to Lucinda and the soldiers*] I follow straight.
          Exeunt, carrying the coffin, all but RODERICK *and* VIOLENTA

[*aside*] What ails this boy?—Why dost thou single me?

VIOLENTA. The due observance of your noble virtue,
Vowed to that mourning virgin, makes me bold
To give it more employment.

RODERICK.   Art not thou
The surly shepherd's boy that, when I called
To know the way, ran crying by me?

VIOLENTA.   Yes, sir,
And I thank heav'n and you for helping me.

RODERICK. How did I help thee, boy?

VIOLENTA. I do but seem boy, sir, and am indeed
          Letting down her hair
A woman, one your brother once has loved
Or, God forgive him else, he lied extremely.

RODERICK. Weep not, good maid. O this licentious brother!

VIOLENTA. I will assure you, sir, these barren mountains
Hold many wonders of your brother's making.
Here wanders (worthy man) Cardenio,

Who lay down sleeping, just as you approached us.

RODERICK. O brother, we shall sound thy depths of falsehood!—
If this be true, no more but guide me to him.
Thou shalt have right, too. Lead me to Cardenio.   *Exeunt*

ACT 5, SCENE 1

Enter QUIXOT *and* SANCHO

SANCHO. I am so starved, when I move my bones clatter.

QUIXOT. Thy lamentations not assist our state.
These storms and thorns of Fortune that affront us,
Soon shall pass. Come, tenderness; our chance will change;
For never good nor ill is durable.

SANCHO. Who comes here? another beating?

Enter BARBER *disguised with a beard, in a Moorish habit*

BARBER. Gentlemen, in the name of courtesy,
Where might a stranger (for I a stranger speak)
That superpowerful knight-errant seek,
Don Quixot of the Mancha?

QUIXOT.   I am he, sir.

BARBER. O happy hunt, and fortunate the finding!
Hearing the high renown spread of your prowess,
I kneel and bring ye greetings from my princess.

QUIXOT. Do not gape, Sancho. Bear thyself more page-like.
—Rise, sir. Whence comes this damsel?

BARBER.   From Africa
Three thousand leagues, three thousand weary leagues,
She's traveled, land and sea; one boon she begs.

SANCHO. Hark you, fellow servant: does your mistress rule over any islands?

BARBER. Yes, millions.—I shall bring her highness straight.   *Exit*

QUIXOT. The face of Fortune now does cease to frown,
And glory beckons, glory and renown.

SANCHO. And islands!

QUIXOT. And naked shameless young-limbed princesses,
Who shall present themselves, like mares to stallions,
For mounting, the which service chivalry must tender,
By way of pity, and of puïssance.
Such are the offices and obligations
Of conquest: doing, doing, doing, doing.

SANCHO. But what shall I do, master? When you promised me an island,
I little thought it should lie in Africa, which is horrible far from my
mother's house, 'twill give me nightmares, master.

QUIXOT. Why, child, you need not live in Africa
  To govern it. You may by deputation,
  As other great adventurers have done,
  Sell your black subjects into slavery,
  Three thousand, or six thousand, or ten thousand,
  And fear no nightmares, neither, but in peace at home
  Live rich, respected, honorèd, adored.

SANCHO. What, may I sell a thousand men and women as though they
  were so many sheep?

QUIXOT. Certainly, Sancho, or a million.
  In mathëmatics men and sheep are equal.   *Flourish within*
  Look, the lady comes.

Enter BARBER, *disguised as before, with* VIOLENTA, *disguised as a
princess, and* CURATE *disguised as her governess, all in Moorish habits*

QUIXOT. [*aside to* SANCHO] Look thou be perfect, pupil.

SANCHO. [*aside to* QUIXOT] Ay, master, for in all the days of my life I
  never saw such a pretty brown face, and in such silk and silver. Lord!
  next to her, all other women are hedgehogs.

VIOLENTA. [*aside to* BARBER] Sure I shall never play a princess right.

BARBER. [*aside to* VIOLENTA]
  Fear nothing, wench. You look as like a princess
  As any woman may, to any man,
  And to this man, whose eyes are now as feeble
  As his imagination strong, you are the pink
  Of princesses. Remember, all ye do is done,
  In charity, to cure him of his madness.
  And it shall help you, too, snare Lord Fernando.

VIOLENTA. [*coming forward and kneeling before* QUIXOT]
  Oh finely ground and bolted flour of knighthood!
  Vouchsafe to patch my virtue with thy valor!

QUIXOT. Rise, lady, rise. O my imagination!   *He kisses her hand. She rises*
  Tell me your name, your grievance, and your wish,
  That I, your champion, may grant your wish,
  Revenge your grievance, and exalt your name.

VIOLENTA. I am the princess of, the princess of—

BARBER. Mycomicon, she would say. Very grief
  Distracts her memory oft, thus violently,
  That she cannot remember her own name,
  Or state, and I must prompt her, that she is
  The heir-apparent by direct descent
  O'th' mighty kingdom of Mycomicon.

VIOLENTA. He says true; I forget myself, for sorrow
  And the quick changes Fortune puts upon me.

QUIXOT. Sweet princess, I forget myself, just so,
    Often enough. But tell your story, if ye can.   *He kisses her hand*

VIOLENTA. I am oppressèd by a lustful giant,
    Y-cleped Fernando, who is all too high
    For my low means to stretch at, and too great,
    Too slipp'ry great, for my small strength to catch.

SANCHO. A giant? My master, kill a giant? Yea, he shall kill him, I can tell ye that, or any other lubberly giant. Have ye but one? Is that all? He would kill twenty.

QUIXOT. Bottlehead! think'st thou 'tis the page's part
    To interrupt the damsel, or to brag thus?
    No matter that thy brags be true.—Princess, proceed.

VIOLENTA. This giant villain, sir, has dispossessed me
    Of all that rightly should belong to me,
    From my home driven me, of friends bereft me,
    And worst of all, sir, oh, he still enchants me.

BARBER. Princess, these tears distract you. You forget—

VIOLENTA. No, I remember.

BARBER.   You must make him vow . . .

VIOLENTA. [*kneeling to* QUIXOT]
    I shall not rise again, sir, till you promise
    You will forsake all other your adventures
    Until you have restored my forfeit state.

QUIXOT. You make your own conditions, and I seal them
    Thus on your virtuous hand.   *He kisses her hand*

VIOLENTA.   Think what you promise.
    I can repay you nothing but myself
    And matrimony, for I need a husband.
    But should you fail in this so righteous quest
    You must confess yourself no knight at all,
    A knight of paper, and old paper too,
    And moldy, one that crumbles at first touch.
    Swear, if you fail, to live forever after
    A private man, retired, and never more raise up
    The hope of miracles that, unperformed,
    Double despair.

QUIXOT.   Lady, what valor may,
    I shall perform.

VIOLENTA.   Nay, swear, sir, on your honor—

QUIXOT. Why, as I am a Christian, and a Spaniard,
    And as my kin have Christians been, in Spain,
    These seven thousand years, and upwards, if—

Which were impossible—but if the noble pronoun
"I," *ego*, should unlawfully cohabit
With the lewd vulgar verb *fallere*, "fail,"
Let me be walled up in my closet, straight,
With "Liar" in red letters on the door,
That all may be forewarned my plague of falsehood.
Rise, lady.

VIOLENTA. [*rising*] May your vow be better kept
Than others I have heard.

BARBER   Her ship attends us
At Cartagena, where we may embark
For Ethiopia, but rest tonight
In a large inn—

QUIXOT.   A princess, in an inn?

VIOLENTA. It but appears an inn, the Castle Inn,
In faith, though, 'tis a castle, and enchanted.

QUIXOT. As I thought.—Sancho, attend her governess.

SANCHO. How comes it, master, that so pretty a princess has in her train
so ugly a hobgoblin?

CURATE. Fie!

SANCHO. Foh! and her face better than her breath.

QUIXOT. Hush, sirrah, 'tis a godly ugliness,
Good for all governesses—Lead on, loveliness!   *Exeunt*

ACT 5, SCENE 2

Enter old DUKE *Ricardo, Don* BERNARD, *and* CAMILLO

CAMILLO. Ay, then your grace had had a son more;
He, a daughter; I, an heir.

DUKE.   Let them go;
They're disobedient children.

BERNARD.   Ay, my lord.
Yet they may turn again.

CAMILLO. Let them e'en have their swing. They're young and wanton.
The next storm we shall have them gallop homeward,
Whining as pigs do in the wind.

BERNARD. Would I had my daughter any way.

CAMILLO. Wouldst thou have her with bairn, man? Tell me that.

BERNARD. I care not, so an honest father got it.

CAMILLO. Ye might have had her so in this good time,
Had my son had her. Now you may go seek

Your fool to stop a hole with.

Enter Lord RODERICK *hastily*

DUKE. O welcome, welcome, welcome, Roderick!

CAMILLO. Do you bring joy or grief, my lord? For me,
Come what can come, I'll live a month or two,
If the gout please, curse my physician once more,
And then,
              "Under this stone
              Lies sev'nty-one."

RODERICK. Senor, you do express a manly patience.—
My noble father, something I have brought
To ease your sorrows.

DUKE. It comes at need, boy, but I hoped it from thee.

RODERICK. The company I bring will bear me witness
The busiest of my time has been employed
On this good task. Now, let me play the chorus,
And present the actors y'ave all come to see.
Come, comedy!

Enter LUCINDA *as a novice, veiled*

              Don Bernard finds beneath
This veil his daughter;

Enter Lord FERNANDO *as a friar*

              you, my royal father,
Beneath this cowl find a wand'ring son.

BERNARD. O my girl! Thou bring'st new life.

DUKE. [*to* RODERICK]   And ye, my son, restore me
One comfort here that has been missing long. –
[*To Fernando*] I hope thy follies thou hast left abroad.

RODERICK. Ay, but they follow him.—Tragedy, enter!

*Enter soldiers carrying a coffin in solemn procession, set it down and
exeunt*

Here is a piece of folly, haunts him.

CAMILLO. 'Tis my poor Cardenio.

RODERICK. Nay, his soul's rich, and paid with peace. Believe me,
He's in a better place.—Are you out, brother?
Your cruelty fitted your friend for this;
Your falsehood drove the nails; why weep you now?
That shepherd boy who plucked my sleeve this morning
Conveyed me to a cave, a dim one, where
The lost Cardenio lay asleep, worn down
With tears, with raging tired, and his long ranging

Through these hard mountains (not so hard as ye),
Lay sleeping, like a babe, near naked, still,
So still I feared his sleep was death, and waked him;
He could scarce speak for weakness, but he knew me,
His madness having like a dream dissolved,
A heavy dream, which leaves the waked soul wearier
Than it lay down; and he bequeathed forgiveness
On those who had forsaken him. I told him,
Lucinda, of your flight into the convent,
Your constancy, your love, your resolution.
He asked that I report him to the world
Still faithful to Lucinda, strong in love
Even when weakest, sound in love when sickest,
Fixed in love when farthest wand'ring—then he sighed
"Lucinda, O!"—sighed, stared, and spoke no more.

DUKE. This sad news breaks the heart of our rejoicing.

CAMILLO. Ay, ay, go on with your rejoicing; weep
Your tears of joy. You've all comforts but I.
You have ruined me, killed my poor boy,
Cheated and choked him, and I have no comfort.

RODERICK. Be patient, senor. Time may guide my hand
To work you comfort too.

CAMILLO.   I thank your lordship.
Would grandsire Time had been so kind t'have done it;
We might have joyed together like good fellows.
But he's so full of business, good old man,
'Tis wonder he could do the good he has done.

DUKE. He mourns it like a man.

CAMILLO. Hang me, sir, if I shed one tear more.
'Od's precious, I have wept so long I'm blind
As justice. When I come to see my hawks—
Which I held a toy next to my son—
If they be but house-high,
I must stand aiming at them like a gunner.

BERNARD. [to LUCINDA]
Nay, child, be comforted. These tears distract me.

DUKE. Hear your good father, lady.

LUCINDA.   Willingly.

DUKE. Obedience is the sacrifice of angels,
Whose form you carry.

BERNARD.   Hear the duke, good wench.

FERNANDO. [to Lucinda] If I have erred, impute it to my love—

LUCINDA. Should I imagine he can truly love me

That like a villain murders my desires?
Or should I drink that wine, and think it cordial,
When I see spiders in't?—My gracious lord,
Let me be so unmannered to request
He would not farther press me with persuasions
O'th' instant hour, but have the gentle patience
To bury this keen suit till I shake hands
With my old sorrows. Let me first but weep
A farewell to my killed Cardenio.

CAMILLO. Blessing be with thy soul whene'er it leaves thee.

LUCINDA. For such sad rites must be performed, my lord,
Ere I can love again. Maids that have loved,
If they be worth that noble testimony,
Wear their loves here, my lord, here in their hearts,
Deep, deep within, not in their eyes or trickments;
Such may be slipped away, or with two tears
Washed out of all remembrance. Mine, no physic
But time or death can cure.

She lays her book on the coffin, and kneels beside it

CAMILLO   Well, wench, thy equal
Shall not be found in haste. I give thee that,
Thou art a right one, ev'ry inch. Thy father—
For, without doubt, that snuff never begot thee—
Was some choice fellow, some true gentleman;
I give thy mother thanks for't. There's no harm done.
Would I were young again, and had but thee,
A good horse under me, and a good sword,
And thus much for inheritance!

Violenta, disguised as a shepherd boy, offers to show herself, but goes back

DUKE.   What boy's that?
Has offered once or twice to break upon us?
I have noted him, and still he falls back fearful.

RODERICK. A little boy, sir, like a shepherd?

DUKE.   Yes.

RODERICK. 'Tis your page, brother; one that was so, late.

FERNANDO. My page?

RODERICK.   E'en so he says, and more and worse,
Your Ganymede; ye stole him from his friends,
And promised him preferment.

FERNANDO.   My Ganymede!

RODERICK. And on some slight occasion let him slip
Here on these mountains, where he had been starved
Had not my people found him as we traveled.
This was not handsome, brother.

FERNANDO.   You are merry.

RODERICK. You'll find it sober truth.

DUKE.   If so, 'tis ill.

FERNANDO. 'Tis fiction all, sir.—Brother, ye must please
    To look some other fool to put these tricks on.
    They are too obvious.—Please your grace, give leave
    T'admit the boy. If he know me, and say
    I stole him from his friends and cast him off,
    Know me no more.—Brother, pray do not wrong me.

    Enter VIOLENTA *disguised as a shepherd's boy*

RODERICK. Here is the boy.

DUKE. [*to* VIOLENTA]   Hear me: what's thy name, boy?

VIOLENTA. Florio, an't like your grace.

DUKE.   A pretty child.—
    Where wast thou born?

VIOLENTA.   On t'other side the mountains.

DUKE. What are thy friends?

VIOLENTA.   A father, sir; but poor.

DUKE. How cam'st thou hither? How, to leave thy father?

VIOLENTA. That noble gentleman pleased once to love me
    And, not to lie, so much to dote upon me
    That with his promises he won my youth
    And duty from my father; him I followed.

RODERICK. How say you now?

CAMILLO. [*to* FERNANDO]   Ay, my lord, how say you?

FERNANDO. [*to the* DUKE] As I have life and soul, 'tis all a trick, sir.
    I never had to do with boys.

VIOLENTA.   O sir,
    Call not your soul to witness in a wrong.
    And 'tis not noble in ye to despise
    What you have made thus.—If I lie, let justice
    Turn all her rods upon me.

DUKE.   Fie, Fernando,
    There is no trace of cunning in this boy.

CAMILLO. A good boy.—Be not fearful. Speak thy mind, child.
    Nature, sure, meant thou shouldst have been a wench,
    And then 't had been no marvel he had bobbed thee.

DUKE. Why did he put thee from him?

VIOLENTA.   That to me
    Is yet unknown, sir. For my faith, he could not;
    I never did deceive him. For my service,
    He had no just cause; what my youth was able,
    My will still put in act to please my master.
    I cannot steal, therefore that can be nothing
    To my undoing; no, nor lie. My breeding,
    Though it be plain, is honest.

DUKE.   Weep not, child.

CAMILLO. This lord's abused man, maid, and child already.
    What farther plot he has, the devil knows.

DUKE. If thou canst bring a witness of thy wrong—
    Else it would be injustice to believe thee,
    He having sworn against it—thou shalt have,
    I bind it with my honor, satisfaction
    To thine own wishes.

VIOLENTA.   I desire no more, sir.
    I have a witness, and a noble one,
    For truth and honesty.

RODERICK.   Go, bring him hither.   *Exit* VIOLENTA

FERNANDO. This lying boy will take him to his heels
    And leave me slandered.

RODERICK.   Here is a letter, brother,
    Produced perforce to give him credit with me;
    The writing, yours; the matter, love—for so,
    He says, he can explain it.

CAMILLO.   Then, belike
    A young he-whore.

FERNANDO. This forgery confounds me!

DUKE. Read it, Roderick.

RODERICK. [*reading*] "Dame Prudence should now teach us to forget
    what the devil indiscretion forged—"

FERNANDO. Hold, sir!

DUKE. [*to* RODERICK] Go on.

FERNANDO. My gracious father, give me pardon.
    I do confess, I some such letter wrote
    (The purport all too trivial for your ear).
    But how it reached this young dissembler's fingers
    Is what I cannot figure. For on my soul
    I never kept about me such a minion.

RODERICK. Why should you do a child this wrong?

FERNANDO.   Go to!
  If ye provoke me thus, I shall forget
  What you are to me. This is a mere practice
  And villainy to draw me into scandal.

RODERICK. Bark no more, puppy.

FERNANDO.   Puppy?

RODERICK.   Here comes a witness
  Shall prove you puppy, through and through. No more.

  Enter the BARBER, *disguised as before*

FERNANDO. Another rascal!

DUKE.   Hold!—Art thou the witness?

BARBER. No, but I bring one, sir.

  Enter LEONELA

FERNANDO.   Ha!

DUKE.   Art thou the witness?

LEONELA. Yes, and I bring another, and a nobler.

  Flourish. Enter VIOLENTA, *dressed again as a Moorish princess*

DUKE. What's here? boy? woman? both? hermaphrodite?

FERNANDO. By all my sins, the injured Violenta.

RODERICK. Now, sir, whose practice breaks? Come, make your answer,
  For as I have a soul I am ashamed on't.

CAMILLO. Is this a page?

LEONELA.   One that has done him service,
  And he has paid her for't, but broke his covenant.

VIOLENTA. My lord, I come not now to rail, or lecture.
  Your pure affection dead, my claim die with it.
  Here, take your ring. Give it to whom you please, sir;
  I'll give place. But let me be your servant,
  Your poor servant, better your poor'st servant
  Than turned out of doors. 'Tis a hard world for women,
  And there's a child now tumbles in my belly
  That begs a father, give it some protection,
  And my last breath shall speak Fernando noble.

FERNANDO. Too good for me! Dare you still love a man
  So faithless as I am?   VIOLENTA *does not answer*
  My gracious father, let my knees confess now
  I have too long too freely giv'n a scope
  To youth and heat; many our best confessors
  Have done the like, or worse, and been forgiven.

But think not that I would engage your virtues
To any cause wherein my constant heart
Attended not my eye. Till now my passions
Reigned in my blood, ne'er pierced into my mind,
But I'm a convertite to most pure thoughts,
And must in sackcloth spend my life to come,
If I possess not her. So much I love.
This is my wife, my flesh, the self-same stuff
Whereof we dukes are made, though clay more browner,
No other would I choose, were she a queen.   *The Duke does not answer*
—Thus, thus, and thus [*kissing Violenta*] I seal my vowed repentance,
Let all men read it here. I know you love me.

CAMILLO. Here's a new change. Bernard looks dull upon't.
Has lost two sons-in-law now, in one day.

FERNANDO. And fair Lucinda, from whose virgin arms
I forced my friend Cardenio, O forgive me!
Take home your holy vows and let him have 'em
That has deserved them. O that he were living!

CAMILLO. This almost melts me. But my poor lost boy—

A watch rings in the coffin

LUCINDA. The watch I gave him! O it mocks my sorrow!   *Lucinda sobs*

CAMILLO. Our sorrows cannot help us, gentle lady.
Let it be as 'tis. I cannot mend it.
One way or other, I shall rub it over
With rubbing to my grave, and there's an end on't.

The sound of knocking from within the coffin

DUKE. What's this now, Roderick? Do ye raise the dead?

RODERICK. Why, father, as you taught me, I have learned:
To use whatever tools are necessary.—
Stand away, all! This may be dangerous.

RODERICK *strikes the lid, and* . . . QUIXOT *bursts from the coffin*

QUIXOT. Ha! Where is this giant? I shall pay him, princess.

DUKE. Who's this?

BARBER. A mad schoolmaster, sir. We take a care
To cure him, if your grace would grant us but two minutes.
He calls himself "Don Quixot of La Mancha,"
And takes her for the princess of Mycomicon.

VIOLENTA. Sir, I am much dismayed by your performance.

QUIXOT. Why, did I not do all as ye directed?
Hide in the coffin, to be carried secret
Into this giant's castle?

VIOLENTA.   But what then?
   Wert thou directed, sir, to fall to sleeping?
   And when a lady looked for action, nothing,
   But heaviness and limpness?

QUIXOT.   Shall we not be married?

VIOLENTA. Was this thy vow? Shriveled antiquity,
   How had I fared, if General Roderick
   Had not stepped in to save me, whilst thou snored
   And thy boy Sancho stole a cheese and ate it?

QUIXOT. Are there no other giants hereabouts?
   Have I no wrongs to right? no function?

VIOLENTA.   None, sir.

QUIXOT. Genius of Amadis, come now to guide me!

RODERICK. You have disgraced the order of knights-errant.

QUIXOT. Wilt thou not whisper, Genius of the book?

RODERICK. Your books have failed you; you have failed your books.
   While you have chased unreal fiery dragons,
   By order of the real Inquisition
   Your neighbors and my soldiers burned your books.
   Give me your sword, old man.—Music, and magic!

Music. Enter above CURATE *as a magician, and enter below black spirits who dance about* QUIXOT, *and bind him*

BARBER. [*sings*]
   Come, ye spirits of black night,
   With amazement bind this knight,
   Wrap astonishment around him,
   Nimbly simply deep confound him.

CURATE. All's told.
   Behold!

Another black spirit brings forth SANCHO, *shackled*

SANCHO. Master, here's no magician, but only old Lopez the parson in a long gown, and there's Fabian the barber, bearded, and these black spirits are General Roderick's soldiers. They go about to cozen you. Speak, grandsire. Have they stolen all your fine long words, too?

QUIXOT. Why dost thou think their human shapes are real?
   Their faces are disguises, mere disguises,
   Mere blood and bone disguises. Foolish pupil,
   Thou seest but poorly. Look, boy, look, my genius,
   My book, that once released me, now has bound me.
   Speak to me, spirit! Spirit, do not leave me!
   Nay, do not close the book!—All is lost, lost.

SANCHO. You promised me an island.

QUIXOT. O Sancho! I have dreamed away my greatness.

BARBER. [*sings*]
   Devils, fly this boy and fool
   Home to ordinary school.
   In that little world remain,
   Trade your sword now for a cane.

   During the song exeunt QUIXOT, SANCHO, BARBER, CURATE, *and
   dancing spirits.* RODERICK *stops the black spirit who brought forth Sancho*

RODERICK. [*to Lucinda*]
   Gentle lady, what think ye of this black-faced spirit?

LUCINDA. He has a face makes me remember something
   I have thought well of. How he looks upon me!
   Poor man, he weeps.—Ha? Stay. It cannot be.
   He has his eye, his features, shape, and gesture.
   Would he would speak!

CARDENIO.   Lucinda.

LUCINDA.   Yes, 'tis he!   *They embrace*

CAMILLO. Now what's the matter? 'twixt the devil and the nun?

RODERICK. Let 'em alone. They're almost starved for kisses.

CAMILLO. Stand forty foot off. No man trouble 'em.—
   Much good may't do your hearts!—What is he, lord?
   What is he?

RODERICK. A certain son of yours.

CAMILLO. The devil he is!

RODERICK.   If he be the devil,
   That devil must call you father.

CAMILLO.   By your leave a little, ho!—
   Are you Cardenio?

CARDENIO. [*kneeling*] My duty tells me so, sir.

CAMILLO. Nay, to't again! I will not hinder you a kiss. 'Tis he!   *He leaps*

DUKE. [*to* CARDENIO *and* LUCINDA]
   E'en as you are, we'll join your hands together.
   [*To* FERNANDO] Ask him forgiveness, boy.

RODERICK   He has it, sir.
   The fault was Love's, not his.

FERNANDO   Once more, my friend?

DUKE. I must, in part, repair my son's offences.
   Cardenio, kneel, and rise a Christian knight,
   Henceforward "Don Cardenio de La Mancha."

We shall invest you with the golden spurs
O'th' ancient order of our caballeros.
Fair Violenta, call me now your father,
Link Ethiopia to Andalusia,
And let me see a grandson ere I die.
A match drawn out of honesty and goodness
Is pedigree enough.—Are ye all pleased?

CAMILLO. All.

BERNARD and FERNANDO. All, sir.

CARDENIO. All.

DUKE. And I not least. We'll now return to court:
A short day's ride, a long night's consummation,
So blessed that lovers, when they read your story,
Shall trace your wanderings to taste such glory.
                              Exeunt, leaving coffin behind

EPILOGUE

Enter QUIXOT *as Epilogue*

O multitude of monarchs! If you please,
Pardon, that I your patient majesties
Dare once more vex thus. Book-bound imitation
I would henceforth forswear—which transmutation
Cannot be performed without you. 'Tis your part,
For charity, to dress me to depart,
To able my unable, till I be
O'th' bondage and invisibility
Of fictions freed. Now, pray you, put me out:
Release me from the durance deep of doubt,
Which prison, though't all power else withstands,
Dissolves, if you magicians clap your hands.

CONTRIBUTORS

Gerald Baker is an independent scholar-director based in South-West London where he directed a staged reading of *Double Falsehood* in April 2010 as well as full stagings of a seven-woman *Henry V* and a two-woman adaptation of *Dr Faustus,* amongst other early modern and contemporary productions. He has also written on the Calverley murder plays and the evidence for role-sharing in early modern drama and is currently enquiring how to identify nonverbal collaboration in early modern plays.

Joyce Boro is Associate Professor of English at Université de Montréal. Her work focuses on the English reception of Spanish romance. An editor of Lord Berners's *Castell of Love* (MRTS 2007) and Margaret Tyler's *Mirror of Princely Deeds and Knighthood* (MHRA forthcoming 2012), she has published on translation, Fletcher, and Grisel y Mirabella.

Terri Bourus is an Associate Professor of English Drama at Indiana University-Purdue University Indianapolis (IUPUI). She is also the Director of the New Oxford Shakespeare Centre at IUPUI and one of the General Editors of that edition. In 2009, Bourus founded Hoosier Bard Productions, for which she directed *Young Hamlet* (2011), *The History of Cardenio* (2012), and two versions of *Measure for Measure* (2013). Bourus has edited multimedia editions of *Hamlet* and *A Midsummer Night's Dream* for Sourcebooks' Shakespeare and digital editions of two John Fletcher plays. She has published on film/stage, the early modern book trade, Shakespeare, Middleton, and most recently, the theatrical evolution of Taylor's reconstruction of *Cardenio* in *The Quest for Cardenio* (2012). Bourus is the recipient of several prestigious teaching and research awards from Indiana University.

Roger Chartier is Professor at the Collège de France, Directeur d'études at the Ecole des hautes études en sciences sociales in Paris, and Annenberg Visiting Professor in History at the University of Pennsylvania. He is one of the world's leading authorities on the history of the book, publishing, and reading in a perspective that associates cultural history and textual criticism. His latest monograph in that field to be translated into English is *Inscription and Erasure: Literature and Written Culture from the Eleventh to the Eighteenth Century* (University of Pennsylvania Press, 2007). In fall 2011 he published in French a book titled *Cardenio entre Cervantes and Shakespeare. Histoire d'une pièce perdue* (Gallimard), published in an English translation in fall 2012.

David L. Gants is Associate Professor at Florida State University, where he also teaches in the interdisciplinary History of Text Technologies program. He is editor of *Publications of the Bibliographical Society of America*, and digital editor of *The Cambridge Edition of the Works of Ben Jonson* (2012). He began his career studying the stationer William Stansby, who printed Jonson's *Works* (1616) as well as Thomas Shelton's translation of *Don Quixote* (1612). Formerly Canada Research Chair in Humanities Computing, he has won fellowships from the National Endowment for the Humanities, the Folger Library, the Houghton Library, and the Newberry Library.

Carla Della Gatta is a doctoral student in the Interdisciplinary PhD in Theatre and Drama program at Northwestern University. Her research focuses on the intersection of contemporary Shakespearean productions and the performance of Latinidad. She studies bilingual Shakespearean adaptations, the role of Shakespeare Festivals in cultural exchange, and Spanish Golden Age theater. She has already published an essay on the Spanish contribution to Greenblatt's multinational *Cardenio* project.

Huw Griffiths is Senior Lecturer in English at the University of Sydney. His contribution to the Oxford University Press *Quest for Cardenio* volume (2012) traces *Double Falsehood*'s hidden histories of male friendship.

Christopher Hicklin is Fletcher scholar and Associate Editor of the Early Modern London Theatres website, an international collaborative project by the *Records of Early English Drama* at the University of Toronto, the Centre for Computing in the Humanities at King's College London, and the English Department of the University of Southampton.

Lori Leigh is Lecturer in the Department of Theatre and Drama at Victoria University of Wellington, New Zealand. She was assistant director of the 2009 production there of Taylor's reconstruction of *The History of Cardenio*, and has published on that text and on Theobald's *Double Falsehood* in *Shakespeare* (2011) and *The Quest for Cardenio* (2012). She has worked on productions and readings of plays both Off-Broadway and regionally in the United States, collaborating as a performer, puppeteer, writer, director, and dramaturg. While in New York, she assisted Shirley Kaplan in productions at Ensemble Studio Theatre, and her production of Lauren Wilson's *Wedding Duet* was a Samuel French Festival Finalist. Lori's play *Lessen* has been produced at the Bailiwick Repertory Theatre in Chicago and her short play *Wi(n)dow on the World* was selected for the Edward Albee/Great Plains Theatre Conference Short Play Lab. In New Zealand, she directed *Dog Sees God* for BATS Theatre and Wellington Summer Shakespeare's production of *The Winter's Tale* in the Wellington Botanic Gardens. She has also served as a dramaturg for Auckland Theatre Company (*Romeo and Juliet*), a script advisor for Playmarket (NZ Agency for Playwrights) and a mentor for Young and Hungry Festival of New Plays. She assists part-time at Shakespeare Globe Centre New Zealand where she has directed *Twelfth Night* and *Much Ado about Nothing*.

John V. Nance has taught at St. John's University in New York City and is currently a PhD student in early modern literature at Florida State University. His article "Gross Anatomies: Mapping Matter and Literary Form" is included in the anthology *The Age of Nashe* (Ashgate, forthcoming).

Vimala Pasupathi is Assistant Professor at Hofstra University. Her work appears in *Research Opportunities in Medieval and Renaissance Drama, Modern Philology, ELH, Early Theatre, Shakespeare*, and *Celtic Shakespeare: The Bard and the Borderers* (Ashgate, 2012).

Kevin C. Robbins is Associate Professor of Early Modern and Modern French History at Indiana University-Purdue University Indianapolis. His research work now extends to the cultural history of art and the history of the print worlds of Paris, especially radical, illustrated serial publications of the modern era.

Emily Schwank has been known to characterize herself at unguarded moments as "stubborn, arrogant, smart, insecure, confident, curious, noisy, and a middle child." A photographer since the age of 13, she strives everyday to see, really see; it seems so many images of grace and tragedy slip by without acknowledgment because the world is unwilling to open its eyes—not only to the obvious, but to the possible.

Elizabeth Spiller is Professor of English and Associate Dean of the College of Arts and Sciences at Florida State University. She is the author of *Reading and the History of Race in the Renaissance* (Cambridge University Press, 2011) and *Science, Reading, and Renaissance Literature* (Cambridge University Press, 2004), and was formerly editor of the *Journal for Early Modern Cultural Studies*. Her first published article was on *Don Quixote*, which is also the subject of a chapter of her most recent book. She has held major year-long fellowships from the National Endowment for the Humanities, Mellon Foundation, and Fulbright Foundation. Her work has been published in such journals as *Renaissance Quarterly, SEL, Criticism, Modern Language Quarterly, South Central Review, Renaissance and Reformation*, and *Renaissance Drama*. Her essay on "Shakespeare and the Making of Early Modern Science" was awarded the Kirby Prize for the best article of 2009 from the South Central MLA.

Gary Taylor is Distinguished Research Professor at Florida State University. He worked for eight years as one of the general editors of the Oxford University Press *Complete Works* of Shakespeare (published in 1986–1987). He is now lead General Editor of the New Oxford Shakespeare project, forthcoming from OUP in 2016. He has also coedited John Fletcher's *The Tamer Tamed*, and was General Editor of OUP's 2007 edition of *The Collected Works of Thomas Middleton* ("our other Shakespeare"), which won the Modern Languages Association prize for a Distinguished Scholarly Edition and the Elizabeth Dietz award for Outstanding Book in Early Modern Studies. He is editor of two series published by Palgrave: "The History of Text Technologies" and "Signs of Race."

Ayanna Thompson is Professor of English at George Washington University. She specializes in Renaissance drama and focuses on issues of race and performance. She is the author of two books: *Passing Strange: Shakespeare, Race, and Contemporary America* (Oxford University Press, 2011) and *Performing Race and Torture on the Early Modern Stage* (Routledge, 2008), and the editor of two books: *Weyward Macbeth: Intersections of Race and Performance* (Palgrave Macmillan, 2010; coedited with Scott Newstok) and *Colorblind Shakespeare: New Perspectives on Race and Performance* (Routledge, 2006). In addition, she is the guest editor of two special editions of scholarly journals: "Shakespeare, Race, and Performance," *Shakespeare Bulletin* (special issue 27.3, Fall 2009) and "Actors of Color in Shakespeare," *Borrowers and Lenders: The Journal of Shakespeare and Appropriation* (special issue 4.1, Spring/Summer 2008). Her essays and reviews have appeared in *Shakespeare Quarterly, Renaissance Quarterly, Seventeenth-Century News, The Eighteenth Century, The Journal of Popular Culture, Textus,* and *Arthuriana.*

Steven Wagschal is Associate Professor and Chair of the Department of Spanish and Portuguese at Indiana University (Bloomington). The author of *The Literature of Jealousy in the Age of Cervantes,* he has published essays on *Don Quixote* in *Cervantes: The Bulletin of the Cervantes Society of America* (2012) and *Cervantes in Perspective* (Madrid, 2013). He has also published essays, in English and Spanish, on Góngora, Calderón, Cristóbal de Castillejo, and on Cervantes's "Romance de los celos."

INDEX

Note: All names indicated in parenthesis as an actor, musician, sound designer, etc. refer to the 2012 IUPUI production of *The History of Cardenio*. Page numbers appearing in italics indicate illustrations and plates.

322   INDEX

Printed and bound by CPI Group (UK) Ltd, Croydon, CR0 4YY